Microsoft 365 and SharePoint Online Cookbook
Second Edition

A complete guide to Microsoft Office 365 apps including SharePoint, Power Platform, Copilot and more

Gaurav Mahajan

Sudeep Ghatak

Nate Chamberlain

Scott Brewster

BIRMINGHAM—MUMBAI

Microsoft 365 and SharePoint Online Cookbook

Second Edition

Senior Publishing Product Manager: Pradeep Sharma

Acquisition Editor – Peer Reviews: Gaurav Gavas

Project Editor: Amisha Vathare

Content Development Editor: Matthew Davies

Copy Editor: SafisE diting

Technical Editor: Karan Sonawane

Proofreader: SafisE diting

Indexer: Manju Arasan

Presentation Designer: Ganesh Bhadwalkar

Developer Relations Marketing Executive: Sohini Ghosh

First published: June 2020

Second edition: February 2024

Production reference: 2070425

Published by Packt Publishing Ltd.

Grosvenor House

11 St Paul's Square

Birmingham

B3 1RB, UK.

ISBN: 978-1-80324-317-7

www.packt.com

Foreword

This book is a "recipes to success" publication. If you are looking for practical guidance on Microsoft 365, you have picked the right book with the right authors. Microsoft 365, SharePoint, Teams, Viva, Power Platform, and more give you the ingredients; this 2nd edition provides over 100 recipes to mix and blend with confidence. Whether you are a beginner or an expert, you will find something useful and interesting on your way to becoming a top Microsoft 365 chef. Now you're cookin'!

The authors are all Microsoft experts with years of real-world experience designing and building Microsoft 365-based solutions (big and small) – and they're gracious enough to point out all the gotchas. Each recipe ensures it is easy to follow and navigates toward photo-worthy results. You will learn how to configure, customize, automate, and integrate Microsoft 365 workloads to enhance your productivity and collaboration. Plus, you'll get tips and tricks along the way.

So, grab your apron and get ready to explore the delicious possibilities of Microsoft 365. Bon appétit! Chefs Gaurav, Sudeep, Nate, and Scott await.

Mark Kashman,
Senior Product Manager - Microsoft

Contributors

About the authors

Gaurav Mahajan is a seasoned technical leader with over two decades of spearheading and delivering Microsoft solutions. As a M365 and Power Platform practice lead in Washington DC, he provides innovative solutions by collaborating with clients across industries. He holds a bachelor's in engineering, Stanford certification in AI, and a PG in management from the coveted IIMs. Gaurav contributes to the tech community through speaking engagements, and his blog gauravmahajan.net. He also co-chaired the M365 & SharePoint Saturday conference in Pittsburgh.

Sudeep Ghatak is a Microsoft MVP in Business Applications and a frequent contributor to the Power Automate Community forum. He works as a principal architect in Christchurch, New Zealand and loves designing solutions based on Office 365 and the Azure platform. He is a certified Solutions Developer (MCSD) and holds a postgraduate degree in instrumentation engineering. He is an active member of the Microsoft community and is often seen speaking at user groups and conferences in New Zealand.

Nate Chamberlain is a technical content creator, solution architect, and trainer, recognized as a 5-year Microsoft MVP. With a background in business analysis and systems administration, Nate has authored seven books and manages his blog, NateChamberlain.com. He holds an array of certifications, including M365 Enterprise Administrator Expert and Microsoft Power Platform App Maker Associate, and is a frequent speaker at user groups and conferences.

Scott Brewster is a Microsoft 365 solutions architect. He has supported numerous government clients focusing on SharePoint and Microsoft 365 since 2008. His focus is on security, administration, migration, governance, and training. Scott has been speaking at conferences and user groups since 2010 and runs the SharePoint User Group of DC.

About the reviewers

Yves Habersaat is a Microsoft **MVP (Most Valuable Professional)** and **MCT (Microsoft Certified Trainer)** with expertise in Microsoft cloud technologies. Yves works for Sword Group in Switzerland, a global leader in technology transformation and a Microsoft Gold Partner, as a business applications consultant. As a consultant, he assists his clients with on-premises migration, deployment, governance, modern software development, low-code/no-code development, and change management.

Yves is passionate about sharing his knowledge and experience with the wider Microsoft community, by participating in many sessions as a speaker and posting regularly on his blog.

Learn more on Discord

To join the Discord community for this book – where you can share feedback, ask questions to the author, and learn about new releases – follow the QR code below:

https://packt.link/powerusers

Table of Contents

Chapter 5: Document Management in SharePoint Online   205

Chapter 7: Microsoft Teams   283

Chapter 8: Power Automate (Microsoft Flow)   365

Chapter 10: Applying Power Apps   473

Preface

We have been working on SharePoint and related technologies since 2007, when Microsoft 365 wasn't around, and we have seen it go through several transformations since then. One of the questions we have often been asked as consultants is "What is SharePoint?" We have, at times, struggled to answer that question because, unlike some other Microsoft products that focus on solving one problem, SharePoint is a platform that can be leveraged to help implement a multitude of business solutions.

The question is even harder to respond to when someone asks "What is Microsoft 365?" because it is even bigger than SharePoint. With this book, our goal is to answer those questions by providing practical guidance on and insights into how to carry out various tasks in all the different areas of Microsoft 365. While we have provided the necessary background and best practices where possible, we have deliberately stayed away from getting too technical to keep the recipes simple for those who are new to Microsoft 365.

Microsoft 365 is an ever-changing platform with frequent updates being made to it. As you can imagine, it is hard to write a book on such a rapidly changing platform. We have tried to keep the book as close to the latest updates as we can. However, *you should expect to see some variations in the steps and images provided in this book*. Having said that, *the underlying concepts that guide these steps should remain the same*.

This comprehensive guide encompasses all major applications within the Microsoft 365 suite, along with an exploration of Copilot, with the aim of providing you with a head start in adapting to Microsoft's adoption of AI features on its platform. To achieve expert status, however, you will require additional study and lots and lots of hands-on practice.

Who this book is for

While writing this book, we had multiple audiences in mind.

On the one hand, we want to help end users become familiar with the many Microsoft 365 services. If you use these services in your business, you'll learn the basic controls as well as some tips and tricks to boost your productivity.

On the other, more administrative, hand, we also wrote recipes with more technical concepts in mind. If you're an IT administrator who wants to understand Microsoft 365 governance, or a business stakeholder or architect wanting to understand the tools of the trade for handling business workflows, there's a lot for you to learn.

What this book covers

Chapter 1, Overview of Microsoft 365, summarizes the products available in the Microsoft 365 suite, what they are used for, and the general licensing information you should know about. You'll learn how to sign in to Microsoft 365 and get to know its user interface.

Chapter 2, Introduction to SharePoint Online, provides recipes for the basic operations when using SharePoint, such as creating and sharing documents. This is useful for anyone who needs guidance on the essentials of using SharePoint.

Chapter 3, Modern Sites in SharePoint Online, explores content management using modern sites. You'll get to know the modern site architecture and features available in SharePoint Online for creating and managing modern sites.

Chapter 4, Lists and Libraries in SharePoint Online, covers the creation and management of lists and libraries in SharePoint Online. These are fundamental components for organizing and storing information.

Chapter 5, Document Management in SharePoint Online, focuses on document management capabilities in SharePoint Online, including versioning, metadata, and document collaboration features.

Chapter 6, OneDrive, discusses the features and functionality of OneDrive, Microsoft's cloud storage solution integrated with Microsoft 365. You'll learn the basics of uploading, syncing, and sharing files.

Chapter 7, Microsoft Teams, explores Microsoft Teams, a collaboration platform that combines workplace chat, meetings, file storage, and application integration. The recipes in this chapter increase in complexity, so you can choose to learn basic controls or more complex topics such as adding connectors, using breakout rooms, and creating registration forms.

Chapter 8, Power Automate (Microsoft Flow), introduces Power Automate, Microsoft's workflow automation tool for creating automated workflows across various applications and services. After creating a workflow, you'll learn how to edit and test the flow before following recipes for exporting, importing, and sharing it.

Chapter 9, Creating Power Apps, guides users through the process of creating custom business applications using Power Apps, Microsoft's low-code application development platform. You'll learn how to create an app based on a template, connect to data sources, and add interactive screens to your app.

Chapter 10, Applying Power Apps, demonstrates how to deploy and integrate apps within your organization. You'll learn how to embed an app in Teams and on a SharePoint page, as well as how to export and import your apps.

Chapter 11, Power BI, provides an overview of Power BI, Microsoft's business analytics tool, for creating interactive reports and visualizations from data sources. While visualizing data is the end goal of Power BI, you'll also learn important steps for transforming and modeling data.

Chapter 12, Overview of Copilot in Microsoft 365 and Power Platform, introduces Copilot, an AI-powered coding assistant, and explores its integration within Microsoft 365 and Power Platform. We'll take a bite-sized tour of Copilot in all the most popular software and what you can do with it.

Please note that the following chapters are only available in the free eBook that supplements this book: https://packt.link/online-sup-book

Chapter 13, Term Store and Content Types in SharePoint Online, discusses the management of metadata and content types using the Term Store in SharePoint Online for improving content organization and search.

Chapter 14, Search in Microsoft 365, explores the search capabilities within Microsoft 365, including Microsoft Search and its integration across various applications.

Chapter 15, Microsoft Delve, provides an overview of Microsoft Delve, a personal search and discovery tool, for surfacing relevant content and connections within organizations.

Chapter 16, Microsoft 365 Groups, explores Microsoft 365 Groups, collaborative workspaces that integrate with various Microsoft 365 services, including Outlook, SharePoint, and Teams.

Chapter 17, Power Automate Desktop for RPA, introduces Power Automate Desktop, Microsoft's **robotic process automation (RPA)** tool, for automating repetitive tasks across desktop applications.

Chapter 18, Copilot Studio (Power Virtual Agents), introduces Power Virtual Agents, Microsoft's no-code chatbot development platform, a predecessor to Copilot Studio used for creating intelligent virtual agents to engage with users.

Chapter 19, Viva Insights, overviews the functionality of the Viva Insights app, including features for organizing your work calendar. As we'll see, this is a "nice to have" application that aims to improve your work-life balance rather than performing staple tasks for your organization.

Chapter 20, Viva Learning, helps you get comfortable with Microsoft's app for training and growing your skills, Viva Learning. You'll learn what Viva Learning is, how to take courses on the app, review your learning activity, and suggest courses for your team.

Chapter 21, Viva Engage, prepares you to use Viva Engage, Microsoft's enterprise social networking platform. You'll find recipes for the basic functionalities of creating and joining Viva Engage communities, using the home feed, following people, and posting messages. In case you need some more administrative knowledge of Viva Engage, you'll learn how to create a network and invite external members to your network.

Chapter 22, Planner, provides an overview of Microsoft Planner, a task management tool, for organizing and tracking work within teams and projects.

Chapter 23, Microsoft To Do, explores Microsoft To Do, a task management app, for organizing tasks and managing to-do lists across devices.

Chapter 24, Microsoft Forms, teaches you the basic features when using Microsoft Forms. As you'll learn in the chapter, Forms is an easy solution for creating forms and quizzes. You'll learn the differences between the two formats and what features are available in each.

Chapter 25, Custom Development – SharePoint Framework, is a more advanced chapter that discusses custom development using the **SharePoint Framework (SPFx)** for building solutions and extensions on the SharePoint platform. This is the only chapter that will require a beginner-level knowledge of JavaScript.

Chapter 26, *Microsoft 365 on Mobile Devices*, explores the features and capabilities of Microsoft 365 applications on mobile devices, enabling productivity on the go.

Note that the *Appendix* is part of the supplementary eBook. It covers niche Microsoft technologies that may be "nice to have" additions to your workspace, such as Microsoft Bookings and Microsoft Loop.

To get the most out of this book

All you need is access to and licenses for the various apps and workloads in Microsoft 365, as well as the right administrative permissions. We'll cover the specific requirements before each recipe. If you already have access to your organization's Microsoft 365 subscription but are still unable to work your way through a recipe, you may need to reach out to your IT department to grant you the appropriate licenses and/or access required to complete the steps in that recipe.

Alternatively, you can also sign up for a Microsoft 365 trial account here: `https://www.microsoft.com/en-us/microsoft-365/try`. This will give you one month's free access to a newly created Microsoft 365 environment. This option is recommended for organizations or users that want to try the service first. You will need to enter your billing information first, but you can cancel the subscription at any time.

Another option is to sign up for the developer program by visiting `https://developer.microsoft.com/en-us/microsoft-365/dev-program`. This will provide you access to a Microsoft 365 environment containing all the workloads and apps, with fictitious user accounts, along with a lot of dummy test content. This environment has a 90-day validity, after which it is deleted unless it is renewed. The developer program provides a great opportunity to learn about Microsoft 365 and its entire suite of apps.

Download the example code files

The code bundle for the book is also hosted on GitHub at `https://packt.link/GitHub-repo`. If there's an update to the code, it will be updated on the existing GitHub repository.

We also have other code bundles from our rich catalog of books and videos available at `https://github.com/PacktPublishing/`. Check them out!

Download the color images

We also provide a PDF file that has color images of the screenshots/diagrams used in this book. You can download it here: `https://packt.link/gbp/9781803243177`

Conventions used

There are a number of text conventions used throughout this book.

`CodeInText`: Indicates code words in text, database table names, folder names, filenames, file extensions, pathnames, dummy URLs, user input, and Twitter handles. Here is an example: "Scaffold a web part template by typing `yo @microsoft/sharepoint` and respond to the questions that are asked."

A block of code is set as follows:

```
Syntax:
Set(variable_name,value)
```

Any command-line input or output is written as follows:

```
npm install -g @microsoft/generator-sharepoint
```

Bold: Indicates a new term, an important word, or words that you see onscreen. For instance, words in menus or dialog boxes appear in the text like this. Here is an example: "Click the **Sync** option in the header menu."

 Warnings or important notes appear like this.

 Tips and tricks appear like this.

Sections

Like any cookbook, we've organized this book into a series of recipes that follow a regular structure. You will find several headings that appear frequently in the recipe format: *Getting ready*, *How to do it...*, *How it works...*, *There's more...*, and *See also*.

To give clear instructions on how to complete a recipe, we've used these sections as follows.

Getting ready

This section tells you what to expect in the recipe and describes how to set up any software or any preliminary settings required for the recipe.

How to do it...

This section contains the steps required to follow the recipe. Don't worry if you've got questions about some of the technical details; we'll cover those in the next section.

How it works...

This section consists of a detailed explanation of what happened in the previous section. This helps to couple your practical skills with a deeper understanding.

There's more...

This section consists of additional information, such as more advanced features for more niche situations.

See also

This section provides helpful links to other useful information for the recipe. This includes links to other resources as well as other relevant recipes elsewhere in this book.

Get in touch

Feedback from our readers is always welcome.

General feedback: If you have questions about any aspect of this book, mention the book title in the subject of your message and email us at customercare@packtpub.com.

Errata: Although we have taken every care to ensure the accuracy of our content, mistakes do happen. If you have found a mistake in this book, we would be grateful if you would report this to us. Please visit www.packtpub.com/support/errata, selecting your book, clicking on the Errata Submission Form link, and entering the details.

Piracy: If you come across any illegal copies of our works in any form on the internet, we would be grateful if you would provide us with the location address or website name. Please contact us at copyright@packt.com with a link to the material.

If you are interested in becoming an author: If there is a topic that you have expertise in and you are interested in either writing or contributing to a book, please visit authors.packtpub.com.

Share your thoughts

Once you've read *Microsoft 365 and SharePoint Online Cookbook - Second Edition*, we'd love to hear your thoughts! Scan the QR code below to go straight to the Amazon review page for this book and share your feedback.

https://packt.link/r/1-803-24317-1

Your review is important to us and the tech community and will help us make sure we're delivering excellent quality content.

1

Overview of Microsoft 365

Microsoft is the reigning leader in business collaboration and productivity. Over 400,000 companies worldwide use Microsoft products and services. Over 100 million monthly active users use SharePoint. Microsoft is a leader in the provision of content services platforms that focuses on the following key areas:

- **Content management:** A **content management system** (**CMS**) (also sometimes known as **enterprise content management,** or **ECM**) lets you store, manage, and optionally share an organization's content, which includes documents and/or web pages. Microsoft's first true CMS came with **Windows SharePoint Services** (**WSS**) 3.0, a product that later came to be known as **SharePoint,** which soon became a widely popular document and content management platform. While SharePoint serves as the document management solution for a team, **OneDrive** is meant to host and manage employees' personal files.

- **Collaboration:** Collaboration is the exchange of information and ideas between *collaborators* within or even outside an organization. More recent advancements in technology allow for those collaborating to be located across different geographical locations and still be able to effectively work together as if they were collocated. **SharePoint** and **Teams,** coupled with your ever-favorite Office apps, such as **Word, Excel, PowerPoint, OneNote,** and so on, are a few of the Microsoft solutions that exist to help boost business collaboration.

- **Communication:** Communication is vital to every business. It reflects the culture of an organization and helps align the goals of individuals within an organization toward a common objective. To effectively communicate with employees, organizations should offer multiple channels for both formal and informal communication. Besides communicating the organization's vision and goals, these channels can be used to update their employees on news, events, and policies to prepare them for a crucial situation, ensure safety, or effectively listen to the opinions and ideas of other employees. Microsoft has several apps that offer communication channels for different engagement levels, such as the following:

  - **Outlook:** For formal communication
  - **Teams:** For instant communication
  - **Engage:** For communication between interest groups

- **Process automation:** Business process automation is the use of technology to execute repeatable tasks or processes. It helps accelerate and standardize business processes, thereby improving the quality of the outcome while reducing costs at the same time. You can streamline both simple and complex processes, such as employee onboarding, accounts payable, contract management, time management, and more. Microsoft provides the following selection of apps, grouped under the **Power Platform** umbrella, to help you build business process automation apps. Power Platform lets experts in the subject build no-code business solutions using the following:

  - **Power Apps:** To build online forms
  - **Power Automate:** To automate repetitive processes
  - **Power BI:** To analyze and visualize data
  - **Power Virtual Agents:** To build chatbots

- **Productivity:** Besides the applications mentioned previously, there are several other applications that target specific use cases, which can be broadly divided into the following categories:

  - **Office Online:** Outlook, Word, Excel, and PowerPoint to author and share content
  - **Project and task management:** Using **To Do** to manage personal tasks, **Planner** to manage simple project tasks, and **Project Online** for more complex scenarios
  - **Digital forms:** Using **Power Apps** and **Forms** to build forms and surveys
  - **Video streaming:** Using **Stream** to upload and manage videos
  - **Copilot:** Microsoft Copilot is the new transformative AI-driven tool that leverages the power of machine learning and natural language processing to optimize productivity, inspire creativity, and elevate collaboration within the Microsoft ecosystem. It simplifies tasks, offers intelligent suggestions, automates repetitive processes, and goes beyond being a mere tool. Designed for Microsoft products like **Microsoft 365, Dynamics 365, Fabric, Sales, Service**, and **GitHub,** Copilot empowers users in various domains.

All these products and services are now integrated and offered as a unified service called **Microsoft 365** (earlier known as **Microsoft Office 365** or **Office 365**). With Microsoft 365, Microsoft has designed a subscription model that allows organizations to provide these services to their employees. It comes with different plans tailored equally well for large, medium, and small companies.

In this chapter, we will first take a closer look at the infrastructure and evolution of Microsoft services. Then it will make sense to see the different plans and licensing models available to us. Once you're aware of the licensing, we can learn a bit more about the apps and interfaces of Microsoft 365. Finally, at the end of this chapter, we will be ready to encounter the many recipes found in this cookbook.

Getting the most out of this book — get to know your free benefits

Unlock exclusive **free** benefits that come with your purchase, thoughtfully crafted to supercharge your learning journey and help you learn without limits.

Here's a quick overview of what you get with this book:

Next-gen reader

Our web-based reader, designed to help you learn effectively, comes with the following features:

🔄 **Multi-device progress sync:** Learn from any device with seamless progress sync.

📖 **Highlighting and notetaking:** Turn your reading into lasting knowledge.

🔖 **Bookmarking:** Revisit your most important learnings anytime.

☀️ **Dark mode:** Focus with minimal eye strain by switching to dark or sepia mode.

Figure 1.1: Illustration of the next-gen Packt Reader's features

Interactive AI assistant (beta)

Our interactive AI assistant has been trained on the content of this book, so it can help you out if you encounter any issues. It comes with the following features:

✦ **Summarize it:** Summarize key sections or an entire chapter.

✦ **AI code explainers:** In the next-gen Packt Reader, click the **Explain** button above each code block for AI-powered code explanations.

Note: The AI assistant is part of next-gen Packt Reader and is still in beta.

Figure 1.2: Illustration of Packt's AI assistant

DRM-free PDF or ePub version

Learn without limits with the following perks included with your purchase:

 Learn from anywhere with a DRM-free PDF copy of this book.

Use your favorite e-reader to learn using a DRM-free ePub version of this book.

Figure 1.3: Free PDF and ePub

Unlock this book's exclusive benefits now

UNLOCK NOW

Take a moment to get the most out of your purchase and enjoy the complete learning experience.

Note: Have your purchase invoice ready before you begin. `https://www.packtpub.com/unlock/9781803243177`

The infrastructure business is changing!

In today's digital landscape, the landscape of business operations and data management has undergone a significant transformation. The days of maintaining in-house data centers with their labyrinthine server rooms, brimming with hardware and requiring constant vigilance, have given way to a more efficient and cost-effective solution: cloud computing.

Traditionally, businesses established these data centers to safeguard their most critical and sensitive information. These centers needed to be fortified with both physical and virtual security measures, making them formidable fortresses against potential threats. Along with security, significant ongoing costs came into play, including server licenses, hardware expenses, the substantial power needed to keep servers running, and the consistent maintenance of the facility itself. As a safeguard, many companies also invested in disaster recovery centers to ensure business continuity in case the primary data center failed.

While the concept of having a private data center, offering full control, might seem appealing, the practicality of maintaining such an infrastructure has proven to be increasingly challenging. Cybersecurity threats loom large, and protecting applications and data from potential attacks demands a level of expertise and resources that many organizations find hard to maintain.

From a financial perspective, it's not cost-effective to keep servers running continuously, especially during periods of low application usage, such as local holiday seasons. Moreover, the burden of maintaining these servers 24/7, including applying patches, installing updates, and ensuring smooth operation, necessitates dedicated staff.

This is where cloud computing and hosting solutions have come to the rescue. The cloud offers scalable and flexible resources, reducing the need for heavy capital investment in hardware and security infrastructure. It allows businesses to pay for what they use, making it cost-effective, and cloud providers take care of the bulk of maintenance, updates, and security. Businesses can now focus on innovation, agility, and their core operations, leaving the technical intricacies to the cloud experts. The transition from traditional data centers to cloud computing has been a game-changer for companies of all sizes, offering a more secure, efficient, and cost-effective approach to data management and IT infrastructure. The term **cloud** refers to the infrastructure and/or services that are hosted and maintained by a provider and that can be accessed over the internet. Microsoft, Google, and Amazon are some of the well-known cloud providers, but there are certainly many more that provide various cloud services. There are primarily three service models that cloud providers offer:

- **Infrastructure-as-a-service (IaaS)**: In this model, instead of purchasing and maintaining their own computing hardware, organizations borrow the necessary infrastructure from one or more service providers by paying a fee. They then install and maintain the required software on this infrastructure.
- **Platform-as-a-service (PaaS)**: In this model, in addition to the infrastructure, the service provider also provides the operating system and development tools required to build applications.
- **Software-as-a-service (SaaS)**: In this model, the applications are provided by the service provider. These applications can be accessed over the internet. The responsibility of upgrading the software and fixing the bugs lies with the service provider.

The evolution of Microsoft 365

The journey of Microsoft's productivity suite started in the 80s when it was first introduced by Bill Gates as **Microsoft Office**, with three applications: Word, Excel, and PowerPoint. Since then, Office applications have captured the corporate world and home users alike. Anyone who has ever used a PC has had some experience with Microsoft Office at some point. It is hard to imagine a world without Word, Excel, and PowerPoint. These applications have transformed the world since the day they were launched.

While one team in Microsoft was busy improving the already popular Office suite of applications, another team was busy shaping an enterprise-scale collaboration and content management platform called **SharePoint**. This platform offers online document storage and enables collaboration between teams. In addition, and since its days of inception, SharePoint has been built to be a highly extensible and customizable platform that allows developers and non-developers alike to extend its capabilities by building business solutions on top of it.

SharePoint was initially released as a standalone application for installation on a server (there are several companies that still use it on-premises) before becoming available on the cloud as SharePoint Online and as a member of the Microsoft 365 family.

Advancements in SharePoint have given birth to other technologies and tools that have now evolved into fully featured products themselves. The following are just some of those products:

- **OneDrive:** Older versions of SharePoint included a service called My Sites. My Sites were personal sites for every SharePoint user, a place where they could store their personal files. My Sites have now been replaced by OneDrive.

- **Microsoft Teams:** Teams has been through several pit stops before becoming Microsoft 365's default communication tool. In 2011, Microsoft acquired **Skype**, a free piece of software that enables you to make VOIP calls and host video conferencing. After the acquisition of Skype, Microsoft replaced the business communication tool named **Lync** with a corporate version of Skype, called **Skype for Business**. Skype for Business has now been deprecated and replaced by Microsoft Teams.

- **Power Automate:** SharePoint as a platform had a workflow solution referred to as **SharePoint workflows**. The workflows were designed using a free tool called **SharePoint Designer**. Although SharePoint workflows were powerful, managing them was hard because of the lack of a visual tool. SharePoint workflows got deprecated with the advent of Power Automate, which had a nice web-based visual designer that was so easy to use that even non-developers could build workflow solutions themselves.

- **Power Apps: Microsoft InfoPath** was a popular tool for designing, editing, and distributing electronic forms. InfoPath forms could be connected to a variety of data sources and were often used along with SharePoint to extend the capabilities of SharePoint list forms. InfoPath has since been deprecated and replaced with a web-based forms designer known as **Power Apps**. Again, with this move, Microsoft has tried to make designing forms easier for non-developers. Going beyond forms, with the help of Power Apps you can build custom business apps that connect to your business data and run seamlessly in the browser or on mobile devices (phone or tablet).

- **Power BI:** In 2006, Microsoft acquired ProClarity and launched PerformancePoint as a business intelligence solution. It was discontinued in 2009 and paved the way for Power BI.

- **Microsoft Viva:** Microsoft Viva is the most recent addition to the Microsoft 365 family, with a growing set of features. It is a platform that combines modules for communication, learning, resources, and insights. For example, **Viva Topics** is used for making knowledge and expertise in an organization available via Teams and SharePoint. **Viva Connections** enables you to create personalized dashboards for your staff. **Viva Learning** lets you build a training hub that brings content from LinkedIn Learning, Microsoft Learn, and other third-party content providers.

  Yet another module is **Viva Insights**, which focuses on your productivity by providing personalized insights about your emails, meeting schedules, calls, and chats. To learn more about Viva, check out two of the eBook chapters: *Chapter 19, Viva Insights*, and *Chapter 20, Viva Learning*.

- **Microsoft Copilot:** Microsoft Copilot a new entry in Microsoft 365 space, revolutionizes productivity by integrating AI into everyday tasks within Microsoft 365 apps. Leveraging advanced **Large Language Models (LLMs)**, Copilot understands user input across Word, Excel, PowerPoint, Outlook, Teams, and more, enhancing specificity through grounding techniques. By accessing content from the Microsoft Graph, Copilot delivers context-aware responses and insights. Eligible for enterprise, business, and education customers with specific licensing requirements, Copilot streamlines workflows, boosts productivity, and enables users to harness the power of AI within the Microsoft ecosystem for enhanced efficiency and innovation.

If you flick to the last pages, you won't find any chapters on Viva. That's because these chapters are part of the *online eBook* that comes with this book! Going ahead, any references to chapters numbered 13 or higher are referring to the eBook.

Over the years, Microsoft has made other strategic acquisitions, such as Yammer and Mover, to consolidate its Microsoft 365 offering. They were soon joined by other online services, such as Stream, Planner, Sway, To Do, and so on.

Hopefully, that provides you with some context on how **Microsoft 365** evolved. The next section explains why Microsoft 365 is right for any organization.

What is Microsoft 365?

Microsoft 365 is a SaaS and PaaS offering by Microsoft. It is a collection of several products, services, and platforms, each tailored for a specific use case. Microsoft 365 applications can be accessed online at `www.office.com`. In addition to online applications, it also lets you download the license-based client version of certain applications, such as Microsoft Office (Word, Excel, and PowerPoint), OneDrive, Teams, and so on.

Moving to Microsoft 365 provides you with the following benefits:

- **One subscription service for everything**: Microsoft 365 provides you with an ecosystem of applications. Every application is designed to cater to a specific use case. You get applications that let you build electronic forms and business process automation, create insights into your business data, and so on. This saves you from buying multiple point solutions for every use case.

- **No installation required**: All Microsoft 365 apps are accessible through a web browser, including the ones that have a web and client version. Client versions are available for some applications, such as Word, Excel, PowerPoint, Outlook, Teams, Power BI, and so on. Although the web versions provide limited features compared to the desktop version, they are catching up with their client counterparts pretty rapidly.

- **Choose your own device**: Microsoft 365 runs on PC, Mac, and Linux machines. It is compatible with all major browsers, such as Microsoft Edge, Internet Explorer 11, Mozilla Firefox, Google Chrome, and Safari 10+. More information on operating system and browser compatibility can be found at `https://packt.link/browser-compatibility`.

- **Mobile friendly**: All Microsoft 365 services are *responsive* (meaning that they adjust to the viewing area of the device) when viewed on mobile browsers. Most of these services also have a mobile app that lets you leverage native mobile features (such as camera and GPS). To read about the mobile compatibility of the various Microsoft 365 apps, visit `https://packt.link/mobile-compatibility`.

- **Always get the latest features:** Microsoft 365 is continuously being updated with new features and capabilities. Users do not have to worry about upgrades; they can experience improvements as soon as Microsoft updates are released to their organization's tenant. Your organization can try new features before they are released to the general public by opting in for **targeted release**. Your IT administrator can designate a set of users to try out these new features before they get rolled out to the rest of the company. You can read more about the **Standard** and **Targeted** releases here: `https://packt.link/first-release`.

- **High availability:** Microsoft 365 offers 99.9% uptime. The information at `https://packt.link/office-continuity` shows uptime data across the world over the last three years. Microsoft notifies you at least five days before any scheduled maintenance job. You also receive notifications in case of unplanned outages. Administrators can check the status of Microsoft 365 services from the administration Service Health portal during partial outages.

- **State-of-the-art security:** One of the main reasons why companies are reluctant to move to the cloud is that they are not sure how secure their data is. Some of these security concerns are as follows:

  - **Who can access my data?:** Your data belongs to you. There are well-laid policies and checks to ensure that no one can access your data without permission. There could be exceptional scenarios where the government or law enforcement agencies can request your data. To read more about this, refer to `https://packt.link/data-access`.

  - **Protect data from hackers:** All Microsoft 365 data is stored in highly secured environments. However, to further secure your Microsoft 365 environment, Microsoft has laid out certain security guidelines (`https://packt.link/security`) that should be followed. These guidelines reduce the risks of hacking, if not eliminating them completely.

  - **Data ownership:** Even though your data is saved on Microsoft infrastructure, they do not own your data. If you cancel your Microsoft 365 subscription, your data gets deleted from their servers after 90 days. During this time, you can renew your subscription or back up the data from Microsoft 365. You can read more about data ownership at `https://packt.link/ownership`.

  - **Compliance and information security:** Microsoft 365 also provides features such as data loss prevention and device management that let you store your company's data and information without the risk of information leakage. It offers additional capabilities surrounding data compliance and information security.

    Since these are very highly specialized areas, focused on the administrative side of Microsoft 365, we have not covered the topics in this book. If you are an administrator and implementing Microsoft 365 for your organization, we recommend that you familiarize yourself with these areas. You can read more about Microsoft 365 compliance features here: `https://packt.link/M365-compliance`. You can read more about Microsoft 365 security features here: `https://packt.link/M365-security`.

Licensing

Adopting Office 365 offers many advantages, but at the same time, it takes a huge effort to find the right balance of cost and features for your organization.

Some licenses provide you with access to a bundle of services or apps while there are individual service plans for a specific app (like Power Apps, Power Automate, etc.).

Microsoft 365 has several subscription plans for the following entities:

- **Small and medium businesses:** In this category, there are **Basic**, **Standard**, and **Premium** plans. The Basic plan offers Office apps (Outlook, Word, Excel, PowerPoint, and OneNote) for online, mobile-only use, and grants 1 TB of storage per user. The Standard and Premium tiers include the corresponding desktop Office apps along with additional services.
- **Schools:** Microsoft offers plans to schools under the "Education" banner. The plans are **A1**, **A2**, and **A3**. A1 offers Office apps (Outlook, Word, Excel, PowerPoint, and OneNote) for online and mobile-only use. The A2 plan additionally provides access to the corresponding desktop apps. Power BI is only available with the A3 plan.
- **Non-profit organizations:** This category includes a **Basic** and a **Standard** plan. The primary difference between the two plans is that the **Standard** plan lets you download Office apps for desktop whereas the **Basic** plan lets you access Office applications only on the web.
- **Home users:** For home users, Microsoft offers a **one-time** purchase or two subscription-based plans (**family** and **individual**) to choose from. The one-time purchase plan lets you use only three apps (Word, Excel, and PowerPoint) on a single device. Family and individual plans offer additional apps.
- **Enterprises:** Enterprises can choose between the E3 and E5 plans. The E5 plan is the premium version that includes all Microsoft 365 apps and services.
- **First-line workers:** The first-line workers are the first ones to represent your organization. Microsoft 365 offers the F3 plan to help such workers stay productive. The F3 plan offers Office web and mobile apps, OneDrive, and a few other Microsoft 365 services.
- **Standalone plans:** Besides the plans mentioned above, some services are also available with standalone plans. These can even be included in plans that do not offer these services by default. The standalone plans are listed here: `https://packt.link/standalone-plans`.

You get access to a set of applications in Microsoft 365 based on the subscription plan assigned to you by your organization. To get access to other applications, you can either ask for your administrator to upgrade you to a higher plan or assign you a license for that specific application. We have mentioned the license requirements in the *Getting started* section of each recipe.

The Microsoft 365 plans get updated from time to time. You can check the plans by browsing to `https://www.office.com/` and looking under the **Products** menu in the top navigation or referring to this page: `https://packt.link/M365-plans`.

Microsoft 365 apps

Microsoft 365 comprises the following key applications and services (in alphabetical order):

- **Calendar:** This app lets you view your daily, weekly, or monthly schedule, book meetings, and share meetings and event times. It also lets you view your organization's shared calendars and the calendars of your colleagues.

- **Delve:** This app uses machine learning and artificial intelligence to display information relevant to you based on what you work on and who you work with. The information is pulled from different applications within Microsoft 365, such as SharePoint, OneDrive, and Teams. Delve is covered in the eBook in *Chapter 15, Microsoft Delve*.

- **Dynamics 365:** Microsoft Dynamics 365 offers customer relationship management and enterprise resource management services. It lets you build business applications for your organization. It comes with purpose-built data models that can then be customized as per your needs.

- **Excel:** Excel is one of the most popular programs that are used for organizing and manipulating data. It lets you connect to various databases and also visualize data using pivot charts and tables. With Microsoft 365, you can access your Excel spreadsheets in a web browser.

- **Forms:** Microsoft Forms lets you create surveys, team quizzes, and opinion polls by designing simple electronic forms using several input options. The responses received can then be analyzed individually or collectively within Forms or by exporting the responses in Excel. To learn more about Forms, check out *Chapter 24, Microsoft Forms*.

- **Viva Insights:** This app provides insights into your work habits by looking into your interactions with people. It also lets you mute notifications that might distract you and book time to focus on your daily calendar.

- **OneDrive:** OneDrive lets you save and share your files in one place. You can share these files securely with your colleagues, vendors, or partners. Your OneDrive files can be downloaded on any device and synchronized with the cloud to ensure that your work is never lost. You can find more details on OneDrive in *Chapter 6, OneDrive*.

- **OneNote:** OneNote is a note-taking app that can capture and organize your notes into notebooks, sections, or pages. It lets you take handwritten as well as audio notes.

- **Outlook:** Outlook lets you stay on top of your emails. It has features such as spam detection and auto-filter. It also has features such as attachment reminders, attendee tracking, and the ability to attach a document as a link (as opposed to a duplicate copy).

- **People:** People lets you maintain a list of your contacts. This includes internal staff, as well as all your friends, family, and acquaintances.

- **Planner:** Planner lets you manage your tasks by organizing them into plans, assigning them to individuals, and notifying people. You and your team can track tasks on a planner board and track them to completion. Planner is covered in the eBook in *Chapter 22, Planner*.

- **Power Automate:** Formerly known as **Microsoft Flow**, this app lets you automate business processes by using conditional logic and connecting a host of data sources. Power Automate is covered in *Chapter 8, Power Automate (Microsoft Flow)*, and *Chapter 17, Power Automate Desktop for RPA*.

- **Power BI:** This app lets you visualize data using built-in and custom visuals, as well as building dashboards and sharing these with others. Power BI is covered in *Chapter 11, Power BI*.

- **Power Virtual Agents:** This service lets you design chatbots for your organization that can integrate with other Microsoft 365 services. Virtual agents are covered in the eBook in *Chapter 18, Copilot Studio (Power Virtual Agents)*.

- **Power Apps:** This app lets you develop electronic forms that allow you to interact with your organization's data. They can be built for both web and mobile. Power Apps is discussed in *Chapter 9, Creating Power Apps* and *Chapter 10, Applying Power Apps*.

- **PowerPoint:** PowerPoint lets you build presentations using visual effects and animations and share them with your colleagues. PowerPoint has both a client and a web version and supports co-authoring.

- **SharePoint:** SharePoint is a platform for your organization to boost team collaboration and document and content management. It lets you securely share content and information with your colleagues and partners. If you want to navigate ahead to recipes about SharePoint, consider the following chapters:
  - *Chapter 2, Introduction to SharePoint Online*
  - *Chapter 3, Modern Sites in SharePoint Online*
  - *Chapter 4, Lists and Libraries in SharePoint Online*
  - *Chapter 5, Document Management in SharePoint Online*
  - *Chapter 13, Term Store and Content Types in SharePoint Online*

- **Stream:** Stream is your company's own video portal, where your staff can upload and share videos of classes, meetings, presentations, and training sessions. It also lets you categorize videos under channels. To learn more about Stream, check out *the appendix found in the supplement eBook.*.

- **Tasks:** The Tasks app lets you manage tasks in Outlook. It lets you assign due dates to tasks and mark them as complete.

- **Teams:** Teams is your collaboration hub with a chat-based team workspace that lets you work collaboratively with your colleagues. It provides features for group chats, online meetings, calling, and web conferencing. *Chapter 7, Microsoft Teams*, covers Teams in detail.

- **To Do:** This app lets you manage, prioritize, and complete the most important things you need to achieve every day. We have covered this in the eBook in *Chapter 23, Microsoft To Do*.

- **Whiteboard:** Whiteboard is an app that lets you use your device as a whiteboard to ideate and exchange ideas. It supports text, shapes, and free-form drawing.

- **Word:** This app lets you create professional documents and share them with your colleagues. The app has a client and a web version and supports the co-authoring of documents.

- **Engage:** Engage is your organization's social network that drives employee engagement in your organization. Engage has been covered in the eBook in *Chapter 21, Viva Engage*.

- **Copilot:** Your AI companion that assists with routine tasks, enhancing productivity within Microsoft 365 apps.

Signing in to Microsoft 365

With that introduction, let's jump right into the service itself.

Microsoft 365 uses a single sign-in for all its apps and services. The initial sign-in page for Microsoft 365 can vary slightly depending on the device that you are signing in from, and the app that you are signing in to. However, you will see a consistent **Sign in** option on all such apps and devices. For example, the initial sign-in page when you use a browser to sign in to Microsoft 365 through its landing page at www.office.com looks like this:

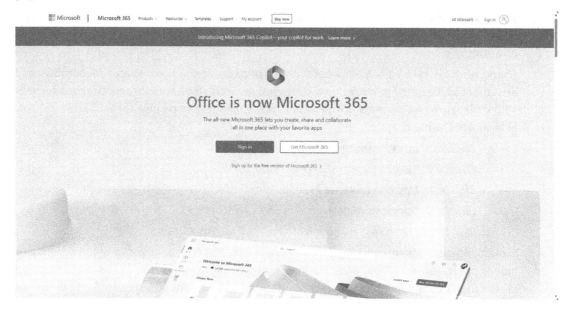

Figure 1.4: Microsoft 365 Sign in link

 This Microsoft support article walks you through the login experience when signing in from apps on various devices:

https://packt.link/M365-signin

The login experience becomes consistent after you click the **Sign in** button. Clicking this button will first prompt you for an email ID. For your work or school subscription, this will be your corresponding work or school email ID. If you have a personal Microsoft account, then this will be your personal email ID.

For work or school accounts, entering the email ID and clicking **Next** will take you to your organization's sign-in page, where you will need to enter your usual password for your organization. Then click **Sign in** again. Note that you may be asked for more information here depending on whether your organization has configured additional security.

If you are navigating to one of the Microsoft 365 services from the browser, you will also be asked if you would like to **Stay signed in?**. Confirming **Yes** to this prompt will mean that you will not need to sign in again every time you access an app or service using the same browser. You can also select **Don't show this again** to reduce the number of times you are prompted to sign in. Please be sure to do this only on devices that belong to you and are not shared with others.

That's it! You are now ready to benefit from all the Microsoft 365 apps and services using this one sign-in. Next, we will explore the various components of the Microsoft 365 user interface in a bit more detail.

Microsoft 365 user interface

Microsoft 365 comes with a very simple and intuitive user interface. You are presented with a landing page that looks like this when you first log in to the Microsoft 365 home page at www.office.com:

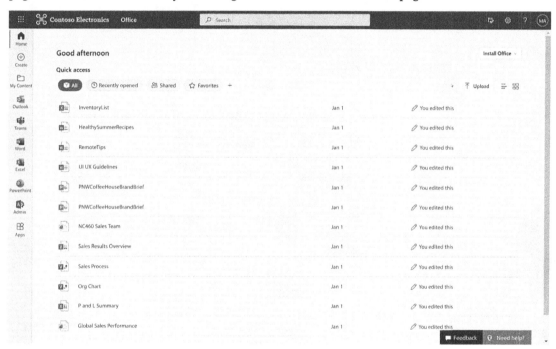

Figure 1.5: Microsoft 365 landing page

Let's look at the various sections of this page in a bit more detail.

Page header — the suite bar

The suite bar appears at the top of all Microsoft 365 apps. The suite bar has the following links:

Figure 1.6: Microsoft 365 suite bar

1. The set of squares on the extreme left is known as the Microsoft 365 **app launcher** (also called the **waffle**). It is the Start menu equivalent to Windows 10. The waffle displays your frequently used Microsoft 365 apps. In addition to the Microsoft 365 apps, your organization can add their own apps in this section. You can then navigate to your apps from here. In addition, you will also see your recent documents if you scroll all the way to the bottom of the app launcher. You can also click **All apps** toward the bottom of the app launcher panel to be taken to a page that shows you a listing of all the apps that you have access to:

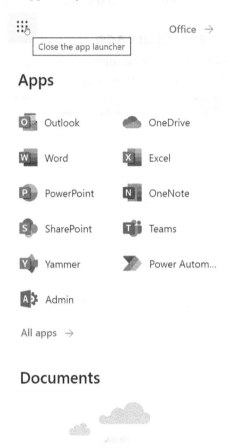

Figure 1.7: Accessing apps

2. The Microsoft 365 **Search** box in the middle lets you search across your organization's entire Microsoft 365 tenant. **Search** allows you to find relevant content from across all SharePoint sites and OneDrive. We will cover **Search** in much more detail in subsequent chapters, but it is worth mentioning here that **Search** will always only show you content that you have access to.

3. Next to the **Search** box are three Microsoft 365 icons:

    a. **Notification icon:** Notifies you when you receive an email.

    b. **Settings icon:** This is explained in the following section.

c. **Help icon:** To get help on Microsoft 365. The help icon is context-aware; clicking this icon will show you help relevant to the area or page that you were browsing when you clicked it.

4. On the right side of the screen is the profile picture (or your initials, if the picture is unavailable). You can update your contact details by clicking on the profile picture and then selecting **My Office Profile.** You can also view your subscriptions and license information and update your account details (privacy settings, password, and so on) from here.

Settings icon

The **Settings** menu is represented by the *gear* icon. The settings icon lets you change your personal preferences, including your notification settings and your password for Microsoft 365, as shown in the following screenshot:

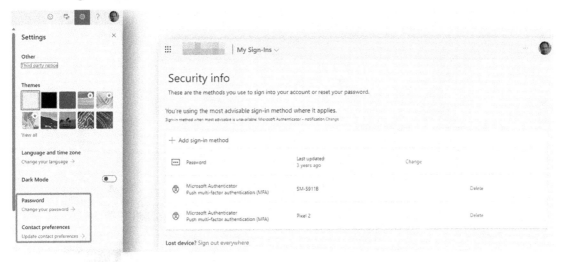

Figure 1.8: Update personal preferences

You can update the following from here:

*   Your personal Microsoft 365 look and feel (if your organization allows this)
*   Certain Microsoft 365 notification preferences
*   Your organization account password
*   Additional security and privacy settings

Further, the settings panel is context-aware, meaning that the settings that you see in this panel will depend on the Microsoft 365 workload or app within which you are working. For example, when you are viewing the settings panel from within a page in SharePoint, you will see settings that are relevant to that specific page or area in SharePoint. We will cover the settings for individual apps separately in the chapters for these apps.

Page content

While the header consistently appears across all the Microsoft 365 workloads, the content for the individual apps varies depending on the type of app. The Microsoft 365 home page contains the following sections (from top to bottom).

The **Install Office** option in the top right-hand corner lets you install Office applications (such as Word, Excel, and PowerPoint) on your machine. This link is visible only if your subscription plan lets you install Office applications.

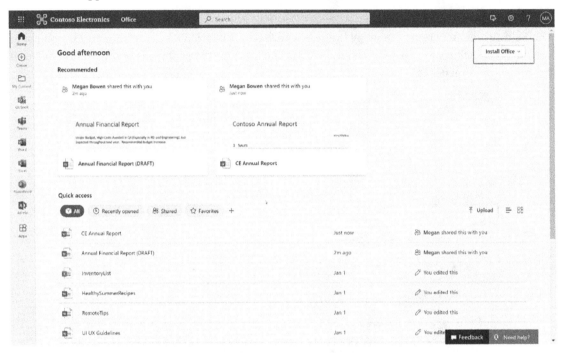

Figure 1.9: Microsoft 365 landing page components

The **Recommended** section displays all the documents that might be relevant to you. Microsoft 365 uses machine learning and artificial intelligence to create a personalized list for each user based on the projects that you are working on and the people you are working with.

Figure 1.10: Recommended results

The **quick access** bar lets you add one or more **content filters**. Content filters let you refine your content based on metadata. It comes with four standard filters: **All**, **Recently opened**, **Shared**, and **Favorites**.

The **Recently opened** link displays the documents in descending order of the last accessed date. This feature is very useful because it lets you start working on documents in order of when you last accessed or updated them.

Figure 1.11: Recently opened documents

The **Shared** view displays the documents that have been shared with you by your colleagues.

Figure 1.12: Shared documents

Toward the bottom of quick access, you will find the **See all My Content** link, which lets you expand your search and filter on specific content using the filters on the left.

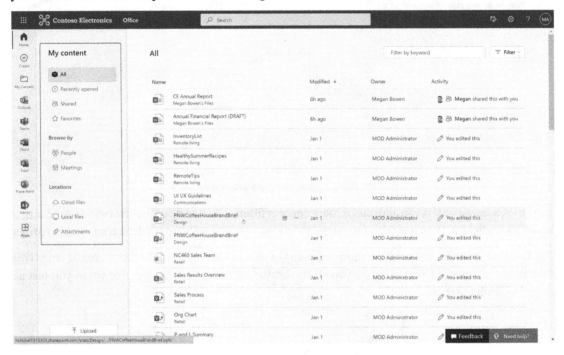

Figure 1.13: Document refinement panel

Microsoft 365 admin interface

Microsoft 365 is a very powerful platform, but with great power comes great responsibility. The Microsoft 365 admin center lets you manage various aspects of the platform. Only designated administrators in your organization can access the admin center. They can access it through the admin app after they log in to www.office.com.

The following screenshot shows the landing screen of the Microsoft 365 admin center:

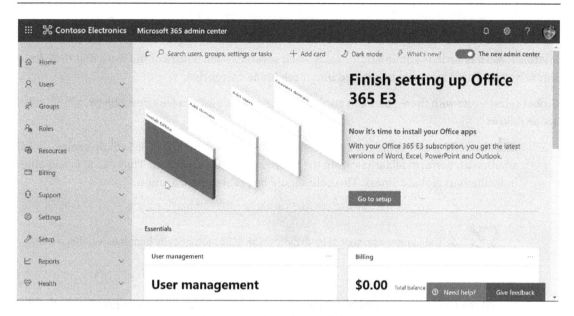

Figure 1.14: Microsoft 365 admin center

You can perform the following actions from the Microsoft 365 admin center:

- Add or remove users in your organization's Microsoft 365 environment
- Manage app licenses for these users
- Manage organization-wide admin role assignments
- Create and manage Azure Active Directory groups and mailboxes
- Manage app licenses and billing information
- Log a support ticket with Microsoft Support
- Register your company domain with Microsoft 365
- View usage and compliance reports and perform audits
- Monitor Microsoft 365 health and performance
- Administer and govern individual Microsoft 365 apps using the corresponding admin center

Since this book is focused on using the different workloads of Microsoft 365, discussing admin capabilities is beyond the scope of this book. However, although the book doesn't cover portal administration recipes, it is good to know about the various roles available in Microsoft 365. We will cover this next.

Microsoft 365 admin roles

Microsoft 365 has various administrator roles, each specific to the nature of the work that the admin is involved in. These roles can be divided into three broad categories.

Global roles: Users with these roles can access all Microsoft 365 admin features. The two global roles are as follows:

- **Global admin:** This is the highest privilege you can get in the Microsoft 365 admin center. Global admins can perform all tasks within the Microsoft 365 admin center. They can also add other individuals as global admins. This role should be granted with caution.

 The person who signed up for Microsoft 365 automatically becomes a global admin.

- **Global reader:** Individuals with this role can view admin features but cannot change them.

Administrator roles: These roles are assigned to individuals responsible for maintaining the different administrative aspects of your Microsoft 365 services, such as licensing, billing, users, helpdesk requests, and so on. Some key roles under this category are as follows:

- **Helpdesk admin:** To reset passwords and manage service requests
- **User admin:** To create users and groups
- **Compliance admin:** To maintain data governance
- **Guest invited:** To provide external users with access to the organization's Active Directory
- **License admin:** To assign licenses to users

Admins for a specific app or workload: It is a best practice to assign individuals admin access only to the services that they are responsible for. Some noteworthy admin roles for specific services are as follows:

- **Exchange admin:** To manage Exchange Online
- **Groups admin:** To manage Microsoft 365 groups
- **SharePoint admin:** To manage SharePoint and OneDrive
- **Teams service admin:** To administer the Teams application
- **Power Platform admin:** To manage Power Apps and Power Automate
- **Power BI admin:** To administer Power BI admin tasks

There are other admin roles in addition to the ones mentioned here. A full list of admin roles and their descriptions is available at `https://packt.link/admin-roles`.

With this high-level summary of administration roles completed, we are ready to begin exploring recipes for different services in Microsoft 365.

Let's get started!

Our aim is to equip you with the necessary knowledge to maximize the benefits of your Microsoft 365 subscription. Understanding the entire Microsoft 365 ecosystem may seem overwhelming, which is why this book is specifically designed to provide explanations on the functionality of each Microsoft 365 application, how to effectively utilize them, and guidance on when to choose one over another.

Microsoft 365 is compatible with various devices, offering a consistent experience across all platforms. However, please note that the screenshots in this book were captured on Windows 10 devices using the Chrome browser. Therefore, if you are using a different operating system or browser, there may be slight differences in the visual presentation.

Although this book comprehensively addresses the key applications in the Microsoft 365 suite, it's important to acknowledge that the technology continues to evolve rapidly. Certain services may become deprecated, while new ones are introduced. In creating this book, our aim was to align closely with the current offerings. We sincerely hope that this book proves valuable to you in your Microsoft 365 pursuits. As a reminder, we encourage you to reach out to us via customercare@packtpub.com and mention the book title in the subject line for any feedback or concerns that you may have. We always welcome your input in helping make this book better.

Best of luck. Let's get started! Our first few chapters will cover one of the most widely used services, SharePoint.

Learn more on Discord

To join the Discord community for this book – where you can share feedback, ask questions to the author, and learn about new releases – follow the QR code below:

https://packt.link/powerusers

2

Introduction to SharePoint Online

SharePoint Online is part of the Microsoft 365 ecosystem that facilitates collaboration and productivity in organizations by empowering its users with tools to create and share content. At its core, SharePoint is a content management system that gives its users *places*, such as sites, lists, and libraries, where they can create and store documents and data. It also lets its users collaborate on this content by allowing it to be securely shared with others within or outside the organization. Users are also able to securely find this content through the powerful **Microsoft Search** capability.

Additionally, SharePoint enables an organization to effectively communicate through rich pages, engaging tools, and **web parts.** We will go over these areas in more detail throughout the book, first introducing them in *Chapter 3, Modern Sites in SharePoint Online*.

SharePoint integrates well with a lot of other tools within and outside of the Microsoft 365 ecosystem, such as Microsoft Teams, OneDrive, and the Microsoft Office suite, to name a few. SharePoint can be accessed through a variety of desktop and mobile browsers, such as Edge, Chrome, Firefox, and Safari. It can also be accessed through native iOS and Android mobile apps.

We briefly discussed in *Chapter 1, Overview of Microsoft 365*, that SharePoint is available both as a standalone e-installation (on-premises) and as a cloud offering through Microsoft 365. The recipes in our book are written with the cloud version in mind, called **SharePoint Online.** While the recipes and related commentary are written for and tested with the cloud version, the key concepts equally apply to both versions of SharePoint. All references to SharePoint in these chapters and in general throughout the book refer to SharePoint Online unless mentioned otherwise.

The following recipes in this introductory chapter will show you how to carry out some of the more common tasks in SharePoint Online:

- Getting to the SharePoint start page
- Creating a modern site
- Viewing site contents
- Creating a list
- Adding an item to a list

- Creating a document library
- Uploading documents to a library
- Deleting and restoring a file
- Sharing a document
- Searching content

While this chapter covers the more commonly used scenarios, dedicated chapters later in this book will dive into many of the different areas of SharePoint in more detail. You will find references to these chapters in the *See also* sections of each recipe in this chapter. By the end of this chapter, you will be able to carry out basic yet common tasks in SharePoint.

Getting to the SharePoint start page

The SharePoint start page is the central location that shows you relevant content from all the SharePoint sites that you have access to in your organization. From here, you can easily get to the sites that you are following, frequently visit, or have recently visited. This page also lets you search for content across all the SharePoint sites that you may have access to.

This recipe shows you how to log in to Microsoft 365 and then browse to the SharePoint Online home page from there.

Getting ready

To be able to browse to the SharePoint start page, your organization should have purchased one of the Microsoft 365 products that contain SharePoint. In addition, they should have assigned you a license to use SharePoint Online.

How to do it...

You can follow these steps to access the SharePoint Online home page:

1. Browse to www.office.com and click the **Sign in** button.
2. Log in using your email ID and password.
3. You will be directed to the Microsoft 365 home page. Click the **app launcher** in the top-left corner, as shown in the following image:

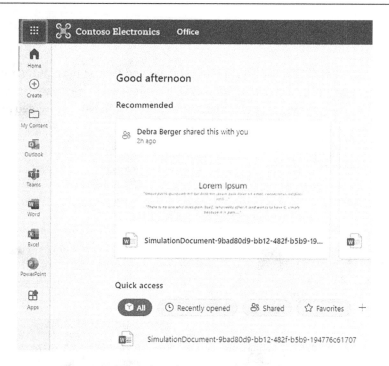

Figure 2.1: The app launcher icon on the Office home page

4. Doing so will expand the app launcher to reveal the suggested and frequently used apps. Then click the **SharePoint** icon, as shown below:

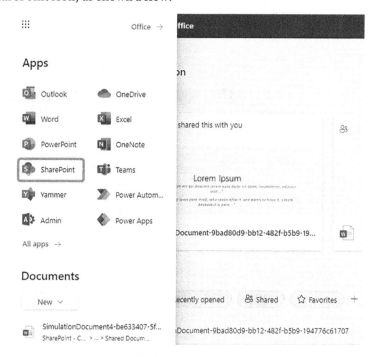

Figure 2.2: Finding SharePoint on the app launcher

5. Doing so will take you to the SharePoint start page, which we will look at in the *How it works...* section of this recipe.

That's it! You just learned how to log on to Microsoft 365 and browse to your organization's SharePoint start page. The content that you see on this page is personalized to you based on various factors, such as, but not limited to, content you've modified or interacted with, news promoted by your organization, your past searches, sites or people you follow, etc.

How it works...

The SharePoint start page shows your interactions across all SharePoint sites that you have access to. In short, this page lets you get to what's most relevant to you, without you having to search for the content.

All pages in SharePoint, including the start page, are comprised of three sections:

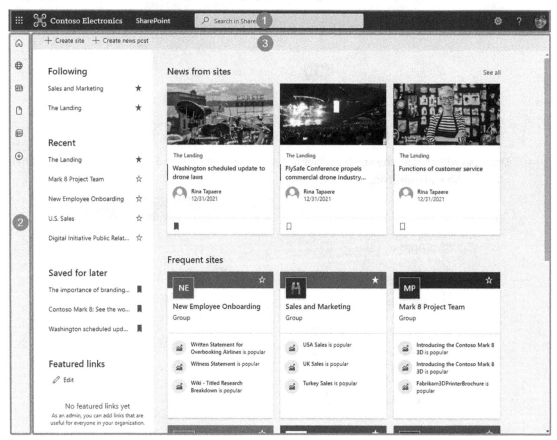

Figure 2.3: The SharePoint start page

1. The **navigation bar**: We discussed the navigation bar as part of *Chapter 1, Overview of Microsoft 365*. One additional detail about the navigation bar for the SharePoint start page is that the search box in the center of this bar allows you to centrally search all your SharePoint and OneDrive content right from within this page.

You will get to know more about searching content in SharePoint later in this chapter. There's also a dedicated chapter later in the book (*Chapter 14, Search in Microsoft 365*) that covers Microsoft 365 Search in greater detail.

2. The **app bar**: The app bar is your gateway to the most relevant content in SharePoint. It allows you to navigate to the sites, news, files, and lists deemed most relevant to you through your interactions with SharePoint and Microsoft 365 in general. It also allows your organization to define global navigation:

Figure 2.4: The app bar on the left of the SharePoint start page

The following list numerically goes through the six different features you can access through the app bar, as shown in *Figure 2.4*:

1. **Home:** The home icon takes you to the SharePoint start page by default. However, as a SharePoint administrator or an owner of the SharePoint home site (see *Types of modern sites* later in this chapter), you can modify the home icon to show cross-site navigation instead.

    Such cross-site navigation in SharePoint is also called **global navigation**. We will read more about global navigation in the *Modifying the top navigation* recipe of *Chapter 3, Modern Sites in SharePoint Online*.

   You can also read more about implementing global navigation through the app bar here: `https://packt.link/home-icon`.

2. **My sites:** Clicking this icon shows you a list of your frequently visited and recently followed sites.

3. **My news:** Clicking this link shows you the recommended news from across all sites.

4. **My files:** This shows you a list of your recently visited documents.

5. **My lists:** This shows you the lists that you have recently worked with or that you have marked as a favorite.

6. **Create:** This link allows you to create:

- Sites within your organization's Microsoft 365 environment.
- News posts, pages, and lists in sites that you have access to.
- Word/ Excel/ PowerPoint files or OneNote notebooks in your OneDrive.

3. The third section on a SharePoint screen is the **main content area:** The navigation bar and the app bar remain stationary as you navigate between various SharePoint sites and pages. What changes, however, is the content that you see within the main area outside of these bars. For the SharePoint home page, this content area contains the following sections:

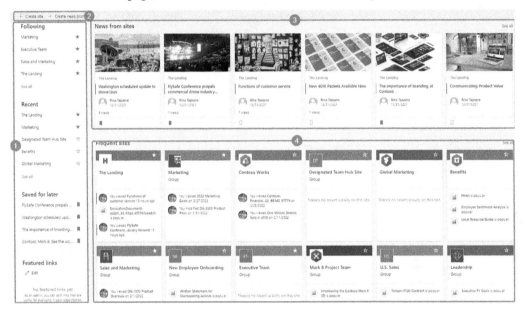

Figure 2.5: The main content area of the SharePoint home page

🔍 **Quick tip:** Need to see a high-resolution version of this image? Open this book in the next-gen Packt Reader or view it in the PDF/ePub copy.

🔒 **The next-gen Packt Reader** and a **free PDF/ePub copy** of this book are included with your purchase. Unlock them by scanning the QR code below or visiting
`https://www.packtpub.com/unlock/9781803243177.`

Let's go through each of these sections of the main content area point by point:

1. **Bookmarks** section: This section allows you to quickly get to content that you have bookmarked or that you have recently interacted with. This section contains the following subsections:

   - **Following:** Here, you can view a list of the sites that you are following. You can then click the site name to directly go to the home page of that site. When you create a site, SharePoint automatically adds it to the list of sites that you are following. To follow an existing site, you can click the **Not following** text toward the top right of any page on that site, as shown in the following image:

Figure 2.6: Toggle following/not following on the top right of a web page

   - **Recent:** This section shows a list of sites that you recently visited. You can click on the site name to quickly get to that site. You can also click the star (☆) image next to the site name to add it to the followed sites list.

   - **Saved for later:** As you browse pages within various SharePoint sites, you can bookmark them by clicking the bookmark (🔖) icon or the **Save for later** link toward the bottom of any news item or a SharePoint page, as shown below:

Figure 2.7: Using the Save for later link to add a page to the Bookmarks section

   - These bookmarked pages then show up in this section. Clicking the page name takes you to the respective page.

   - **Featured links:** Your organization can add links that are useful for everyone in this section. These links are visible to everyone in the entire organization. These could be links to your organization's website, timesheet system, payroll, or other resources that would prove useful for everyone. Only users that have certain admin privileges can create or edit these links.

2. **Create site** and **Create news post**: Clicking **Create site** starts the new SharePoint site creation wizard. We'll discuss this in more detail as part of the *Creating a modern site* recipe later in this chapter.

   Clicking **Create news post** takes you to the **Create news post** page within a site of your choice.

These options only show up if your organization has turned them on. We'll discuss this in more detail as part of the *Adding a page* recipe in *Chapter 3, Modern Sites in SharePoint Online*.

3. **News from sites:** As the title suggests, this section brings together news from all your sites in one single place. From here, you can simply click the news item to go to the details page. You can also bookmark (save for later reading) a news item so that it shows up in your list of **Saved items** on this page.

4. **Frequent sites:** As the title suggests, this section shows you *tiles* containing information about your most visited sites. In addition to the name of the site and a link to it, each tile shows a quick glimpse of what's the latest and what's popular on the site.

See also

- *Chapter 1, Overview of Microsoft 365*
- The *Creating a modern site* recipe in this chapter
- The *Adding a page* recipe in *Chapter 3, Modern Sites in SharePoint Online*

Creating a modern site

SharePoint provides various templates or site types so that you can create sites. These templates use similar building blocks but create slightly different sites in the end that help target different collaboration and communication goals. These templates differ from each other in various ways, such as how they store information, how they present it, and even the features that they offer.

This recipe shows you how to create a site using the **Team site** template, which is the most commonly used site template for team collaboration.

Getting ready

Your organization should do the following before you can create sites from the SharePoint start page:

- Grant you access to SharePoint as part of the Microsoft 365 suite
- Enable the creation of sites from the SharePoint start page
- Enable the creation of modern sites in your Microsoft 365 environment

How to do it...

To create a new site from the SharePoint start page, follow these steps:

1. Browse to the SharePoint start page, as described in the previous recipe.
2. Click on the **Create site** option and then **Team site**, as shown in the following screenshot:

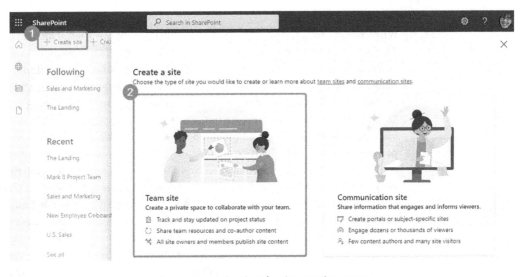

Figure 2.8: Navigating the site creation screen

 If you can't see the **Create site** option, your organization has likely disabled site creation for you.

3. Click **Standard team** and then click **Use template**:

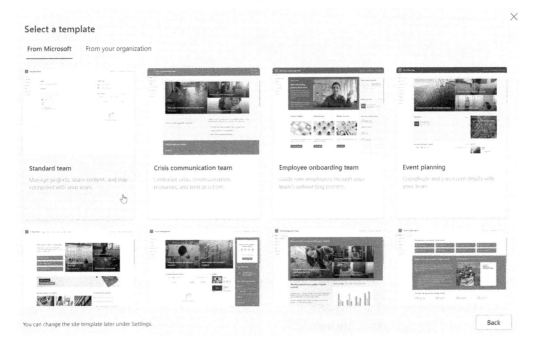

Figure 2.9: Selecting a template for your site

When you create a site, it comes with a standard set of libraries, lists, and pages. The lists, libraries, and pages that get created as part of the standard team and communication site templates are very minimal. SharePoint offers additional templates which contain pre-populated pages, page templates, web parts, and other artifacts that may be better suited to the specific needs of the site being created. Your organization can also create templates which you can apply when creating your sites. Like the templates provided by Microsoft, these templates can have pre-built content which can be specific to your custom needs. Please note that exporting a site as a template and creating a site template from scratch both require development knowledge. Also note that these templates are subject to change and will grow over time. It is worth checking for the latest built-in site templates currently available here: `https://packt.link/site-templates`. Finally, you can always start with one template and apply a different template on top of it later, through the site settings menu. We discuss the site settings menu in the *Viewing and changing site settings* recipe of *Chapter 3, Modern Sites in SharePoint Online*.

4. Fill in **Site name**, **Site description**, confirm or change the pre-selected **Group email address**, and then click the **Next** button:

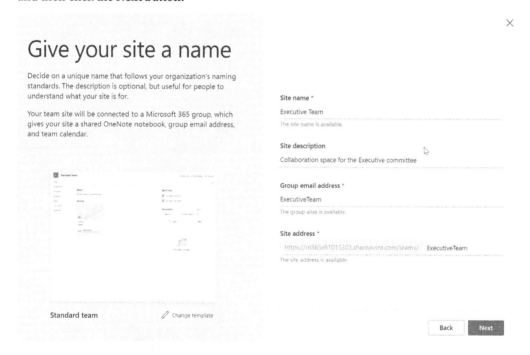

Figure 2.10: Entering details for creating a team site

5. Choose the **Privacy settings**, **Select a language** (more about these settings later in this recipe). Then, click the **Create site** button.

The group email address that you can see in the previous screenshot is used for the corresponding Microsoft 365 group that gets created along with the team site. You can read more about groups in *Chapter 16, Microsoft 365 Groups*.

Furthermore, you should carefully choose the **Privacy settings** on this screen. Choosing **Private** for this setting means only selected members that you allow on the next screen will have access to view and modify content within the site. Selecting **Public** would mean that *everyone* in your organization will be able to view and modify content within this site. You can always change the site's permissions after it has been created.

6. At this point, SharePoint will start creating the site in the background.

7. Even as it does that, SharePoint will prompt you to optionally invite other users to your site. These users are typically people from your organization who you'd like to grant owner or member access to this site. Coworkers you add from here are added as **Members** by default. You can change their access level on the site by selecting the word **Member** against their name and then changing the role to **Owner**. This can be seen in the following screenshot:

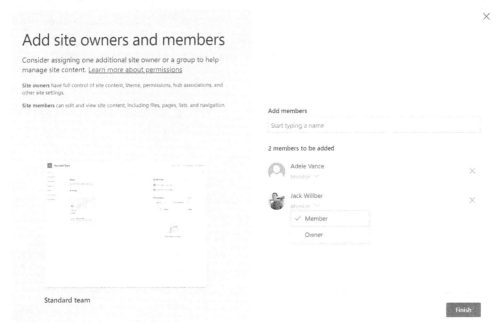

Figure 2.11: Adding members to a team site

Owners and members who are added through this screen are granted two different levels of permissions in SharePoint. Members can add, update, or delete content (documents, pages, and/or list items) on your site. They can also view all the content within your site that others may have authored. In comparison, site owners can do everything that members can do. In addition they are able to alter site permissions, add and customize pages, and change other key elements of the site. This access is usually only granted to a select few users from the team.

There is also a third permission setting, visitor access. Visitors to your site can view the content within your site. This content can be presented through informational lists, documents, or pages within your site.

8. Clicking **Finish** will then redirect you to the home page of this newly created site. You may also be prompted to apply a custom template to your site, but we will talk about that in the next section.

Congratulations! You just created a new site in SharePoint Online.

How it works...

At its core, a SharePoint site is a website that lets us store information and then present it in different ways. Information can be stored as data in lists and in the form of documents and/or files in libraries within the site. SharePoint uses pages and, optionally, web parts in these pages to show this information in a variety of formats. When you create a new site in SharePoint, it automatically creates one or more of these artifacts for you within that site. Finally, every site that gets created comes with search capabilities built into it. Microsoft Search in SharePoint is a quick way to find information relevant to you, not only from within your site but also other sites and workloads that your organization may have enabled in Microsoft 365. We will learn more about Search as part of the *Searching content* recipe in this chapter and then go through it in more detail as part of *Chapter 14, Search in Microsoft 365*.

Types of modern sites

At the time of writing this book, Microsoft has made a variety of templates available for modern sites. Let's go over them now.

Team site

This type of site is primarily used for collaboration within a team or a department that is actively working on a shared project or goal. As mentioned earlier, this is by far the most common type of site template used for creating SharePoint sites. SharePoint team sites are also connected to Microsoft 365 groups, which, in turn, are connected to other Microsoft 365 workloads such as Microsoft Teams, Planner, and Outlook. Examples of team sites include sites created for individual project teams to collaborate on, sites created to work with external partners or vendors, and sites created for departments within the organization (such as the Human Resource department or Finance department) for their team collaboration. This means your organization would typically have a lot of team sites.

 While this recipe described creating a group-associated team site, you can also have your designated SharePoint admin(s) create modern team sites for you without an underlying group. They can create such team sites through the SharePoint admin center.

Communication site

This type of site is used to broadcast a message or simply tell a story to your organization. Communication sites can be used to share news, reports, strategies, and other information in a visually compelling way. The content in a typical communication site will be shared with a large audience (potentially the entire organization). Examples of communication sites include your intranet landing site, a training site, a site where members in your organization would view key business metrics, and a site that's created to gather information for an organizational merger. This means your organization would typically have very few communication sites.

Hub site

 SharePoint hub sites are a way to bring together (roll up) information such as news and activity from a family of related sites. As a site owner, you can either register your site as a hub site or associate it with an existing hub. If you choose to associate your site with an existing hub, your site will inherit the look and feel of the hub site.

Your site will also inherit other properties of the hub site, such as the navigation bar, additional navigation links, applications, or custom lists with specific columns.

Additionally, users who have been granted access to the hub site will start seeing content, news, and activity being rolled up from your site, along with any other sites that are associated with that hub site. This makes it easier for users to discover related content from across all these sites. An example of a hub site could be an enterprise Sales portal providing shared resources for the organization-wide Sales teams and connecting multiple regional Sales team sites and communication sites.

 Hub sites need special permissions to be created and cannot be created by end users through the SharePoint start page. They can only be created by special users designated as SharePoint admins by your organization. You can read more about the SharePoint admin role here: `https://packt.link/SP-admin`.

Home site

A home site is your organization's designated intranet landing site. Behind the scenes, a home site is just another communication site, but with the following differences:

- It aggregates content from your entire organization through news, events, videos, conversations, and other resources.
- The search experience in the home site defaults to the entire organization. This means that if you perform a search from the home site, it will bring back results from the entire organization.
- You can only designate one site from your entire organization as the organization's home site.

It is highly recommended that you create a home site as a place to aggregate content that is of utmost importance to your organization.

You can read more about the home site and the best practices surrounding its setup here: `https://packt.link/home-site`.

Site creation next steps

After you create a site, you are provided with a menu to carry out additional actions for it:

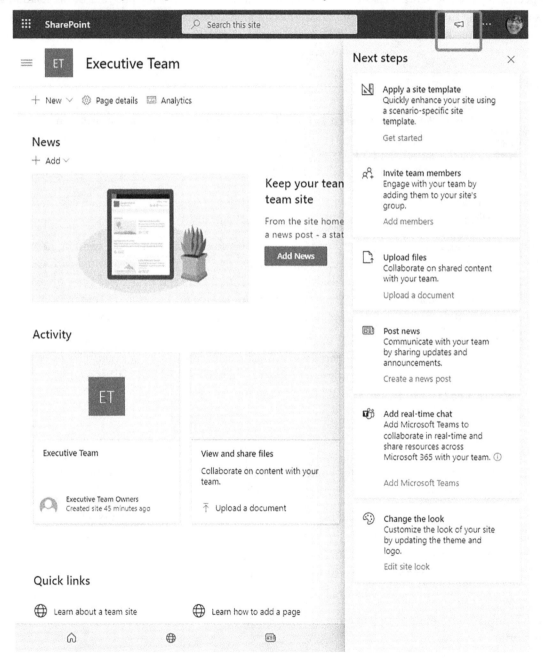

Figure 2.12: Additional actions menu for a created site

Let's go through each of these options:

- **Apply a site template:** When you create a site, it comes with a standard set of libraries, lists, and pages. The lists, libraries, and pages that get created as part of the standard team and communication site templates are very minimal. SharePoint offers additional templates that you can apply on top of these standard sites. These templates contain pre-populated pages, page templates, web parts, and other artifacts that may be better suited to the specific needs of the site being created. The following image shows the different templates that are currently available in SharePoint:

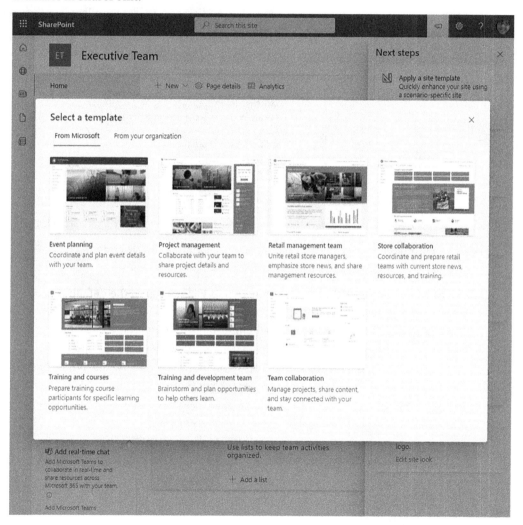

Figure 2.13: Selecting a template for your site

As you can see from the image, your organization can also create templates that you can apply when creating your sites. Like the templates provided by Microsoft, these templates can have pre-baked content that can be specific to your custom needs built into them.

As we hinted at before we delved into the different types of modern sites, these templates are subject to change. It is worth checking for any built-in site templates currently available that might suit your purpose: `https://packt.link/site-templates`.

This Microsoft article provides a walk-through of the steps you can use to create your own templates: `https://packt.link/create-site-template`.

Please note that exporting a site as a template and creating a site template from scratch both require development knowledge.

- **Invite team members:** You can use this action to grant access to others to your site. Please note that this option is called **Share this site with others** for communication sites:

 Share this site with others
Get help managing site content
by adding site owners and
members, then share the site
with visitors.

Add owners, members, and
visitors

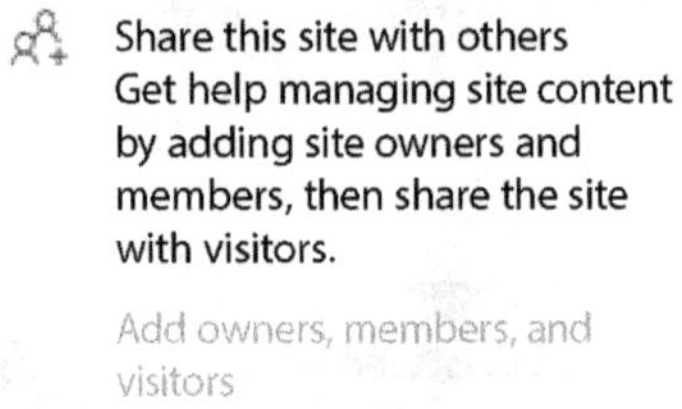

Figure 2.14: Invite team members option is named differently for communication sites

We will discuss permissions and access in more detail in the *Determining and revoking permissions in a site* recipe of *Chapter 3, Modern Sites in SharePoint Online*.

- **Upload files:** Clicking **Upload a document** simply takes you to the default document library for the site so you can upload the relevant document(s) to it. You will learn about document libraries and uploading documents to them through subsequent recipes in this chapter.
- **Post news:** Clicking **Create a news post** creates a draft **News post** page, and takes you to it. You will learn more about creating news posts in the *News post and news link* topic of the *Adding a page* recipe in *Chapter 3, Modern Sites in SharePoint Online*.
- **Add real-time chat:** Clicking **Add Microsoft Teams** creates a new team and links this site to it. You will learn all about Teams in *Chapter 7, Microsoft Teams*.
- **Change the look:** Clicking **Edit site look** allows you to apply a theme to your site, as well as changing its header, footer, and navigation settings. You will learn more about these topics through multiple recipes in *Chapter 3, Modern Sites in SharePoint Online*.

There's more...

In this section, we will briefly review the concept of site collections. We will then look at the difference between the deprecated classic user interface versus the more modern experience.

Site versus site collection

As noted earlier, what we created through this recipe is actually called a **site collection**. Fundamentally, as the name suggests, this is a *collection* of one or more sites that are under the same URL. More often than not, all sites within a site collection will share identical navigation, branding, audience type, and sometimes even similar security.

When you first create a site collection, SharePoint will create a top-level site, or what is known as the **root site**, for you. You can then create as many **subsites** as you'd like to under this root site.

Microsoft no longer recommends creating subsites. Everything in the modern SharePoint experience is based on top-level sites (or site collections, as they are called). In fact they have altogether eliminated the words *site collections* and *subsites* from their terminology and just use the word *site* instead.

You can read more about this change as part of the *How it works...* section of the *Creating a subsite* recipe in *Chapter 3, Modern Sites in SharePoint Online*.

Modern versus classic experience

SharePoint supports two different **user interface** (UI) experiences:

- The more modern, fluid, and mobile-friendly experience
- The classic experience, which is now being phased out

The modern experience makes it easy for you to create dynamic sites and pages that automatically adjust to the resolution of the device that they are being viewed on and are, hence, mobile-friendly. The modern site experience also includes a newer, modern way of working with lists and libraries. Since the classic experience is being deprecated and is no longer recommended for creating new content, we will only be discussing the modern experience in this book. For those of you with an inquisitive mind, here is a great article on the SharePoint community blog explaining the modern experience and why you should use it for creating new content: `https://packt.link/why-modern`.

While it is strongly recommended to use the modern site experience, your SharePoint admins can create classic sites using the SharePoint admin center if there's a really compelling reason for it. The steps to create sites using one of the classic templates are listed here: `https://packt.link/create-classic-site`.

Reusing a site as a template

 This is an advanced topic and requires some development knowledge.

You may want to save your existing site as a template so you can reuse the functionality, structure, and/or some or all content from it. The way you would have achieved this in the classic SharePoint experience was by saving the site as a *template* and then creating new sites using that template. This capability, however, is now deprecated in the modern SharePoint experience.

There are two ways to export existing sites as templates in the more modern experience, and we will look at both here.

Export site using a site script

Site designs and site scripts allow you to create sites using a complex and customizable provisioning experience. They are a great way to create standardized sites from scratch. You can also use site scripts to export your existing site and its settings so you can use the generated script to create a new site.

Please refer to the `Get-SPOSiteScriptFromWeb` command here to export your site as a script: `https://packt.link/Get-SPOSiteScriptFromWeb`.

 The `Get-SPOSiteScriptFromWeb` command is part of the SharePoint Online PowerShell module. You can read more about SharePoint Online PowerShell in the *PowerShell* section of the *Appendix*.

Once the site is exported as a script, you can use it in a site design for users to create a new site based on that template.

In addition to using PowerShell for site designs and site scripts, you can also use the Microsoft 365 Rest API to carry out the same tasks, as described here: `https://packt.link/site-design-REST-API`.

Export site using PnP provisioning

The PnP engine has made developer and admin commands available that can be used to save a site of your choice as a template. You can then optionally make changes to the features of the saved site template and then use similar PnP commands again to provision one or more sites using the saved template.

 You can read more about **PnP** (**Patterns and Practices**) in the *SharePoint PnP* topic of the *Office Development Frameworks* section in the *Appendix*.

You can use the `Get-PnPSiteTemplate` command to export the site as a template, as described here: `https://packt.link/Get-PnPSiteTemplate`.

You would then use the `Invoke-PnPSiteTemplate` command to use this template to create a new site: `https://packt.link/Invoke-PnPSiteTemplate`.

You can read more about the PnP provisioning engine and its templating capabilities here: `https://packt.link/PnP-provisioning-engine`.

See also

- *Chapter 3*, *Modern Sites in SharePoint Online*
- The *SharePoint PnP topic in the Office Development Frameworks section of the Appendix*

Viewing site contents

The **Site contents** page in SharePoint provides a one-stop view of all the lists, libraries, and other apps within the site. Any subsites within that site will also appear here. Provided you have appropriate access, you can also add new lists, libraries, pages, apps, and subsites to the site from this page.

Getting ready

You should have at least **Read** or **View** access to a site in order to be able to view the contents within that site.

How to do it...

To view the contents of your site, follow these steps:

1. Browse to your site in SharePoint.
2. Click on the **settings icon** in the top-right corner of any page on the site and then click **Site contents**, as shown in the following screenshot:

Figure 2.15: Opening the site settings to reach the Site contents page

3. You will be directed to the **Site contents** page, as shown in the following screenshot:

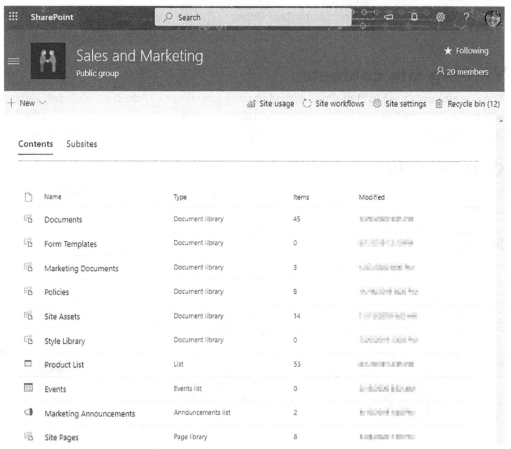

Figure 2.16: Viewing Site contents from Site settings > Site contents

That's it! You can now view the various assets of your site from here.

How it works...

The **Site contents** page lets you view a list of all the lists and libraries within your site. The view shows various information for each list and/or library, including its name, type, the number of items in that list or library, and when anything was last modified in it.

If the site has subsites, you can also view a list of such sites through this page. The view shows the following details for each subsite: its name, description, the number of user views, when the site was created, and when anything was last modified in it.

In addition to this, you can also perform multiple actions from this page as shown in the image below:

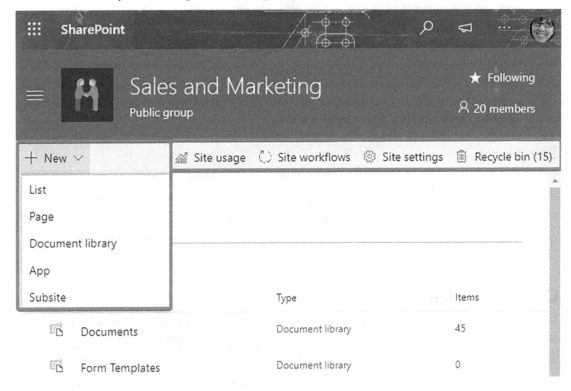

Figure 2.17: Exploring the options on the Site contents page

Let's go over these actions here:

- **New:** You can use this menu to create or add a **List, Page, Document library, App,** and **Subsite.** We will discuss these items through various recipes in this chapter and in *Chapter 3, Modern Sites in SharePoint Online.*

- **Site usage:** You can view these reports to understand how users interact with your site and what content is popular among the users of your site. Assuming you have the required access, this is also where you can generate and view reports about the content permissions within your site. You can read more about site usage reports here: https://packt.link/usage-data.

- **Site workflows:** SharePoint workflows are now deprecated. We will also briefly discuss them as part of the *SharePoint workflows* topic in the *Appendix*. However, if you are still using Share-Point workflows and have appropriate access in SharePoint, you can click this link to view the site workflows.

 The modern way to implement process automation and workflows is to use **Power Automate** in Microsoft 365. We will discuss Power Automate in great detail in *Chapter 8, Power Automate (Microsoft Flow).*

- **Site settings:** You can view and change the site's settings through this link. We'll discuss site settings in detail in the *Viewing and changing site settings* recipe in *Chapter 3, Modern Sites in SharePoint Online*.

- **Recycle bin:** The SharePoint recycle bin is just like the recycle bin on your computer; it lets you view the items that have been deleted from your site. We will return to the recycle bin in the *How it works...* section of the *Deleting and restoring a file* recipe, later in this chapter. Please refer to the *See also* section for other recipes in this chapter where we have covered artifact deletion and the recycle bin in greater detail.

See also

- The *Deleting a list* topic in the *Creating a list* recipe, later in this chapter
- The *Deleting an item* topic in the *Adding an item to a list* recipe, later in this chapter
- The *Deleting and restoring a file* recipe, later in this chapter
- The *Viewing and changing site settings* recipe in *Chapter 3, Modern Sites in SharePoint Online*
- *SharePoint workflows* in the *Appendix*

Creating a list

A SharePoint list is a table-like container that stores information similar to an Excel spreadsheet or a database table. A key difference between Excel files or database tables and lists is that the information in lists is automatically shared with and available to other users that have access to those lists.

This recipe shows you how to create a new list from scratch. For illustrative purposes, we will use this list to store details of the products from our company's product line. This list will contain the following columns to store the product information:

- **Title**
- **Code Name**
- **Product Line**
- **Date Released**
- **Notes**

Getting ready

You will need either **Edit**, **Design**, or **Full Control** permission on the site where you'd like to create the list. You will usually have this permission if you are part of the *Site owners* or *Site members* groups for the site where you would like to create the list.

How to do it...

You can follow these steps to create a new SharePoint list:

1. Browse to the site within which you'd like to create the list.

2. Click the **New** menu, click **List**, and then click **Blank list**:

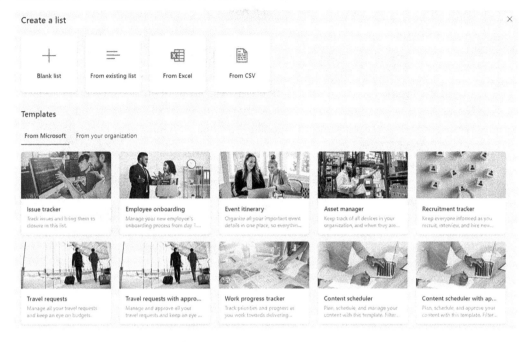

Figure 2.18: The Blank list option from New menu > List

 Instead of creating a new list from scratch, you can also choose to start from an existing list, create a list based on an Excel/ CSV file, or use one of the pre-defined templates to create the list. Doing so creates a list with pre-defined columns and settings. We will further explore these options in *Chapter 4, Lists and Libraries in SharePoint Online.*

3. Provide a descriptive name for the list so that others can identify the nature of the information that it stores. We are going to use Products as the name for our list.

4. Enter a description for the list and leave the **Show in site navigation** box checked. This will result in the list being shown in the site's quick launch navigation area toward the left. Then click the **Create** button:

Figure 2.19: Adding description and visibility options for the Products list

This will create the new list and take us to it in the browser. You will notice that the list already has a **Title** column created for us. We can now add the remaining columns to our list.

5. To add the **Code Name** column, click the **Add column** option and select **Single line of text**. Then, enter Code Name as the column name, optionally provide an appropriate description for the column, and click the **Save** button.

6. To add the **Product Line** column, click on the **Add column** option and enter Product Line in **Name**. Then select **Choice** as the column type and enter Computers & Tablets, Gaming, and Home Theater on three separate lines in the **Choices** field. Then, click the **Save** button, as shown in the following screenshot:

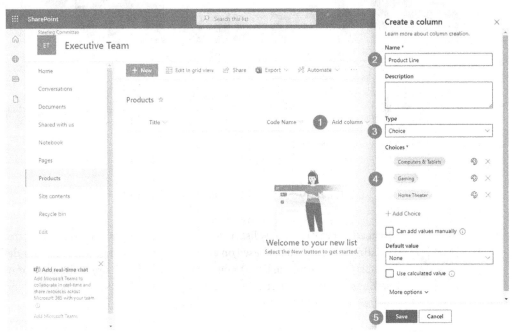

Figure 2.20: Filling in the fields for Create a column

7. To add the **Date Released** column, click the **Add column** option and select **Date** as the column type. Then, enter Date Released as the column name and click the **Save** button.

8. To add the **Notes** column, click on the **Add column** option and select **Multiple lines of text** as the column type. Then, enter Notes as the column name, optionally enter a description, and click the **Save** button.

When a new list is created in SharePoint, it creates a few additional columns that are not shown to the users by default. The **Modified** and **Modified By** columns are two such columns that get created with the list. We are going to add them back to the view of the list so that we can track who added the items to the list and when.

9. Click on **Add column** and then **Show/hide columns**. As shown in the following screenshot, then select the **Modified** and **Modified By** columns:

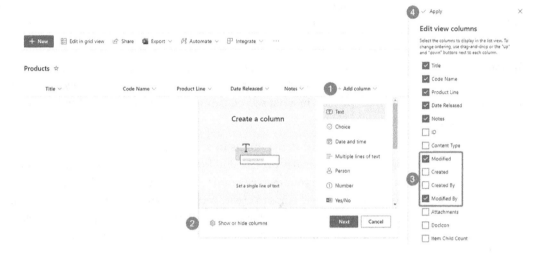

Figure 2.21: Selecting columns to appear in our list

This is what your list will look like:

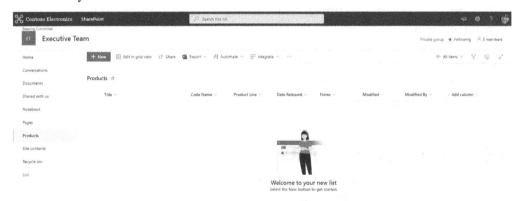

Figure 2.22: Displaying a custom list

Congratulations! You just learned how to create a custom list and added new columns to it.

How it works...

SharePoint uses lists as the primary way to store information that users create. Almost all information in SharePoint is stored in some type of a list. A list in SharePoint helps you to store data in a way that enables you and your co-workers to organize and share information flexibly. Just like a spreadsheet or a database table, it lets you add and manage columns so that you can store and display various types of information such as text, number, date, and currency. For each column, you can also specify properties, such as making the column required or optional, setting a default or calculated value for the column, etc. The properties you can specify for each column type vary based on the type of column. The *Adding a column* recipe in *Chapter 4, Lists and Libraries in SharePoint Online*, discusses list columns in greater detail.

In addition to the ability to define columns, SharePoint lists also let you create multiple *views*, which allow you to organize and show the underlying list data in various forms. List views enable you to filter, sort, group, and format the data in a list so you can easily present and highlight information that's most important to your audience.

Content in lists exists in the form of list items. Items in a list can include file attachments, people, and links. Furthermore, SharePoint provides pre-created forms that you can use to add or update the information in lists. You can also create your own customized forms to add or edit information in lists. You can use tools such as Microsoft Power Apps to create mobile-friendly forms and apps around this data. Additionally, you can configure email alerts for when list items are added, updated, or deleted. We will look at alerts as part of the *Adding alerts* recipe in *Chapter 4, Lists and Libraries in SharePoint Online*.

Deleting a list

You can delete a list by browsing to the **List settings** page. Please refer to the *How it works...* section of the *Viewing and changing list settings* recipe in *Chapter 4, Lists and Libraries in SharePoint Online*, for more information about browsing to the **List settings** page and deleting a list.

See also

- The *Deleting an item* topic in the *Adding an item to a list* recipe, later in this chapter
- The *Deleting and restoring a file* recipe, later in this chapter
- *Chapter 4, Lists and Libraries in SharePoint Online*

Adding an item to a list

You can add items to lists in various ways. This recipe will show the most used method to add items to the representative list we created as part of the previous recipe. The other methods to add list items will be covered in greater detail in *Chapter 4, Lists and Libraries in SharePoint Online*. Even though this recipe uses the **Products** list as an example, the steps provided here can be used to add items to any list.

Getting ready

You will need *Contribute* permissions or higher for the list you would like to add the new item to. You will usually have this permission if you are part of the *Site owners* or *Site members* groups for the site containing the list.

How to do it...

To add a new item to a list, follow these steps:

1. Browse to the list where you'd like to add the new item.

 You can also access the lists and libraries through the **Site contents** page. The *Viewing site contents* recipe earlier in this chapter shows you how to navigate to this page.

2. Click the **New** button above the section that shows the title of the list.

3. Enter information for the required fields (highlighted by a red asterix) and, optionally, the non-required fields.

4. Assuming they are enabled for your list, you can also optionally add file attachments for this item by clicking the **Add attachments** hyperlink toward the bottom of the form. File attachments include a variety of file types – images and documents, to name a few.

5. Click the **Save** button, as shown below, to add the item to the list:

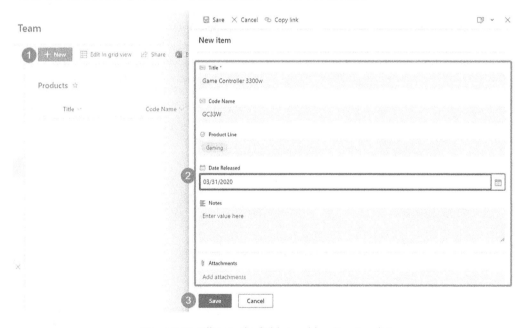

Figure 2.23: Filling in the fields to add an item to a list

Congratulations! You just added a new item to a SharePoint list.

How it works...

You can imagine a list item as a single row in an Excel spreadsheet, except that this row can hold a variety of rich information. Each list comes with a set of forms to add, edit, and view these items. Each list item can optionally also contain one or more attachments.

Furthermore, the forms to add, edit, and view list items can be customized to meet specific user needs. Every time an item is added or edited in a list, SharePoint also stores additional information (or metadata) for that item. This metadata includes information such as who created or edited the item and when was it created or edited. Further, you can use **Power Automate** to set up automated actions when certain things happen in the list. For example, you can set up an automated approval and notification workflow that kicks in when a new item is added to a list or when an existing item is updated. We will discuss Power Automate in depth in *Chapter 8, Power Automate (Microsoft Flow)*.

There's more...

Provided you have appropriate access, you can also carry out additional actions on the item you just created, and other such items in the list. We will discuss these in the sections to follow:

Viewing and editing items

There are a couple of ways in which you can view and edit the newly created item. To view the item:

1. Simply click on the title of the item.
2. Double-click anywhere else on the item.
3. Right-click anywhere on the item and click **Open**.
4. Click the three dots next to the item and then click **Open**:

Figure 2.24: Opening an item

5. Select the item and click the ⓘ icon towards the right of the screen:

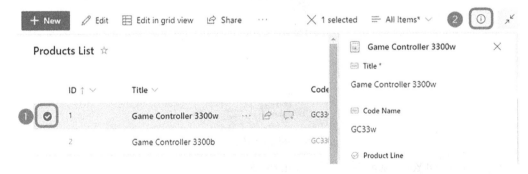

Figure 2.25: Reaching item metadata

To edit the item:

6. Simply click **Edit all** when viewing the item:

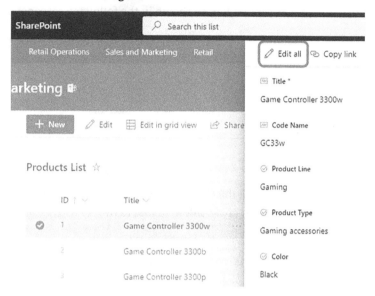

Figure 2.26: Editing item metadata

7. Right-click anywhere on the item and click **Edit**.
8. Click the three dots next to the item and click **Edit**.
9. Select the item and click **Edit** from the list menu bar:

Figure 2.27: Editing an item

Deleting an item

To delete a list item, simply browse to your list, select the file you would like to delete, and then click the **Delete** option from the list's menu bar, as shown in the following screenshot:

Figure 2.28: One method of deleting an item

Alternatively, you can also right-click the list item or click the three dots to the right of the **Title** field to open the context menu and then click **Delete** to delete the item. This is shown in the following screenshot:

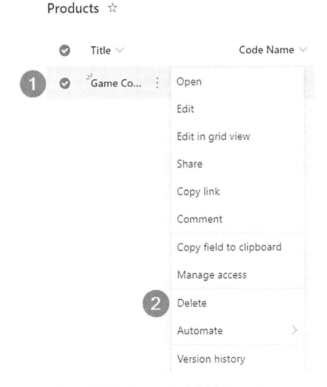

Figure 2.29: Another method of deleting an item

Deleting an item from a list or library sends it to the recycle bin, where it stays for a couple of days until it gets moved to the second-stage recycle bin or gets permanently deleted. You can restore deleted items if they are still in the recycle bin and have not been permanently deleted. Please refer to the *Deleting and restoring a file* recipe, later in this chapter, to read more about the site recycle bin.

Other actions

You can carry out many other actions for list items in addition to viewing, editing, and deleting them. You can view these actions by right clicking the item or clicking the three dots next to it, as shown below:

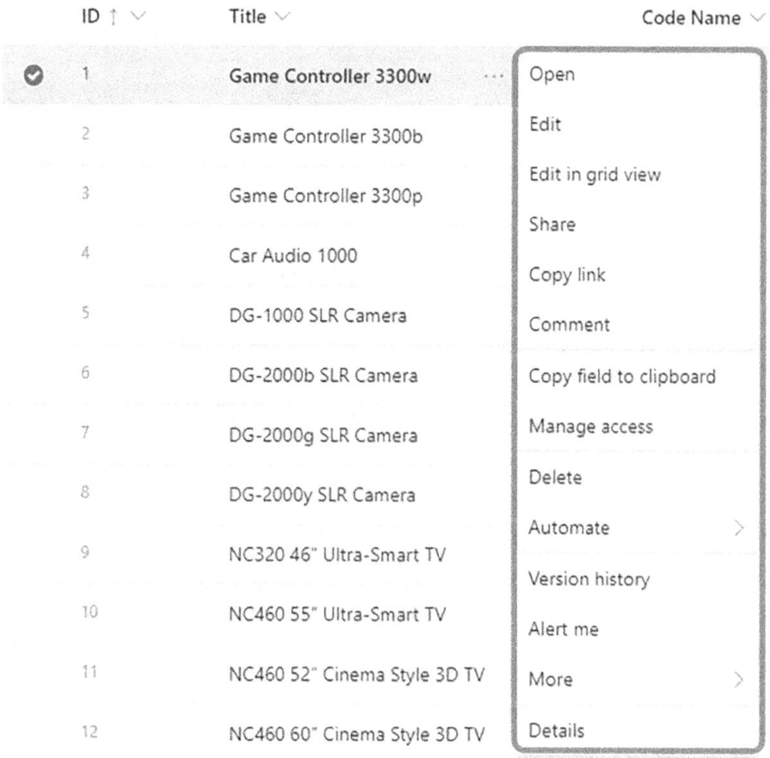

Figure 2.30: Viewing item actions

We will cover many of these in detail in subsequent chapters, but here are a few key ones in addition to **Open**, **Edit**, and **Delete**, which we discussed previously:

*   **Edit in grid view:** Allows the item to be edited in grid view. You will learn more about this in *Chapter 4, Lists and Libraries in SharePoint Online*.
*   **Share** and **Copy link:** Allow you to get and email a sharable link to the item. You will learn more about this later in this chapter.

- **Comment:** Comments are a great way to have discussions around items. You can even @ mention your colleagues in the comments to get their attention. Doing so sends them an email with your comment and a link to the item. The following screenshot shows the two places from where you can create and access comments and what the commenting experience looks like:

Figure 2.31: Adding comments

- **Copy field to clipboard:** You can right-click any field to copy its value to the clipboard. Clicking ••• and then clicking **Copy field to clipboard** copies the value of the **Title** field for that list item.
- **Manage access:** This option allows you to manage permissions for the item. You only see this option if you have owner-level permissions to the item. You will learn more about list and item permissions in *Chapter 4, Lists and Libraries in SharePoint Online*.
- **Automate:** This option allows you to create and/or run automation workflows on the item. You will learn more about this in *Chapter 8, Power Automate (Microsoft Flow)*.
- **Version history:** SharePoint allows you to maintain and view a history of all the changes that have happened to the item since it was created. You will learn more about versioning in *Chapter 5, Document Management in SharePoint Online*.
- **Alert me:** You can set up alerts on the item to get notified when changes happen to the item. You will learn more about alerts in *Chapter 4, Lists and Libraries in SharePoint Online*.
- **More:** This option contains legacy and other advanced sub-options which are beyond the scope of this options.
- **Details:** Opens a detailed view of the item, which allows you to view the item properties and managed permissions to it. This is the same view which opens when you select the item and click the ⓘ icon to view it.

See also

- The *Deleting a list* topic in the *Creating a list* recipe, earlier in this chapter
- The *Deleting and restoring a file* recipe, later in this chapter
- The *Using Edit in grid view to bulk-edit list items* recipe in *Chapter 4, Lists and Libraries in SharePoint Online*
- The *Sharing a document* recipe, later in this chapter
- The *Viewing and changing list permissions* recipe in *Chapter 4, Lists and Libraries in SharePoint Online*

- *Chapter 8, Power Automate (Microsoft Flow)*
- The *Versioning settings, content approval, and document checkout* recipe in *Chapter 5, Document Management in SharePoint Online*
- The *Adding alerts* recipe in *Chapter 4, Lists and Libraries in SharePoint Online*

Creating a document library

A library is a secure place in SharePoint where you can upload, create, edit, and manage files for online sharing and collaboration with your team. Just like lists, each library comes with key built-in columns that automatically store default information about each file, such as who created the file and when, and who last modified it and when. You can always add your own columns to the library, just as you would for a list. Each SharePoint site ships with one or more libraries to enable you to store files within the site. Libraries can be of different types. A **document library** is the most used type of library. As the name suggests, it is used to store, manage, and share documents. The **Site pages** library is used to store and manage pages and news items. The *Inbuilt list and library templates* topic of the *Creating a list using a built-in list template* recipe in *Chapter 4, Lists and Libraries in SharePoint Online*, provides a list of all the inbuilt templates.

For this recipe, we will create a document library from scratch. We will use this library to store marketing documents. This library will also enable you to classify each document using the **Document Type** and **Document Classification** columns.

Getting ready

You will need either **Edit**, **Design**, or **Full Control** permission on the site where you'd like to create the library. You will usually have this permission if you are part of the *Site owners* or *Site members* groups for the site where you would like to create the library.

How to do it...

You can follow these steps to create a new document library:

1. Browse to any page within the site where you'd like to create the library.
2. Click the **New** menu and then click the **Document library** option.
3. Provide a name and description for the library so that others can identify the nature of the documents that it stores. We are going to use `Marketing Collateral` as the library name and `This library contains collateral for use of the Marketing team` as its description.
4. We will leave the **Show in site navigation** box checked. This will result in the library being shown on the left-hand side navigation menu for the site.
5. We will then click the **Create** button to create the new document library. This will create the new library and redirect us to it in the browser.
6. You will notice that the library comes with the following columns already created for us: **Name**, **Modified**, and **Modified By**. We can now add the remaining columns to our library.

7. To add the **Document Type** column, click on the **Add column** option and select **Choice** as the column type. Then, enter `Document Type` as the column name. Enter `Campaign`, `Case Study`, `Product Overview`, and `Product Pitching` in four separate lines in the **Choices** field.

8. Then, click **More options**, set **Require that this column contains information** to **Yes**, and click the **Save** button, as shown in the following screenshot:

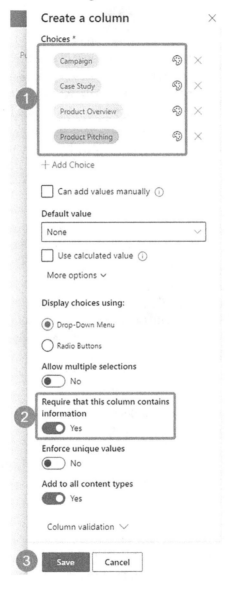

Figure 2.32: Filling in the options for creating a column

9. Similarly, to add the **Document Classification** column, click the **Add column** option again and select **Choice** as the column type. Then, enter `Document Classification` as the column name. Enter `Confidential`, `Restricted`, `Internal use`, and `Public` in four separate lines in the **Choices** field.

10. Then, click **More options**, set **Require that this column contains information** to **Yes**, and click the **Save** button.

11. We will also change the position of the two newly created columns so that they show up next to the **Name** column (before the **Modified** and **Modified By** columns). To do so, simply click on the **Document Type** column name and drag it to the left, before the **Modified** column. Do the same for the **Document Classification** column, as shown in the following screenshot:

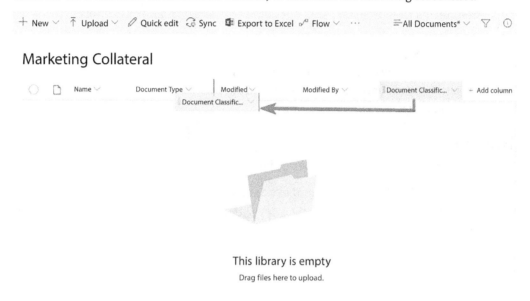

Figure 2.33: Rearranging the columns of a list

That's it – congratulations! You just created and configured your first SharePoint document library.

How it works...

We discussed lists in the two previous recipes. A **document library** is a special type of list that is centered around documents. Just like a list, it lets you add, edit, view, and delete documents, and metadata related to those documents. One of the more popular and widely used features that document libraries enable is the ability for multiple users to concurrently view and edit documents that it stores. Users can not only concurrently edit documents but can also view each other's edits in real time. SharePoint also lets you create complex approval workflows surrounding these documents. Like regular lists, you can set email alerts so you are notified when relevant documents in a library are added, updated, or deleted.

Just like lists, SharePoint comes with a number of pre-built libraries. Some notable examples of such libraries are the **picture library**, **form library**, and **site pages library**.

See also

- *Chapter 4, Lists and Libraries in SharePoint Online*
- *Chapter 5, Document Management in SharePoint Online*

Uploading documents to a library

SharePoint lets you create new documents directly within a library through the **New** menu. It also lets you upload documents that have been authored offline.

In this recipe, we are going to learn how to upload an existing document to a document library and then associate metadata to it. Even though this recipe uses the **Marketing Collateral** library, which we previously created as an example, the steps here work for any SharePoint library.

Getting ready

You will need **Contribute** permissions or higher to the library where you would like to upload the document. You will usually have this permission if you are part of the *Site owners* or *Site members* groups for the site containing the library.

How to do it...

Here's how to upload a document to your document library:

1. Browse to the library where you'd like to upload the document.

2. Click **Upload** and then choose the **Files** option to open the file selection dialog, as shown in the following screenshot:

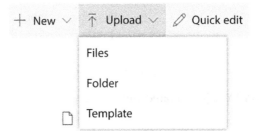

Figure 2.34: Choosing an item to upload to a document library

3. Browse to the file that you'd like to upload and click the **Open** button.

 SharePoint also supports drag-and-drop capabilities, which work with a wide variety of browsers. Simply drag and drop the files or folders anywhere in the browser window when viewing the library. This will result in SharePoint uploading the folders, subfolders, and any files within them to the library.

4. This will initiate the file upload process. SharePoint will show the newly uploaded file in the library, as shown in the following screenshot:

Figure 2.35: Uploaded file in a document library

5. You will notice that SharePoint shows information about the file as well as a preview.

 Clicking the preview in the right-hand side pane activates the file and lets you view the entire contents of the file right from within that pane.

6. You will need to enter information in the required fields for this document before it becomes visible to anyone else in your site or your organization (depending on how the site's security has been configured). You will also want to give your file a friendly title at this point. Click the **Edit all** link in the details pane toward the right. Make sure the document is selected if you can't see the details pane.

7. Enter or select the required information for the document and click the **Save** button, as shown in the following screenshot:

Figure 2.36: Required information and Save button on the details pane

After you've uploaded the document, SharePoint will maintain a history of all edits that have been made to that document. You can view the previous versions of the document, when and who modified it, and even roll back the document to a previous version. This is particularly useful when a document is being updated by multiple users and you need to "undo" a small set of changes because they were inaccurate or incorrect.

That's it! You have now uploaded your first document to a SharePoint document library. We will learn how to view and modify these documents in the *Viewing and editing documents in the browser* recipe in *Chapter 5, Document Management in SharePoint Online*.

How it works...

Documents are stored in libraries one document at a time. SharePoint also lets you upload or delete multiple documents at a time. If your documents have associated metadata, SharePoint lets you edit the metadata of multiple documents at once. The metadata that you associate with the documents will also show up in the information panel in regular desktop Office apps such as Microsoft Word, Excel, or PowerPoint, as shown in the following screenshot:

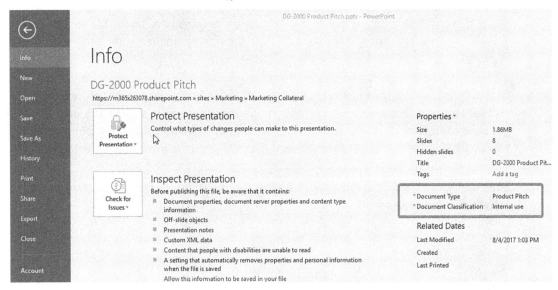

Figure 2.37: Associated metadata of a document

In addition to custom metadata, SharePoint will also store and show you additional information about who created or last modified the document and when. SharePoint also lets you create follow-up actions when documents are added, modified, or deleted. You can do this by using **Power Automate**. For example, if a user uploads an expense report, you can send it through an automated approval process in your organization. Please refer to *Chapter 8, Power Automate (Microsoft Flow)*, for more details.

Finally, SharePoint enforces some restrictions on file sizes and paths. You can view those restrictions here: `https://packt.link/file-size-path-restrictions`.

Uploading a folder

You can upload an entire folder along with any subfolders and their contents to a SharePoint document library. To do so, simply browse to your library, click **Upload**, and choose the **Folder** option. You will then be prompted to select a folder from your computer. Selecting the folder will create a copy of that folder in the document library and copy all the contents of that local folder to the newly created folder in SharePoint online. Note, as mentioned earlier in this recipe, that you can also simply drag and drop folders into your document library view. Doing so will recreate the folders and their contents within the document library.

There's more...

We discussed the different actions you can carry out on list items. You can similarly carry out additional actions on documents. We will look at some of these additional actions in this section.

Document actions

Just like list items, you can carry out many actions on documents in addition to viewing, editing, and deleting them. You can view these actions by right-clicking the item or clicking the three dots next to it, as shown below:

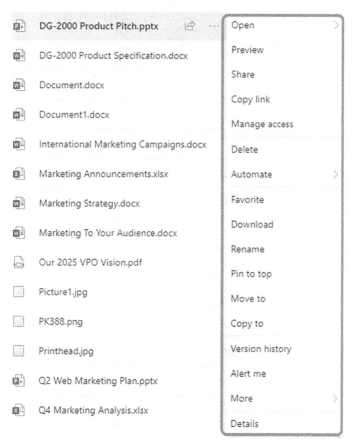

Figure 2.38: Document actions

We covered a lot of these actions in the *Adding an item to a list* recipe, earlier in this chapter. Here, we will cover the remaining options not covered earlier:

- **Preview:** Opens the document for viewing in the browser.
- **Favorite:** Marks the document as a favorite. You can view your favorite documents from all sites together from various places, such as in OneDrive, Delve, or on https://office.com. You will learn more about these in more detail in the appropriate chapters.
- **Download:** Downloads an *offline* copy of the document to your device.
- **Rename:** Allows you to rename the file.
- **Pin to top:** *Pins* the document to the top of the library. Pinned documents then always show up on the top like this:

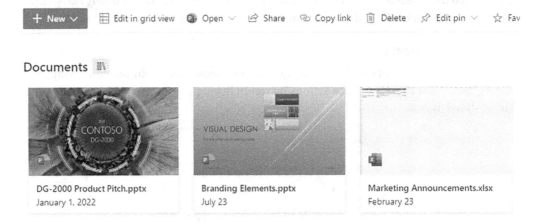

Figure 2.39: Pinned documents

- **Move to** and **Copy to:** Allow you to move or copy the file to a different folder within this library or an altogether different library or site. You will learn more about this in *Chapter 5, Document Management in SharePoint Online*.

See also

- *Chapter 5, Document Management in SharePoint Online*
- The *Other actions* topic in the *Adding an item to a list* recipe, earlier in this chapter
- The *Adding alerts* recipe in *Chapter 4, Lists and Libraries in SharePoint Online*

Deleting and restoring a file

In this recipe, you will learn how to delete a SharePoint document and then restore it from your site's recycle bin.

Getting ready

You will need to be able to access a document library in a SharePoint site for which you have at least **Contribute** permission or higher. You will usually have this permission if you are part of the *Site owners* or *Site members* groups for the site containing the library.

How to do it...

To delete a file:

1. Select the ellipsis (...) next to a file, then **Delete**.

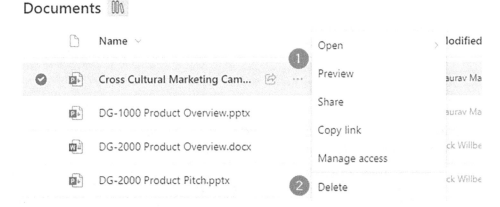

Figure 2.40: Deleting a file from an item's context menu

2. Confirm the deletion on the pop-up dialog by selecting **Delete**. Watch for the status notification in the upper-right corner letting you know the file was successfully deleted:

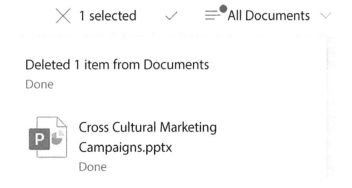

Figure 2.41: Deletion notification

To restore a file:

3. Select **Recycle Bin** from the left-hand navigation menu (team sites only) or follow the *Viewing site contents* recipe earlier in this chapter to browse to the **Site contents** page and then click **Recycle bin:**

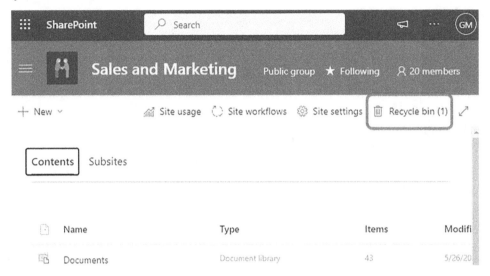

Figure 2.42: Recycle bin

4. Select the file you wish to restore by clicking the circle that appears to its left when hovering your mouse over the file. Then choose **Restore:**

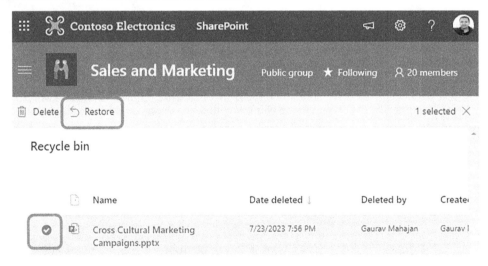

Figure 2.43: Restoring an item from the recycle bin

How it works...

Steps 1-2 move a file from its original location to the site's recycle bin shared by all site members. At this point, a countdown of 93 days begins, after which the file will automatically be permanently deleted.

If, during those 93 days, you choose (or a fellow site member chooses) to restore a deleted file, you can follow *steps 3-4* to move the file back to its original library.

Just like the recycle bin on your computer, you can either restore deleted items or permanently delete them from here. However, there are several key differences between the recycle bin on your computer and the site recycle bin, as follows:

- **Types of deleted items:** The site recycle bin not only contains deleted files and folders but also *deleted items of other types*, such as list items, calendar items, contacts from the contact lists, entire lists or libraries, and even subsites. In that sense, it is a catch-all for anything that gets deleted from your site.

- **Permission-dependent:** You can only view content that you have access to *depending on your permissions* within a site. So, unless you had permission to specific content before it was deleted from the site in the first place, you will not see it in the site recycle bin. An exception to this rule is for the site admins – since site admins have access to all content on the site, they also can view and restore any and all content that was deleted from the site.

- **Second-stage recycle bin:** In addition to the primary recycle bin that you can see within a site, site admins also have access to *a second-stage recycle bin* (or the site collection recycle bin). This is where items go once they've been deleted from your recycle bin. Just as in the primary recycle bin, admins can restore or permanently delete items from the second-stage recycle bin.

> Deleted subsites are stored in the second-stage recycle bin and can only be restored from there by the site owner. You can learn more about restoring items from the site collection recycle bin here: https://packt.link/2nd-stage-bin.
>
> We also read about site collections as part of the *Creating a modern site* recipe earlier in this chapter. Deleted site collections will need to be restored by a designated SharePoint admin from your organization.

- **Retention period:** The total retention period for items in the recycle bin is *93 days*. You can restore content or have your site admins restore content within the site for 93 days. After that, the content is permanently deleted.

- **Auto-purge on quota:** Files in the site recycle bin still count against site storage quotas, and the recycle bin can only hold 200% of that quota before it will begin to *auto-purge* the oldest items. The second-stage recycle bin (when the recycle bin is empty, or deleted files are deleted from the recycle bin) does not count against site storage quotas and is only accessible to site owners. You can read more about managing site storage limits here: https://packt.link/site-storage-limits.

- **Back up data:** In addition to the above, Microsoft retains *back ups of your site data* for 14 days beyond the actual deletion. Such data is only available via a request to Microsoft Support by your organization's administrators.

There's more...

As with most things in SharePoint, you can accomplish the outcome of this recipe in multiple ways. For example, instead of selecting a document's ellipsis (...) and then **Delete**, you can instead simply right-click the document and choose **Delete**. You can also select the file (clicking the circle to the left of the file) and choose **Delete** from the top ribbon menu.

You can also multi-select to delete several files at once and restore them through the same method.

Keep in mind that the recycle bin is shared by all site members, so another member may choose to restore a file you deleted (and you can restore files others deleted). All these actions are always dependent on having appropriate edit permissions to involved content and locations.

Emptying the recycle bin

If you know you won't need any deleted items in your recycle bin, you can choose **Empty recycle bin**, which is effectively the same as deleting a file a second time, but from your recycle bin:

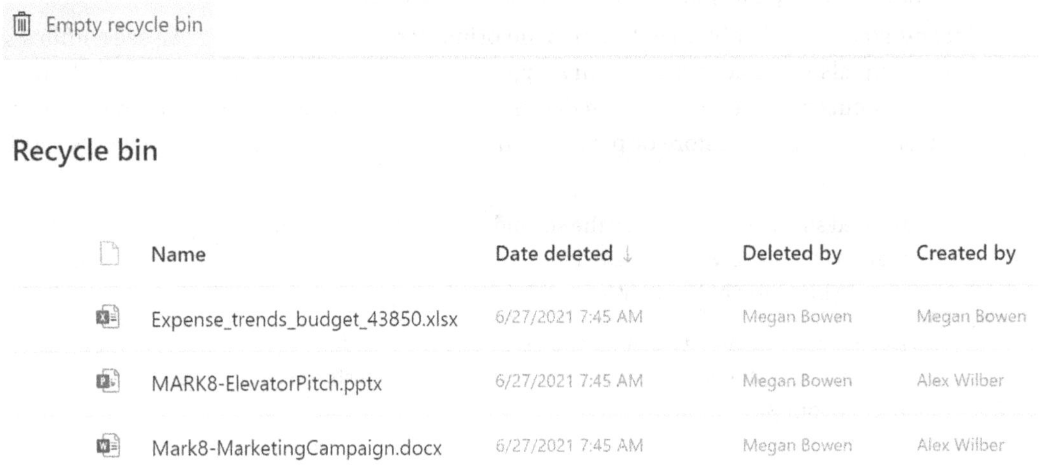

🗑 Empty recycle bin

Recycle bin

	Name	Date deleted ↓	Deleted by	Created by
📊	Expense_trends_budget_43850.xlsx	6/27/2021 7:45 AM	Megan Bowen	Megan Bowen
📊	MARK8-ElevatorPitch.pptx	6/27/2021 7:45 AM	Megan Bowen	Alex Wilber
📄	Mark8-MarketingCampaign.docx	6/27/2021 7:45 AM	Megan Bowen	Alex Wilber

Figure 2.44: Button to empty the recycle bin

This moves all content in your site's recycle bin to the site's second-stage recycle bin, only accessible to site owners:

Figure: 2.45: Items in the second-stage recycle bin

Files can still be restored from here by a site owner unless a file has been in either recycle bin for a total of 93 days, after which it's permanently deleted. Note that files restored from the second-stage recycle bin still return to the original location (not the first recycle bin).

File deletion in OneDrive

Deleting files in OneDrive is very similar to this process. In fact, the deletion and restoring process is nearly identical.

For those closely monitoring their storage space in OneDrive, second-stage recycle bin files will not count toward the storage being used. However, this should not be used as a permanent storage solution to bypass a storage limit. After 93 days, files in either recycle bin (first or second-stage) are permanently deleted.

Restoring a library

Rather than restoring one file, you may wish to "undo" many changes made over a period of time. In SharePoint document libraries (and your OneDrive), you can choose **Settings** > **Restore this library**. This allows you to specify a point in time to which you'd like to revert the entirety of the library (or your OneDrive).

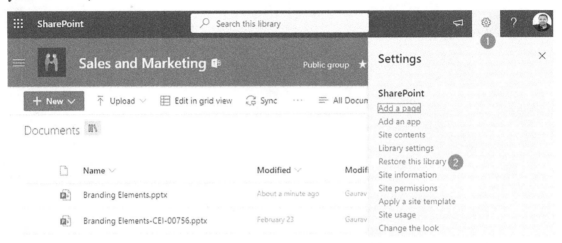

Figure 2.46: Option to restore library under SharePoint in the site Settings menu

When restoring a library, you choose a point in time to which you'd like to return. You can restore to:

- Yesterday
- One week ago
- Three weeks ago
- Custom date and time

Once you've made a selection for the point in time, you'll see all individual changes (file modified, file deleted, etc.) that will be undone before you proceed with the restoration, as seen at the bottom of the following screenshot:

Restore Mark 8 Project Team - Documents

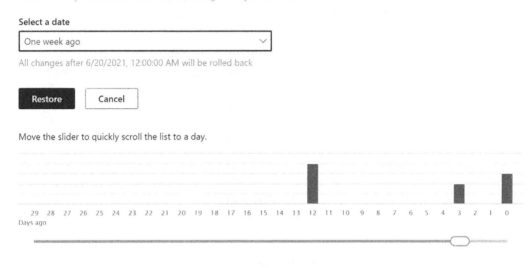

If something went wrong, you can restore this library to a previous time. Select a date preset or use the slider to find a date with unusual activity in the chart. Then select the changes that you want to undo.

Select a date

| One week ago | ⌄ |

All changes after 6/20/2021, 12:00:00 AM will be rolled back

[Restore] [Cancel]

Move the slider to quickly scroll the list to a day.

29 28 27 26 25 24 23 22 21 20 19 18 17 16 15 14 13 12 11 10 9 8 7 6 5 4 3 2 1 0
Days ago

Select a change in the list below to highlight it and all the changes before it. Then select the Restore button to undo all the highlighted changes.

⌄		Change	File name
	⌄	Today - 6/27/2021 (3)	
✓	🗑	Deleted by Megan Bowen 9:45:28 AM	📄 Mark8-MarketingCampaign.docx
✓	🗑	Deleted by Megan Bowen 9:45:27 AM	📄 MARK8-ElevatorPitch.pptx

Figure 2.47: Rolling back changes to a library by restoring the library from a certain date

Once you click **Restore**, it may take some time to complete depending on the size and complexity of all involved changes.

Deleting library columns

It's worth noting that if you should ever delete a column of metadata from a library (such as **Category**, **Due Date**, etc. that may have been used for organization), that column is not retrievable or restorable. Once deleted, it is permanently gone.

One idea to consider is just hiding the column so the metadata is retrievable in version histories or for auditing. You can even rename these unneeded columns with a prefix like **ARCHV-Category** to keep them sorted together and available if needed.

Deleting previous file versions

If you delete a specific version of a file (for example, version 2, when the current version is 6), that version goes through the recycle bin independently in the same process as a normal file and can be restored. You'll see it noted with the original filename, but appended with the version number in parentheses:

Recycle bin

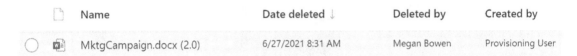

	Name	Date deleted ↓	Deleted by	Created by
	MktgCampaign.docx (2.0)	6/27/2021 8:31 AM	Megan Bowen	Provisioning User

Figure 2.48: Deleted items have a version number after their name in the recycle bin

And after 93 days (or if manually deleted sooner), that version will be permanently deleted and non-restorable just as with a normal file.

See also

- The *Deleting a list* topic in the *Creating a list* recipe, earlier in this chapter
- The *Deleting an item* topic in the *Adding an item to a list* recipe, earlier in this chapter

Sharing a document

Once you've uploaded your document to SharePoint Online, you can simply use **Share** or **Copy link** to easily share it with your colleagues. This recipe shows you how to share a link to a document using the **Share** feature.

Getting ready

You should have at least **Read** access to the document you'd like to share.

How to do it...

To share a document with a member of your team, follow these steps:

1. Browse to the document you'd like to share.
2. Click the **Share** ( ) icon next to the document. Alternatively, select the document and then click the **Share** option on the top menu bar, as shown in the following screenshot:

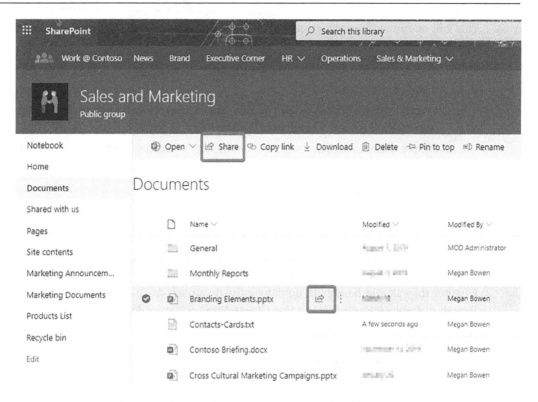

Figure 2.49: Icon for sharing an item on the right of the item name

3. On the pop-up box that appears, click the gear icon on the right of the filename to open **Sharing settings**:

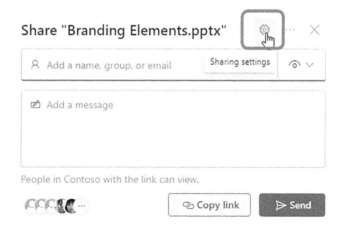

Figure 2.50: Opening Sharing settings with the icon to the right of the filename

4. This will open the **Sharing settings** dialog, which allows you to select one of the following options:

    •   **Anyone:** This option is for anonymous link sharing and is enabled only if your organization allows this

    •   **People in <your organization's name>:** This option creates a link that allows the entire organization to view or edit your document

    •   **People with existing access:** This option simply creates a link for people who already have access to the document

    •   **People you choose:** This option allows you to specify names of people with whom you'd like to share the document

    We will cover these options in more detail in the *How it works...* section of this recipe. For now, select the last option to generate a link for specific people.

5. Select whether the person you are sharing this document with should be able to edit it and whether they should be able to download the document (or be able to view it only online). For our example, we will deselect the **Allow editing** option and select **Block download** so the generated link grants view-only access to the document through the browser:

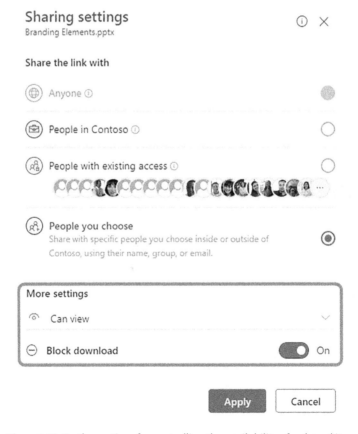

Figure 2.51: Further options for controlling the availability of a shared item

Your organization can control the options that are enabled and selected by default in the **Sharing settings** box shown in the preceding screenshot. Most organizations have the **Can view** option set as the default option. This means that the people who you are sharing the document with will be able to view it but will not be able to edit it.

You can additionally select the **Block download** option to prevent users from being able to download the documents. When this option is selected, they can only view the documents in the browser. This is especially useful when you do not want users to maintain a local copy of the document. Note that the **Block download** option is only available when you are sharing the document with a view-only link.

6. Click the **Apply** button and then enter the names of the people you would like to share the document with.

7. Enter a message to be sent with the sharing invitation email and click the **Send** button, as shown in the following screenshot:

Figure 2.52: Option to send a message with a shared file

Depending on how your organization has been set up, in addition to sharing documents with individuals, you may be able to share them with entire groups or teams (see how the link is being shared with the **Executive Team Members** in the preceding figure).

Also note that you can copy the link from this dialog and send it to members via a tool of your choice, such as an email or Microsoft Teams message. The copied link is only valid for the members selected on this screen.

8.   SharePoint then sends the recipients an email with your message and a link to the document, as shown in the following screenshot:

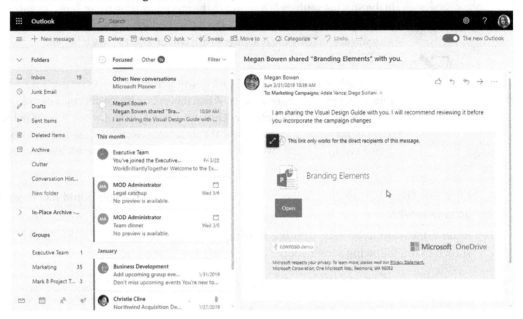

Figure 2.53: Shared item and message are notified to the recipient via email

Congratulations! You just learned how to share a document with other members within your organization. The recipients of your sharing invitation can now view or edit this document, depending on the permission that was granted to them.

How it works...

There are a few things that happen when a document is shared:

- SharePoint checks to see if the person that the document is being shared with already has the required permissions. If not, SharePoint alters the permissions for the document so that the appropriate rights (**Read** or **Edit**) are granted to the person that the document is being shared with. You can read more about managing document permissions in the *Viewing and changing document permissions* recipe in *Chapter 5, Document Management in SharePoint Online*.

SharePoint also checks *your* permissions during the sharing process. If you do not have permission to edit the document and try to share it with the **Can edit** option selected, SharePoint will send an approval request email to the site owners. An email with a link to the document will then only be sent to the requested users after the sharing request gets approved. The request reviewer will also be able to change the level of access that will be granted to the requested user(s). They can restrict permissions and inversely grant greater access than what you had originally requested.

- It generates a link specific to the people with which the document is being shared.
- It sends an email with the generated link, along with a message, if you specified one.

Types of links

This recipe showed you how to share a document with specific people. Three other sharing options that you will see in the **Sharing settings** dialog are as follows:

- **Anyone:** Use this option to share the document with anonymous users that are outside your organization. People with this link can view or edit the document without having to sign in to Microsoft 365. Since this option enables you to share your organization's content with *anonymous* external users, there's a chance that it may have been disabled by your SharePoint site or organization administrators. When sharing a link through this option, it is recommended to set an expiration date, along with a password, for added security:

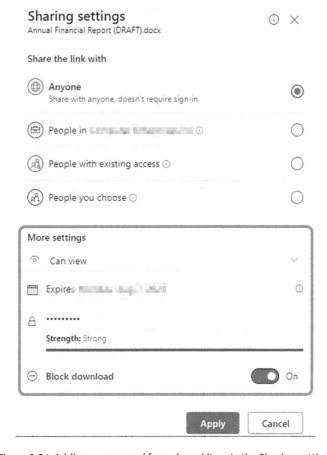

Figure 2.54: Adding a password for a shared item in the Sharing settings

If you do decide to password-protect your file, remember to share the password with people who will use the link. They will be prompted to enter the password before accessing the file, as shown in the following screenshot:

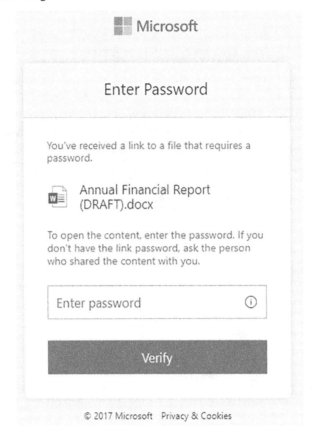

Figure 2.55: Recipient must enter a password to access the shared item

- **People in <your organization's name>**: This option generates a link that anyone in your organization can use to view or edit the document. Note that unlike the previous option, users of the link will be required to sign in to the site.
- **People with existing access**: This option enables you to simply get a link to the document without changing its permissions. This should be your first choice if you know that people who will view the link already have access to the document.

There's more...

As we just saw, the **Share** option sends an email message with a link to the intended recipients. You may, however, need to just copy the link so that you can then share it through different means (such as a Teams channel or even an existing email chain). The **Copy link** menu option, which is right next to the **Share** option, enables you to do just that.

Copy link

You can access the **Copy link** option from either the top navigation bar or the context menu for a list or library item:

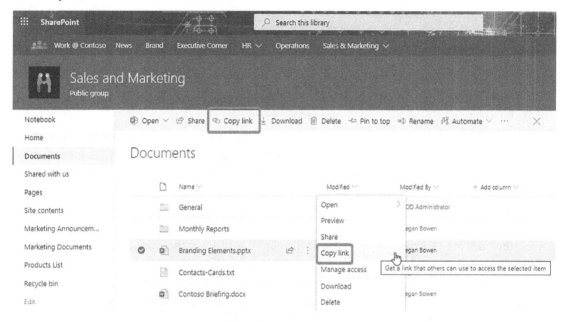

Figure 2.56: Two methods of copying the link of an item

Once you select this option, you can optionally go through steps similar to the **Share** option described in this recipe, to adjust the permissions of the generated link.

See also

- The *Creating a new document* recipe in *Chapter 5, Document Management in SharePoint Online*
- The *Determining and revoking permissions in a site* recipe in *Chapter 3, Modern Sites in SharePoint Online*
- The *Sharing a file* recipe in *Chapter 6, OneDrive*

Searching content

Search is a core part of the SharePoint user experience. It enables users to find relevant business information and documents more quickly and easily than ever before.

For this recipe, I am going to act as a marketing manager who would like to search for our visual design guide, which I remember is called "Branding Elements."

Getting ready

All you need is **Read** access to the site where you will be performing your search. The results that SharePoint returns are **security trimmed**, which means you will only see content that you have access to through direct or indirect permissions.

How to do it...

To perform a search within a site, follow these steps:

1. Browse to any page on the site where you'd like to perform the search. In our example, I will browse to my Sales and Marketing site.

2. Start typing your search keywords to see the relevant results. In this case, we will start typing `Branding Elements`. We'll notice that we immediately start seeing the results after entering the first two letters. At this point, we can click the appropriate result if we've found what we're looking for.

3. Otherwise, we can finish entering the search keyword(s) and then click the **Show more results** link, towards the bottom, to be taken to the search results page to see the matching results from the current site. Note that these results are sorted in order of their predicted relevance to you.

    As shown in the image below, we have the following five options on this page:

    1. The ability to change the scope of the search results to show results from the hub or entire organization, instead of just from within this site.

    2. By default, this page shows you all result types. You can, however, select one of the tabs on the top to further narrow down the results to **Files**, **Sites**, **News**, or **Images**.

    3. Depending on the selected tab, you can apply additional filters such as the modified date.

    4. Each result shows you a preview of where your search keyword occurred and also an image of the relevant file or site result.

5. Finally, the three dots toward the top right of the result row allow you to perform certain actions on the result. These actions vary depending on the type of search result. The options that you see in the screenshot below are relevant to the file result type.

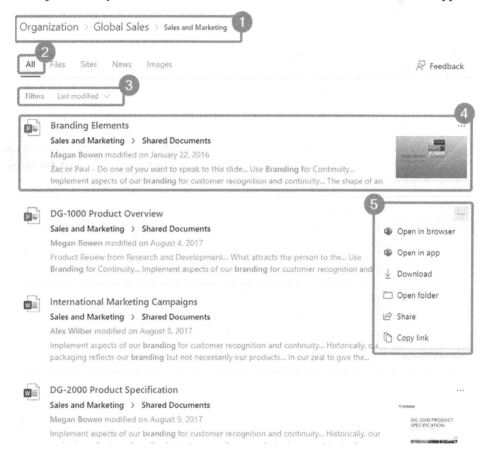

Figure 2.57: The show results page, with areas numbered to match the above list respectively

The whole SharePoint search experience is customizable by your organization. For example, your organization can define additional filters that you can utilize. Other possible search customizations are acronym searches, bookmark searches, location searches, and Q&A searches, which help return the right results when users look for acronyms, certain keywords, office locations, or look for answers to questions. Finally, the results you will initially see are those from within the site where you performed the original search. Clicking the **Global Sales** link at the top, however, brings back results from the *hub* that this site is part of.

You learned about hub sites in the *Creating a modern site* recipe earlier in this chapter.

Furthermore, clicking the **Organization** link at the top will expand the scope to show results from all sites in the entire organization. Bear in mind that the results you see are always security-trimmed, which means that you will only see documents and content that you have access to in the first place.

How it works...

Microsoft Search is the component of Microsoft 365 that helps you find information that you already have access to but do not know where to look for. This information could be a document that you had previously created, or it could be information that was shared by your colleagues.

In addition to lists and libraries, SharePoint Search indexes content in pages and the profiles of the employees in your organization. It then lets you **search** this indexed content using advanced filter criteria. Finally, it lets you **view the results** through a user-friendly presentation experience.

Some of the salient features of the search results page shown in the preceding screenshot are as follows:

- **Search scopes**: Earlier, we discussed the ability to expand the scope of the search results from the current site to the current hub, and then to the entire organization. Searching from within the Microsoft 365 home page or the SharePoint start page automatically defaults the search scope to the organization level. Similarly, performing a search from the hub site defaults the scope to the entire hub, meaning that it will show you results from all the sites within that hub.

- **Search result verticals**: The various tabs shown in the preceding screenshot are also commonly known as search verticals. Verticals are a way to group content of different types. The preceding screenshot shows verticals for **Files** (which only shows file and folder results), **Sites** (which only shows matching sites), and **News** (which only shows matching news posts). The **All** vertical shows combined results from all the verticals. In addition to these, you may also be able to see a **People** vertical, which, as the name suggests, will show you matching people results. The **People** vertical is only shown when you expand your search scope to the organization level. We'll discuss **People** search in more detail in the *Finding experts and people* recipe in *Chapter 14, Search in Microsoft 365*.

- **Unified experience**: Microsoft provides a unified search experience through all the Microsoft 365 workloads. This means that no matter which workload or app you search from, you will find the identical experience everywhere, regardless of whether you perform the search from SharePoint, Outlook, Teams, Word, or other workloads and apps in Microsoft 365.

Microsoft has been investing heavily in Search, resulting in numerous improvements being made to it. These improvements include things such as showing results based on their relevance to you. This relevance score could be based on the things you work on the most, the people you interact with the most, and the freshness of the content, to name a few. Recent enhancements to the platform have resulted in users being able to get results back instantly, even as you click in the search box and start typing your keywords, and even before you click the search button to perform an actual search.

See also

- *Chapter 14, Search in Microsoft 365*
- *Chapter 15, Microsoft Delve*

Unlock this book's exclusive benefits now

This book comes with additional benefits designed to elevate your learning experience.

Note: Have your purchase invoice ready before you begin. `https://www.packtpub.com/unlock/9781803243177`

3

Modern Sites in SharePoint Online

In the previous chapter, we looked at some basic recipes explaining how you can interact with a site in SharePoint. This chapter dives deeper into the workings of these sites. We will review various site customization options, such as changing a site's theme, modifying the navigational elements, working with pages of a site, and working with web parts on those pages. We will then go through a few additional scenarios, such as modifying site permissions and creating a subsite.

In this chapter, we will cover the following topics:

- Changing the look
- Adding a page
- Adding a web part
- Adding an app
- Modifying the top navigation
- Modifying the left navigation
- Viewing and changing site settings
- Determining and revoking permissions for a site
- Creating a subsite

Let's get started!

Changing the look

SharePoint lets you apply custom styles and colors to your site so that it closely aligns with the branding guidelines defined by your organization. It also allows you to customize the site header and navigation elements.

In this recipe, we will look at how to change the look and feel of a SharePoint site, primarily by changing its theme.

Getting ready

You will need to be a site owner, or have design or full control permissions on the site, to be able to apply a theme to a modern site. You will also need these permissions to change the header and navigation settings.

How to do it...

To change the theme of your site, browse to the site and follow these steps:

1. Click on the **Settings** gear icon in the top-right corner.
2. Click **Change the look**, as shown in the following screenshot:

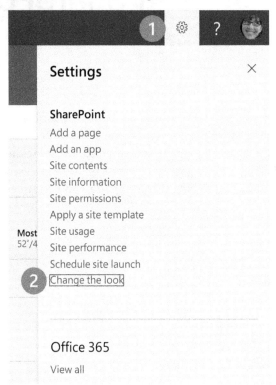

Figure 3.1: Option to change the theme from the Settings pane

3. Click **Theme** and select the theme you would like to apply. As you select the theme, your site's look changes side by side to help you preview these changes.

> The options you can see here can be controlled by your organization. A lot of organizations have a set of pre-created company themes available for their users to select from. Some organizations also lock down the themes entirely so that users cannot change them. Also, if your site is connected to a hub site, the theme settings are managed there.

4. Optionally, click **Customize** if you'd like to change the theme colors; otherwise, just click **Save**:

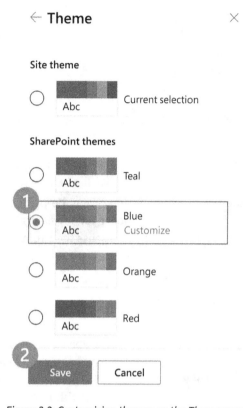

Figure 3.2: Customizing themes on the Theme menu

Congratulations! You just changed the theme for your site.

How it works...

There are multiple ways in which you can "brand" a SharePoint site so that it matches other sites and areas in your organization's Microsoft 365 tenant. The following is a list of some of the customizations you can make to your SharePoint site:

- Changing the logo for your site
- Changing the header area at the top
- Changing the top and left navigation
- Applying a footer (only for communication sites)
- Defining and applying a custom color scheme or theme
- Creating custom page templates
- Advanced branding using custom code and third-party tools

In addition to providing the option to change the theme colors, the **Change the look** setting allows you to further change the styling for the following site elements:

- Site header layout and styling. This option allows you to change the following elements of the site header area:

    - The height and layout
    - The background color scheme
    - The visibility of the site's title
    - The site's logo and thumbnail

- The site navigation visibility and style. This section allows you to set the visibility of the site's navigation. Further:

    - For team sites, you can choose to show the navigation vertically toward the left or horizontally toward the top.
    - For team and communication sites, when the visibility is set to show the navigation at the top, you can additionally choose for the navigation to be shown as a mega-menu or as a cascading menu. We will discuss the two menu types in the *Modifying the top navigation* recipe later in this chapter.

- The footer visibility and style. You can only set the footer options for communication sites. Through this setting, you can change the footer layout, logo, display text, and background color scheme.

The options that are available to you depend on the type of site (team versus communication), your role in the organization, and the permissions that have been granted to you. If you have been granted access to brand your site, you will want to make sure that it adheres to your organization's branding and theming guidelines. That way, it will align better with the other sites in your organization and thus give your site's users a more consistent and familiar experience. Here's a great infographic from the Microsoft support team on how to customize your site: `https://packt.link/customize-site-infographic`.

An important caveat to making these changes is that Microsoft pushes updates to Microsoft 365 and SharePoint online from time to time. You will therefore want to ensure that if such changes are being made through custom code or third-party tools, they adhere to Microsoft's guidance for branding and compatibility with such updates.

Finally, we previously discussed the classic experience as part of the *Modern versus classic experience* topic of the *Creating a modern site* recipe in *Chapter 2, Introduction to SharePoint Online*. If you are working with the classic experience, this support article will show you how to change the look for such a site: `https://packt.link/classic-design`.

See also

- *Modifying the top navigation* recipe in this chapter

Adding a page

Pages in SharePoint are a means to display information and content to the users of your site. As an owner or member of the site, you are granted access to modify them through easy-to-use page editing tools that are built right into the platform. You can use these tools to format and style the pages, as well as to maintain a variety of content on them.

In this recipe, you will learn how to add a new page to your site. In later recipes in this chapter, we will also see how to add meaningful content to this page.

Getting ready

You will need to be a site owner, or member, or have been assigned the following permission levels on your site: **Contribute**, **Edit**, **Design**, or **Full Control**.

How to do it...

To add a new page to your site, browse to the site's home page and follow these steps:

1. Click **New** and then **Page** from the navigation bar, as shown in the following screenshot:

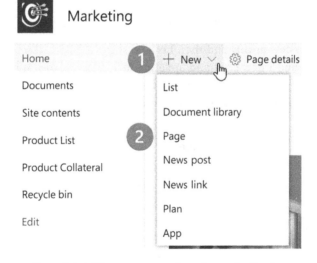

Figure 3.3: Adding a new page from the navigation bar

2. You will then be prompted with the following options if you are creating a page on your site for the first time:

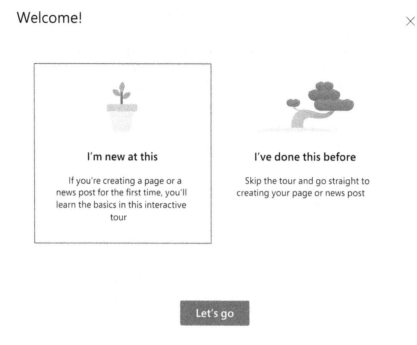

Welcome!   ✕

I'm new at this

If you're creating a page or a news post for the first time, you'll learn the basics in this interactive tour

I've done this before

Skip the tour and go straight to creating your page or news post

Let's go

Figure 3.4: Option for a guided tour when creating a page

Selecting **I'm new at this** and then **Let's go** starts a guided tour that walks you through the steps of creating a new page and updating its key properties. It is a good way to learn if you are creating a page for the first time. Whether you select this option, or **I've done this before**, the steps that follow will remain the same.

3. We will first select a template from the list of available page templates. For our example, we will select the **Blank** page template.

A page template is a pre-created design layout for your page. Instead of having to design a page from scratch, selecting a page template lets you get started with a design and theme that closely matches the anticipated design/layout needs for your page. In addition to the templates available through SharePoint, your site owner might have pre-created templates based on the common needs across your organization.

4. Click **Create page** to create the new page.
5. SharePoint will then take you to the newly created page. Here, you can give it a title, add an image for your page, and optionally, add content to it.
6. You can then click the **Save as draft** button toward the top-left corner to save the page.
7. SharePoint will now generate a URL for the page.

Draft pages are not visible to the *visitors* of your site, but they do help you save the progress while you are working on them. It is recommended that you keep saving the draft page as frequently as possible. This will ensure that you don't lose your work. Note that anyone with **Contribute** access or higher to the Site Pages library (more on this shortly) will be able to view such drafts. To restrict draft page access to just yourself and the site owners, select the **Create as a private draft** option towards the bottom of the template selection page, which shows up as part of the page creation wizard:

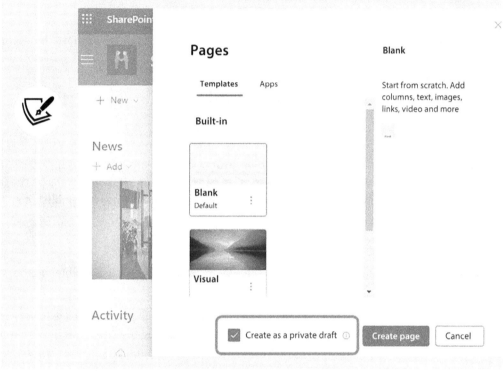

8. Optionally, you can click **Publish** toward the top right of the page once you have completed your edits to it and are ready to share it with others.

Congratulations! You just published your first page.

How it works...

Except for a few key differences, pages in SharePoint are like other documents that live in a document library. The few key differences between the two types of files are:

- SharePoint pages have a special .aspx extension (unlike the usual .docx, .pdf, and .xlsx extensions for documents).
- These pages are typically stored in a special Site Pages library.
- The permissions needed to edit pages are different from the permissions required to edit documents in a library.

- You can edit the content of a page using tools built right into SharePoint.

These traits can help us develop and manage our SharePoint pages. Below, we will look at some essential steps for making changes to a page. For example, once you've created a page, you can start to enter or modify some of its basic information. After exploring this, we will turn our attention to how to publish the changes made to a page, and how to view the Site Pages library.

Entering basic page information

You can make the following edits to the properties of SharePoint pages:

- Give it a title
- Change the name of the contact person for the page (or completely remove that information from the page)
- Change the layout for the title area
- Show or hide the date when the page was published
- Enable or disable page comments

Beyond this, you can also start adding content to your page. You can add content to your pages through several types of **web parts**. We will cover web parts in more detail in the next recipe. Please also see the section titled *Components of a SharePoint page* later in this recipe for more details on the layout of a SharePoint page. Once you have added content to the page, you will need to publish it so that it is visible to other users.

Publishing a page

A page can go through various stages in the publishing process before it is visible to others in your organization.

When you create a new page, the page gets saved as a draft. At this point, the page is only visible to you and to others who have member, owner, or contribute access to the Site Pages library (unless you selected the **Create as a private draft** option while creating the page). The site visitors will not see any draft pages or versions.

You can then continue to edit the page and save it as a draft until you are satisfied with the changes. You can publish the page once you have finalized its content. If your site owner has enabled scheduling on the Site Pages library, you can also choose a time when your changes go live:

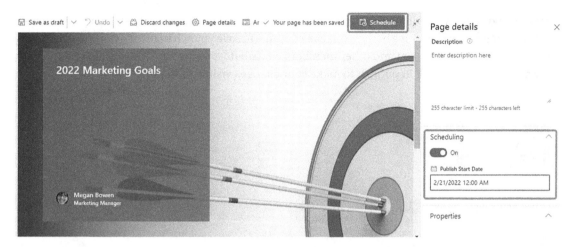

Figure 3.5: Scheduling when a page will publish changes

Once your page goes live, its status is automatically changed to **Published.** The page and its content now become visible to others that have access to your site. The added or changed content from your page will now also start showing up in the relevant searches. You may also now want to add a link to your page from one of the navigation menus or from another page so that users can easily locate it. We'll discuss the SharePoint navigation in more detail as part of the *Modifying the top navigation* and *Modifying the left navigation* recipes later in this chapter.

After the page has been published, you can come back to it any time in the future and edit it to make changes. To do so, simply browse to your page and click the **Edit** button in the top-right corner of the screen, as shown in the following screenshot:

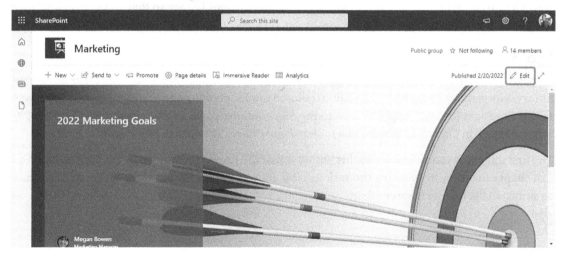

Figure 3.6: The button for editing a published page

From that point on, you will go through the same editing and publishing process that you followed while creating a new page. Like before, you can continue to save your changes as drafts (which means they will *only* be visible to you and other members/contributors of the site). Once you are done with your changes, simply click **Republish** to make your changes visible to visitors:

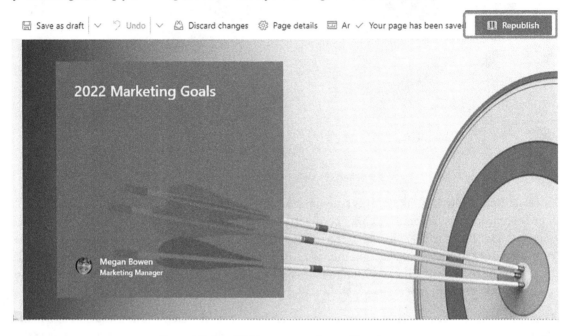

Figure 3.7: Republishing a page after making changes

You can also configure the publishing process via the Site Pages library so that all the pages on your site go through a formal approval workflow before they become visible to others.

The Site Pages library

All pages get stored in a special library called **Site Pages**. This library is just like any other document library, except that it has certain capabilities tailored toward creating and managing pages. To browse to the Site Pages library, simply browse to the **Site contents** page, as described in the *Viewing Site contents* recipe in *Chapter 2, Introduction to SharePoint Online*. Then, click **Site Pages**.

The first thing that you will notice in this library is that the pages are grouped by the page author. You can change this view by selecting the various view options toward the top-right corner of the library, as shown in the following screenshot:

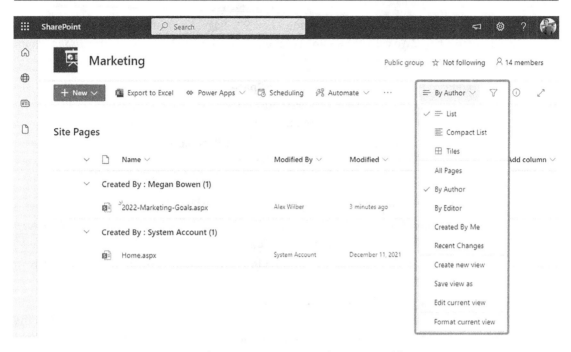

Figure 3.8: Changing view options in the Site Pages library

We'll discuss views and related options in more detail in the *Creating a custom list view* recipe in *Chapter 4, Lists in SharePoint Online*.

You will also notice the following menu options toward the top of the **Site Pages** library:

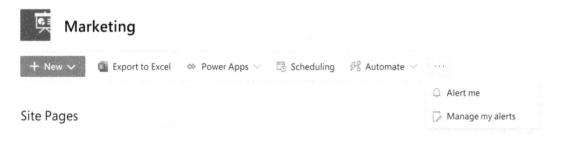

Figure 3.9: Menu options in the Site Pages library

 If you are not seeing these options, it's likely that you do not have access or you are viewing the site in the classic experience. To exit out of the classic experience, simply click **Exit classic experience** towards the bottom left of the page.

- **New:** You can click the **New** menu to create a new **Site Page**. You can also use this menu to link to an existing page. We will discuss link creation in *Chapter 5, Document Libraries in SharePoint Online*. In addition to these options:

  - Modern sites have an option to create a **Space**. *Spaces* in SharePoint is a web-based, immersive platform, which lets you create and share mixed reality experiences by using 3D web parts. We will learn more about SharePoint Spaces in the *Appendix*.

  - Team sites show the **Wiki Page** and **Web Part Page** options, in addition to the usual option to create a **Site Page**. However, these page types are now deprecated and are not suitable for a modern site. They are therefore not covered in the book.

- **Export to Excel:** Clicking this option will open the list of pages in Excel on your device.

- **Power Apps:** Allows you to work with Power Apps. You will learn more about this in *Chapter 9, Creating Power Apps, and Chapter 10, Applying Power Apps*.

- **Scheduling:** Allows page authors and editors to schedule a time for new pages or edits to existing pages to go live.

- **Automate:** Allows you to create workflows against your pages using Power Automate. We will learn more about this in *Chapter 8, Power Automate (Microsoft Flow)*. You can further click the **Configure page approval flow** submenu option to automatically send new pages for approval. We will read more about this in the section to follow.

Alert me and **Manage my alerts:** You can set up alerts in SharePoint to get notified when pages (or, for that matter, list items or documents) are added, edited, or deleted. We will learn more about alerts in the *Adding alerts* recipe in *Chapter 4, Lists and Libraries in SharePoint Online*.

There's more...

In this section, we will look at the structure of a SharePoint page. We will then understand a little bit about the page approval workflow before reviewing a special type of modern SharePoint page called a **news post**. Finally, we will see how to delete a page from a site.

Components of a SharePoint page

When a user reaches your site, they are first presented with the **home page** of that site. If you are the site owner, you should carefully plan the information and layout of your site's home page. The information that may be presented on the home page can vary significantly, depending on the purpose and type of your site. For a department site, for example, the home page could show key department updates, key documents and forms, department events, important contacts, KPIs, and/or links to key information and areas within the site.

Every page of a SharePoint site consists of standard sections, as shown below:

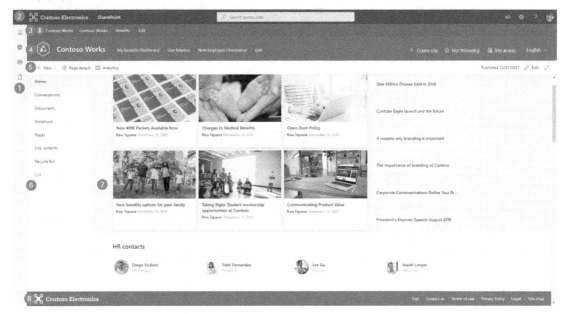

Figure 3.10: Standard sections (numbered) of a SharePoint page

Let's go through the sections below, with numbers matching those in *Figure 3.10*:

1. **The App Bar:** The app bar is your gateway to the most relevant content in SharePoint. We reviewed the App Bar in detail in *Chapter 2, Introduction to SharePoint Online*.

2. **The Office Suite Bar:** The Office Suite Bar gives you a consistent navigation experience across all workloads of Microsoft 365. It also gives you access to context-aware settings and your profile details, among other things. We discussed the Office Suite Bar in detail in *Chapter 1, Overview of Microsoft 365*, and again in *Chapter 2, Introduction to SharePoint Online*.

3. **Hub navigation:** This area is visible only on sites that are part of a hub. It is used for cross-site navigation between various sites that are part of the hub. We discussed hub sites as part of the *Creating a modern site* recipe in *Chapter 2, Introduction to SharePoint Online*.

4. **Site header and top navigation:** The site header appears on every page on the site. It contains the site logo and the site title. Clicking the site title from any page within that site will take you to the home page for that site. For communication sites, and optionally for team sites, it also contains the top navigation for that site. We will discuss the top navigation as part of the *Modifying the top navigation* recipe later in this chapter. Towards the right side of this section, you will find menu options that will allow you to do the following:

   • **Create site:** This option is only available on hub sites (as shown in the screenshot above). Clicking this link creates a new site collection and associates it with the selected hub.

   • **Follow or unfollow a site:** We learned about this as part of the *Getting to the SharePoint home page* recipe in *Chapter 2, Introduction to SharePoint Online*.

- **Site access:** This option is only available on communication sites or hub sites that are based on the communication site type. It allows you to view existing site access and invite others in the organization to your site:

Figure 3.11: Sharing a communication site

As you can see in the image above, you can select the permissions to grant and optionally send a message to the invitee when sharing the site with them. Please note that sharing a site, document, page, or list item may alter its underlying permissions. We will review sharing and permissions in greater detail in the *Determining and revoking permissions for a site* recipe later in this chapter.

- **English:** This text indicates the language for sites where the multi-lingual capabilities have been enabled. You can then select the drop-down to view the site in any of the other enabled languages. You can read more about multilingual SharePoint sites, pages, and news here: `https://packt.link/create-multilingual-SP-pages`

- **Group privacy and membership count:** These are only available for group-connected team sites. The group privacy text indicates whether the site is linked to a **Public** group (which means everyone in your organization can join the group) or a **Private** group (only limited people have access to it). For such group-connected sites, you can also see the current member count for that group:

Figure 3.12: Privacy type and member count of a group

- Clicking the member count further allows you to view and manage the members in that group. We will learn more about Microsoft 365 Groups in *Chapter 16, Microsoft 365 Groups*.

5. **New menu and page editing toolbar:** This section contains the following options:

    - **New menu:** Clicking this menu lets you add new lists, libraries, pages, posts, and other types of apps and artifacts to your site.
    - **Page details:** Clicking this link lets you view and edit various properties of the page.
    - **Published status and date:** This text shows whether you are viewing a published page or whether you have the page open in editing mode (provided you have access to edit the page in the first place). On communication sites, it also shows the last date when the page was first published or updated.
    - **Edit:** Clicking this option lets you make changes to the page and republish it. We will learn how to add and edit pages as part of the *Adding a page* recipe later in this chapter.

6. **Left navigation menu:** This section lets you define the navigation menu in order to help users easily navigate between the various lists, libraries, pages, and other areas on your site. The left navigation menu is only available for team sites or hub sites based on the team site template. We will discuss the left navigation menu as part of the *Modifying the left navigation* recipe later in this chapter.

7. **Page content:** This section contains the actual page content. The layout of this section and the content in it can vary vastly across different sites and for the pages on those sites. You can modify the layout and content of modern pages by using the **page editing tools** that come built into SharePoint. We will discuss this in more detail as part of the *Adding a web part* recipe later in this chapter.

8. **Page footer:** The footer appears at the bottom of all the pages within your site. You can enable or disable the footer for your site via the **Site settings** menu. You may remember the footer as part of the *Changing the look* recipe earlier in this chapter.

Please note that the options mentioned here and the actions that you can perform through these options are highly dependent on the type of site and your level of access to that site.

Content approval

A lot of large organizations require that page additions and modifications go through an approval process before new pages or changes to existing pages become visible to others. The **Configure page approval flow** option enables you to do just that. We will learn more about automating such approval tasks in *Chapter 8, Power Automate (Microsoft Flow)*. Please read this Microsoft Docs article if you want to learn more about the page approval flow: `https://packt.link/page-approvals`.

You will start seeing the **Submit for approval** button instead of the **Publish** and **Republish** buttons once you turn on approvals for your library:

Figure 3.13: Button to start an approval flow before publishing changes to a page

Clicking **Submit for approval** will result in the approval flow starting, which lets you add a message and submit the page for approval:

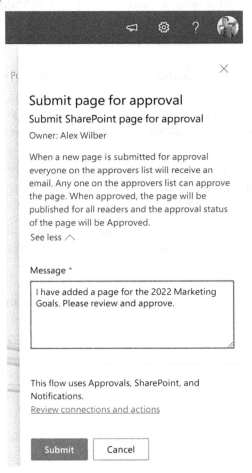

Figure 3.14: Adding a message to the approval request

The status of the page will now be changed to **Pending approval:**

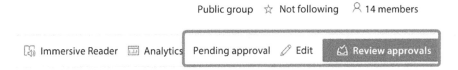

Figure 3.15: Status of a page pending approval

Additionally, the respective approvers will receive an email, notifying them of the approval request. They can then click the **Approve** link from that email to view the approval request or approve the page through Power Automate:

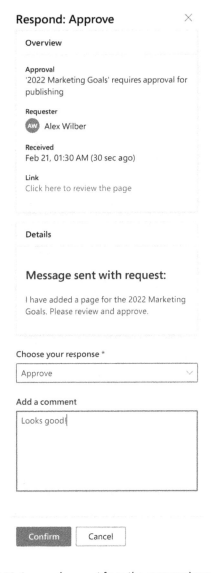

Figure 3.16: Approval request from the approver's perspective

Approvers will also see a **Review approvals** button, which they can click to act upon the approval request, as shown below:

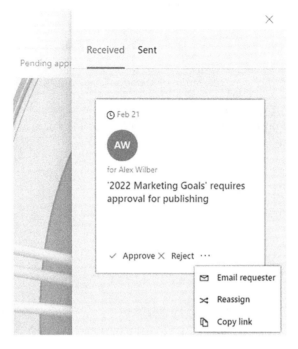

Figure 3.17: Notification to respond to an approval request through the Review approvals button

Once approved, the changes you made to the page will become visible to the site's visitors.

To turn off page approvals again, simply turn off the **Content Approval** setting from the **Versioning** settings page for the library. Please refer to the *Versioning settings, content approval, and document checkout* recipe in *Chapter 5, Document Management in SharePoint Online*, to learn more about how to do that.

News posts and news links

A **news post** is a type of page that enables you to publish news, announcements, and updates, and create engaging stories about your department or organization. This published content can then automatically surface in different places through the various web parts and channels within and outside of SharePoint. The two ways that a news post differs from a regular site page in SharePoint are as follows:

- News posts surface through pre-built web parts and other means, such as on the SharePoint mobile app.
- You cannot create news posts directly using the **New** menu from the Site Pages library. However, you can create them from the **Create news post** option at the top of the SharePoint home/start page. Please refer to the *Getting to the SharePoint home page* recipe in *Chapter 2, Introduction to SharePoint Online*, for details on how to browse to the SharePoint home page. You can also create news posts by clicking the **New** menu option and then **News post** from the top of any page of your modern team or communications site.

One of the other options that you will notice when you click the **New** menu on your site's home page is **News link**:

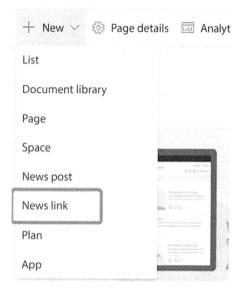

Figure 3.18: Adding a link that acts like a News post

While a news post lets you create and publish new content as a news post, a news link lets you create a link to existing content and surface it as a news post. In addition to promoting content from within your SharePoint sites, you can also promote external content such as the news from your external site.

Creating, maintaining, and having news posts or news links surface in various places is a relatively large topic and beyond the scope of this book. You can, however, refer to the following Microsoft support articles for more details on how to do that:

- *Create and share news on your SharePoint sites*: `https://packt.link/create-news`
- *Use the News web part on the SharePoint page*: `https://packt.link/news-web-part`
- *Create an organization news site*: `https://packt.link/news-site`

Finally, this resource lists some compelling use cases for creating SharePoint news pages: `https://packt.link/SP-news`.

Deleting a page

You have two options to delete a page.

- **Option 1**: Edit the page, click **Page details**, then expand **More details** towards the bottom right corner in the **Page details** pane and then click **Delete page**. Please note that this option will not show up if the page you are trying to delete is the home page for the site or if you don't have permissions to delete it.

- **Option 2:** Browse to the **Site Pages** library within the site, select the page you would like to delete **(1)**, and then click the **Delete** option from the library menu **(2)**, as shown in the following screenshot:

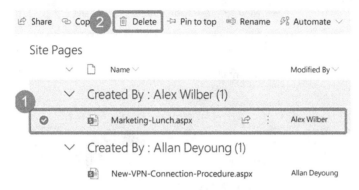

Figure 3.19: Page navigation for deleting a page

In general, this is also how you can delete documents from within any document library, or items from within any list in SharePoint. Please refer to the *Deleting an item* section of the *Adding an item to a list* recipe in *Chapter 2, Introduction to SharePoint Online,* for more details about deleting items and documents from SharePoint lists and libraries. Additionally, the *Viewing Site contents* recipe in *Chapter 2, Introduction to SharePoint Online,* discusses the site recycle bin. The site recycle bin is where deleted pages are stored until they are permanently deleted.

Please note that this method allows you to delete your site's home page. If you delete the home page, your site may not be accessible for the site's users. Worry not though, you can always restore the deleted page from the site's recycle bin.

See also

- The *Viewing Site contents* recipe in *Chapter 2, Introduction to SharePoint Online*
- The *Audience targeting* topic of the *Adding a web part* recipe later in this chapter
- The *Creating a custom list view* recipe in *Chapter 4, Lists and Libraries in SharePoint Online*
- The *Versioning settings, content approval, and document checkout* recipe in *Chapter 5, Document Management in SharePoint Online*
- *Chapter 8, Power Automate (Microsoft Flow)*

Adding a web part

Web parts are the smallest building blocks of a page. Each web part is a self-contained widget that lets you add text, images, files, videos, and other dynamically generated content to your page. This content can exist within your Microsoft 365 environment or can even exist externally.

In this example, we will add a news web part to our recently created page. This news web part will show a summary of all the news items within the current SharePoint site or from other SharePoint sites within your tenant.

At the time of writing, it has recently been announced that the editing experience for SharePoint pages will be upgraded. So, the content described in this section may be different to what you will experience. Unfortunately, no further details are currently available.

As mentioned in the preface, it is common for cloud platforms to undergo changes over time. That said, the underlying concepts covered in this chapter will stay the same.

Getting ready

You will need to have either owner or member permissions on your site to edit pages and add web parts to them. Alternately, you can also have one or more of the following permission levels (more on this later) on your site to do so: Contribute, Edit, Design, or Full Control.

How to do it...

To add a web part, browse to the page to which you'd like to add it and follow these steps:

1. Click the **Edit** link from the page editing bar in the top-right corner of the page that you'd like to edit.

2. Click the + symbol at the bottom of the title area to reveal a list of web parts that you can add to your page.

3. Select a web part you would like to add. In this case, we will add the **News** web part, as shown in the following screenshot:

Figure 3.20: Page navigation for adding a news web part

4. Click **Edit web part** (the pencil icon) to the left of the web part to optionally edit properties for the web part:

Figure 3.21: Customizing the layout of the news web part

> The properties you see will vary, depending on the type of web part that you are editing. For the **News** web part, you can select the source of news, its layout within the section, any filters you'd like to apply to it, and how you'd like to organize it.

5. You can then either save your changes as a draft or publish the modified version of your page so that your changes are visible to other users.

That's it! You just learned how to add a web part to a page in SharePoint.

How it works...

When you edit a page, its status changes to **Draft** as an indicator. Your site's visitors will continue to see the previously published version of the page. The changes that you make to the page aren't visible to them unless you publish it again. Remember that other site owners and members will still be able to see the latest saved version of the page, including any drafts that you may not have published yet.

A page in SharePoint can have multiple horizontal **sections**. Each section, in turn, can be subdivided into one or more vertical subsections or **columns**. You can then add web parts to the appropriate columns in these sections. You can add a section by clicking the + sign toward the left of your page:

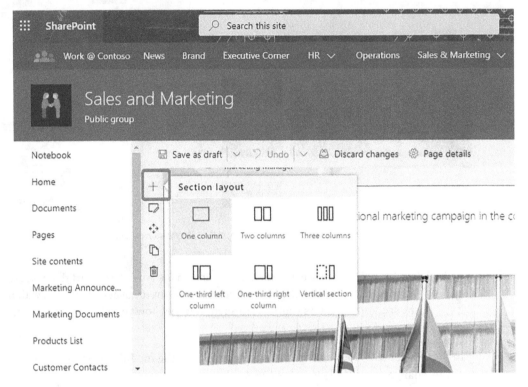

Figure 3.22: Section layout subdivided into columns

SharePoint offers a variety of web parts that you can add to your page. For example, you can add web parts that let you:

- Enter text or wiki-like markdown on your page
- Show current weather information for a given address
- Embed images, documents, or content from secure (HTTPS only) third-party websites (such as YouTube)
- Show commonly used links using the **Quick links** web part
- Show content from existing lists or libraries on your site using the corresponding list or document library web parts

Your organization can also develop custom web parts using one of the modern SharePoint development frameworks, such as the SharePoint Framework, which will be discussed in greater detail in *Chapter 25, Custom Development – SharePoint Framework*. Additionally, you can download a variety of third-party apps and web parts from the SharePoint store. We will discuss this in more detail in the *Adding an app* recipe later in this chapter.

This is just a limited subset from the list of all the web parts that SharePoint has to offer. There are a ton of other web parts that enable interesting capabilities, which we encourage you to explore. You can view the complete list of web parts and an overview via this Microsoft support article: `https://packt.link/web-parts-list`.

Remember that each web part comes with a set of properties that you can use to somewhat customize you and your customers' experience.

There's more...

In this section, we will look at the concept of audience targeting, which lets you provide relevant content to users based on their profile attributes, such as their department or role, to name a couple. Please note that while this recipe is specific to web parts, audience targeting applies to other areas of SharePoint too, which we will cover below.

Audience targeting

Audience targeting in SharePoint enables you to serve up relevant content to your users. It does this by allowing you to selectively restrict access to a *targeted* set of users for the following content:

- **Navigation links:** You can use audience targeting for navigation to set the visibility of menu items to specific audiences. For example, you could potentially set a target audience on the **HR** menu link, from the top navigation menu, so that it only shows up for members of the HR department.
- **Pages and news:** You can similarly target pages and news posts toward specific groups. For example, you can set the target audience for a marketing news page so that it only shows for the members of the Marketing department.
- **Web parts:** Turning on the target audience filter for the News and **Highlighted content** web parts enables these web parts to use the target audience values that have been defined for the published news posts or various SharePoint lists or library items.

Please note that audience targeting, in a sense, employs *security by obscurity* to only show relevant content to the targeted users. This means that it does not change the underlying permissions of the content but merely *hides* it from being shown up in the UI for users who are not part of the groups that the content is targeted at. For example, even if you set the audience for the HR site navigation link so that the link is only visible to HR department users, users that are not part of the HR department can still directly browse to the HR department site if they know the URL.

 To ensure that only users from the HR department have access to the site and its content, you should secure it through appropriate permissions in SharePoint. We will learn more about permissions and security through the *Determining and revoking permissions for a site* recipe later in this chapter.

Using audience targeting is a great way to create a personalized experience for the users of your site. For example, you could have a similar set of web parts on your site's home page and yet show different content to various users, depending on the departments or teams that they belong to.

The following Microsoft support articles provide in-depth details of the various concepts and details of audience targeting:

- *Overview of audience targeting in modern SharePoint sites*: `https://packt.link/audience-targeting-overview`
- *Target navigation, news, and files to specific audiences*: `https://packt.link/audience-targeting-uses`

Adding an app

You can extend the functionality of your SharePoint site by adding apps to it. Just like the apps on a mobile device, SharePoint apps are ready-to-use standalone widgets or applications that help address specific business needs. You can add apps that your organization might have developed in-house, or you can add apps from the SharePoint Store.

In this recipe, we will learn how to add an app from the SharePoint Store.

Getting ready

You need to have Owner or Full Control access to the site you would like to add the app to.

How to do it...

To add an app from the SharePoint Store, follow these steps:

1. Browse to the home page of your site.
2. Click **New** from the page editing menu and then click **App**, as shown in the following screenshot:

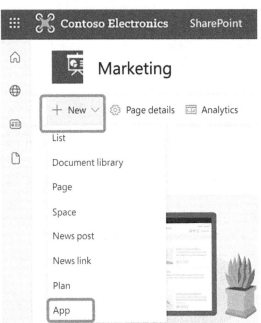

Figure 3.23: Menu navigation for adding an app

3. Doing so will take you to the **Apps you can add** screen of the **My apps** page. Here, you can view a list of apps that your organization has created or previously purchased, which can be added to your site. You can add an app from this screen by simply clicking on the app:

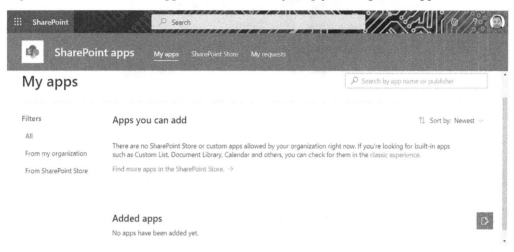

Figure 3.24: List of an organization's created or purchased apps

 If needed, you can also add built-in classic SharePoint apps through the classic experience of the app store. To do so, simply click the **classic experience** hyperlink on the **My apps** page.

4. Next, click the **Find more apps in the SharePoint Store** link to be taken to the SharePoint app store. Here you can perform a keyword search for your app or look it up by one of the categories on the left.

5. We will search using the text Calendar Overlay for our example.

6. This will bring up a list of search results. We can click on each app to view the app details.

 You might receive a message indicating that some of the apps will only work in the *classic experience*. You can switch to the classic app experience to add such an app to your site. You can read more about the classic app store experience here: https://packt.link/classic-app

7. Click **Request** on the app details page once you are satisfied with the description of the app and would like to add it to your site. You will then need to submit a reason for the request so the administrators can accordingly review it:

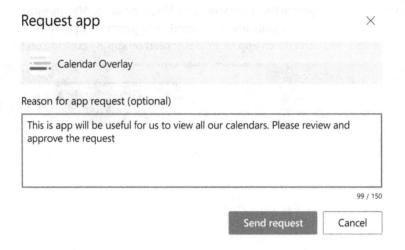

Figure 3.25: Sending a request for an app to the SharePoint administrators

8. Your SharePoint administrators can then review the app in greater detail, including the security permissions it requires. They can then approve or decline your request:

App Info

App Name	**Publisher**
Calendar Overlay	Cloudwell
Release Date	**Lastest Version**
February 2022	2.3.1.0
Rating	**Legal**
★ ★ ★ ★ ★ 5 (7 Ratings)	Terms and Conditions
	Privacy Policy

About

Are you ready to elevate your calendar game? Designed to make your life easier regardless of industry, our app makes it easy to **overlay SharePoint lists and libraries, Exchange calendars, and Planner plans** in one place. Use it with...

See more

Comments

Message to person requesting this app (optional)

> Add message here

Approve and add this app   Decline request

Figure 3.26: Request for an app from the approver's perspective

While approving it, they can also automatically enable it for all sites, including yours. If they don't want it to be automatically added to all sites, they can just enable it for use across all sites without adding it to the sites:

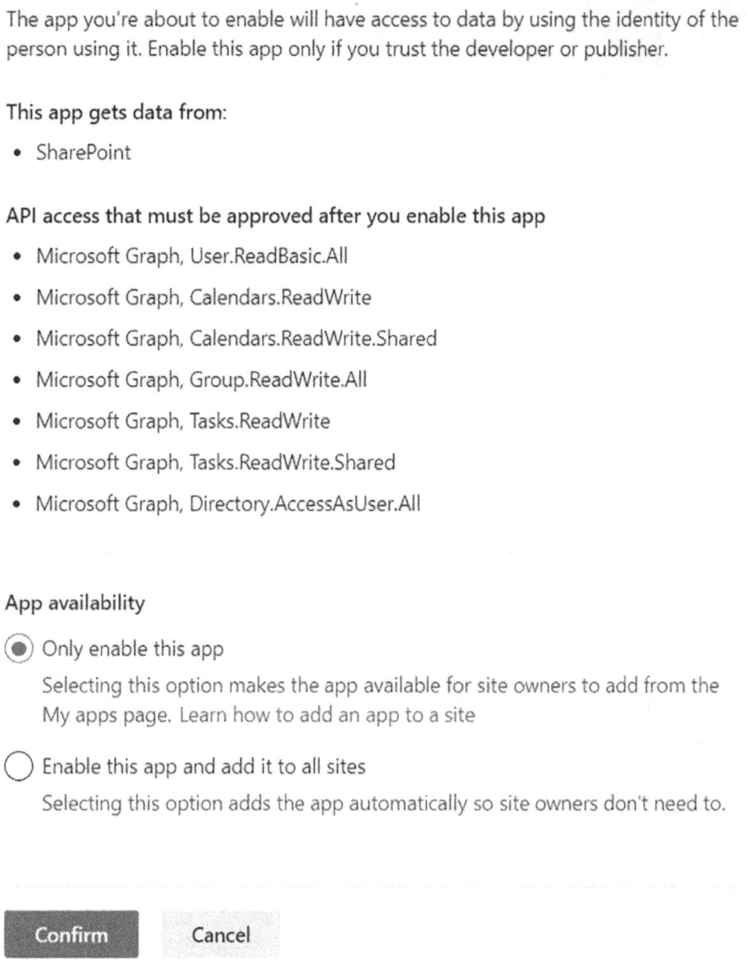

The app you're about to enable will have access to data by using the identity of the person using it. Enable this app only if you trust the developer or publisher.

This app gets data from:

- SharePoint

API access that must be approved after you enable this app

- Microsoft Graph, User.ReadBasic.All
- Microsoft Graph, Calendars.ReadWrite
- Microsoft Graph, Calendars.ReadWrite.Shared
- Microsoft Graph, Group.ReadWrite.All
- Microsoft Graph, Tasks.ReadWrite
- Microsoft Graph, Tasks.ReadWrite.Shared
- Microsoft Graph, Directory.AccessAsUser.All

App availability

(●) Only enable this app

Selecting this option makes the app available for site owners to add from the My apps page. Learn how to add an app to a site

( ) Enable this app and add it to all sites

Selecting this option adds the app automatically so site owners don't need to.

[Confirm]   [Cancel]

Figure 3.27: Administrator's choice to either enable or enable and add an app

9. Once the app is approved for use on the organization screen, you will now start seeing it on the **My apps** page:

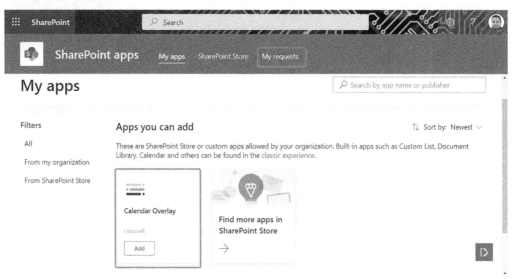

Figure 3.28: Approved app appears now in SharePoint

Note that you can also click the **My requests** tab on this page to see all your requests and their status.

10. The app will now start showing up on the **Site contents** page. If it supports being added as an app part to the pages of your site, you will be able to do so now, as shown in the example image below:

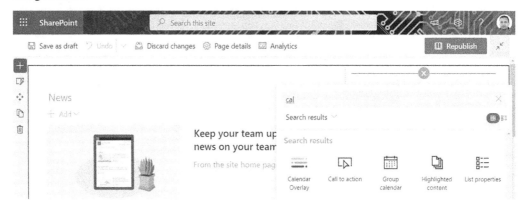

Figure 3.29: Adding the approved app as an app part

Congratulations! You just learned how to request an app from the SharePoint Store and add it to your site. From this point on, depending on the type of app, you can either add it as an app part to a page on your site or click the app to explore its functionality. Some of the more complex apps may require your company administrators to perform further configuration before the app you purchased can work. Besides this, someone in your organization may need to procure the appropriate licenses from the app vendor.

How it works...

In addition to adding apps using the **New** menu from a page on your site, you can add SharePoint apps from the following places:

*   By clicking on the gear icon in the top-right corner of your site and then clicking **Add an app**, as shown in the following screenshot:

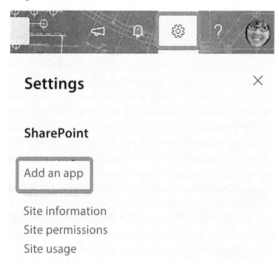

Figure 3.30: Adding an app through Settings instead of the New menu

*   By using the **New** menu option of the **Site contents** page. Please refer to the *Viewing Site contents* recipe in *Chapter 2, Introduction to SharePoint Online*, for more details on the **Site contents** page.

Types of apps

SharePoint custom apps are also sometimes known as **add-ins**. From a functional perspective, SharePoint add-ins are of three different types:

*   **App parts:** Commonly also known as web parts, these usually provide small blocks or units of functionality that can be embedded in a page. We looked at web parts as part of the previous recipe in this chapter. An example of this could be an app that shows the local weather of your office.

- **Full-page apps:** These are usually more complex apps that provide a single-page or multi-page experience for implementing a larger business functionality. These apps are usually meant to automate more complex business processes.

- **SharePoint extensions:** These types of apps can be used to extend SharePoint's features, such as adding to the existing ribbons, menus, or buttons.

Your organization can decide to create its own add-ins. Please refer to *Chapter 25, Custom Development – SharePoint Framework*, to learn more about how to create your own add-ins, along with other aspects of SharePoint development.

Removing an app from your site

Site owners can remove add-ins that were previously deployed to their site by browsing to the **Site contents** page, clicking the three dots next to the app (1), and then clicking **Remove** from the context menu (2), as shown in the following screenshot:

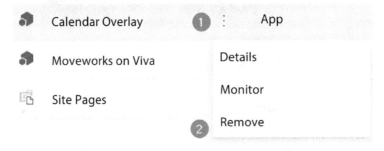

Figure 3.31: Option for removing an app through the app's context menu

Please note that at the time of writing, you will receive the following message when you try to remove the app from the **Site contents** page:

Action isn't supported in this view   ✕

We are working to add that functionality to this page. In the meantime, please go to classic SharePoint to complete this task.

Figure 3.32: Redirection message when removing an app from Site contents

While this is expected to change in the future, for now, you will need to click the **Return to classic SharePoint** button to be taken to the **Site contents** page in *classic* SharePoint. You will then need to follow similar steps to delete the app from the classic **Site contents** page, as shown by steps 1 and 2 in the following screenshot:

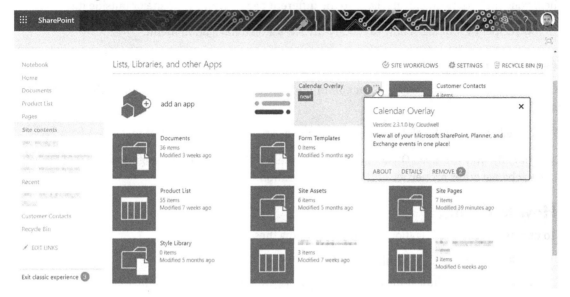

Figure 3.33: Removing an app through the classic SharePoint design

You will then need to click **Exit classic experience**, as shown by *step 3* in the preceding screenshot, to return to the modern SharePoint experience.

 While removing the app completely removes any files that it uses internally, the app may have created artifacts in your site that may still be in use and will likely not be deleted by this operation. An example is as follows: if your app created custom pages or provisioned custom lists or libraries on your site, there's a good chance that you will need to manually delete those pages and/or lists from your site.

Please note that even once you remove the app from your site, the app will still be available for other site owners to use on their sites. This is because when the app was first installed, it was *licensed* to be used for the entire organization.

See also

- The *Viewing Site contents* recipe in *Chapter 2, Introduction to SharePoint Online*
- *Chapter 25, Custom Development – SharePoint Framework*

Modifying the top navigation

When you create a new communication site or register a site as a **hub**, SharePoint creates a navigation menu at the top of the site. This menu is called the **global navigation** menu. You can use this menu to help your site's users quickly navigate to the different pages within your site or outside it.

In this recipe, we will learn how to modify the site's global navigation menu.

Getting ready

Global navigation is only available for communications sites (or a communications site registered as a hub).

You can edit items in the global navigation menu as an owner or member of that site.

Additionally, you will need Owner access or be granted Full Control or Design permissions for your site to change other properties of the global navigation.

How to do it...

To update the global navigation on your site, follow these steps:

1. Browse to any page within the site.
2. Click the **Edit** link at the end of the top navigation bar, as shown in the following screenshot:

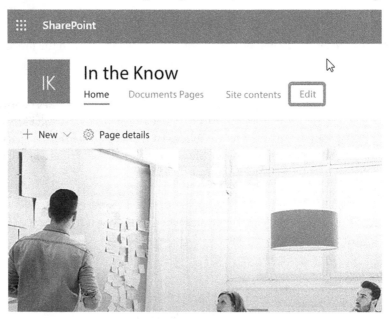

Figure 3.34: Edit button in the top navigation bar

3. This results in the global navigation opening in **Edit** mode. Position the mouse cursor below an existing item where you would like to add a new menu item.

4. Click the + sign and then select the **Header** option from the **Choose an option** dropdown, as shown in the following screenshot:

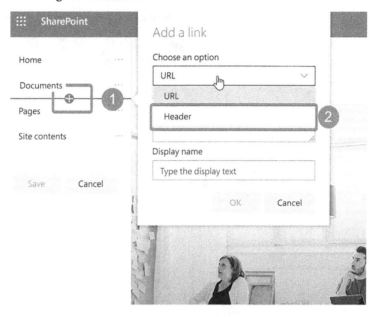

Figure 3.35: Option for creating a new header in the global navigation menu

5. Give your menu a **Display name** and then click the **OK** button. This will result in a new header being created.

6. To add a link underneath the newly created header item, position the mouse cursor directly below it.

7. Click the + sign and then select **URL** from the **Choose an option** dropdown.

8. Enter values for the **Address** and **Display name** textboxes, as shown in the following screenshot:

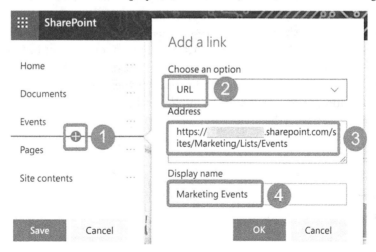

Figure 3.36: Adding a link to the newly created header

9. Click the **OK** button to save your URL.
10. Click the three dots next to your newly added link menu.
11. Click the **Make sub link** menu option, as shown in the following screenshot:

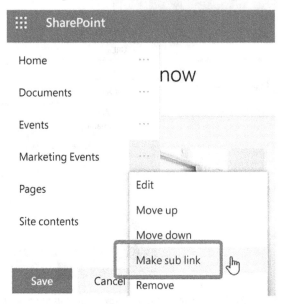

Figure 3.37: Menu option to make the header a link

12. Then, click the **Save** button to save your changes.

Congratulations! You just added new navigation items to your global navigation.

How it works...

Communication and **hub** sites are typically used for organization-wide communication or intranet-type scenarios, where users are likely to be presented with content from across multiple pages and/or sites. Such sites are typically designed so that users can easily get to the content they are looking for, and the top navigation is usually where users start their search for relevant content. Creating a robust cross-site global navigation in such scenarios aids the user experience by helping users quickly browse to the information they are specifically looking for. It is therefore even more important to carefully plan global navigation. If you are especially implementing global navigation for a mid-sized or large organization, it is recommended that your organization goes through an upfront effort to clearly define this navigation in a way that helps your users to easily get to the content that they are looking for.

There's more...

SharePoint lets you create global navigation using two different widely accepted styles. We will discuss these menu styles in the following section.

Cascading menus and mega menus

SharePoint global navigation can be styled as either **cascading menus** or **mega menus**. A cascading menu uses classic multi-level navigation to help you display your navigation hierarchy using multiple sub-level menus, as shown in the following screenshot:

Figure 3.38: Example of the cascading menu layout

On the other hand, the **mega menu** option lets you display multiple levels of navigation without you having to go through the various flyouts, as shown in the following screenshot:

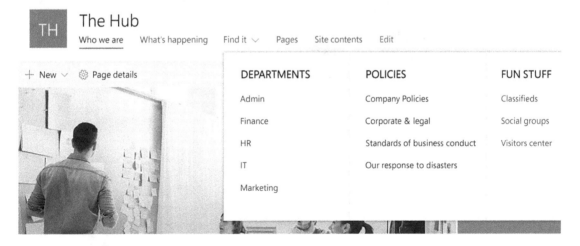

Figure 3.39: Example of the mega menu layout

You can switch between either of these menu styling options through the **Change the look** setting, which was described earlier as part of the *Changing the look* recipe.

See also...

- The *Audience targeting* topic of the *Adding a web part* recipe, earlier in this chapter

Modifying the left navigation

When you create a new team site, SharePoint also creates a navigation menu toward the left of the page. This menu is called the **Quick Launch** menu. The purpose of the **Quick Launch** menu is to help the users of your team site quickly get to the different areas *within* your site.

In this recipe, we will learn how to modify the Quick Launch menu on your site and how to add a link to an existing list within the site.

Getting ready

The Quick Launch menu is only available for team sites (or a team site registered as a **hub**).

You can edit items in the Quick Launch menu as an owner or member of that site.

Additionally, you will need Owner access or be granted Full Control or Design permissions for your site to change other properties of the Quick Launch menu.

How to do it...

You can follow these steps to edit items in the Quick Launch menu of your site:

1. Browse to any page on your team site:

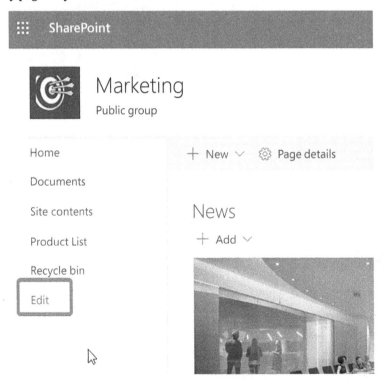

Figure 3.40: Edit button on a team site

2. Click the **Edit** link in the Quick Launch menu on the left-hand side.

3. Click the + sign below an existing item and then select **URL** from the **Choose an option** drop-down.

4. Enter the link address and a display name for the link. Then, click the **OK** button.

5. In the end, click **Save** to save your changes, as shown in the following screenshot:

Figure 3.41: Steps for adding a link to the Quick Launch menu

That's it! You just learned how to modify the Quick Launch menu for your site.

How it works...

The purpose of a team site is to facilitate collaboration within a team. Users of a team site are expected to navigate to pages within the site rather than across multiple sites. The Quick Launch navigation menu helps to facilitate this *intra-site* navigation.

In addition to defining custom links, SharePoint also provides you with a list of pre-defined links to choose from, such as the ones shown in the following screenshot:

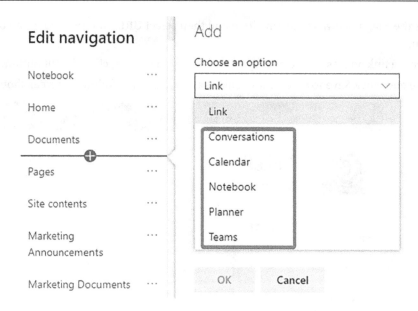

Figure 3.42: Predefined links to add to the Quick Launch menu

Clicking **Planner** in the preceding screenshot, for example, will automatically add a link to the plan for the site. The Quick Launch menu also allows multiple levels of submenus to help you better organize the navigation within your site. To make a menu item a submenu, simply click the three dots next to the menu item and then click **Make sub link**, as shown below:

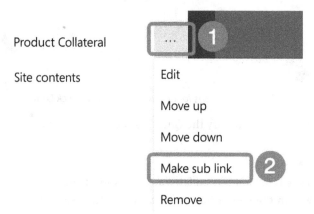

Fig 3.43: Option for demoting a menu item to a submenu item

You can similarly promote sub links by clicking the **Promote sub link** option in the context menu.

There's more...

You can completely disable the Quick Launch navigation or change it so that it shows at the top instead.

Hiding Quick Launch or changing orientation

You will need Owner access or be granted Full Control or Design permissions for your site to hide the Quick Launch menu or change its orientation to horizontal. To do so:

1. Click on the settings gear icon in the top-right corner of the screen.
2. Click **Change the look**:

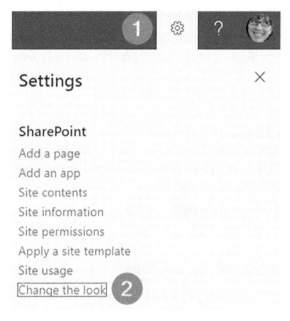

Figure 3.44: Customizing navigation options

3. Click **Navigation**.
4. You can then completely turn off the site navigation from here or change it so that it shows up horizontally at the top, instead of the default vertical navigation that you see on the left. Optionally, you will also be able to change the style of your menu when you choose the horizontal orientation:

Figure 3.45: Options for choosing the navigation style

See also...

- The *Viewing and changing site settings* recipe later in this chapter
- The *Audience targeting* topic of the *Adding a web part* recipe earlier in this chapter

Viewing and changing site settings

You can view and modify your site settings and properties after it's created.

In this recipe, we will learn how to view and change the basic information of a site, such as its title, description, or logo. We will also learn how to change the advanced settings of a site, such as changing the time zone for the site.

Getting ready

Which settings you are allowed to change depends on your permissions within the site. Member access or the Edit and Design permission levels allow you to change certain features, such as the ability to edit site navigation and the site theme. Owner access or the Full Control permission level gives you the greatest control over various site settings.

This recipe assumes that you have Owner or Full Control access to the site.

How to do it...

To change the time zone that your site uses for the date/time fields:

1. Browse to the site for which you would like to change the settings.
2. Click on the settings gear icon in the top-right corner.
3. Click **Site information,** as shown in the following screenshot:

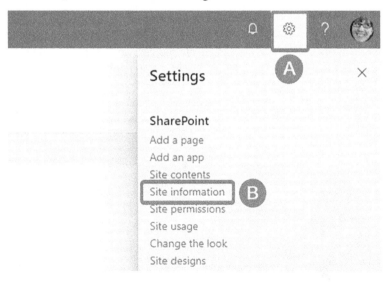

Figure 3.46: Changing site settings through Site information

4. This brings up the panel for editing site information. You can carry out the following actions in this panel:

    •   Change the site logo, name, and description
    •   Change the privacy settings of the site (on a group-based modern team site)
    •   Change the hub association for the site (refer to the *Creating a modern site* recipe in *Chapter 2, Introduction to SharePoint Online*, to learn what a hub site is)
    •   View or change advanced site information
    •   Delete the site (you can use this link to delete a site if you have Full Control access to it)

5. Click **View all site settings**, as shown in the following screenshot:

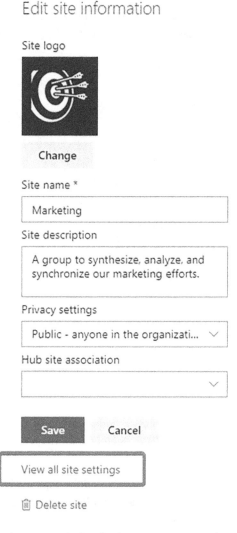

Figure 3.47: Finding further site settings to edit

6.   Click **Regional settings** under the **Site Administration** heading.

7.   Change the time zone to your desired time zone and click the **OK** button at the bottom.

That's it! You just learned how to change the time zone of your site. All created and modified times on your site will now follow the changed time zone.

How it works...

You can change the various properties and settings of your site after it has been created. The type of settings that you can change not only depends on your permissions within the site but also on the type of site you have.

The following image shows other settings that you can access through the settings gear icon:

Figure 3.48: Settings pane for a SharePoint site

We've discussed most of these settings and actions in the various recipes in this chapter and the previous chapter, *Chapter 2, Introduction to SharePoint Online*. Here, we will briefly mention the remaining settings from this menu:

*   **Site usage:** Takes you to the site usage analytics page. Here, you can view and export various reports on the site's traffic and how users have interacted with the site. You can read more about these reports here: https://packt.link/SP-usage-analytics

In addition to usage analytics, you can also view a permissions report, listing all site-level permissions and any unique permissions defined at the list/library or list item/document level. These permissions can be viewed by clicking the **Run report** link under the **Shared with external users** section. Also note that for a hub site, this page shows you the hub usage data report by default. You can switch to the site usage data report by clicking the dropdown at the top right of this page:

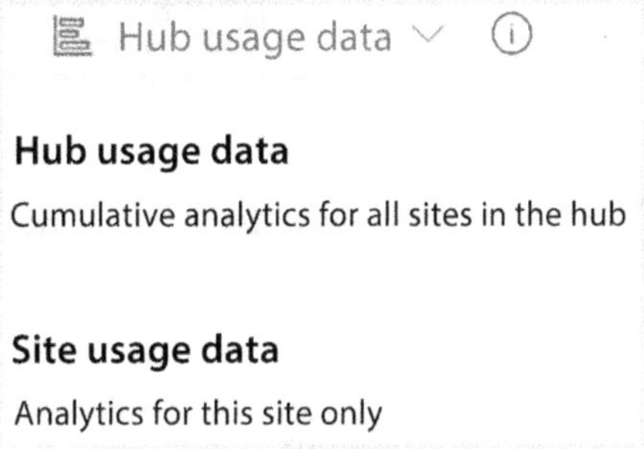

🏛 Hub usage data ∨ ⓘ

Hub usage data

Cumulative analytics for all sites in the hub

Site usage data

Analytics for this site only

Figure 3.49: Switching between hub and site analytics

If you are a site owner and you do not see the **Shared with external users** section, please make sure that you are viewing the site usage data and not the hub usage data report.

- **Site performance:** This is an advanced capability that can be used (typically by developers) to troubleshoot slowness due to apps or customizations on specific pages. You can read more about it here: `https://packt.link/SP-page-diagnostics`

- **Schedule site launch:** This is also an advanced capability that allows you to schedule the launch of a large high-traffic communications portal (site) to a subset (or wave) of users at a time. You can read more about it here: `https://packt.link/SP-launch-scheduler`

- **Office 365 – View all:** You can click this link to update a few key Office 365 settings, as shown in the following image:

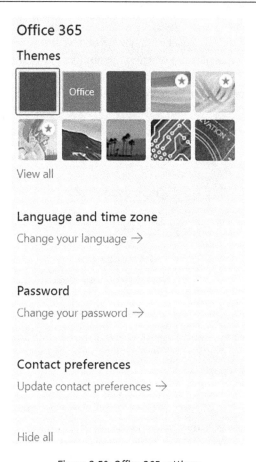

Figure 3.50: Office 365 settings

Note that the themes in question are not site themes, which we discussed in the *Changing the look* recipe earlier in this chapter, but rather apply to the overall Office 365 theme personalization for you, which applies to areas such as the Office 365 top bar and other common areas in Office 365.

- Finally, clicking the gear icon, **Site information**, and then **View all site settings** takes you to the classic **Site settings** page, which allows you to tune many more settings for your site:

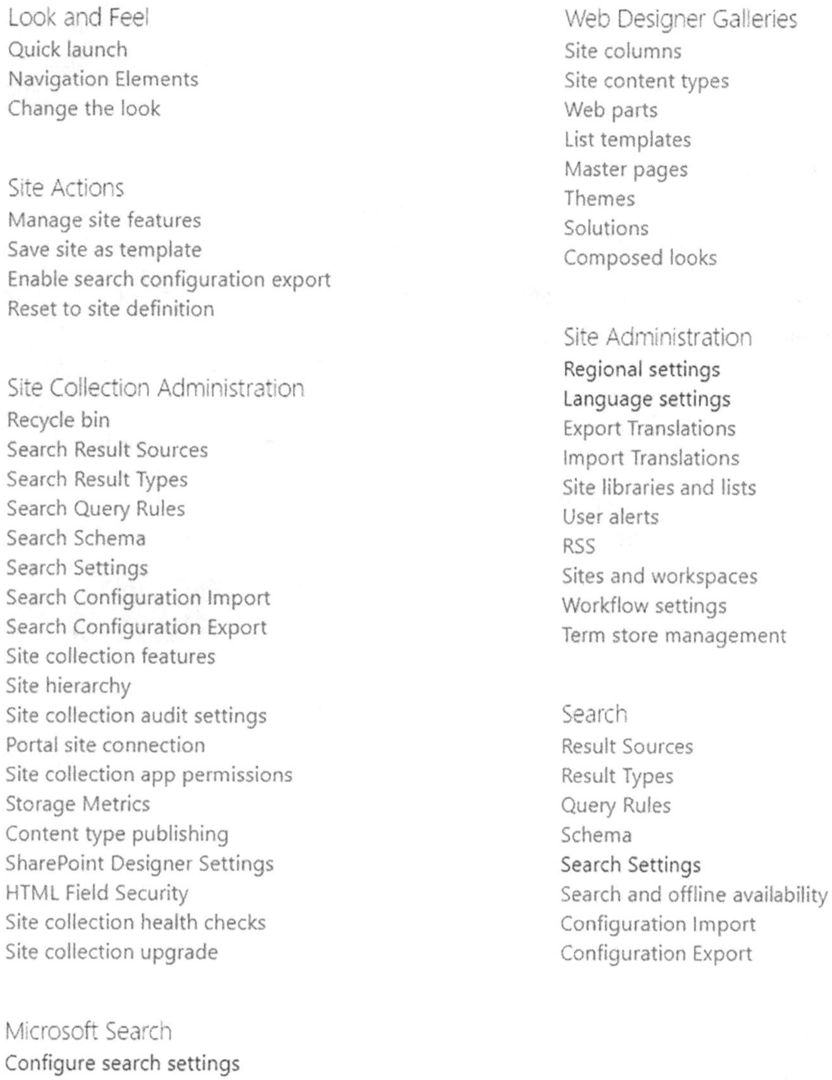

Look and Feel
Quick launch
Navigation Elements
Change the look

Site Actions
Manage site features
Save site as template
Enable search configuration export
Reset to site definition

Site Collection Administration
Recycle bin
Search Result Sources
Search Result Types
Search Query Rules
Search Schema
Search Settings
Search Configuration Import
Search Configuration Export
Site collection features
Site hierarchy
Site collection audit settings
Portal site connection
Site collection app permissions
Storage Metrics
Content type publishing
SharePoint Designer Settings
HTML Field Security
Site collection health checks
Site collection upgrade

Microsoft Search
Configure search settings

Web Designer Galleries
Site columns
Site content types
Web parts
List templates
Master pages
Themes
Solutions
Composed looks

Site Administration
Regional settings
Language settings
Export Translations
Import Translations
Site libraries and lists
User alerts
RSS
Sites and workspaces
Workflow settings
Term store management

Search
Result Sources
Result Types
Query Rules
Schema
Search Settings
Search and offline availability
Configuration Import
Configuration Export

Figure 3.51: Classic site settings page showing all site settings

Most of the settings on this page are advanced admin settings available only to the site owners and are beyond the scope of this book. Others, such as **Site columns**, **Site content types**, and **User alerts**, are covered throughout the various chapters and recipes in this book.

Determining and revoking permissions for a site

SharePoint lets you view who has access to your site and what level of access they have.

This recipe will show you how to determine the level of access that a user may have to your site. We will also learn how to use SharePoint permissions management to revoke permissions for an existing user of the site.

Getting ready

You will need at least **Read** access to the site where you'd like to check user permissions. You will need **Full Control** access to be able to view advanced permissions or revoke user permissions on your site.

For this recipe, we will assume that you have **Full Control** access to the site where you'd like to check permissions.

How to do it...

To view and update user permissions on a site, browse to your site and follow these steps:

1. Click on the **Settings** gear icon in the top-right corner.
2. Click **Site permissions**, as shown in the following screenshot:

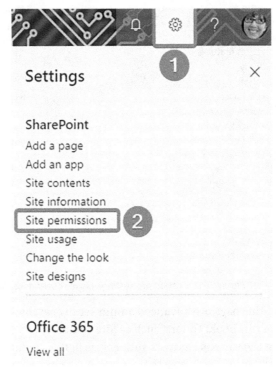

Figure 3.52: Reaching Site permissions through the Settings icon

3. Here, you can see the three types of permissions that you can assign to your site users:

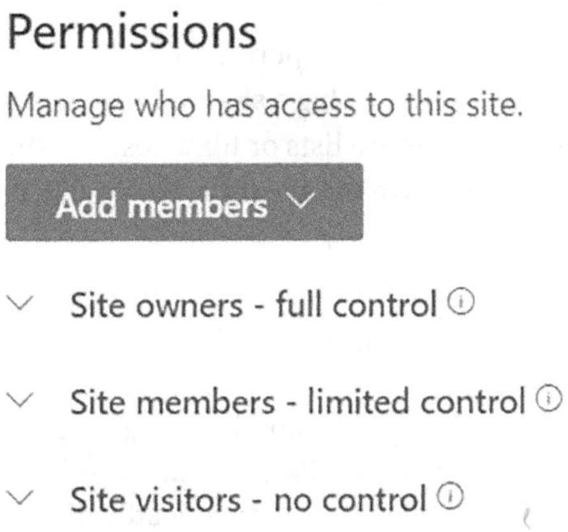

Permissions

Manage who has access to this site.

Add members ∨

∨ Site owners - full control ⓘ

∨ Site members - limited control ⓘ

∨ Site visitors - no control ⓘ

Figure 3.53: Viewing the three permission types for site users

4. You can then expand each type and view, change, or completely revoke the permissions of a user. In the screenshot below, for example, I can click the **Edit** option and then click **Remove** to completely remove Alex from the **Site members** group:

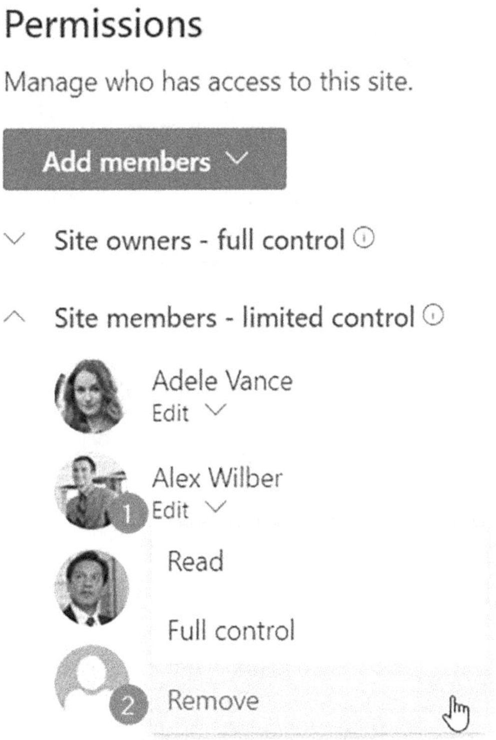

Permissions

Manage who has access to this site.

Add members ∨

∨ Site owners - full control ⓘ

∧ Site members - limited control ⓘ

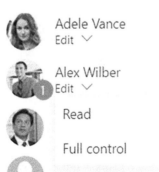

    Adele Vance
    Edit ∨

    Alex Wilber
    Edit ∨

    Read

    Full control

    Remove

Figure 3.54: Managing permissions for an individual

5. To completely remove a person, you will need to ensure that they are not present in all three groups.

6. Many times, this will suffice to revoke permissions for a person from your site. However, more often than not, your site users will have shared links to individual items (usually documents/list items but it can even be entire lists or libraries). Further, there's a possibility that permissions might have been granted to the site through advanced ways, such as SharePoint or **Active Directory** groups.

 Active Directory (known as AD for short) groups are a way for your organization to categorize together members with similar permissions or roles. Often, organizations use AD groups to centrally manage user permissions and access to disparate applications, instead of having to manage them individually for each application, including SharePoint, or, for that matter, the other workloads in Office 365.

In such cases, SharePoint will show you a message with a link to the **Advanced permissions settings** page, as shown below:

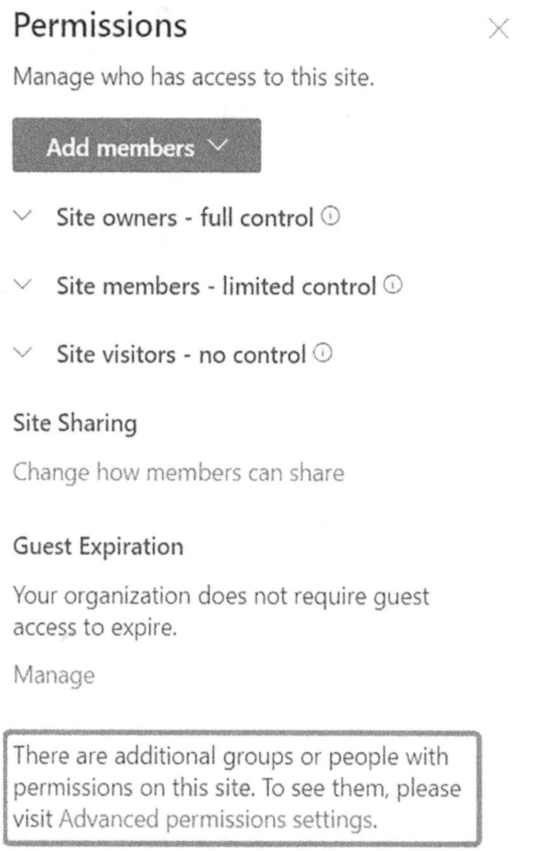

Permissions   ✕

Manage who has access to this site.

Add members ⌄

⌄   Site owners - full control ⓘ

⌄   Site members - limited control ⓘ

⌄   Site visitors - no control ⓘ

Site Sharing

Change how members can share

Guest Expiration

Your organization does not require guest access to expire.

Manage

> There are additional groups or people with permissions on this site. To see them, please visit Advanced permissions settings.

Figure 3.55: Message indicating permissions have been given to the site through other sources

The link to where you can view advanced permissions will only be visible to you if you are the site owner or have been granted the **Full Control** permission level on the site.

7. Click the link and then click on **Check Permissions** from the menu at the top.
8. Enter the name of the user or group that you would like to check the permissions of and click **Check Now.**
9. You can now view the permissions that have been granted to this user:

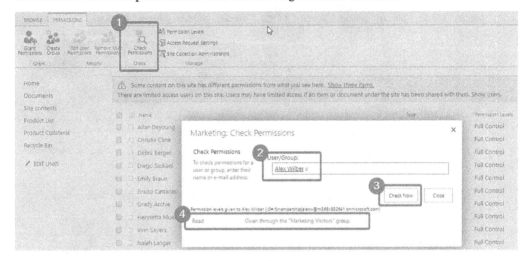

Figure 3.56: Reviewing permissions granted to a user

10. Note the names of any such groups that the user is part of. In this case, the user, **Alex Wilber**, has been granted **Read** access through the **Marketing Visitors** group.
11. Close this dialog box and click on the **Marketing Visitors** group from the **Permissions** screen.
12. Select the checkbox against the user's name from the list of users that shows in the **Marketing Visitors** group.
13. Click the **Actions** menu and then **Remove Users from Group,** as shown in the following screenshot:

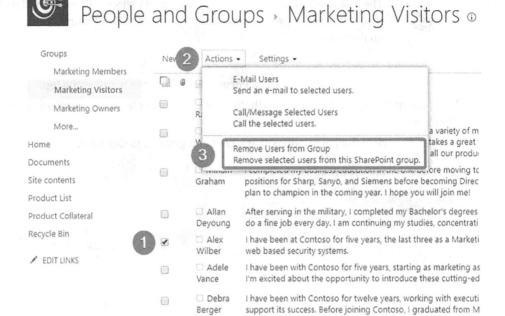

Figure 3.57: Removing a user from a group entirely through the Actions menu

14. Click **OK** on the confirmation message that appears.

Congratulations! You've learned how to determine and update user permissions for your sites.

How it works...

SharePoint offers very granular permission and access controls not only for your site but also for lists and document libraries, and even for the items, documents, and files in those lists and libraries. We will review the various permission-related settings here.

Site permissions

Permissions in SharePoint start at the site level. There are typically three permission groups that get created along with the site:

- **Site Owners:** Members of this group have **Full Control** access to the site and all content in it.
- **Site Members:** Members of this group have **Edit** access to the site.
- **Site Visitors:** Members of this group have **Read** access to the site.

In addition to these groups, which are created by default, you can grant or revoke site permissions for individual users or groups of users through the **Site permissions** page.

We will review various aspects of permissions in SharePoint later in this topic.

Permission levels

Full Control, Edit, and **Read** are called **Permission Levels.** These can be accessed through the **Site permissions** page. SharePoint comes with five pre-defined permission levels, with each permission level shown in the following screenshot:

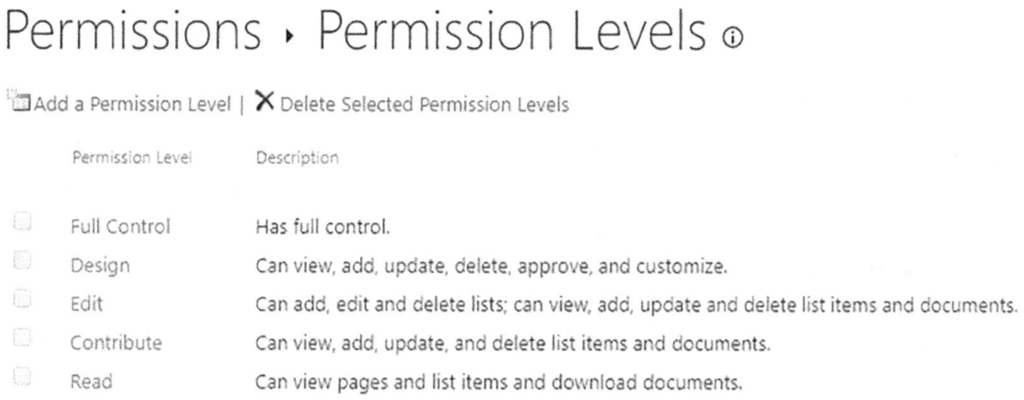

Permissions ▸ Permission Levels ⓘ

⬚Add a Permission Level | ✕ Delete Selected Permission Levels

Permission Level	Description
Full Control	Has full control.
Design	Can view, add, update, delete, approve, and customize.
Edit	Can add, edit and delete lists; can view, add, update and delete list items and documents.
Contribute	Can view, add, update, and delete list items and documents.
Read	Can view pages and list items and download documents.

Figure 3.58: Viewing pre-defined permission levels

Each permission level includes or excludes several individual permissions. Permissions on the add/edit **Permission Levels** page are categorized under the following headings:

- **List Permissions:** This subsection contains all permissions related to lists and list items, such as whether this permission level allows users to add/edit or delete items. The following screenshot shows various permissions that can be controlled within this category and the permissions that are selected by default for the **Edit** permission level:

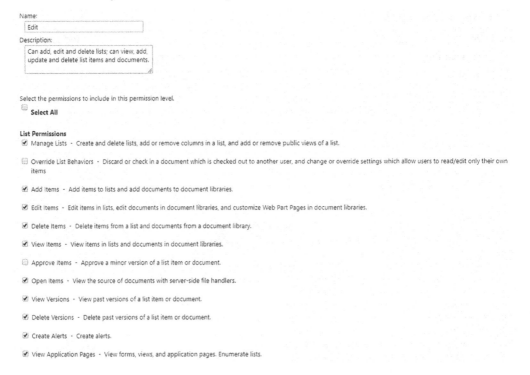

Figure 3.59: Permissions in the List Permissions category

- **Site Permissions:** This subsection lists all permissions that can be controlled for a site. The following screenshot shows various permissions that fall under this category and the permissions that are selected by default for the **Edit** permission level:

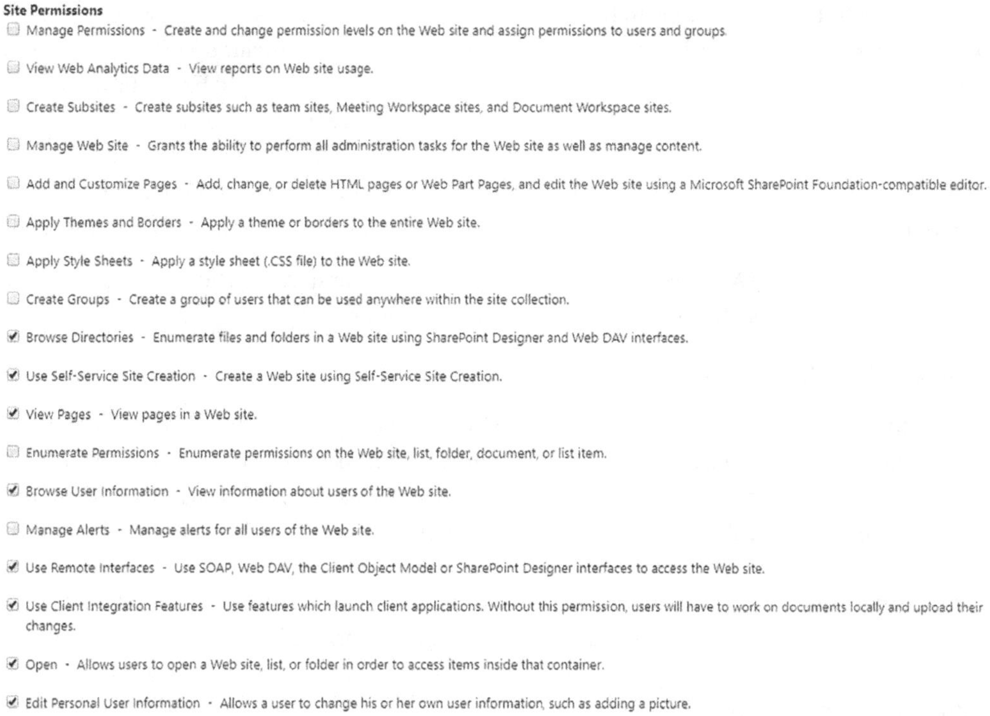

Site Permissions

☐ Manage Permissions - Create and change permission levels on the Web site and assign permissions to users and groups.

☐ View Web Analytics Data - View reports on Web site usage.

☐ Create Subsites - Create subsites such as team sites, Meeting Workspace sites, and Document Workspace sites.

☐ Manage Web Site - Grants the ability to perform all administration tasks for the Web site as well as manage content.

☐ Add and Customize Pages - Add, change, or delete HTML pages or Web Part Pages, and edit the Web site using a Microsoft SharePoint Foundation-compatible editor.

☐ Apply Themes and Borders - Apply a theme or borders to the entire Web site.

☐ Apply Style Sheets - Apply a style sheet (.CSS file) to the Web site.

☐ Create Groups - Create a group of users that can be used anywhere within the site collection.

☑ Browse Directories - Enumerate files and folders in a Web site using SharePoint Designer and Web DAV interfaces.

☑ Use Self-Service Site Creation - Create a Web site using Self-Service Site Creation.

☑ View Pages - View pages in a Web site.

☐ Enumerate Permissions - Enumerate permissions on the Web site, list, folder, document, or list item.

☑ Browse User Information - View information about users of the Web site.

☐ Manage Alerts - Manage alerts for all users of the Web site.

☑ Use Remote Interfaces - Use SOAP, Web DAV, the Client Object Model or SharePoint Designer interfaces to access the Web site.

☑ Use Client Integration Features - Use features which launch client applications. Without this permission, users will have to work on documents locally and upload their changes.

☑ Open - Allows users to open a Web site, list, or folder in order to access items inside that container.

☑ Edit Personal User Information - Allows a user to change his or her own user information, such as adding a picture.

Figure 3.60: Permissions in the Site Permissions category

- **Personal Permissions:** The actions in this section pertain to changes that users can make to their personal views. These actions do not alter the content that other users see on the site. Through the permissions in this section, you can control the actions that the users can perform on their personal views. The following screenshot shows various permissions that fall under this category and the permissions that are selected by default for the **Edit** permission level:

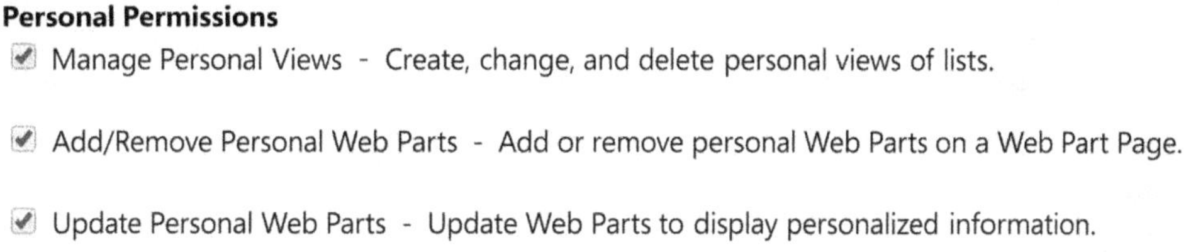

Personal Permissions

☑ Manage Personal Views - Create, change, and delete personal views of lists.

☑ Add/Remove Personal Web Parts - Add or remove personal Web Parts on a Web Part Page.

☑ Update Personal Web Parts - Update Web Parts to display personalized information.

Figure 3.61: Permissions in the Personal Permissions category

You cannot edit the permissions in the SharePoint default permission levels, but you can create your own permission levels by selecting the permissions you'd like to include in those permission levels. This means you can be very specific about what kind of access you would like to have for each permission level in SharePoint. For example, one of the frequently requested features is the ability for users to be able to edit or contribute content but not to be able to delete it. This can simply be achieved by creating a permission level by copying the **Edit** permission level (shown in the preceding screenshot) and then deselecting the **Delete Items** permission under the **List Permissions** category.

Here's a recommended Microsoft article if you would like to understand SharePoint permission levels in greater detail: `https://packt.link/permission-levels`.

Permission inheritance

When you create a new subsite, list, or library within a SharePoint site, it *inherits* the permissions from the parent site. This means the object uses the same permissions as the site that it was created within. These permissions further trickle down to the item level in a list or to the individual document level in a document library. This means that items in lists or documents in document libraries automatically inherit permissions from the parent list or library. SharePoint, on the other hand, allows you to stop inheriting permissions and assign unique permissions to individual lists/libraries or items/documents within them. This enables you to set different permissions for individual lists or libraries within your site. The *Viewing and changing list permissions* recipe in *Chapter 4, Lists and Libraries in SharePoint Online*, discusses this in more detail.

> It is not recommended to *break* permission inheritance too frequently since it tends to confuse users. It can also quickly become a maintenance nightmare when you are trying to figure out permissions for different objects within a site.

Permission groups in SharePoint

Permission groups in SharePoint are a way to manage a set of users that are expected to have the same permissions in SharePoint. You will have one or more users in a SharePoint group that you can then assign permissions to. Just like the site owners, members, and visitors groups we mentioned earlier, you can create additional groups of your own in SharePoint and assign them custom permissions.

In addition to assigning permissions to users through SharePoint groups, you can also assign permissions to users that are part of *Active Directory domain* groups in your organization. This way, you can utilize the user's categorization through those AD groups, provided that your organization is actively maintaining them. Similarly, you can use Office 365 Groups to grant permissions to a group of people to your site. While you can directly grant these AD groups or Office 365 groups appropriate permissions through the **Advanced permissions settings** page, it is recommended to grant access by adding these groups to the appropriate Owners, Members, or Visitors SharePoint groups. This helps avoid having to manage too many direct permissions down the road.

Site collection administrator

When a site is created, there is one permission *role* that gets created in addition to the three groups mentioned earlier. This role is the **site collection administrator**. Site collection administrators not only have full access to all content within all sites and any subsites in that site collection, but they also have access to additional settings and admin functionality for the site. This list of site collection administrators can be managed through the **Site settings** page. Only existing site collection administrators or the global **SharePoint Admins** that have been designated by your organization can manage the site collection administrators list.

There's more...

In addition to managing permissions within the site, site owners can also manage what content users within their site can share. If your organization allows link sharing with external users (or guests), you can manage the expiration of such links.

Site sharing and guest link expiration

The **Site permissions** panel, which you can open by clicking the gear icon and then clicking **Site permissions**, allows you to manage access to the site. As a site owner, it additionally allows you to manage the following settings:

- **Site sharing settings** and **Access requests:** In this panel, you can control what your site members can share:

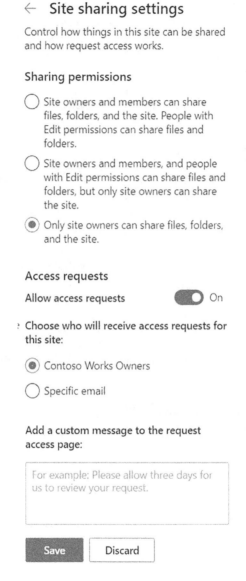

← **Site sharing settings**

Control how things in this site can be shared and how request access works.

Sharing permissions

○ Site owners and members can share files, folders, and the site. People with Edit permissions can share files and folders.

○ Site owners and members, and people with Edit permissions can share files and folders, but only site owners can share the site.

◉ Only site owners can share files, folders, and the site.

Access requests

Allow access requests   ⬤ On

Choose who will receive access requests for this site:

◉ Contoso Works Owners

○ Specific email

Add a custom message to the request access page:

> For example: Please allow three days for us to review your request.

[Save] [Discard]

Figure 3.62: Panel for managing what can be shared by site members

In addition, when users that currently do not have access to the site try to browse to your site, they receive an access denied message. Along with the message, they are allowed to submit a request for access, along with a reason for requesting the access. You can control from this panel whether such requests are allowed and who should be able to respond to such requests.

- **Guest expiration:** Your organization may have required all guest links to expire at the end of a certain period. As a site owner, you can override the expiration of such links for your site. This panel allows you to either terminate the guest links right away or extend the expiration time on these links. You can read more about guest link expiration here: `https://packt.link/SP-guest-links`.

See also...

- The *Sharing a document* recipe in *Chapter 2, Introduction to SharePoint Online*
- The *Viewing and changing list permissions* recipe in *Chapter 4, Lists and Libraries in SharePoint Online*

Creating a subsite

SharePoint lets you create subsites under existing sites. Subsites are useful when you want to organize content through a subset of lists, libraries, or pages but the audience that will have access to this content is the same as or a subset of the users of the parent site. For example, a large organization might have a site for the HR department, and they are likely to have a payroll subsite within it for a small set of members that help manage the organization's payroll.

This recipe shows you how to create a subsite using the modern team site template.

Getting ready

You need **Full Control** access to the site that you would like to create the new subsite for.

How to do it...

To create a subsite, follow these steps:

1. Browse to the site that you would like to create the subsite for.
2. Click on the **Settings** gear icon in the top-right corner and then **Site contents**.
3. Click **New** and then **Subsite**.
4. On the **New SharePoint Site** page, enter or select the following:
    - A title, description, URL name, language, and template for your site.
    - Whether or not the site will use the same permissions as the parent site. Clicking **Use unique permissions** will let you specify permissions that are different from that of the parent site.
    - Whether or not the site will show up on the **Quick Launch** menu of the parent site (typically set to **No**).

- Whether or not the site will show up on the global navigation menu of the parent site (typically set to **Yes**).
- Whether or not the site will use the same global navigation menu as the parent site (typically set to **Yes**):

Site contents › New SharePoint Site

Title and Description

Title:

DG-2000 Drone Launch

Description:

This is a team collaboration site for the DG-2000 Drone Launch

Web Site Address

URL name:

https://m365x882641.sharepoint.com/sites/Marketing/ DG2000Launch

Template Selection

Select a language:

English ▼

Select a template:

Collaboration | Enterprise | Duet Enterprise

Team site
Team site (classic experience)
Blog
Project Site

A site with no connection to an Office 365 Group.

Permissions

You can give permission to access your new site to the same users who have access to this parent site, or you can give permission to a unique set of users.

Note: If you select **Use same permissions as parent site**, one set of user permissions is shared by both sites. Consequently, you cannot change user permissions on your new site unless you are an administrator of this parent site.

User Permissions:

◉ Use same permissions as parent site
○ Use unique permissions

Navigation

Display this site on the Quick Launch of the parent site?
○ Yes   ◉ No

Display this site on the top link bar of the parent site?
◉ Yes   ○ No

Navigation Inheritance

Use the top link bar from the parent site?
◉ Yes   ○ No

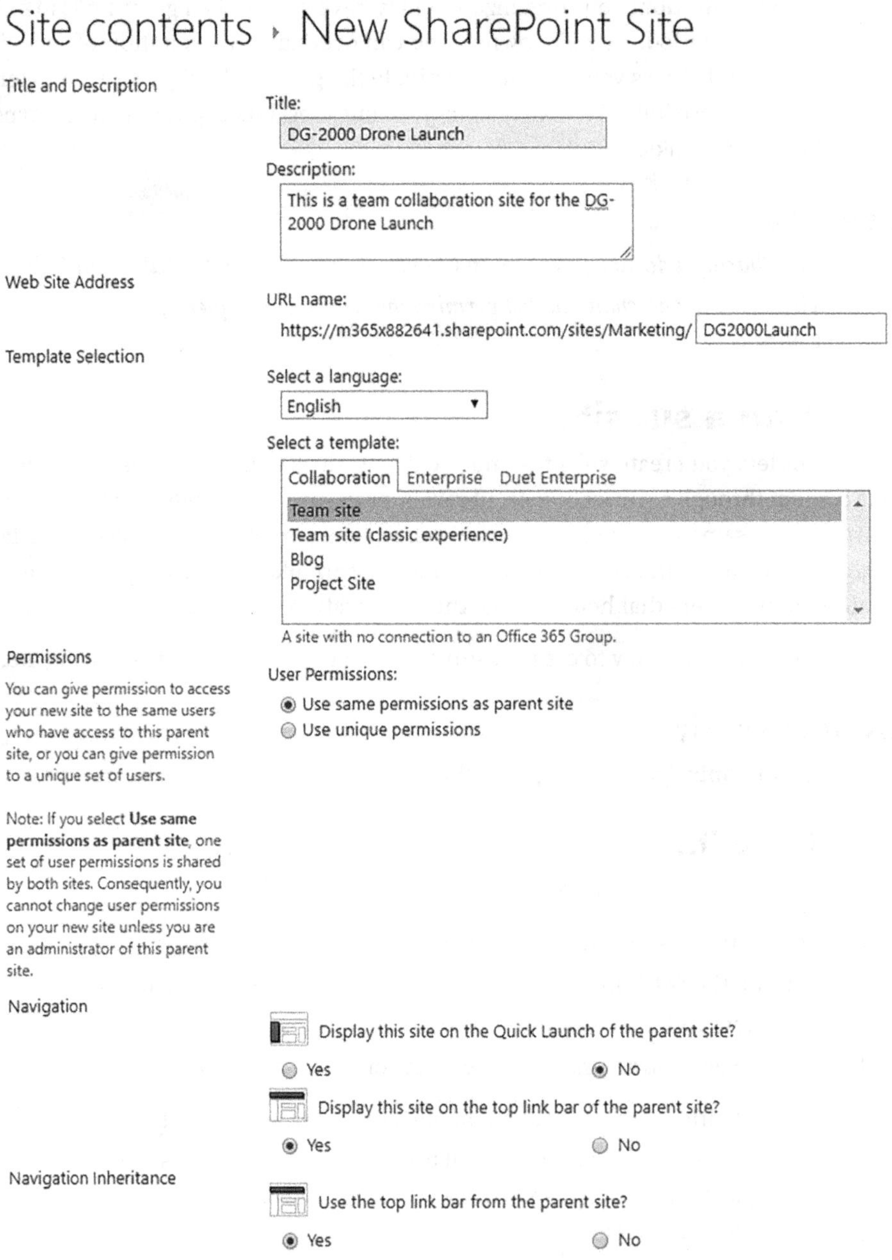

Figure 3.63 Creation page for making a subsite

5. Click the **Create** button once you have finished setting this up or confirmed the information you provided here.

Congratulations! You just created your new subsite.

How it works...

For reasons beyond the scope of this book, the general guidance from Microsoft at the time of writing is to not create subsites. Microsoft recommends creating sites (that is, site collections) instead to accomplish your goals and using a hub to connect related sites. Having said that, subsites may still make sense in some scenarios. One such scenario was described at the onset of this recipe, with the HR site and the payroll subsite. Another example could be a temporary collaboration area within a team site used for research, with a smaller team to collaborate on a new idea or upcoming product. Here is some good independent guidance on the pros and cons of each: `https://packt.link/why-subsites` and `https://packt.link/why-sites`. At the time of writing, the maximum number of subsites that you can have within a SharePoint site collection is 2,000. On the other hand, the maximum number of site collections per organization tenant is 2 million.

See also...

- The *Creating a modern site* recipe in *Chapter 2, Introduction to SharePoint Online*

Learn more on Discord

To join the Discord community for this book – where you can share feedback, ask questions to the author, and learn about new releases – follow the QR code below:

`https://packt.link/powerusers`

4

Lists and Libraries in SharePoint Online

SharePoint lists enable you to organize and view your information in a tabular format, just as you would organize it in an Excel spreadsheet or a database table. Just like spreadsheets or database tables, lists have columns and rows. Columns identify the type of information that gets stored in the lists and rows (also called **list items**) are responsible for storing this information. SharePoint comes with a set of ready-to-use *list templates* that can be used to create lists with pre-built functionality. Examples of such lists are the **Issue tracker**, **Employee onboarding**, **Recruitment tracker**, and **Asset manager** list templates. Your organization can also create organization specific reusable list templates for you to use. All lists come with some standard and useful features, such as the following:

- Adding or removing columns of different types
- Viewing and editing individual rows through *list forms*
- Grouping, filtering, and sorting tabular multi-row *list views*
- Specifying validations for the columns (such as required fields, field lengths, and so on)
- Embedding information from these lists into other pages in Microsoft 365
- Allowing read/edit permissions to be specified for the entire list or individual rows within the list
- Performing a *security-trimmed search* for items within lists or across all lists that you have access to, so you will only be shown those items in the search results that you have access to via appropriate permissions
- Maintaining a version history (or a record of changes) for each item
- Subscribing to alerts for changes to the items in the list

Lists can be further extended as libraries, which are lists centered around documents. We will learn more about libraries in *Chapter 5, Document Management in SharePoint Online*. However, for this chapter, it is sufficient to note that almost all concepts that apply to lists also apply to libraries. The recipes that we will cover in this chapter therefore also apply to libraries.

The following recipes in this chapter will show us how to work with lists in SharePoint:

- Creating a list from an existing Excel file
- Adding a column
- Creating a custom list view
- Using **Edit in grid view** to bulk-edit list items
- Viewing and changing list settings
- Viewing and changing list permissions
- Adding alerts

Creating a list from an existing Excel file

In *Chapter 2, Introduction to SharePoint Online*, we saw how to create a custom list from scratch. If your team or you have been collaborating using Excel files, it may be a good idea to convert one or more of those spreadsheet(s) to lists in SharePoint. This will not only allow your team to collaboratively work with the data in those lists but will also make available the numerous advantages of Office 365 in general and SharePoint Lists in particular.

In this chapter, we'll see how to create a list from an existing Excel file. The Excel file can exist on your computer or within a document library in a SharePoint site. For our recipe, we will convert a marketing announcements spreadsheet from our site to a SharePoint list. Doing so will further enable us to easily share news, updates, and announcements about the marketing department with others. You will also be able to use the inbuilt rich text editor to add images, links, and rich formatting to these announcements. You can then add this list as a web part to the home page of your site so that the announcements are prominently visible to your site's visitors. You can additionally set an expiration date for each announcement so that it *drops off* the list after that date.

Getting ready

You will need **Edit**, **Design**, or **Full Control** permissions on your site to be able to create lists. Alternately, you will need to be a member of the **Site Owners** or **Site Members** group to create lists on your site.

The Excel spreadsheet that you want to convert will need to have data in a *tabular format*. If you don't know how to convert your data to a tabular format, click the search bar at the top and then type `format as table`, as shown below:

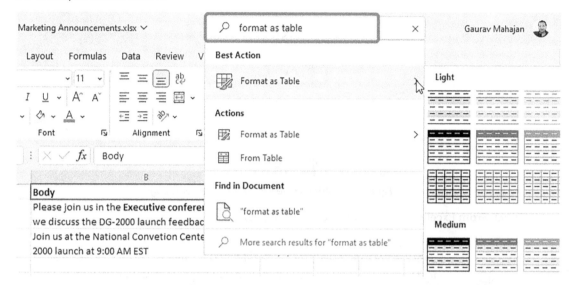

Figure 4.1: Entering text into the search bar at the top of the screen

Then follow the guided steps to convert your data into a tabular format. Note that the first row of your table will need to contain column headers. Excel will add a new row with column headers if your data does not have a header row. SharePoint will give you an error while creating the list if the Excel file is missing column headers.

How to do it...

The steps below will create a new list from an existing Excel file:

1. Browse to the home page of the site in which you would like to create the list.

2. Click **New** and then **List:**

Figure 4.2: Creating a new list from a site home page

3. Click **From Excel** on the pop-up screen that appears.

 Similar to creating a list from an Excel file, you can also create a list from a CSV file. The steps described in this recipe will also apply to creating a list from a CSV file. Simply select the appropriate option in the pop-up. Note that you will not need to convert your data to a tabular format when creating a list from a CSV file.

4. You will now be prompted to either select an Excel file from a library within your site or upload a new file to a library on your site. In our case, we will select the Marketing Announcements. xlsx file from the **Documents** library:

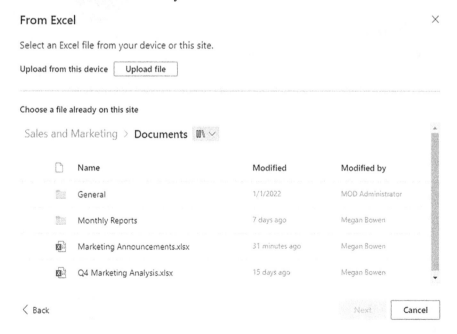

Figure 4.3: Selecting an Excel file from a library

You can download the sample spreadsheet used for this recipe here: `https://packt.link/c4-sample-excel`

5. The next screen will require you to select a table from your Excel workbook. If there are multiple worksheets with tables in them, they will all be listed in the table selection dropdown. You will also be prompted to confirm the data type for each of your columns. Then, you will also see a preview of the data from the table on this screen:

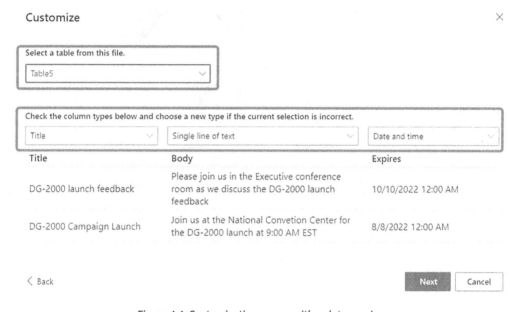

Figure 4.4: Customization screen with a data preview

 Note that date values are usually stored as numbers in Excel. You will therefore manually need to change the data type of such columns on this screen from **Number** to **Date and time.**

6. Click **Next** once you have selected the appropriate table and adjusted the column types as needed.

7. The wizard will then take you to the final screen, where you can specify a name, a description for your list, and whether you would like it to appear in the site navigation. The list name will automatically be set to the name of your Excel file, but you can always change it. In our example, it will be set to **Marketing Announcements.** We will choose the default name and click the **Create** button to create the new list.

The name you enter while creating a list or a library is also used for the URL of your list. Names having spaces or other special characters can result in odd URLs. For example, the list we just created would have the characters %20 in its URL:

```
https://tenant-name.sharepoint.com/sites/Marketing/Marketing%20
Announcements/
```

For that reason, you should avoid entering spaces or other special characters when creating lists or libraries in SharePoint. Doing so will ensure that the URL for your list is clean and does not contain any special characters. In the preceding example, you would want to enter `MarketingAnnouncements` (without a space) as the list name. This would create a list with the following URL: `https://tenant-name.sharepoint.com/sites/Marketing/MarketingAnnouncements`

Once the list is created, you can rename it to add the spaces and special characters as desired (`Marketing Announcements` in our example, with a space in between). Renaming the list after it's created does not change the URL of the list, and your users would still see the same clean URL that got generated while creating the list, at the same time benefiting from a more user-friendly title.

To update the list name after it's created, simply click on the list name after it's created, enter the new name, and then click **Save**, as shown:

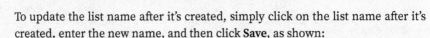

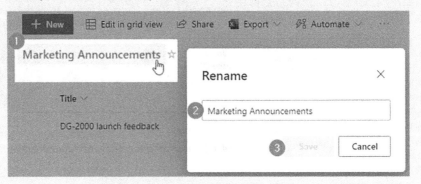

Figure 4.5: Updating a list name

Congratulations! You just created a SharePoint list using the columns and data from your existing Excel file.

How it works...

This way of creating lists is very useful for people who have been working with Excel files and now want to bring their data over to SharePoint online, due it the many benefits listed earlier. SharePoint *infers* the column types from the Excel file, creates the columns using those column types, and then imports the data from the Excel file. After the list is created, it is highly recommended that you review the settings for each column to ensure they are appropriately set. As an example, you may want certain columns to be required or may want to adjust the number of decimals for numeric columns. From that point on, your list will function like any other list that was created from scratch.

There's more...

In addition to creating blank lists from scratch and creating lists using Excel files, SharePoint also offers the following ways to create lists.

Creating a list from a template

Microsoft provides a few list templates that get you started with relevant columns, color formatting, and functionality. Lists created using these templates are generally geared toward addressing very focused needs so that you can start using them right away. If required, however, you can also customize them to meet your specific requirements. At the time of writing, there are 11 templates, a couple of notable examples being:

- **Issue tracker:** Lists created using this template can be used to log, track, and get notified about issues.
- **Event itinerary:** Lists created using this template contain columns, formatting, and some management functionality.

Microsoft is constantly adding new templates and you can visit this link for more information on the various list templates in Microsoft 365: `https://packt.link/list-templates`

This link shows you how to create lists using the M365 list templates: `https://packt.link/create-list-from-template`

In addition to the templates provided by Microsoft, your organization can create custom reusable templates to meet your organization's specific needs. Further, you can limit access to custom templates to specific users or security groups. This link walks you through the process of creating a custom template: `https://packt.link/create-list-template`

Creating a list from an existing list

Instead of creating a new list from scratch, you can also choose to start from an existing list. Doing so will show you a list of existing sites that you have access to. Selecting the site will then show you all the lists from that site. You can then click on an existing list and click **Create**. Doing so will create a new list with the same columns, views, and formatting as the list that you had selected.

You can read more about this capability here:

`https://packt.link/create-list-from-list`

Saving a list as a template

The previous topic discussed how to create a new list based on an existing list. For the most part, you should be able to use it to recreate an existing list with its columns, views, and formatting. There are, however, a few limitations to that approach:

- When selecting the source list, you will only see sites and lists that you have access to via permissions. Consequently, you will not be able to see or create lists based on other lists that you do not have access to.

- You will not be able to copy over data using this approach.
- You will be unable to copy over any list settings that you may have changed from the defaults.
- You cannot use this approach if you would like to automate the creation of certain predefined lists when provisioning new sites.

This is where some of the additional methods discussed in this recipe come in handy. Using these methods, your SharePoint admins, or others who have access to the existing list, can export it as a template and share it with you so that you can recreate a new list in your site based on that template. The one drawback of these methods is that you will require administrator or developer help to be able to use them to export and import your lists.

We will briefly discuss these additional methods of saving existing lists as templates and then reusing them to create new lists. Note that you can reuse the exported list templates to not only recreate lists within the same site or other sites in your organization but even across organizations/tenants if you need to do so.

Exporting a list using site scripts

We discussed site designs and site scripts as part of the *Custom provisioning using site designs and site scripts* topic of the *Creating a subsite* recipe in *Chapter 3, Modern Sites in SharePoint Online*.

We can use the `Get-SPOSiteScriptFromList` command to export the list as a script. For more details, go to the following link: `https://packt.link/Get-SPOSiteScriptFromList`.

> The `Get-SPOSiteScriptFromList` command is part of the SharePoint Online PowerShell module. You can read more about SharePoint Online PowerShell in the *PowerShell* section of the *Appendix*.

Once the list is exported, you can import it to an existing site or make it part of a site's design to be provisioned to a new site.

Remember that in addition to using PowerShell for site designs and site scripts, you can also use the Microsoft 365 **REpresentational State Transfer** (**REST**) **application programming interface** (**API**) to carry out the same tasks, as described here: `https://packt.link/Site-Design-REST-API`.

Exporting a list using PnP

The **PnP** (short for **Patterns and Practices**) provisioning engine also gives us commands for exporting your lists as reusable templates.

> You can read more about PnP in the *SharePoint PnP* topic of the *Office development frameworks* section of the *Appendix*.

You can use the `Export-PnPListToProvisioningTemplate` command to export the list, as described here: `https://packt.link/export-PnP-list-to-provisioning-template`.

You would then use the `Invoke-PnPSiteTemplate` command to recreate the list in a new or existing site, as described here: `https://packt.link/apply-PnP-provisioning-template`.

You can read more about the PnP provisioning engine and the templating capabilities here: `https://packt.link/PnP-Provisioning-Engine`.

Exporting a list using list settings

Finally, you can also use the **Save list as template** list setting to save a list as a template. To do so, browse to the **List settings** page, as described in the *Viewing and changing list settings* recipe later in this chapter. Then, click the **Save list as template** heading under the **Permissions and Management** heading.

 If you are not seeing this option under list settings, your site administrator might need to allow **Custom Scripts**. Please refer to this article from Microsoft to enable **Custom Scripts** on your site: `https://packt.link/custom-script`.

You can read more about saving and using list templates here: `https://packt.link/manage-list-templates`.

Please note that this way to export lists is now considered legacy and Microsoft can remove this option in SharePoint Online at any time.

See also

- The *Creating a list* recipe in *Chapter 2, Introduction to SharePoint Online*
- The *There's more...* section of the *Creating a subsite* recipe in *Chapter 3, Modern Sites in SharePoint Online*
- The *SharePoint PnP* topic in the *Office development frameworks* section of the *Appendix*

Adding a column

Columns define the nature and type of information that is stored in lists. We briefly saw how to create new columns for a list as part of the *Creating a list* recipe in *Chapter 2, Introduction to SharePoint Online*.

In this recipe, we'll see how to add a new column to the `Marketing Announcements` list that we just created. We will add a new `Announcement Start Date` column to the list. We will then discuss some more advanced concepts around column creation in the sections to follow.

Getting ready

You will need **Edit** permissions or higher for the list to be able to add columns to it. You will usually have this level of access to the list if you have Owner or Member access to your site.

How to do it...

To add a new column to your list:

1. Browse to the list for which you would like to add the new column.
2. Click **Add column** to see a list of the types of columns that you can add to the list.
3. Click **Date and time** to create a column that lets you store dates or date-time values and click **Next**.
4. In the **Create a column** window, enter the name for your new column.

 Every time you create a column in SharePoint, it creates two names for it: an *internal* name and a *display* name. It uses the *internal name* to internally reference the column. The internal name of a column does not have spaces, and never changes once the column is created. The *display name,* on the other hand, is the name of the column as you see it. It can have spaces, and you can change it even after you create the column. Both the internal and display names have to be unique within the list or library for columns created locally within that list or library.

5. Then enter, or select values for, various column properties, as shown in the following screenshot (you will need to click **More options** to see all settings from the screenshot below):

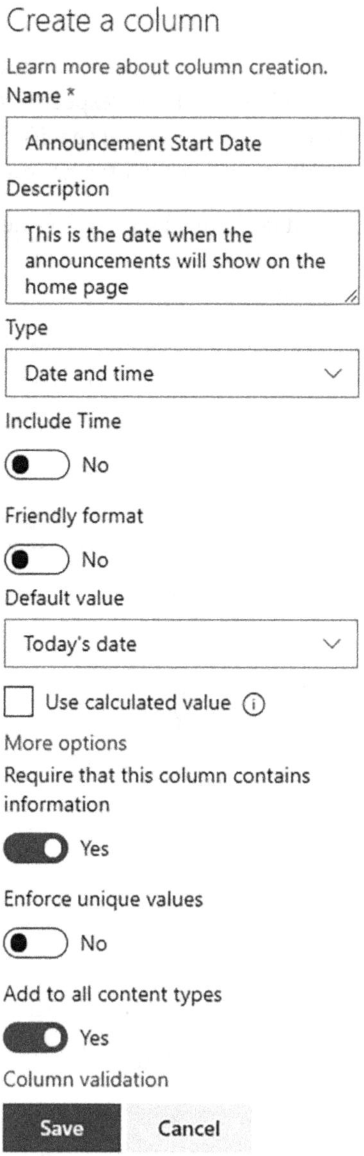

Create a column

Learn more about column creation.

Name *

> Announcement Start Date

Description

> This is the date when the
> announcements will show on the
> home page

Type

> Date and time   ⌄

Include Time

(●) No

Friendly format

(●) No

Default value

> Today's date   ⌄

☐ Use calculated value ⓘ

More options

Require that this column contains
information

(●) Yes

Enforce unique values

(●) No

Add to all content types

(●) Yes

Column validation

Save	Cancel

Figure 4.6: Column properties when creating a column

6.   Click the **Save** button to save the properties and create your new column.

That's it! You just learned how to add a new column to your list.

How it works...

Columns allow information to be associated with items in your list. For document libraries, column values act as metadata that gets associated with the respective document. Just as with columns in an Excel worksheet, SharePoint lists and libraries let you specify the type of information these columns can hold. Similarly, you can sort, filter, and group information using SharePoint list columns.

SharePoint supports various types of columns, as shown in the following screenshot:

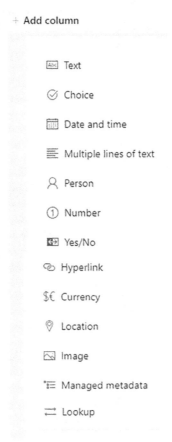

Figure 4.7: Column types available in SharePoint

After you select a column type, you can choose to specify additional properties for that column. For example, for the **Text** column type, you can specify the maximum number of characters that the users can enter (with an upper limit of 255 characters). In addition to such column-specific properties, SharePoint also lets you specify some common properties, such as whether a column value is required or optional. You can view detailed descriptions of the different types of columns and their properties through this support article: `https://packt.link/column-types`.

The **Content type** option listed at the end of *Figure 4.6* does *not* pertain to columns. We will discuss this in detail in online *Chapter 13, Term Store and Content Types in SharePoint*. In the meantime, you can read more about this option here: `https://packt.link/add-list-content-type`.

Once a column is created, you can view and edit any of its properties through the **List settings** page. You can also delete the column from this page if you no longer see the need for it. The **List settings** page also lets you specify the order of columns to be shown in the data entry form. The *Viewing and changing list settings* recipe later in this chapter covers the **List settings** page in greater detail.

There's more...

In this section, we will learn about a few more actions that you can perform with columns. We will also learn about how to make your columns reusable across various lists and libraries on your site through the use of site columns.

Editing or deleting a column

Once a column is created, you can easily make changes to it, or even completely delete it. To do so, simply click on the column name, then click **Column settings** and then **Edit** to view the column in **Edit** mode:

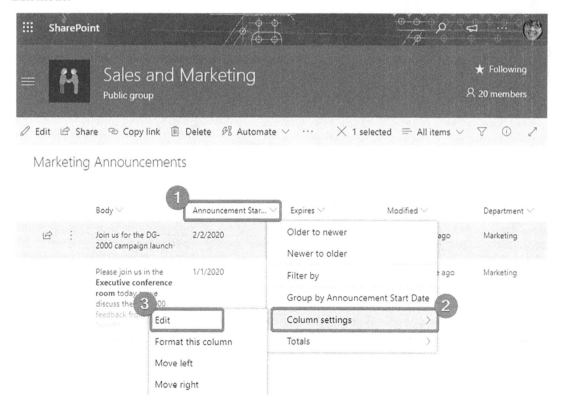

Figure 4.8: Navigating to the Edit option in Column settings

This will show you the **Edit column** screen, just like the one you saw when creating the columns. Here, you can make changes to the column and then click **Save** to save those changes. You can also delete the column by simply clicking the **Delete** button toward the bottom of the screen:

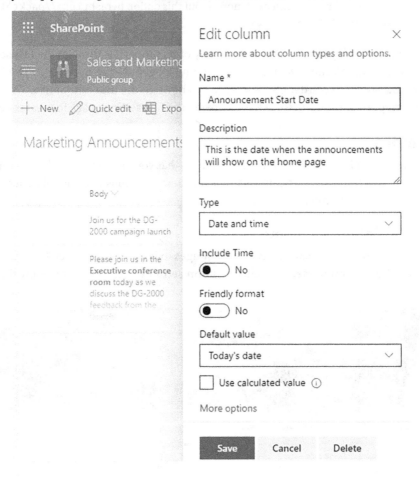

Figure 4.9: Edit column options with buttons to Save or Delete

Clicking **More options** from the **Edit column** screen lets you set additional properties for the column:

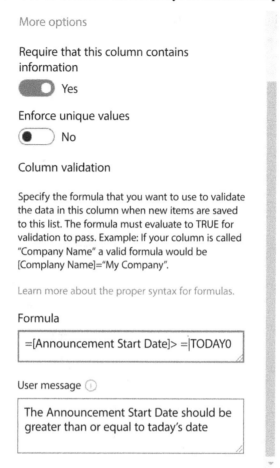

Figure 4.10: Additional properties on the Edit column screen

As shown in the preceding screenshot, in addition to specifying whether or not the column is mandatory and whether it should enforce unique values, you can also set validation for the values that the column would allow. In the example from this screenshot, we are validating for the start date to be greater than or equal to today's date (the date on which the item is being created or edited). We are also providing a message that SharePoint will display to users if the selected start date does not meet the validation criteria.

 While the Microsoft documentation illustrates the use of *Display name* in the validation formulas, the formula does not work if you changed your column's display name before creating the formula. If that happens, you may want to try using the column's *Internal name* for the formula.

Other column settings

In addition to editing a column, clicking on **Column settings** lets you perform a couple of other actions with the column:

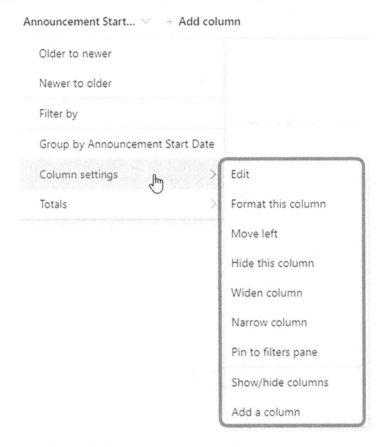

Figure 4.11: Navigating to the other options in Column settings

Here's a brief description of these settings:

- **Format this column:** See the *Column Formatting* section below.
- **Move left/Move right:** Moves the column toward the left or right in the view. You can also simply *drag* the column to reposition it within the view.
- **Hide this column:** Hides the column from the *current* view. Note that since the column is simply hidden and not deleted, it can still be shown in other views and/or forms.
- **Widen column:** Increases the display width of the column.
- **Narrow column:** Reduces the display width of the column.

- **Hide this column:** Hides the column from the *current* view. Note that since the column is simply hidden and not deleted, it can still be shown in other views and/or forms.
- **Pin to filters pane:** This allows the column to be pinned to the filters pane for the current view. We have discussed this in more detail through the *Filters pane* topic in the next recipe, *Creating a custom list view*.
- **Show/hide columns:** Clicking this option opens a list of all the columns from the list or library and enables you to select or deselect columns to be shown in the current view.
- **Add a column:** You can add a new column to the list using this option.

Column formatting

Column formatting allows you to customize the display of column information in a list or library view. In the following screenshot from Microsoft's sample library (link below), column formatting was used to implement inline approval functionality. Clicking the inline approve/reject buttons in the **Approval** column results in the color-coded **Item Status** column values being dynamically updated. Along with that, the **Approval Action By** column is updated with the name of the person who carried out the action, all this without writing a single piece of code:

Description ∨	Approval ∨	Item Status ∨	Approval Action By ∨
Item 1	This item is approved	Approved	Michel Mendes
Item 2	This item is rejected	Rejected	Michel Mendes
Item 3	This item is approved	Approved	Michel Mendes
Item 4	✔ Approve ⊘ Reject	Pending	
Item 5	✔ Approve ⊘ Reject	Pending	

Figure 4.12: Adding approval functionality by using column formatting

Column formatting is very similar to view formatting, which we describe in greater detail as part of the *Advanced view formatting* topic in the next recipe, *Creating a custom list view*. Column and list view formatting are slightly advanced topics, and you will need some knowledge of HTML and JSON (a lightweight *declarative* format for specifying configuration and data) to benefit from this capability. You can read more about column formatting at `https://packt.link/about-column-formatting` and `https://packt.link/use-column-formatting`.

This GitHub repo contains a ton of code examples for various scenarios where you can apply column formatting: `https://packt.link/git-column-formatting`.

List form customization

Similar to column and list view formatting (which we will see in the next recipe), SharePoint also allows you to customize list or library forms to a certain extent, all without having to write any custom code (although you will need to know HTML and have a basic knowledge of JSON). This allows you to create a more dynamic and customized view of your list item create/edit/view forms, as shown in the following image from the Microsoft samples library:

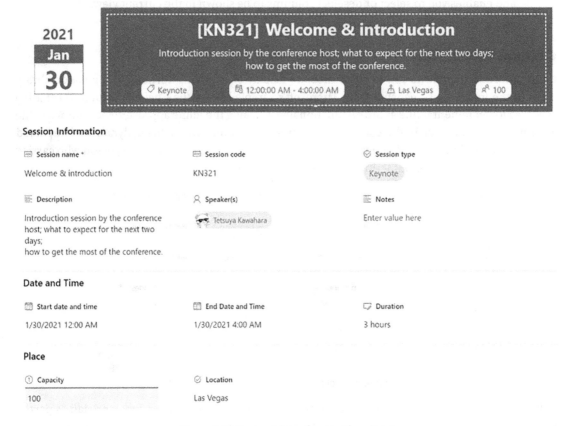

Figure 4.13: Customizing a form in SharePoint

Through this, you can:

- Show or hide columns in a list/library form based on data in the list item being edited
- Apply formatting to the form header and make it more dynamic
- Change the layout of the body of the form by defining custom sections within the form
- Build a custom footer for the form

You can read more about list form configuration at `https://packt.link/list-form-show-hide-columns` and `https://packt.link/list-form-customize`

For advanced readers, this GitHub repo contains various samples of column formatting: `https://packt.link/list-form-customization-samples`

Site columns

One disadvantage of creating columns in the way we have done previously is that they are specific to that list or library. This means if someone else needs a similar column in another list or library on the site, they will have to create a similar column elsewhere. In addition to effort duplication, this also often leads to inconsistencies between columns that are similar to each other but have subtle differences because they were created independently of each other. These inconsistencies are further amplified in **Choice** type fields where users have to select one value from a list of predefined values. For example, one list could contain Human Resources as a department, while another list could contain HR as a choice for the department name. Furthermore, if you need to make changes to such a column that is recreated across multiple lists and libraries, you will now need to go to each list and make changes to the column within that list.

This is where **site columns** shine compared to one-off list columns. Site columns are quite similar to list or library columns, but they are defined and maintained at the site level. You will need **Design** or **Full Control** permissions on the site to be able to create site columns.

Creating a **site column** is almost always recommended instead of creating a column that is local to a list or library. Furthermore, it is now recommended to create site columns through the **Content type gallery** versus creating it just for your individual site. That way, your column can be used across multiple sites within your organization's tenant. There is a chance that you might not have access to create a column in the content type gallery and that you might have to reach out to your SharePoint admins for it. Even though that's an added step, creating a site column is the recommended way to go when possible. You will learn more about the content types and content type gallery in *Chapter 16, Term Store and Content Types in SharePoint Online*.

If you do want to create a column for your site (instead of the content type hub), you can do so by browsing to the **Site Settings** page and then clicking the **Site Columns** link under the **Web Designer Galleries** heading. We discussed the **Site Settings** page as part of the *Viewing and changing site settings* recipe in *Chapter 3, Modern Sites in SharePoint Online*. Once you are on the **Site Columns** page, you will see a list of the existing site columns for your site. You will also be able to click on the **Create** link at the top of the page to create a new site column:

Figure 4.14: Button for creating a new site column

From this point on, the steps to create the site column will be similar to the steps earlier in the recipe. The only difference will be that you will be prompted to choose a **Group** for your site column, as shown in the following screenshot:

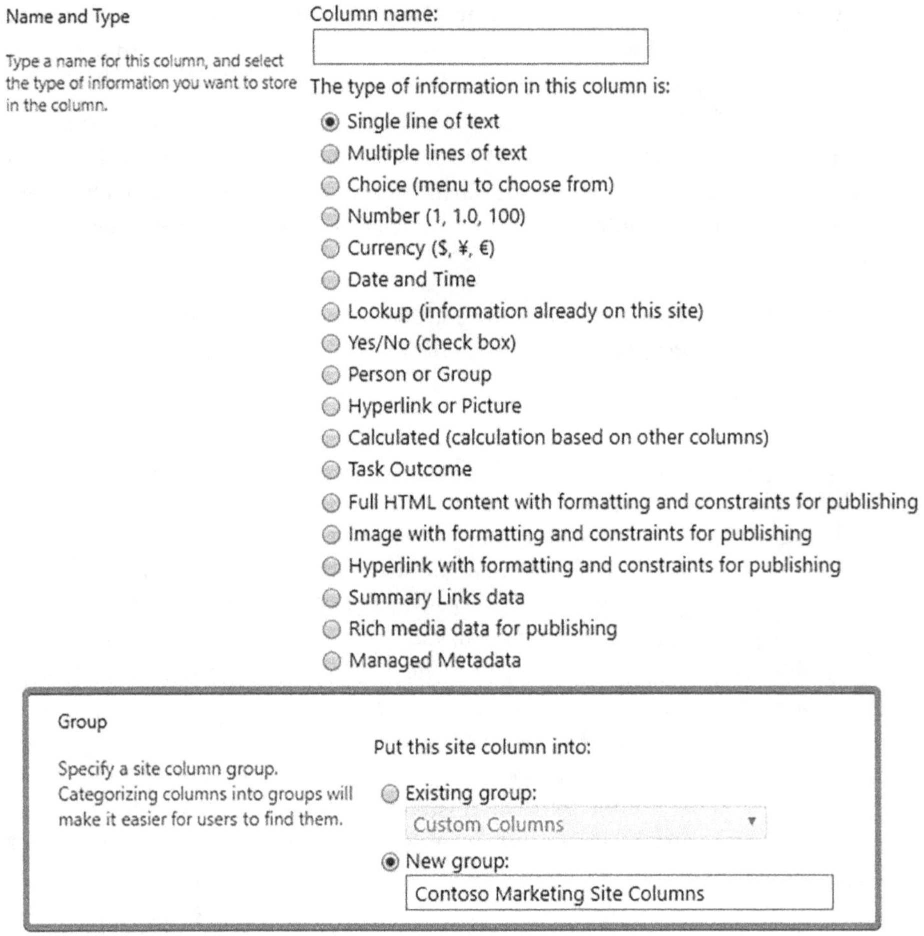

Name and Type

Type a name for this column, and select the type of information you want to store in the column.

Column name:

[   ]

The type of information in this column is:

- ● Single line of text
- ○ Multiple lines of text
- ○ Choice (menu to choose from)
- ○ Number (1, 1.0, 100)
- ○ Currency ($, ¥, €)
- ○ Date and Time
- ○ Lookup (information already on this site)
- ○ Yes/No (check box)
- ○ Person or Group
- ○ Hyperlink or Picture
- ○ Calculated (calculation based on other columns)
- ○ Task Outcome
- ○ Full HTML content with formatting and constraints for publishing
- ○ Image with formatting and constraints for publishing
- ○ Hyperlink with formatting and constraints for publishing
- ○ Summary Links data
- ○ Rich media data for publishing
- ○ Managed Metadata

Group

Specify a site column group. Categorizing columns into groups will make it easier for users to find them.

Put this site column into:

- ○ Existing group:
    Custom Columns ▾
- ● New group:
    Contoso Marketing Site Columns

Figure 4.15: Option for grouping site columns

A **Group** is just a logical means of grouping site columns under one heading. It does not have any impact on the functionality of the site column. Once your site column is created, you can go back to your list and add it to the list through the **Add from existing Site Columns** link on the **List settings** page. We will discuss the **List settings** page in more detail in the *Viewing and changing list settings* recipe later in this chapter.

See also

- The *Creating a list* recipe in *Chapter 2, Introduction to SharePoint Online*
- The *Viewing and changing site settings* recipe in *Chapter 3, Modern Sites in SharePoint Online*
- The *Viewing and changing list settings* recipe in this chapter
- The *Creating a managed metadata site column* recipe in *Chapter 13, Term Store and Content Types in SharePoint Online*

Creating a custom list view

Views in SharePoint enable you to organize and show list or library items that are the most relevant for you and your users. Through views, you can select which columns to show to users, filter data based on various criteria, and select the order in which to show your data. Every list or library in SharePoint comes with an inbuilt view called **All Items**. Unless a list admin or a site admin assigns a different view as the default view for the list, this view is shown by *default* any time a user browses to a list or library. For this reason, it is also sometimes known as the *default view* for that list or library. We can create additional *custom views* for our list to meet our data display needs. We can then show or hide columns in the custom view, change the sort and/or filter criteria, group by one or more fields, and add formatting to a view.

In this recipe, we will see how to create a custom view for the Marketing Announcements list that we just created. We will then save the view as the default view so that anyone who browses to the list will see the new view that we created.

Getting ready

You will need **Edit** permissions or higher for your list to be able to create public views for it. You will usually have this access if you are part of the Site owners or Site member groups for that site.

You can create a personal view for any list to which you have **Contribute** access.

How to do it...

To create a new view for your list, follow these steps:

1. Browse to the list for which you would like to create a new view.

 SharePoint automatically saves changes to your views as you make those changes. So, you will first want to save the current view under a different view name if you don't intend to make changes to it. Unlike list items, list views are not versioned, so there's no way to revert changes you have made to a list view.

2.   Click **All items** and then **Save view as** toward the top-right corner of the page, as shown in the following screenshot:

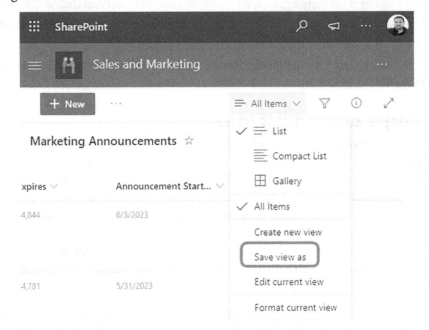

Figure 4.16: Navigating to the option to save a view from All items

3.   Give your view a name (for example, **Current Announcements**) and click **Save**. This will create a new view. Next, we will add columns to it.

4.   Click **Add column** and then **Show/hide columns**, as shown in the following screenshot:

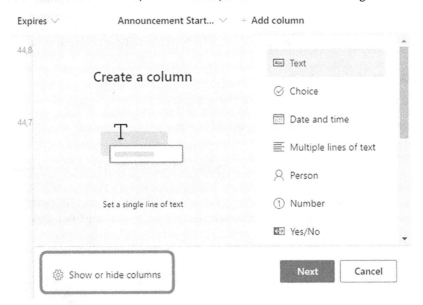

Figure 4.17: Option for showing or hiding a column from + Add column

5. Select the columns you would like to show on the new view, and deselect the columns you would like to hide. For the `Marketing Announcements` list that we created earlier, we will deselect the **Modified** column, then select the **Body, Expires,** and **Announcement Start Date** columns. Then, we will click the **Apply** button on the top. This is shown in the following screenshot:

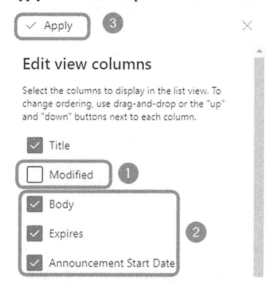

Figure 4.18: Deselecting columns to hide them from the view

6. Then, drag the **Expires** column toward the extreme right from the main view, as shown in the following screenshot:

Figure 4.19: Moving columns in the main view

7. Next, we will add a filter to the view so that we only see current announcements. Click **Current Announcements** and then **Edit current view**, as shown in the following screenshot:

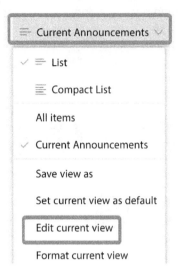

Figure 4.20: Option to Edit current view from Current Announcements

8. Scroll down on the **Edit View** page to the **Sort** section, and change the value in the **First sort by the column** dropdown option to **Announcement Start Date**. Then, select the **Show items in ascending order** option to sort the announcements in ascending order of the **Announcement Start Date**.

9. Scroll down further to the **Filter** section and change the filter values to the ones shown in the following screenshot:

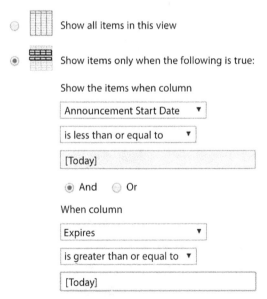

Figure 4.21: Changing filter values for showing items

10. Scroll to the bottom of the page and click **OK** to save your changes.

11. Finally, click on the **Current Announcements** view and then click **Set current view as default**. Doing so will make this new view the default view for the list:

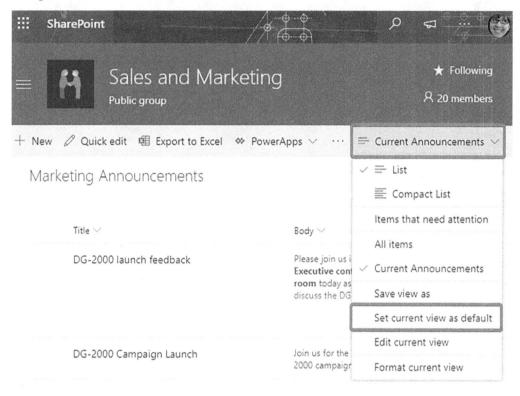

Figure 4.22: Setting a view as the default view

Congratulations! You just learned how to create a new view and then modify it for basic column ordering and sorting. You then saw how to edit the view, create a filter, and sort the items in that view. Specifically, for the Marketing Announcements list, the **Current Announcements** view only shows announcements where today's date lies between the **Announcement Start Date** and the date indicated by the **Expires** column. Finally, we set the new **Current Announcements** view as the default view so that users browsing this list will always see the **Current Announcements** by default. They will be able to change the view to the **All items** option if they want to see past announcements or others that happened to be filtered due to the criteria specified in the new view.

How it works...

Views are the presentation layer for information stored in lists and libraries. You can create multiple views to easily organize this information for varied purposes (such as different audience types, for example). You can create public views that are visible to anyone who has access to the list, or you can create personal views that are only visible to you.

Views don't have permissions associated with them *per se*; you can create filters on views to hide certain items. Users can still get to such items through direct links, creating/ modifying new or existing views, and through search results, if they have access to these items via appropriate permissions.

In this recipe, we saw how to edit a view to filter and sort information in it. There are a few additional actions you can carry out when editing a view from the **Edit View** page, as shown in the following screenshot:

⊞ Sort

⊞ Filter

⊞ Tabular View

⊟ Group By

Select up to two columns to determine what type of group and subgroup the items in the view will be displayed in. Learn about grouping items.

First group by the column:

None ▼

◉ Show groups in ascending order
(A, B, C, or 1, 2, 3)

◯ Show groups in descending order
(C, B, A, or 3, 2, 1)

Then group by the column:

None ▼

◉ Show groups in ascending order
(A, B, C, or 1, 2, 3)

◯ Show groups in descending order
(C, B, A, or 3, 2, 1)

⊞ Totals

⊞ Style

⊞ Folders

⊞ Item Limit

⊞ Mobile

By default, show groupings:
◉ Collapsed ◯ Expanded

Number of groups to display per page:

30

Figure 4.23: Additional options on the Edit View page

Some of the more prominent actions are as follows:

- Select or deselect the columns that get shown in the view and specify the order of those columns from left to right
- Specify a multi-column filter and sort criteria (we saw this earlier in this recipe)
- Group the items up to two group levels
- Specify some basic styles for the view
- Specify whether to show items in folders or to show them without the folders

- Specify a limit on the number of items shown per page or, optionally, a limit on the total number of items that get shown in the view
- Specify whether to show a separate view for mobile requests and basic settings for the mobile view

Finally, you can also delete a view from this page. To do so, simply click the **Delete** button in the top- or bottom-right corner of the page:

Figure 4.24: Deleting a view

Note that you can only delete the view if it's not currently set up as the default view for the selected list or library.

There's more...

In this section, we will see the additional things that you can do with list views.

Microsoft Teams document library views

When a new team is created in Microsoft Teams, a site is provisioned for it in SharePoint. Along with that, a default **Documents** library is also created within the site to store files from various channels in the team. Every time a *public* channel is created within the team, a folder corresponding to the channel name is created in this **Documents** library.

This site setup is slightly different for *private* and *shared* channels in that a separate SharePoint site is provisioned for each private and shared channel that is created.

 You will learn more about the different channel types and how they work in *Chapter 7, Microsoft Teams*.

However, beyond this, the setup is similar – a **Documents** library is created in each of these sites to store the files from the corresponding channel.

If you browse to a **Documents** library that was created as part of the team, you will see all such channel folders grouped under an **In channels** category in the default view of the library. For a team that's set up as follows, with **General** and **Monthly Reports** being public channels, **Private Channel** being a private channel and **Shared Channel** being an example shared channel:

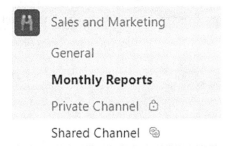

Figure 4.25: Example of a private and a shared channel

The library view will be shown, as in the image below:

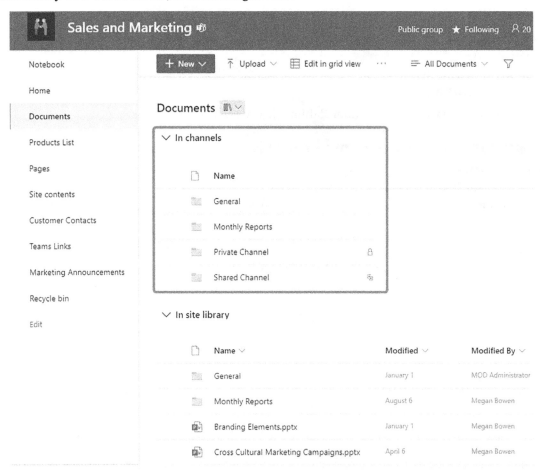

Figure 4.26: Example of a library view

Note the following in the screenshot above:

- The folders for each channel are shown together under the **In channels** category. This includes folders for all public, private, and shared channels for the team.
- The **Private Channel** and **Shared Channel** are indicated as such by the icons next to their names.
- Clicking the private or shared channel folders takes you to the corresponding libraries on the respective SharePoint site.
- The **In site library** category contains the folders for public channels for the Team, along with any files that might have been directly uploaded to the **Documents** library from within SharePoint (and not through the **Files** tab in the Teams channels).

It is recommended that you revisit this topic after reviewing *Chapter 7*, *Microsoft Teams*, if this section seems confusing to you.

The Items that need attention view

SharePoint will provide various indicators if you have items in your list or library that are missing the required information. As shown by **A**, **B**, and **C** in the following screenshot, it will indicate this by showing the following icons:

- **A**: A *missing metadata* icon next to the **Title** field
- **B**: A *required info* notification on the specific column
- **C**: A red dot against the view name:

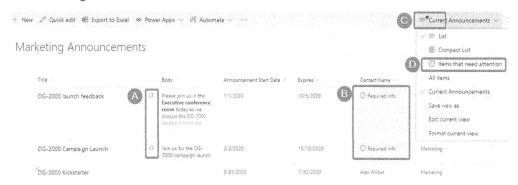

Figure 4.27: Different icons indicating an item needs attention

However, sometimes, a view may contain many items, or, for a document library, it may contain items nested within folders, making it difficult to find and work with just the items that are missing values. You can use the **Items that need attention** view, shown by **D** in the preceding screenshot, in such situations.

    In document libraries, this view is called **Files that need attention**.

Switching to this view will only show you those items that are missing values. You can then easily work with such items in either the regular or the **Quick Edit** view, which we discuss in the next recipe.

Bulk-editing properties

SharePoint lets you select multiple items and bulk-edit their properties. This is particularly useful when you need to backfill the property values after these items have been created. To bulk-edit multiple items, simply select the checkboxes next to them to open the details pane, as shown in the following screenshot:

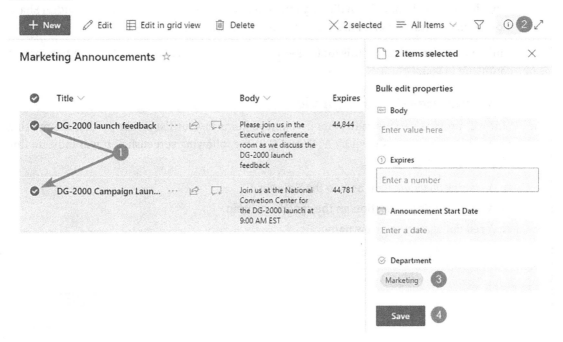

Figure 4.28: Selecting multiple items and bulk-editing their properties

Then, simply enter or select values for the properties that you'd like to change, and click the **Save** button toward the bottom.

Exporting to CSV or Excel

SharePoint also lets you export the list items from the current view if you'd like to work with them in a **Comma-Separated Values (CSV)** file or an Excel file. To do so, simply click **Export** and then **Export to CSV** or **Export to Excel**.

Clicking **Export to CSV** downloads a CSV file containing all items from the current view. Meanwhile, clicking **Export to Excel** generates and downloads a .iqy file, as shown in the following screenshot:

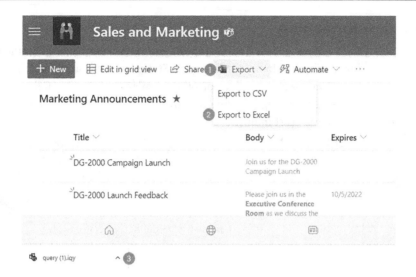

Figure 4.29: Generating a .iqy file by clicking Export to Excel

Opening the `.iqy` file will open the items from the view in an Excel workbook, as shown in the following screenshot:

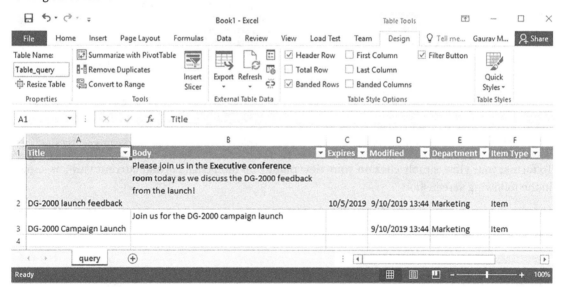

Figure 4.30: Opening the SharePoint items in an Excel workbook

You can now work with this information just as you would with any other spreadsheet.

 The `.iqy` file or *Internet Query File* is a file that contains a one-way read-only connection to the SharePoint List. This means it will refresh the data with the latest information from the corresponding SharePoint list whenever you refresh the connection in Excel. However, any changes you make to the data in Excel will not be pushed back to the corresponding list.

Advanced view formatting

Modern lists enable you to enhance the visual display of your views easily, and significantly. A very common use of such formatting is when your list has a **Status** column, and you'd like to highlight the items in the view based on the status values or other similar criteria. The following screenshot shows an example where we have highlighted the **Announcement Start Date** column of the Marketing Announcements list, based on the start month:

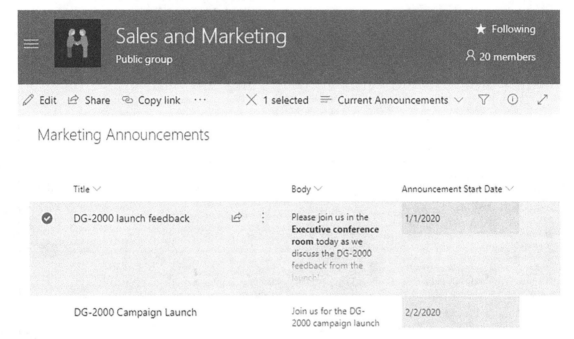

Figure 4.31: Highlighting the Announcement Start Date column in the Marketing Announcements list

To format your view, simply click on your view name and then click **Format current view,** as shown in the following screenshot:

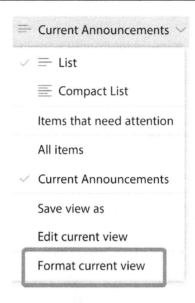

Figure 4.32: Navigating to the Format current view option from the view name

Then, select whether you would like the formatting to be applied to one of the columns or the entire row. Selecting an entire row will let you either specify alternating row styles or rule-based conditional styling to be applied to the entire row, as shown in the following screenshot:

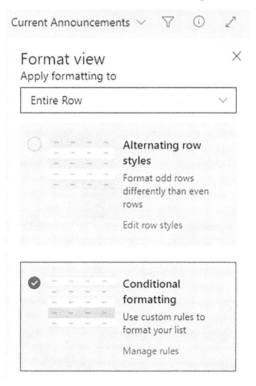

Figure 4.33: Selecting the option to use custom formatting rules for an entire row

If you choose to apply the formatting to just a single column, SharePoint will show you options based on the type of column that you selected. In the following example, we are seeing the two different options that can be specified for date columns:

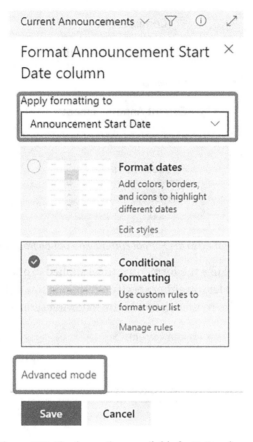

Figure 4.34: Viewing options available for Date columns

You can then specify formatting, as in the rule shown in the following screenshot:

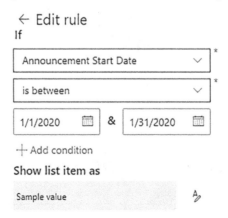

Figure 4.35: Editing the formatting of a rule

You can also click the **Advanced mode** link toward the bottom of the **Format view** pane to define more complex formatting for the view. An example of such advanced view formatting is shown below, where you could potentially use basic code to convert the view display from an unformatted view to one that is more appealing. Let's look at the view display below:

Figure 4.36: Example of a standard view display

With a little bit of coding knowledge, you could make the display richer and easier to read:

Figure 4.37: Example of a view display with formatting edits

Advanced view formatting involves writing a little bit of code using HTML and **JSON (JavaScript Object Notation)**, and hence is beyond the purview of this book. You can, however, learn more about JSON view formatting through these Microsoft support articles:

* Formatting list views: `https://packt.link/formatting-list-views` and `https://packt.link/formatting-list-views-2`

- Advanced list view formatting: `https://packt.link/formatting-list-views-adv`
- Use column formatting to customize SharePoint: `https://packt.link/Use-Column-Formatting`
- PnP list view formatting samples: `https://packt.link/PnP-list-formatting-samples`

In-place view filtering, sorting, and grouping

The steps in the *Creating a custom list view* recipe showed you how to filter and sort your view using the view settings page. SharePoint also lets you filter and sort the current view of your list by columns from within the view itself. To sort a view by a particular column order, simply click the column name and then select a sort order. The sort options that you see will depend on the type of column that you are sorting by. These are shown by **A** in the screenshot that follows. You can only sort your view by one column at a time using this option.

To filter the view based on a column, click the column name and then click **Filter by** to reveal the values that you can filter on. This is shown by **B** in the screenshot that follows. Unlike sorting, you can filter by multiple columns. You can also use the filters pane, discussed in the next topic, for advanced filtering.

To group by a column, select the **Group by Column name** option, shown by **C** in the screenshot that follows. You can only group by one column using this approach. You can use the view settings page described in the preceding *How it works...* section to group by an additional column. Further, you can also show group totals and an overall total by clicking the **Totals** option, shown by **D**, **E**, and **F** in the following screenshot:

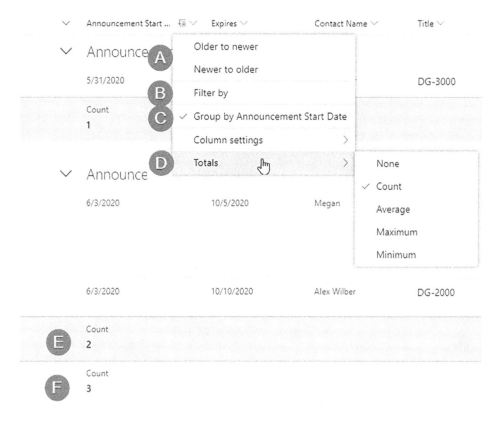

Figure 4.38: Navigation areas for various sort options

Further, the aggregation options that you will see under the **Totals** menu will depend on the type of column. The options shown in the preceding screenshot are those for a date column. A text column would only have shown **Count** as the aggregation option.

Filters pane

As we saw in the *Creating a custom list view* recipe, you can apply some basic filters on individual columns to create a filtered view. In addition to that, you can also create advanced filters on multiple columns in the view. As shown in the following screenshot, you can click the *filter* icon **A** toward the right of your list or library menu to open the filters pane:

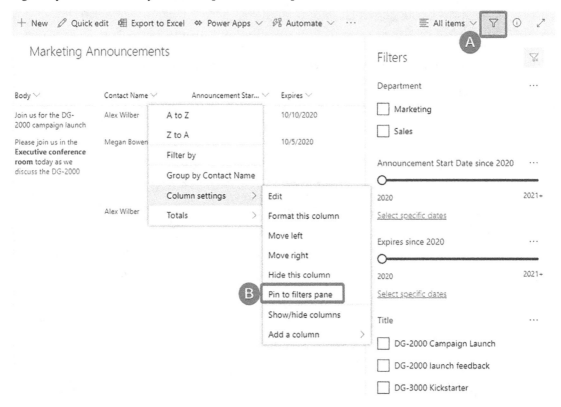

Figure 4.39: Navigation to the Pin to filters pane option

Here, you will see a list of columns with values that you can filter on. Only columns from your view will be shown here. You can add columns to the filters pane by clicking on the corresponding column name, then clicking **Column settings**, and then **Pin to filters pane** (**B**). Once the column is added to the filters pane, you can choose to filter your view using the values from this column in combination with the others already present in this pane. To make your filters permanent, simply save the view by selecting the view name, and then click **Save view as**, as described earlier in the recipe.

 Note that not all columns are filterable. In the example above, the **Body** column cannot be filtered. So, if you are not seeing your column in the **Filters** pane, that might be the reason why.

The following support articles provide additional details regarding the features and limitations of the filters pane:

- What is the list and library filters pane?: `https://packt.link/filters-pane`
- Use filtering to modify a SharePoint view: `https://packt.link/use-filters`

Working with large lists and libraries

You can store millions of items in a SharePoint list or library (30 million items, to be precise, at the time of writing). However, due to technical reasons beyond the scope of this book, there are special considerations to keep in mind when the number of items grows beyond 5,000. When that happens, you will be restricted from carrying out certain tasks in the list or library, including the following:

- Being able to show more than 5,000 items in a single view
- Programmatically retrieving more than 5,000 items through a single request
- Adding columns

There are multiple ways to overcome these limitations, including organizing documents within folders in a document library, but the most recommended approach is to create one or more *indexed columns* on your list. You will need to create the indexed column(s) before the items in your list or library exceed the 5,000-item limit. It is recommended that you index all columns that are being used or are anticipated to be used for filtering or sorting items in your list or library. As a list or library owner, you will, therefore, want to put some upfront thought, especially when you are expecting the information in your lists or libraries to grow beyond the 5,000-item limit.

You can read more about this important topic through these Microsoft support articles:

- Manage large lists and libraries in SharePoint: `https://packt.link/large-lists`
- Add an index to a SharePoint column: `https://packt.link/add-column-index`

Using Edit in grid view to bulk-edit list items

The grid view is a special view that resembles an Excel worksheet and allows you to work with multiple list items. In this recipe, we will see how to use **Edit in grid view** to modify multiple list items. We will use the previously created `Marketing Announcements` list as an illustration for this recipe.

Getting ready

You can use this view to bulk-edit items if you have Contribute access or higher to the list. You will usually have this access if you are part of the Site owners or Site member groups for that site.

How to do it...

1. Browse to the list for which you would like to bulk-edit the items.
2. Click **Edit in grid view** in the navigation bar.

If you are viewing a classic (and not a modern) list or if you are viewing a modern list in the classic view, you will see the **Edit this list** menu option instead of the **Edit in grid view** option. Both options eventually work the same way.

3. Doing this reveals the *grid view* of the list. You can now directly enter and edit items in the list through this view, just like you would in an Excel spreadsheet.

4. Point to the first cell in the last row and simply start typing or double-click the cell to make it editable.

 You can use the *Tab* key, the arrow keys on the keyboard, or the mouse to move to the next cell in the row.

You can also use the arrow keys to navigate to other rows in the list. Doing so saves the current row, as long as you have entered all required information for that row.

5. Enter values for the other cells in the row, as shown in the following screenshot for the Marketing Announcements list:

Figure 4.40: Entering cell values

6. Click the cell in the **Expires** column in the first row of the list shown in the preceding screenshot. Then, use the *Ctrl + C* keys to copy the date value from the selected cell.

7. Select the two empty cells in the **Expires** column for the last two rows and paste the copied value, as shown in the following screenshot:

Figure 4.41: Pasting a value into the Marketing Announcements list

Just like Excel, **Edit in grid view** also lets you drag the corners of a cell or multiple cells to bulk-copy the cell values.

That's it! You just learned how to use **Edit in grid view** to bulk-edit your list items.

How it works...

Working with lists is somewhat identical to working with database tables and Excel worksheets. **Edit in grid view** lets you work with list items just as you would work with information in an Excel worksheet. Like in Excel, you can click individual cells in a list to edit the items in those cells. Also similarly to Excel, you can carry bulk copy-paste operations in these cells. You can even add new columns through the datasheet view by clicking the + **Add Column** toward the top-right corner of the datasheet view.

Viewing and changing list settings

SharePoint lets you view and change a variety of settings for your list.

In this recipe, we will use the `Marketing Announcements` list that we created earlier to add validation rules for the information that users can add to your list. We will add validation rules to ensure the following:

- The **Announcement Start Date** value is greater than the current date
- The **Expires** date entered by the users is greater than the **Announcement Start Date** value

Getting ready

You will need **Edit, Design,** or **Full Control** access permissions to the list for which you'd like to view or change settings. You will usually have this access if you are part of the Site owners or Site member groups for that site. The settings that you will have access to will depend on the level of access you have to the site and ultimately to the list itself.

How to do it...

1. Browse to the list for which you would like to view or change the settings.
2. Click the settings gear icon in the top-right corner.

3.   Click **List settings**, as shown in the following screenshot:

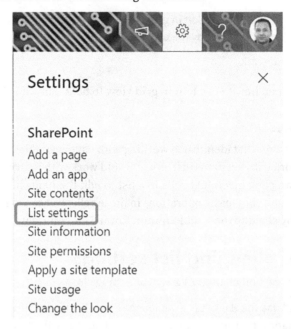

Figure 4.42: Navigating to the List settings option

4.   On the **Settings** page, click the **Validation settings** link under **General Settings**.

5.   Enter the desired validation formula in the **Formula** textbox. We are going to add the following formula for our example:

```
=AND([Announcement Start Date]>=TODAY(), [Expires]>=[Announcement Start
Date])
```

 SharePoint provides a ton of formulas for you to work with. You can find a list of all such formulas via this support article: `https://packt.link/list-formulas`.

6.   Enter text in the **User Message** textbox to indicate details about the validation error. We are going to enter the following message for our example:

One or more of the following validation errors occurred:

1.   The announcement start date should be greater than or equal to today's date.

2.   The Expiration date should be greater than or equal to the Announcement Start Date.

Please fix these errors and try submitting the form again.

7. The **Validation Settings** screen should then look like this:

Settings ‣ Validation Settings

Formula

Specify the formula you want to use to validate data when new items are saved to this list. To pass validation, the formula must evaluate to TRUE. For more information, see Formulas in Help.

Example: =[Discount]<[Cost] will only pass validation if column Discount is less than column Cost.

Learn more about proper syntax for formulas.

User Message

Type descriptive text that will help site visitors understand what is needed for a valid list item. This description will be shown if the validation expression fails.

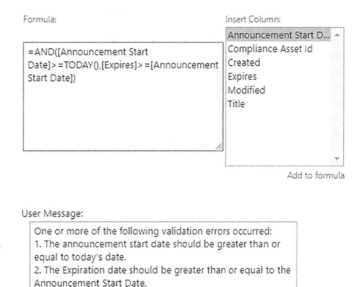

Formula:

=AND([Announcement Start Date]>=TODAY(),[Expires]>=[Announcement Start Date])

Insert Column:

Announcement Start D...
Compliance Asset Id
Created
Expires
Modified
Title

Add to formula

User Message:

One or more of the following validation errors occurred:
1. The announcement start date should be greater than or equal to today's date.
2. The Expiration date should be greater than or equal to the Announcement Start Date.
Please fix these errors and try submitting the form again.

Save   Cancel

Figure 4.43: Adding a user message to the Validation settings screen

8. Click the **Save** button to save the changes.

 Note that you can only perform one validation and show a single validation message for the entire form. This means you will need to perform an AND operation if you'd like to validate multiple fields, as we did in the preceding example. As also shown in our example, you will want to make the information in the **User Message** textbox detailed enough to list all the possible causes that may result in a validation error.

9. Browse to your list again.

10. Click the **New** menu option to add a new item to your list.

11. Enter information in the list so that it satisfies the error condition. For our example, we are going to enter a past date for the **Announcement Start Date** field.

12. Click the **Save** button.

13. Notice the validation error message toward the top of the form, as shown in the following screenshot for our example:

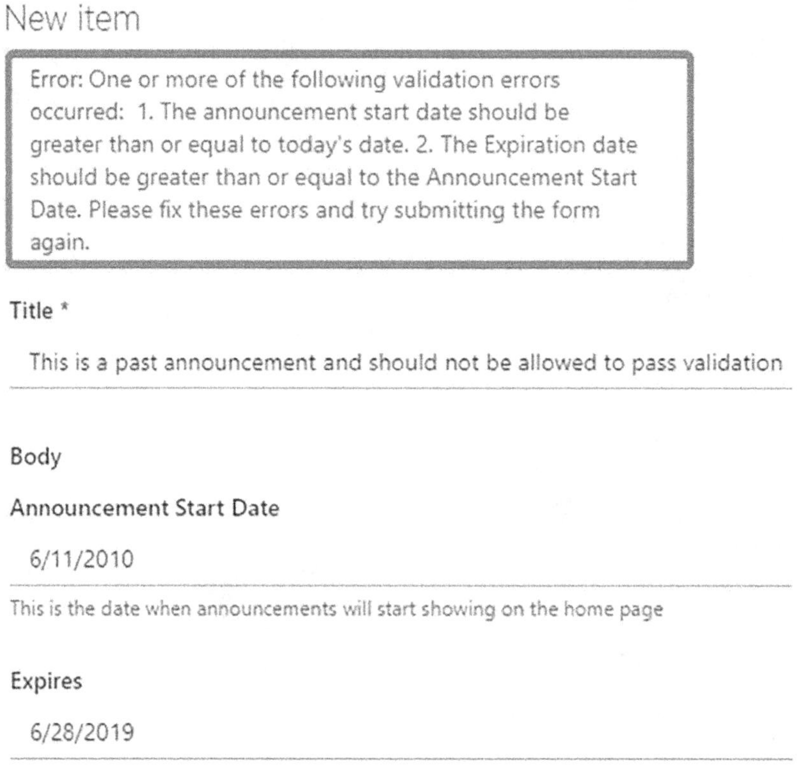

New item

> Error: One or more of the following validation errors occurred: 1. The announcement start date should be greater than or equal to today's date. 2. The Expiration date should be greater than or equal to the Announcement Start Date. Please fix these errors and try submitting the form again.

Title *

This is a past announcement and should not be allowed to pass validation

Body

Announcement Start Date

6/11/2010

This is the date when announcements will start showing on the home page

Expires

6/28/2019

Figure 4.44: Example of the created error message

 Note that this validation also works when editing items and also in the grid view, which we saw in an earlier recipe.

Congratulations! You just saw how to view and modify settings for a SharePoint list. You also saw how to set up validation for your list.

How it works...

SharePoint lets you manage your lists and libraries through various settings. We've already seen a couple of these important list settings in some of our previous recipes. Here are a few other more common list settings that we have not discussed so far:

- **List name, description, and navigation:** This is where you can change the title and description for your list. Note that the list URL remains the same even after you change the list name. This is where you can also specify whether or not to show the list in the site's **Quick Launch** (refer to the *Modifying the left navigation* recipe in *Chapter 3, Modern Sites in SharePoint Online*).

- **Versioning settings**: This allows us to control whether or not to keep a version history of the changes to the list items. We will look at versioning in greater detail in a subsequent chapter.
- **Advanced Settings** (the more commonly used ones):
  - **Content types**: We will learn about content types in a subsequent chapter but at this point, it is sufficient to be aware that this setting is part of the list's/library's **Advanced Settings**.
  - **Item-level Permissions**: This setting allows you to define individual permissions for each item in the list. This setting is only applicable to lists (and not to libraries). We will discuss item-level permissions as part of the next recipe.
  - **Attachments**: Whether or not allow attachment uploads for the lists. It is a good governance practice to consider enabling or disabling this setting every time a list is created. This setting is also available only for lists (and not document libraries).
  - **Comments**: Whether or not allow comments for list items. Comments are enabled on list items by default and are a great way to have discussions around individual list items.
  - **Folders**: Whether or not folder creation should be enabled for the list. Again, you should make a conscious decision as to whether or not to enable this setting for every list or library that gets created.
  - **Search**: This option defines whether items from this list should show up in the search results. For most use cases, you will set this option to **Yes**. Instead of excluding items from just the search results, you should instead update the list or item permissions if you would like to hide items from other users. Once you change the list permissions, items from this list will also not show up in search results for users that don't have access to them. If, however, you have a compelling case to not show the list items in search results but still allow users to be able to access them, you simply change this setting to **No**. Doing so will hide the items from this list in the search results, while still allowing them to have direct access to them when they browse to the list or access them through shared links. Please refer to the *Viewing and changing list permissions* recipe later in this chapter for details on how to modify list and item permissions.
  - **Reindex List**: Microsoft Search should automatically pick up new items from this list as part of the search results. Also, items that get deleted from this list should get dropped from the search results. If, however, for any reason you are not seeing appropriate items from this list in the search results and you have waited sufficiently long enough for the search crawler to crawl and index this list, you can click the **Reindex List** button to completely delete and recreate the index as a way to fix the search results. Please refer to *Chapter 14, Search in Microsoft 365*, for more details on the different components of Microsoft Search and how it works in general.
  - **Quick property editing**: Enables or disables the **Edit in grid view** feature.
  - **List experience**: This lets you deviate from the default list experience setting for the site. Here, you can choose to explicitly use the classic list experience or the new modern experience for your list or library. Please see the next section in this recipe for the details of the modern versus classic list experience.

- **Delete this list:** Clicking on this link deletes the list and sends it to the recycle bin of that site. Deleting a list or library sends it to the recycle bin, where it stays for a couple of days until it gets moved to the second-stage recycle bin or gets permanently deleted. You can restore deleted lists or libraries, as long as they are still in the recycle bin and have not been permanently deleted. Please refer to the *Viewing site contents* recipe in *Chapter 2, Introduction to SharePoint Online,* to read more about the site's recycle bin.

- **Workflow settings:** This allows us to specify workflow settings for the lists and libraries. Workflows are being replaced by **Microsoft Power Automate**. We have covered Microsoft Flow as part of a subsequent chapter. We will briefly discuss workflows as part of the *Appendix in the online eBook.*

- **Columns:** This section lists the different columns for the list or library. You can click on the column names to view and change column settings.

- **Create column:** This link allows you to create a new column for the list.

- **Add from existing Site Columns:** Click this link to add a previously created site column to this list or library. We discussed site columns as part of the *Adding a column* recipe earlier in this chapter.

- **Column ordering:** Click this link to specify or change the order of the columns as shown from top to bottom in the **Details** pane or the add/edit forms for this list or library.

- **Indexed columns:** Specifying column indexes improves list performance when using filtered views. These are especially useful for large lists. You can read more about indexed columns and their impact on performance here: `https://packt.link/indexed-columns`.

- **Views:** This section shows the views currently configured for the list or library. You can edit existing views or create new views from this section.

The following support article provides a comprehensive listing of all the settings that are available for lists in SharePoint: `https://packt.link/list-settings`

There's more...

SharePoint is an ever-evolving platform. Microsoft recently introduced a more modern, flexible, and mobile-friendly user experience for SharePoint. Modern lists and libraries are part of this new experience. Next, we will briefly review the difference between the two types of experience as it pertains to lists and libraries.

Modern versus classic list and library experience

Modern lists are faster, easier to use, and mobile friendly. Some of the key benefits of modern lists and libraries are as follows:

- Easier to create and upload files and folders
- Easily add, sort, filter, and organize columns and views
- Easy access to file previews and information
- A better search experiences
- Easy customizations to the view display using column and list view formatting

- Ability to pin important documents to the top of the screen
- Ability to add files as links instead of having to copy them across sites
- A responsive experience

The classic experience is now deprecated, and the modern experience is the default for newly created lists or libraries. To switch to the classic list experience, click **Return to classic SharePoint** from the bottom-left corner of the view page of your list or library. Note that while Microsoft lets you switch to the classic list experience, it is recommended that you continue to use the enhanced modern list and library experience unless there's an extremely compelling and well-thought-out reason not to do so.

See also

The *Adding an item to a list* recipe in *Chapter 2, Introduction to SharePoint Online*

- The *Viewing site contents* recipe in *Chapter 2, Introduction to SharePoint Online*
- The *Adding a column* recipe in this chapter
- The *Creating a custom list view* recipe in this chapter
- The *Viewing and changing list permissions* recipe in this chapter
- The *Adding a content type to a list or library* recipe in the online *Chapter 13, Term Store and Content Types in SharePoint Online*
- *Chapter 14, Search in Microsoft 365*

Viewing and changing list permissions

Just as in a site, you can adjust permissions on a list in a manner that allows control over who can view the list or edit items in it.

In this recipe, we will see how to view and change permissions in a SharePoint list.

Getting ready

You will need **Full Control** access to the list for which you'd like to view or change the permissions. You will usually have this access if you are in the *Site owners* group for the site.

How to do it...

To modify list permissions, follow these steps:

1. Browse to the list for which you would like to view or change the settings.

    Libraries in SharePoint are special types of lists, hence a lot of settings that you can configure for lists are also relevant for libraries. This includes the permission settings discussed in this recipe.

2. Click the settings gear icon in the top-right corner.

3. Click **List settings**, as shown in the following screenshot:

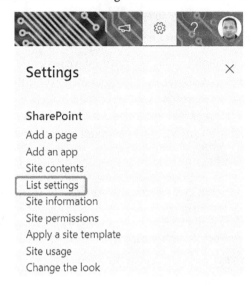

Figure 4.45: Finding List settings under the gear icon

4. On the **Settings** page, click the **Permissions for this list** link under **Permissions and Management.** You can now view the current permissions for that list on this screen.

5. Click **Stop Inheriting Permissions** from the **PERMISSIONS** tab in the top navigation menu, as shown in the following screenshot:

Figure 4.46: Navigating to the Stop Inheriting Permissions button

6. Click **OK** on the confirmation message.

 As with the message states, by choosing to stop inheriting the permissions, you will have created unique permissions for your list. This means that the permissions for the list will have to be managed independently of the permissions for the site. Changes made to the permissions at the site level will not automatically be reflected in the permissions on the list. You can always reverse this setting and turn inheritance back on by clicking the **Delete unique permissions** menu option on the **Permissions** tab. Note that this option only appears if you are not inheriting permissions on the selected object.

7. You can now independently adjust the permissions on this list by carrying out one or more of the following actions:

    •   Granting permissions to additional users or groups

    •   Changing permissions for selected users or groups that already have access

    •   Completely revoking access for existing users or groups that have access to the list

8. Select one or more existing users and click the **Edit User Permissions** menu option, as shown in the following screenshot:

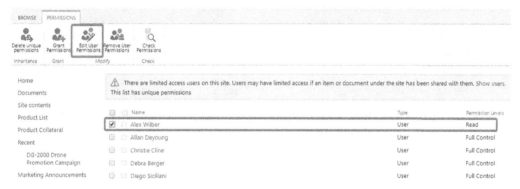

Figure 4.47: Editing permissions for a selected user

9. Change the permissions for the user and click the **OK** button, as shown in the following screen-shot:

Figure 4.48: Options available when editing permissions

Congratulations! You just set up permissions for your list in a way that is different from the parent site.

How it works...

We saw permissions management in great detail in the *Determining and revoking permissions in a site* recipe in *Chapter 3*, *Modern Sites in SharePoint Online*. We encourage you to review the recipe and related notes for more details on permissions in SharePoint, but to summarize, we covered the following:

*   We reviewed permission levels in SharePoint.
*   We saw how these permission levels relate to things that you are allowed to do and not allowed to do in SharePoint.
*   We learned how to configure and adjust SharePoint permissions using these permission levels.

Permissions management in a list or library is similar to permissions management on a site. When new lists and libraries are created, they *inherit* the security settings from the site, meaning that whatever access users have to your site, they will have the same level of access to the list. If, for example, a user has **Visitor** or **Read** access to your site, they will by default have **Read** access to the list. After the list or library is created, however, you can alter these permissions using the steps mentioned in this recipe.

 Caution: While you can change permissions for each list and library, it is generally not recommended to do so for many lists and libraries in your site. Creating and managing individual permissions can very soon become a governance and maintenance nightmare. Each situation differs, but you will likely be better off segregating audiences by way of creating different sites targeted toward solving the needs of those audiences.

There's more...

The permission hierarchy explained previously and its subsequent management further trickles down to the item level. This means that every item in a list and every document in a library by default *inherits* its permissions from the parent list or library. You can, however, break away from the inherited permissions and define distinct permissions for individual items. We discuss this and other related areas in the topics to follow.

Item permissions

Just as lists and libraries inherit permissions from their sites, items in lists and documents in libraries by default inherit permissions from the corresponding lists or libraries. SharePoint, however, lets you deviate from the norm and specify unique permissions for individual list items or documents. There are essentially two unique scenarios where you might want distinct permissions on individual items or documents within lists and libraries:

The first scenario is where for all items in a list, you may want users to only see their submissions to that list. An example of such a scenario could be a time-off request form, where individual department employees would submit their time-off requests and department managers would approve or deny them. Such a scenario in SharePoint is easily handled by simply enabling item-level permissions through the list settings. To enable item-level permissions in your list, browse to the **List settings** page, as described in the previous recipe. Then, click **Advanced settings** link in the **General Settings** section. You will then see the **Item-level Permissions** section, as shown in the following screenshot:

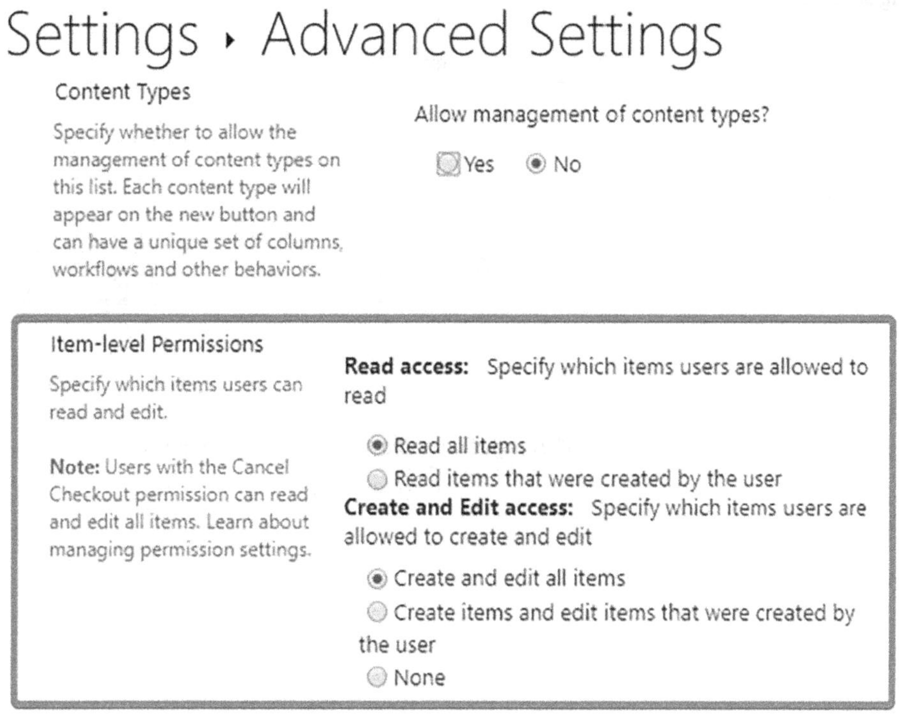

Settings ▸ Advanced Settings

Content Types

Specify whether to allow the management of content types on this list. Each content type will appear on the new button and can have a unique set of columns, workflows and other behaviors.

Allow management of content types?

○ Yes   ● No

Item-level Permissions

Specify which items users can read and edit.

Note: Users with the Cancel Checkout permission can read and edit all items. Learn about managing permission settings.

Read access: Specify which items users are allowed to read

● Read all items
○ Read items that were created by the user

Create and Edit access: Specify which items users are allowed to create and edit

● Create and edit all items
○ Create items and edit items that were created by the user
○ None

Figure 4.49: Item-level permissions under Advanced Settings

You can specify the following settings in this section:

- **Read access:** You can specify whether individual items can be read by everyone or can only be read by the users who created them.

- **Create and Edit access:** This is where you specify whether or not users can edit items created by others.

Please note that you will need **Design** or **Full Control** access to be able to update these settings. Also, worth noting is the fact that users with certain access levels, such as those having **Design** and **Full Control** access, will be able to view and edit all items in the list, irrespective of these settings. Also, these settings are only available for lists. You cannot configure item-level permissions for document libraries such as this. We'll cover how to apply unique permissions to documents in the next scenario.

The second scenario is where you may want to deviate from the permissions norm for a single list item or for one or more documents in a library (since the item-level permissions described previously are not applicable to document libraries). Let's say that you'd like to get internal reviews done in a presentation before sharing it with a wider audience that has access to it via the parent container library. Until then, you would like to only share it with a few colleagues for their review. For such scenarios, SharePoint lets you stop inheriting permissions from the parent library and specify custom permissions for the document in question. To do so, follow these steps:

1. Click the ellipsis next to the document and then click **Manage access**, as shown in the following screenshot:

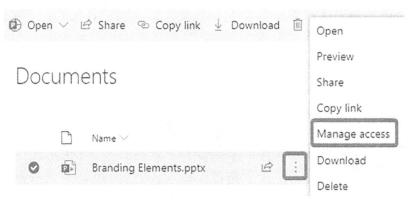

Figure 4.50: Navigating to the Manage access option

2. Click the three dots (**...**) toward the top right of the **Manage Access** panel and then click **Advanced settings**, as shown in the following screenshot:

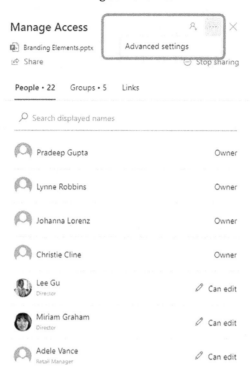

Figure 4.51: Navigating to advanced permissions from the Manage Access screen

3. This will take you to the **Permissions** screen for that document. Here, you can view the existing permissions and modify them as needed.

The steps to modify document permissions from this point on are the same as the steps to modify the list permissions, which we described earlier in this recipe.

Navigation and search visibility

Modifying the permissions for lists or libraries and corresponding items or documents within them automatically ensures that the corresponding objects are not visible anywhere in the quick launch or global navigation. Furthermore, search results in SharePoint are also security trimmed to only show items that users have at least read access to. Any time permissions on a document get updated, the search results will almost immediately reflect the permissions change and users will only see the document in search results if they still have permission to at least view it.

See also

- The *Viewing and changing list settings* recipe in this chapter
- The *Determining and revoking permissions in a site* recipe in *Chapter 3, Modern Sites in SharePoint Online*
- The *Searching content* recipe in *Chapter 2, Introduction to SharePoint Online*

Adding alerts

If you so desire, SharePoint can notify you by email when list or library items are added, edited, or deleted.

In this recipe, we will see how to create email alerts for SharePoint lists and libraries.

Getting ready

You will need at least **Read** access on the list or library for which you'd like to get alerted.

How to do it...

1. Browse to the list for which you would like to view or change the settings.

2. Click **Alert me**, as shown in the following screenshot:

Figure 4.52: Option to add an alert for a list

3. This shows the **Alert me** dialog box. Here, you can specify various properties and settings for the alert to be created:

    - **Alert Title:** Specify a title for the alert which is descriptive of what the alert is for. The title will be shown in the subject line of the email alert that the selected users will receive.

    - **Send Alerts To:** Users with **Full Control** access to the list, such as the list owners, see this additional option. This option enables you to subscribe other users to receive these alerts. Note that only users that have at least **Read** access to the list will be able to receive alerts from it.

    - **Delivery Method:** The alert delivery method defaults to email. Note that even though the screen shows a **Text message (SMS)** option, that option is no longer enabled for SharePoint Online (at least, at the time of writing).

- **Change Type:** Here, you can specify the kind of change that triggers the alert. You can choose to get notified for all changes to the data in that list or you can choose to get alerted only if items are specifically added, modified, or deleted.

- **Send Alerts for These Changes:** This setting lets you specify additional filters for when you would like to get alerted. You can narrow down the alerts to when someone else changes items that you have created or modified.

- **When to Send Alerts:** This final option lets you select the alert frequency. You can choose to receive an immediate alert or schedule a daily or weekly summary alert. If you opt to receive a daily or weekly summary alert, you can also choose the time at which you receive the summary notification email.

How it works...

Alerts in SharePoint are a very handy way to get notified about changes in a list or library. **Announcements, Issue Tracking, Tasks** lists, and **Calendar** are examples of where you might want to get notified of such changes. In addition to setting up alerts on entire lists and libraries, SharePoint also lets you set alerts on individual list items and/or documents, as shown in the following screenshot:

Figure 4.53: Option to add an alert for a list item

This can be handy when, for example, you are collaborating with your team on important documents and would like to stay up to date on any changes made to them.

Once you've created a list- or item-level alert, you can modify and/or delete it through the **Manage my alerts** menu option, as shown in the following screenshot:

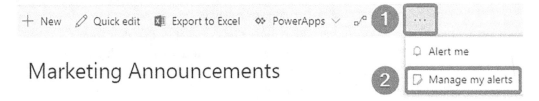

Figure 4.54: Option to manage alerts for a list

Clicking **Manage my alerts** will take you to the following screen, which will show you your alerts for all the lists, libraries, items, and documents across the entire site:

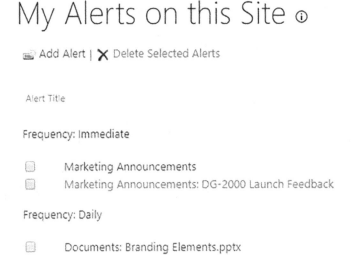

Figure 4.55: Screen for managing alerts related to a list

Clicking the alert name will enable you to make changes to it. Selecting one or more alert(s) and clicking **Delete Selected Alerts** will delete the alert(s). Note that unlike various other information types in SharePoint, deleted alerts don't go to the recycle bin and hence cannot be recovered.

There's more...

When you sign up for alerts in SharePoint, you receive detailed email notifications every time that the alert is triggered. These emails contain details about the item itself and metadata surrounding the triggering event. In the next section, we will look at these emails in more detail. We will then see how, as a site administrator, you can view and manage alerts that other site users may have subscribed to.

Notification emails

SharePoint sends two types of emails for alerts:

- **An email notifying you that the alert has successfully been created:** When you sign up for alerts on a list or library, SharePoint sends a confirmation email letting you know that an alert has been created. The following screenshot shows an example of such an email:

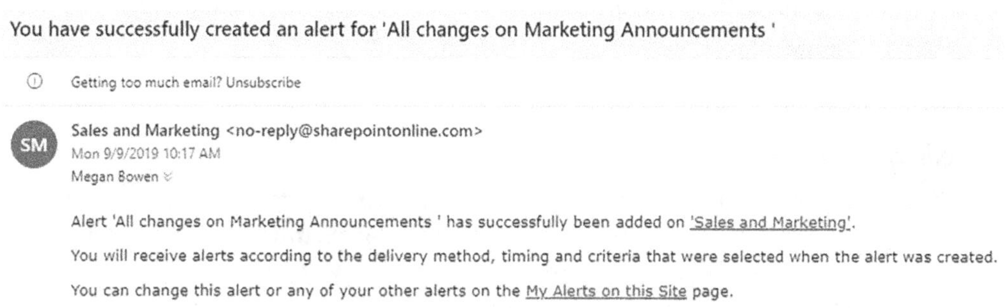

You have successfully created an alert for 'All changes on Marketing Announcements '

ⓘ Getting too much email? Unsubscribe

SM Sales and Marketing <no-reply@sharepointonline.com>
Mon 9/9/2019 10:17 AM
Megan Bowen ⌄

Alert 'All changes on Marketing Announcements ' has successfully been added on 'Sales and Marketing'.

You will receive alerts according to the delivery method, timing and criteria that were selected when the alert was created.

You can change this alert or any of your other alerts on the My Alerts on this Site page.

Figure 4.56: Example of an email notification about a created alert

- As you can see from the preceding example, the notification email contains the following information:

  - The name of the list or library that the alert is for
  - A link to the site that contains the list or library
  - A link to the view/ manage alerts page that we discussed in the preceding section

- **The actual alert email:** SharePoint sends an alert email when an activity occurs that matches your specified criteria. The following screenshot shows an example of an alert notification email:

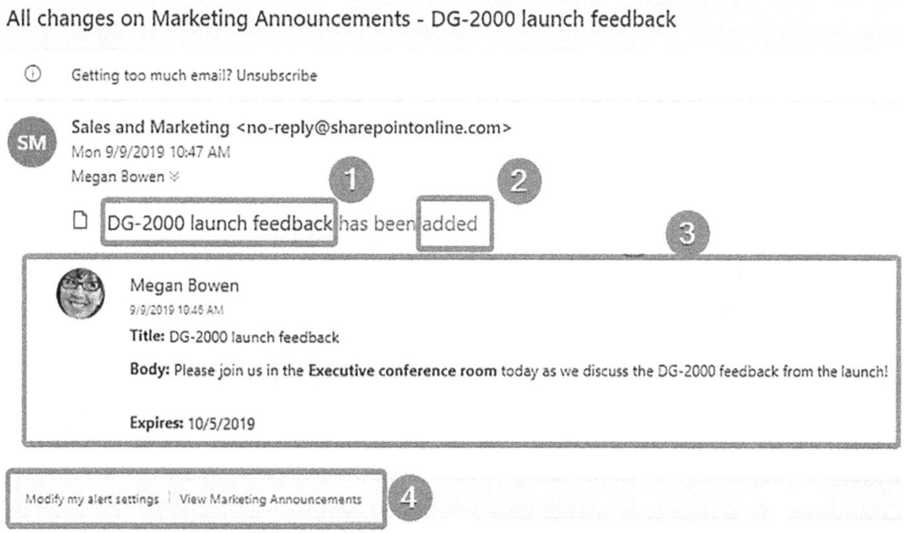

All changes on Marketing Announcements - DG-2000 launch feedback

ⓘ Getting too much email? Unsubscribe

SM Sales and Marketing <no-reply@sharepointonline.com>
Mon 9/9/2019 10:47 AM
Megan Bowen ⌄

DG-2000 launch feedback has been added

Megan Bowen
9/9/2019 10:46 AM
Title: DG-2000 launch feedback
Body: Please join us in the **Executive conference room** today as we discuss the DG-2000 feedback from the launch!
Expires: 10/5/2019

Modify my alert settings | View Marketing Announcements

Figure 4.57: Example of an alert email notification

- As you can see from the preceding example, the notification email contains the following information:

  - The name of the item that the alert is for—the name hyperlinks to the corresponding item in the list
  - The type of change that triggered the alert
  - Details of the item, including who triggered the action and when
  - A hyperlink to modify the alert settings
  - A hyperlink to view the corresponding list

Finding and deleting other users' alerts

As a site administrator, you can not only view and manage your alerts, but you can also view and delete alerts for other users of your site. To do so, browse to the **Site Settings** page of your site, as described in the *Viewing and changing site settings* recipe in *Chapter 3, Modern Sites in SharePoint Online*. Then, click **User Alerts** under the **Site Administration** heading. This will take you to the **User Alerts** page, as shown in the following screenshot:

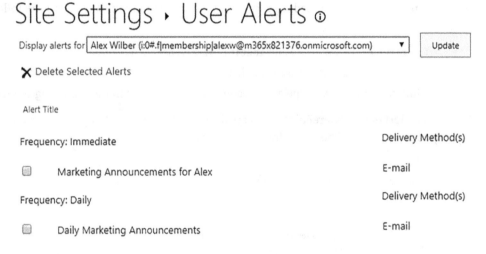

Figure 4.58: Viewing other users' alerts as an admin

Here, you can select a user from the **Display alerts for** dropdown option and click **Update** to view alerts that they are subscribed to. You can then select appropriate alerts and delete them by clicking **Delete Selected Alerts**.

See also

- The *Viewing and changing site settings* recipe in *Chapter 3, Modern Sites in SharePoint Online*

Unlock this book's exclusive benefits now

This book comes with additional benefits designed to elevate your learning experience.

Note: Have your purchase invoice ready before you begin. https://www.packtpub.com/unlock/9781803243177

5
Document Management in SharePoint Online

A **library** in SharePoint is a special type of list built specifically for managing files and the metadata around them. Libraries carry over the following similarities from lists:

- Just like you work with individual *items in lists*, libraries contain *files* that you can work with.
- Just as *columns* in lists define the *information* that gets stored as part of each list item, columns in libraries define the *metadata* that you can associate with each file. Once the columns for a library are defined, you can tag individual files with the appropriate metadata.
- Just like you can manage items individually or by selecting multiple items in lists, you can manage metadata in libraries for a single file or together for multiple files.
- Just like you would manage permissions for list items, you can also manage permissions individually for each file in a library.

From these perspectives (and in a lot of other ways), lists and libraries are similar to each other. The one main difference between lists and libraries is that while list capabilities are focused on list items, all the functionalities in libraries are focused on files. From that perspective, libraries are an extension of lists, with added capabilities for working with documents and other types of files. A few notable examples of such capabilities are as follows:

- The file editing and sharing experience
- In-place file previews
- Downloading, copying and moving files
- Ability to pin important files to the top
- Check in/check out, versioning, and approval experience
- Synchronizing files or folders locally for a desktop editing experience

Libraries typically contain documents, but they can also contain various other file types. SharePoint Online provides three pre-built libraries that are used to fulfill distinct needs:

- **Document library:** The document library allows you to store and share documents. SharePoint provisions a default document library for each site that gets created. Document libraries allow you to efficiently work with Office files and other types of files. We got some insight into working with document libraries and documents as part of *Chapter 2, Introduction to SharePoint Online*.

- **Site Assets library:** This library is used to store reusable assets for your site (such as images that you insert into pages, stylesheets, and the site's OneNote notebook).

- **Site Pages library:** The purpose of this library is to store pages within a site. This is also where the news posts of your site live as pages.

In *Chapter 4, Lists and Libraries in SharePoint Online*, we looked at lists in great detail. We saw how to add columns, modify views, and modify other settings in a list. Since a library is a special type of list, almost all the guidance applicable to lists also applies to libraries. Before proceeding with the recipes in this chapter, it is highly recommended to review that chapter if you have not already done so. In this chapter, we will discuss recipes that we haven't discussed before since they are unique to libraries.

In this chapter, we will discuss the following recipes:

- Creating a new document
- Associating a document template
- Viewing and editing documents in the browser
- Viewing and editing documents in the client
- Downloading documents
- Moving and copying documents
- Viewing and changing document library settings
- Versioning settings, content approval, and document checkout

Creating a new document

In *Chapter 2, Introduction to SharePoint Online*, we saw how to upload existing documents and folders to a document library. In addition to uploading existing documents, you can create new documents from scratch within a document library.

There are two ways to create a new document within a library:

- Create it using the **New** menu in the library
- Create it using one of the desktop Microsoft Office apps (MS Word, Excel, and so on.)

This recipe will show you how to create a new Word document using these approaches.

Getting ready

You will need **Contribute** permissions or higher for the library in which you would like to create a new document. You would have this permission if you were part of the Owners or Members group for the site.

How to do it...

To create a document using the **New** menu in a document library, follow these steps:

1. Browse to the library where you would like to create the new document.
2. Click the **New** menu from the navigation bar at the top of the library:

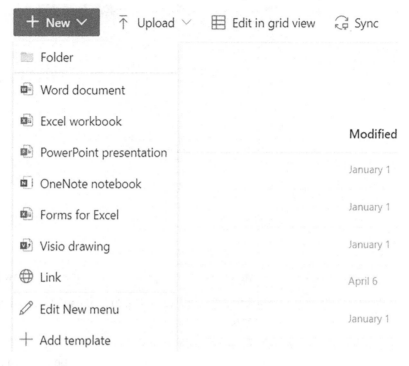

Figure 5.1: Clicking the New menu to create a Word document

3. Click on the type of document you would like to create. We will choose a **Word document** template for our example. Doing so will create a blank Word document in the library and will open it for editing in a new browser window.
4. Click on the **Document - Saved** text at the top of the screen (above the ribbon menu):

Figure 5.2: Clicking on the name field for a document

5. Give a name for your document and then press the *Enter* key or click anywhere outside the text box to save the change:

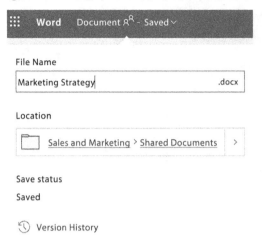

Figure 5.3: Naming a document

To create a new document using the Microsoft Office app on your computer, follow these steps:

1. Open the Office desktop application locally. We will open Microsoft Word since we are creating a Word document in this example.
2. Create or edit content in it like you typically would.
3. Click the **File** menu and then click **Save** or **Save As**. You will now be shown a list of your recent locations. These recent locations could be your online SharePoint and OneDrive libraries, or local folders on your computer:

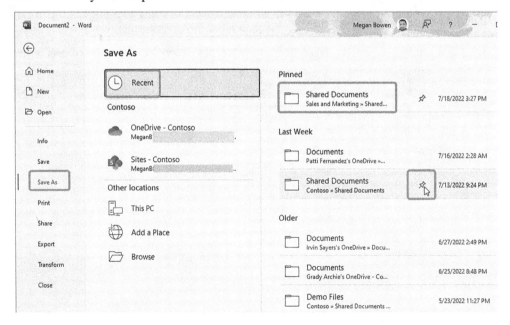

Figure 5.4: Viewing recent locations for saving a document

Notice that you can click the pin icon alongside your frequently used locations, so they are pinned to the top of the list.

4. If you see your SharePoint Online library here, you can select it, enter a name for your file, and then save it here, as shown in the following screenshot:

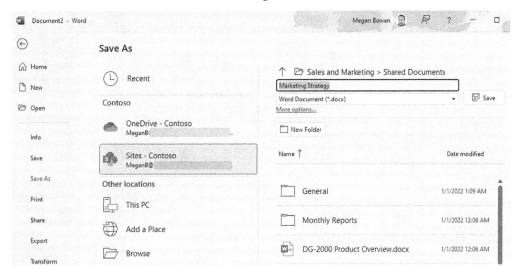

Figure 5.5: Saving a file into a SharePoint library

5. If you did not find your library in the list of recent libraries, you can click the **Sites** – (your organization name) option to view a list of your frequently accessed or followed sites:

Figure 5.6: Saving into frequently accessed sites

6. Clicking a site name then shows you the document libraries on those sites. You can then select a library and then save your document there, similar to the figure shown in *step 4*.

7. Finally, if you do not see your site on this list, you can click the **Browse** button to open the **Save As** dialog. Then enter the URL of the library (without the trailing `Forms/AllItems.aspx`) and click **Save**, as shown in the following screenshot:

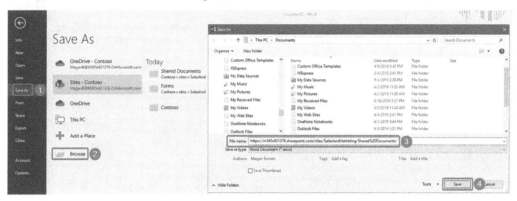

Figure 5.7: Saving via the Browse button

🔍 **Quick tip:** Need to see a high-resolution version of this image? Open this book in the next-gen Packt Reader or view it in the PDF/ePub copy.

🔓 The **next-gen Packt Reader** and a **free PDF/ePub copy** of this book are included with your purchase. Unlock them by scanning the QR code below or visiting `https://www.packtpub.com/unlock/9781803243177`.

8. This takes you to the default view of the library (just like you would see it in the browser).

 Note that you may be prompted for credentials at this point, especially if you are doing this for the first time or not using your work computer. Please be careful to not save/remember the credentials if you are using a public computer to do this.

9. Enter a filename and click **Save** again to save the document to the library.

10. If your library contained mandatory columns for additional metadata, you will be prompted to enter values for those columns before you can save the document. If that happens, you will need to select or enter the required metadata and then click the **Retry Save** button:

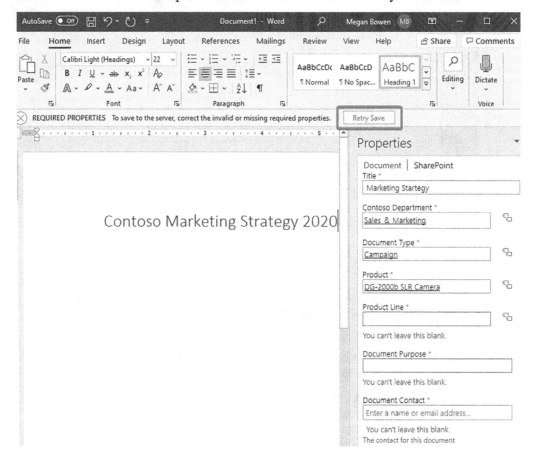

Figure 5.8: Checking mandatory metadata columns in the Properties panel

 You can find the option to open the **Properties** panel by clicking **View** in the top ribbon.

11. Doing so will save the document to the location that you had previously selected.

Congratulations! You just created a new document in the library. You learned how to do so by using the **New** menu from within the library or by using the appropriate Microsoft Office desktop app.

How it works...

One difference between storing a document in SharePoint Online versus storing it locally is that when you store a document in a SharePoint document library, it automatically becomes available to anyone else who has access to that library. Other users that have access to the document can also immediately work on it in parallel. Among its other benefits, storing documents online also makes it easy to share them with others by merely emailing them links to those documents using the **Share** or **Copy link** functionality in SharePoint Online. We saw how to share documents in the *Sharing a document* recipe of *Chapter 2, Introduction to SharePoint Online*.

There's more...

Governance and information architecture

Your site's members can create lists and libraries within it. They can further create columns within the libraries, create folders, customize library views, and change other settings for these libraries. This can quickly lead to several lists and libraries all over your site. Along with that, many dispersed columns, folders, and list views can also get created within those libraries.

For this reason, if you are a site owner or owner of a library, you should put some upfront thought into planning the permissions for your site and/or lists and libraries within the site. Also, you will want to plan the structure and organization of content that will be hosted within these sites. You should ideally do this before users start creating or uploading files in the library. As a site owner, you should think about whether content should be hosted in one library or multiple libraries. Further, as a library owner, you should think about the following:

- The columns (a.k.a. metadata) that should be captured for the documents in the library
- The views that should be created for the library
- Whether you need to create folders to organize the files
- Versioning, checkout required, and other such settings for the library

In addition to this, you should think about the different user types that will interact with your library or, better yet, your site on the whole, and accordingly plan the permissions for who can do what within the site.

See also

- The *Uploading documents to a library* recipe in *Chapter 2, Introduction to SharePoint Online*
- The *Sharing a document* recipe in *Chapter 2, Introduction to SharePoint Online*
- The *Associating a document template* recipe in this chapter
- The *Adding a column* recipe in *Chapter 4, Lists and Libraries in SharePoint Online*
- The *Adding alerts* recipe in *Chapter 4, Lists and Libraries in SharePoint Online*
- The *Creating a content type* recipe in *Chapter 13, Term Store and Content Types in SharePoint Online*

Associating a document template

The **New** menu in a library lets you create documents using the standard inbuilt document types:

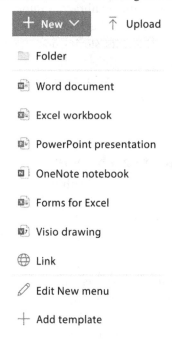

Figure 5.9: Creating a document via the New menu

Clicking any of these document types will result in a blank document being created for you of that document type. There are times, however, when you want your users to create documents using the standard document templates defined by your organization. These templates may contain pre-defined branding, standard cover pages, headers, and footers specific to your organization. You can modify the **New** menu to enable document creation using company-defined templates and also optionally hide the inbuilt blank document types.

This recipe will show you how to associate a pre-created document template with the **New** menu in your library. We will also see how to show this template at the top of the list of options on the **New** menu and then disable the inbuilt **Word document** option.

Getting ready

You will need the **Edit** permission or higher to be able to edit the **New** menu for a library. You would have this permission if you were part of the Owners or Members group for the site.

How to do it...

To add a new template to the list of options in the **New** menu:

1. Click the **New** option in the menu bar.

2. Click **Add template** toward the bottom of the menu:

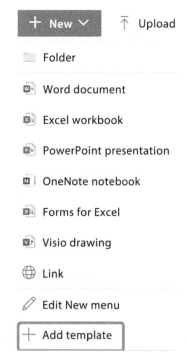

Figure 5.10: Option to add a template at the bottom of the New menu

This opens the usual file selection dialog box for your computer.

3. Browse to the appropriate document template and then select it.

 Creating document templates is beyond what we can cover in this book, but this Microsoft article provides guidance on how to work with document templates: `https://packt.link/create-document-template`.

4. This will add the new document template to this menu, as shown in the following screenshot:

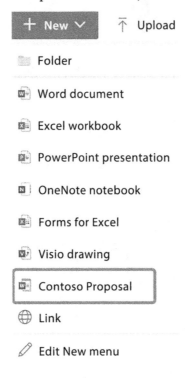

Figure 5.11: Viewing an added document template

To modify the order of the different document types that the users see in the **New** menu, or to completely hide them:

1. Click the **New** option from the menu bar.
2. Click **Edit New menu** towards the bottom.

This brings up the **Edit New menu** panel. Here, you can hide the existing menu options, reorder them, or completely delete the custom options by clicking the ellipses to the right of the options:

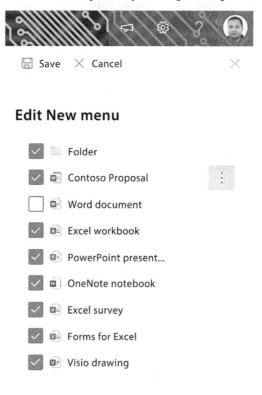

 You cannot delete an inbuilt option – you can only hide it by unchecking the checkbox to its left.

Figure 5.12: Editing the New menu

3. You can then click the **Save** button to save your changes to the **New** menu.

Congratulations, you just learned how to associate a document template with the **New** menu in your library. You then learned how to rearrange the order of various menu options and then hide the options that were not needed.

How it works...

It is usually a good idea to integrate your organization's templates instead of your site users creating blank documents from scratch. This further ties into the discussion of governance and information architecture from the previous recipe in this chapter. Doing so, where possible, helps to further improve the quality of content and consistency within your site, and in your organization beyond that. Please note that SharePoint cannot validate whether the documents uploaded to your library were created using a template. Your users can still upload documents that may not be based on a document template defined for that library.

See also

*   The *Creating a new document* recipe in this chapter

Viewing and editing documents in the browser

Microsoft 365 conveniently enables you to view and edit files directly in the browser, without even having to download a local copy. This recipe will show you how to do that.

Getting ready

You will need **Read** permissions or higher on the document which you'd like to view and **Contribute** permissions or higher on it if you'd like to edit it. Alternatively, you will need to be at least part of the Visitors group to view documents and the Members or Owners group to edit them.

How to do it...

To open a document in the browser, follow these steps:

1.   Browse to the library that contains the document which you'd like to view or edit.
2.   Click on the document you'd like to view or edit. This will open the document in a new browser window.

> It may happen that clicking the document will prompt you to open the desktop app instead of opening it in the browser. This can happen if the library owner has changed the *default open behavior* for documents in that library. To open a document in the browser for such a library, click the ellipses next to it, then click **Open**, and then **Open in browser.**
>
> If you are the owner of such a library, we will discuss later in this chapter how you can change this behavior for your library.

3.   Depending on your permission level for the document, you will directly be able to view it or edit it in place in the browser.

That's it! You just learned how to view and edit documents from a SharePoint library in the browser.

How it works...

Office for the web (previously known as Office Online or Office Web Apps) is the online Office suite that enables viewing and editing files in the browser. It supports hundreds of file types for viewing in the browser. This link provides a list of all such file types: `https://packt.link/preview-file-types`.

In addition to the ability to view files within the browser, Office for the web also enables you to edit a subset of these file types right from your browser. At the time of writing, the ability to edit documents in the browser was available for most Microsoft Office file types, such as `.docx`, `.pptx`, and `.xlsx`, and most text file types, such as `.txt`, `.css`, `.html`, and `.js`.

Please note that even though there is a limit on the file types that can be viewed or edited in the browser, there's practically no limit on the file types that can be uploaded to it. In addition, the browser viewing and editing experience slightly varies depending on the type of file. Further, if SharePoint is unable to render a file type in the browser, clicking on the file will prompt you to download it to your computer. You can then open the file as you usually would on your computer using the native app for that file type.

Some advantages of browser editing are as follows:

- **No additional licensing or software is required**: Office for the web is included with your Microsoft 365 subscription without an additional cost (a.k.a. free). Further, it does not require any software to be installed (not even the Microsoft Office desktop software) and simply works out of the box with almost all commonly used browsers.
- **Quick and convenient**: It is certainly very convenient to be able to edit the documents from within the browser instead of having to download them first. You can not only view and edit these documents on your desktop browser but also with a variety of mobile browsers and Office mobile apps on a variety of other devices as well. Further, your changes to such files are automatically saved so you don't need to manually save them.

The one main limitation of using Office Online to view or edit your documents in the browser is that not all features of the corresponding desktop apps are available in Office Online. For example, not all transitions and animations are available in PowerPoint Online. Having said that, the capabilities available in Office Online still cover the most common usage scenarios. This article provides a detailed comparison of features that are available in the client apps versus those available in the corresponding web apps: `https://packt.link/office-online-service-description`.

There's more...

We will discuss the online viewing, editing, and co-authoring experience in SharePoint Online in the next few topics.

Editing and Viewing modes

When you open a Microsoft Office document in SharePoint, and you have *edit* rights to it, the document opens in **Editing** mode by default. This is indicated by the *mode* indicator on the document menu bar, as shown below:

Figure 5.13: Excel file in Editing mode

When a document opens in **Editing** mode, any changes you make to it are automatically saved to it. This further results in your name being shown as the name of the person who last modified the document. For Excel files, a simple action like switching to a different sheet within the Excel file can trigger the **Save** event. This can get annoying, especially if the intent was not to modify the document. In such scenarios, you can switch the document to **Viewing** mode, as shown in the following figure:

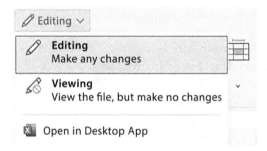

Figure 5.14: Switching between Editing and Viewing mode

Switching to this mode will make the document read-only and prevent you from making any changes to it, as shown in the following figure:

Figure 5.15: Viewing mode causes a file to be read-only

 Microsoft Word also allows for a **Reviewing** mode that allows documents to be shared for review. Documents shared this way will have tracking and comments turned on by default for receivers of the sharing link. You can read more about this feature announcement from Microsoft here: https://packt.link/SP-reviewing-mode.

Co-authoring documents in the browser

Co-authoring is two or more people working on a document at the same time. Co-authoring in Office not only enables multiple people to simultaneously work on the same document but also lets them see each other's changes in real time. You can co-author MS Word, PowerPoint, Excel, or OneNote files that are stored in SharePoint Online or OneDrive. The following screenshot shows an example of co-authoring:

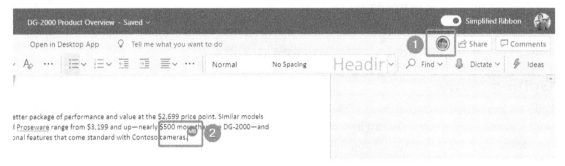

Figure 5.16: Viewing co-authors and their activity on a file

In the example shown in the preceding screenshot, a user, Alex, is making changes to a Word document. As shown in the screenshot, another user, Megan Bowen, is simultaneously editing the same document. Alex can see that Megan is editing the document by way of her image showing up in the top-right corner of the document (illustrated by the rectangle marked number 1). Further, Alex can also see the changes that Megan is currently making in real time by way of a cursor that shows her initials – **MB** (illustrated by the rectangle marked number 2).

 Office provides various indicators when multiple people are co-authoring a document. In addition to the indicators mentioned here, Office will explicitly notify you when someone else starts editing a document that you are already presently editing. It will also notify you when they exit that editing experience. Please note that you do **not** get notified when others open documents in view-only mode (you only get notified when they open the document in edit mode).

In the same way, Megan will also see the changes that Alex is making in real time through a presence indicator along with a cursor showing his initials. If more than two users were editing this document, Word would similarly indicate their presence along with the real-time updates that they were making to the documents.

This support article provides more details on co-authoring: `https://packt.link/co-authoring`.

See also

- *Adding an item to a list* recipe of *Chapter 2, Introduction to SharePoint online*
- The *Viewing and editing documents in the client* recipe in this chapter
- The *Adding alerts* recipe in *Chapter 4, Lists and Libraries in SharePoint Online*

Viewing and editing documents in the client

In addition to the ability to view and edit documents in the browser, SharePoint also lets you view and edit online documents in the corresponding desktop applications. There are two ways to open an online document in the desktop app:

* Browse to the library and then open the document from there
* Directly open an online document from the app

In this recipe, we will see how to use both methods to view and edit a document that was uploaded to a SharePoint library in the corresponding desktop application.

Getting ready

You will need **Read** permissions or higher on the document that you'd like to view and **Contribute** permissions or higher on it if you'd like to edit it. Alternatively, you will need to be at least part of the Visitors group to view documents and the Members or Owners group to edit them.

How to do it...

To open the online document from a library, follow these steps:

1. Browse to the library that contains the document that you would like to view or edit.
2. Click the ellipses next to the document (**1**), mouse over the **Open** submenu option (**2**), and then click **Open in app** (**3**), as shown in the following screenshot:

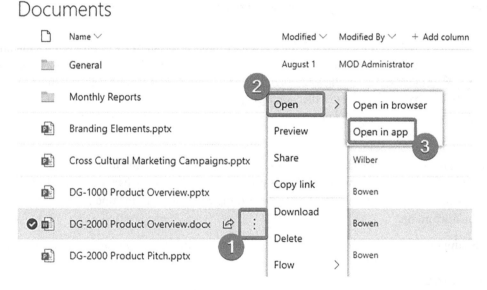

Figure 5.17: Opening a SharePoint document in the desktop Word app

3. If you are opening a Word document, like we are in the preceding screenshot, click **Open Word** on the prompt that appears to confirm that you'd like to open the document in Word.

     Anything you do in SharePoint, and Microsoft 365 in general, requires you to be authenticated and have appropriate access configured through permissions. This is true for documents that you are opening in the client as well. You will be prompted for credentials the first time you open any document in a client app (or if your credentials have changed since the last time). Your credentials will then be remembered from there on, provided you were able to successfully authenticate yourself. From that point on, SharePoint will use the saved credentials every time you try to open a document (even though it will still check to make sure you have permission to do so).

4. The selected document will now open in the Word desktop or mobile app. If you have the right to edit the document, you can start making changes to it and your changes will automatically be saved to the document library in SharePoint.

To open the document directly from the client app, follow these steps:

1. Open the corresponding desktop app, like you usually would.
2. Once you open the app, you will be shown the **Home** tab. Here, you can see all your recently opened documents, which include documents from Office online. Click the document to open it if you see it here. Otherwise, we can move on to the next step.
3. Depending on the option you are seeing, click the **Open** tab or click the **File** menu and then click **Open**.
4. You will now see a list of your recent files. If you have previously connected your Microsoft 365 account through the desktop client, you will also see a list of organizations that you have recently accessed.

5. Clicking the organization name will show you your frequent and followed sites from the organization:

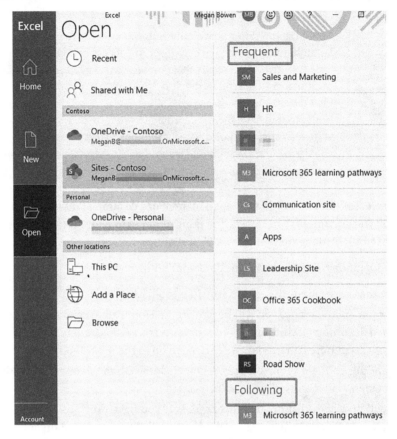

Figure 5.18: Selecting a file to open from Frequent and Following

6. You can then click the site name and the corresponding library to view all the folders and documents from it.
7. If you found your document here, you can click on the name to open it. If not, we will move on to the next step.
8. Click the **Browse** button to open the usual file selection dialog box.
9. Enter the URL of your site and then click **Open** to see a list of the libraries on that site.

You need to ensure that the URL points to the file and not any libraries or pages underneath it. For example, a URL like this will result in an error because it points to a page (and not a site): `https://<OrganizationName>.sharepoint.com/sites/SalesAndMarketing/SitePages/Home.aspx`.

The correct URL to enter in the file dialog for this site is `https://<OrganizationName>.sharepoint.com/sites/SalesAndMarketing/`

10. Select the library that contains your document and then click **Open** to view a list of documents in that library.

11. Select the document you'd like to open, and then click **Open**, as shown in the following screenshot:

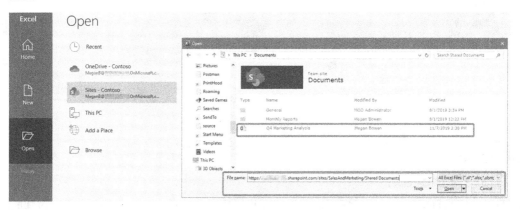

Figure 5.19: Selecting and opening a file from a SharePoint library in a desktop app

12. Doing so will open that document in the desktop client. If you have the right to edit the document, you can start making changes to it and your changes will automatically be saved to the document library in SharePoint.

Congratulations! You just learned how to directly view and edit documents from a SharePoint library in a client app. Please note that you can currently only open Microsoft Office documents this way.

How it works...

Being able to edit documents online is very convenient. However, it lacks the advanced editing controls that Microsoft Office desktop apps provide. The client editing capability brings together the best of both worlds. It lets you store and share your documents on the cloud, where they are easily accessible to everyone. Also, you can use the rich client capabilities to make modifications to your documents in that you see more editing and formatting options in the ribbon menus. As of now, you can only edit Microsoft Office documents connected to the cloud this way. All other file types that you would like to edit using the client applications will first need to be downloaded, edited, and then uploaded back to the library.

In addition to directly opening online documents in a desktop app, you can also use the **Open in Desktop App** option to open, in the corresponding desktop app, any online documents that you may be viewing or editing in your browser.

The Open in Desktop App option

When editing documents in the browser, SharePoint Online presents an **Open in Desktop App** menu option in the **Editing** *mode switcher* menu, as shown in the following screenshot. Clicking this option also opens the document in the corresponding desktop app:

Figure 5.20: Opening a file in the desktop app from within the file

There's more...

We discussed auto-save and co-authoring as part of the last recipe. These discussions in the previous recipe were focused more on a browser-based experience in that all users were using their browsers to work with the documents. In the context of the current recipe, it is also possible to use the corresponding Microsoft Office desktop apps to auto-save and co-author documents. We will discuss these in the topics to follow.

AutoSave in the client app

When you open a Microsoft Office document stored in SharePoint Online or OneDrive in the desktop app and you have *edit* rights to the document, your changes to such documents are automatically saved to the appropriate library in SharePoint or on OneDrive. Like the online Office document authoring experience, you can turn off the auto-save feature in the desktop app as well. To do so, simply click the **AutoSave** toggle shown towards the top-left corner of your Office app, as shown below, to switch it from **On** to **Off**:

Figure 5.21: AutoSave toggle

If you recall from the previous recipe, turning off **AutoSave** in the browser editing experience changes the document authoring mode from **Editing** to **Viewing**. The experience is slightly different in the client app in that it stops your document from being automatically saved and your document will only be saved when you manually save it using the *Ctrl + S* shortcut or by clicking the **Save** () icon.

 When you open documents stored locally (and not from SharePoint Online or OneDrive), such documents are always opened with the **AutoSave** toggle set to **Off**. Additionally, you cannot turn on **AutoSave** and will always need to manually save changes to such documents.

Co-authoring documents in the client app

While you edit the document in a desktop app, your co-workers could either be using the browser or a desktop app to view and edit the same document. The Office desktop app would provide you with similar notifications and indicators to not only show you who else is editing the document but also show their edits in real time (provided both of you have **AutoSave** turned on).

 The editing experience differs depending on the type of document that you are editing and the type of app that you are using. This support article provides a good reference to troubleshoot any issues that you may have with the co-authoring experience: `https://packt.link/troubleshooting-co-authoring`.

One added benefit of using the desktop app for co-authoring is that clicking a person's presence indicator in the app lets you perform the following additional actions:

- Go to the location that the person is at in the document
- Email the person
- View their contact information

Document metadata

When the document library containing the document is configured with columns to store additional metadata/information for the document, Microsoft Office lets you edit that metadata from within the client application. Further, if any of those columns are mandatory, the client application will require you to enter that information before you can save the document. It shows these columns through the **Properties** pane, as shown in the following screenshot:

Figure 5.22: Mandatory metadata in the Properties pane

This **Properties** pane is also sometimes referred to as the **Document Information Panel**. The Office client will save your document to SharePoint once you update its properties through this panel.

See also

- The *Viewing and editing documents in the browser* recipe in this chapter
- The *Adding alerts* recipe in *Chapter 4, Lists and Libraries in SharePoint Online*
- The *Versioning settings, content approval, and document checkout* recipe in this chapter

Downloading documents

In addition to viewing and editing documents in browsers or client apps, you can also download them for offline viewing. This recipe shows you how to do that.

Getting ready

You will need **Read** permissions or higher on the document that you'd like to download. Alternatively, you will need to be at least part of the Visitors group to download documents within the site.

How to do it...

To download a document, follow these steps:

1. Browse to the library that contains the document that you would like to download and then select it by checking the checkbox next to it.

2. Click the **Download** option from the library menu:

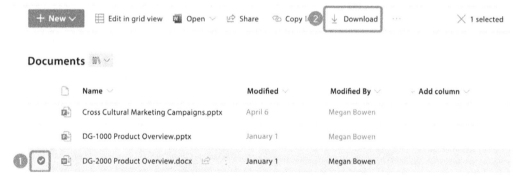

Figure 5.23: Download option in a SharePoint library

 When you select a document, the options that you see in the top menu bar are also available to you when you click the ellipses next to the document. In this case, for example, you can also click the ellipses to reveal the **Download** menu option.

That's it! You just downloaded a copy of the document for offline use.

How it works...

You can download any file for offline viewing and editing. For file types that you can view in the browser, Office 365 provides two additional ways of downloading the files when you are viewing or editing them, depending on the file type:

- For Microsoft Office documents, once you have the document open in your browser window, you can click the **File** menu, then **Save As**, and then **Download a Copy**. You will also see some additional options depending on the type of Office document that you are viewing (Word, Excel, or PowerPoint). Word, for example, additionally presents a **Download as PDF** option:

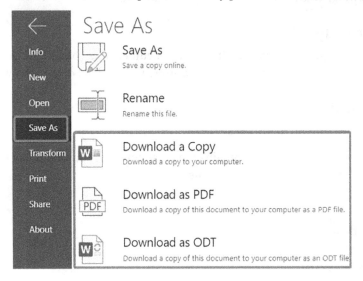

Figure 5.24: Options for downloading a file for offline use

- When working on a document with the Office client app, you can use the app's **Save a Copy** menu to download the files locally to your computer:

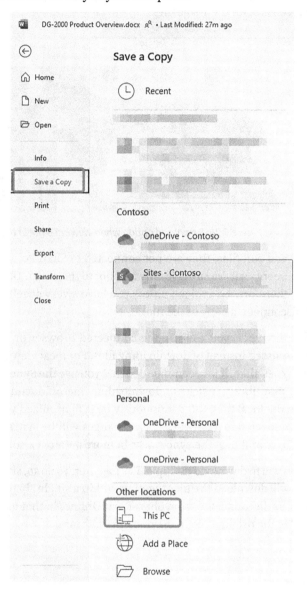

Figure 5.25: Downloading a file to the PC from within a desktop app

For all other file types, you will be able to download the file by clicking the **Download** option in the top menu bar, which appears when viewing those files in the browser, as shown in the following screenshot for an image file:

Figure 5.26: Download option when viewing a file in the browser

When you download and edit files, they are not connected to SharePoint Online, meaning that your local edits to the documents will be saved locally and not to the cloud. Downloading files and editing them locally should, therefore, be avoided unless you have a very specific need that requires you to use an offline and disconnected copy of the file.

For Microsoft Office file types, you can use the connected browser or desktop editing experience that we previously discussed instead of downloading files. For local viewing and editing of Office and other non-Office file types alike, it is recommended that you use the **Sync** menu option to locally sync the documents from your library instead of downloading one-off documents. Once you do that, any changes you make to the local files will continuously be synchronized with the online document. If you are offline (not connected to a network), your changes will be synced once you go online again. We will discuss **OneDrive** and how the sync works in more detail in a subsequent chapter.

SharePoint also allows you to download multiple files together. To do so, simply select the files and click **Download**. Doing so will download the files together within a single zip file. As mentioned previously though, the files will be disconnected from SharePoint Online, in that any changes to such files will not be synchronized to the original file in the document library.

See also

*   *Chapter 6, OneDrive*

Moving and copying documents

You can copy or move your documents from one site to another site in your tenant. In this recipe, we will see how to copy a document to a different library on another site.

Getting ready

To *copy* a document, you will need **Read** access to the library from which you are copying the document. If you are *moving* a document, you will need **Contribute** permissions or higher from where you are moving the document.

In addition, you will need **Contribute** access to the library to which you are moving or copying the documents.

Alternatively, you will need to be at least part of the Visitors group of the source site and the Members or Owners group of the destination site.

How to do it...

To copy or move one or more documents, follow these steps:

1. Browse to the library that contains the documents that you'd like to copy or move.

> You would follow the same steps if you'd like to copy files over from your OneDrive to a library in SharePoint.

2. Select one or more documents that you'd like to move or copy and click the **Move to** or **Copy to** options in the library menu, as shown in the following screenshot:

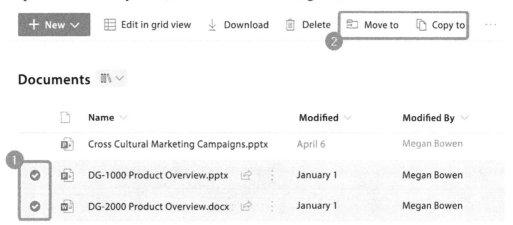

Figure 5.27: Options for moving and copying a file in a SharePoint library

3. Choose a destination to move or copy your file to. You can choose from multiple options, as shown in the following screenshot:

   • Create a copy of the file within the same library
   • Move or copy the file over to a folder in your OneDrive
   • Choose a library from a list of recently used sites

- Browse to a site not shown in the list of recently used sites

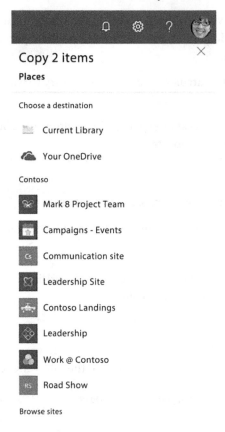

Figure 5.28: Selecting a site to copy the files to

4. We will select the **Road Show** site for this example.
5. We will then select a library on this site.
6. If needed, we can further create new folders or select existing subfolders, and then click **Move here** or **Copy here** to move or copy the files over to the selected library:

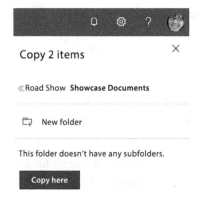

Figure 5.29: Selecting a library within a SharePoint site

The copied files will automatically inherit permissions from the destination library, even if the source library or documents have a different set of permissions.

That's it! You just learned how to copy or move files in SharePoint to another destination within SharePoint or OneDrive.

How it works...

Copying or moving files in SharePoint Online is quite like copying or moving files on your computer. If you are moving a file, the source file is deleted. If you are copying a file, the source file is maintained, and a new copy of the file is created in the destination. Just like when you copy or move files locally on your computer, SharePoint provides appropriate indicators when the file operation starts and then when it succeeds or fails. The one difference between the copy and move operations in SharePoint is that since copying effectively creates a new file in the destination, certain properties of the file, such as the version history, do not carry over. Moving the file, on the other hand, results in the version history also being brought over to the destination file.

 Please refer to the *Versioning settings, content approval, and document checkout* recipe later in the chapter to find out more about versioning and version history.

Also, if you have custom metadata associated with the document being copied or moved, that metadata is copied over along with it as long as the destination library has the same column as the source to store that information.

Finally, please note that at the time of writing, SharePoint restricts the maximum size of a copy or move operation to 100 GB when the operation is across two sites. You can read more about this here: `https://packt.link/move-copy-limits`.

Viewing and changing document library settings

We saw several list settings as part of the *Viewing and changing list settings* recipe in *Chapter 4, Lists and Libraries in SharePoint Online*. As mentioned earlier, libraries are an extension of lists, and hence these settings also inherently apply to libraries. They also, however, have a few additional settings of their own that are relevant to the way you work with files and documents.

We will look at some of these settings as part of this recipe. As an example, we will see how to change the default way that browser-enabled documents open. When you click a document within a library, the default setting results in the document opening in the browser. However, as described in the *Viewing and editing documents in the browser* recipe earlier in this chapter, the browser editing experience has its limitations. You may, therefore, require the documents in a particular library to open in the corresponding Office clients so your site's users can get that rich editing experience every time they open a document from the library. This recipe will show you how to do that.

Getting ready

You will need **Edit**, **Design**, or **Full Control** access to the library for which you'd like to view or change the settings. Alternatively, you will need to be at least part of the Members or Owners group of the site to modify the list settings.

How to do it...

To change the default open behavior for documents in a library, follow these steps:

1. Browse to the library for which you would like to change this behavior.
2. Click on the settings gear icon in the top-right corner.
3. Click **Library settings**, as shown in the following screenshot:

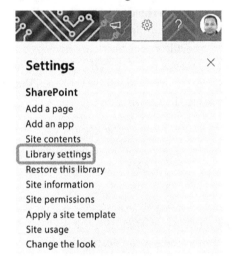

Figure 5.30: Opening Library settings from the Settings menu

4. This takes you to the **Settings** page for the library. Here, you can view and modify various settings for the list.
5. Click the **Advanced settings** link and scroll down to the **Opening Documents in the Browser** setting.
6. Select the **Open in the client application** option.
7. Click the **OK** button at the bottom of the screen.

You just changed the default open behavior for browser-enabled documents. Clicking a document in the library will now prompt you to directly open it in the corresponding client app.

How it works...

As we saw in earlier recipes, working on the client has its advantages as well as drawbacks. This means you will want to carefully choose the default open behavior based on the specific needs of your team. Also, note that since you can only edit Microsoft Office documents directly in the client, this setting will only impact those file types.

Other files will continue to open in the browser (for file types that support browser viewing) or will get downloaded, based on the file type.

Some of the other settings relevant to documents are as follows:

- **General Settings – Advanced settings – Offline client availability**: This setting prevents documents in this library from being synced locally using the OneDrive sync. Note that users can still download these documents – it's just that they will not be synced through the OneDrive sync client.

> We will learn more about OneDrive and the sync client in *Chapter 6, OneDrive*.

- **General Settings – Column default value settings:** This is one of the more useful but overlooked settings in SharePoint Online. This settings page helps you to define default metadata values for your library, based on the folder that the documents are being saved to. As an example, let's assume there's a `Policies` library on your intranet site that is used to share the policies across various departments in your organization. The library has department-based folders (such as `Communications`, `Finance`, and `HR`) and then sub-folders to hold relevant policy documents. Let's also assume the library has a metadata column called `Department` so you can tag each policy document by the department it belongs to. You can now define default values for this column so that any documents uploaded to the library get automatically tagged by the department name depending on the folder they are being uploaded to. An example of this is shown in the following screenshot:

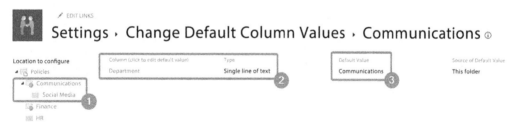

Figure 5.31: Setting default values for document metadata

In the preceding screenshot, **1** represents the folder (and any subfolders) for which the default metadata is being defined, **2** represents the metadata column (and its type) for which the value is being configured, and **3** represents the default value that will be applied when documents are uploaded to the folder.

- **Permissions and Management – Manage files which have no checked-in version:** This page shows a list of all files that do not have a checked-in version. We will learn about this setting as part of the next recipe, *Versioning settings, content approval, and document checkout*.

There are a lot of other settings that are not mentioned here so we stay focused on what's important for everyone. Readers are, however, encouraged to independently explore the many other settings through the library settings page.

See also

- The *Viewing and changing list settings* recipe in *Chapter 4, Lists and Libraries in SharePoint Online*
- The *Viewing and editing documents in the browser* recipe in this chapter
- The *Viewing and editing documents in the client* recipe in this chapter
- The *Enabling versioning and requiring checkout* recipe in this chapter
- The *Adding a content type to a list or library* recipe in *Chapter 13, Term Store and Content Types in SharePoint Online*

Versioning settings, content approval, and document checkout

The **Versioning Settings** page lets you control various settings related to document life cycle management, such as document versioning, approval, checkout, and draft document visibility.

In this recipe, we will change the versioning settings to require document *checkout*. Enabling this option results in the users having to first *check out* the document before they can make changes to it. This essentially locks down the document exclusively for their editing use. Once a document is checked out, other users will not be able to edit that document unless it's checked in again by the user editing it. Anyone with **Read** access or higher can still view the document. However, the version of the document that they will see is the one that was last checked in. They will not see the edits that the user who checked out the document is currently making until after they *check in* the document.

Getting ready

You will need **Edit**, **Design**, or **Full Control** access to the library for which you'd like to view or change the versioning settings. Alternatively, you will need to be part of the Members or Owners site groups to edit these settings.

How to do it...

To require *check out* for the documents in a library, follow these steps:

1. Browse to the **Settings** page as described in the previous recipe.
2. Click **Versioning settings** in the **General Settings** section.
3. On the **Versioning Settings** page, scroll all the way down to the **Require Check Out** section.
4. Select **Yes** for **Require documents to be checked out before they can be edited?**.
5. Click **OK** to save your changes.

6. Go back to the library by clicking on the library name in the breadcrumb navigation, as shown in the following screenshot:

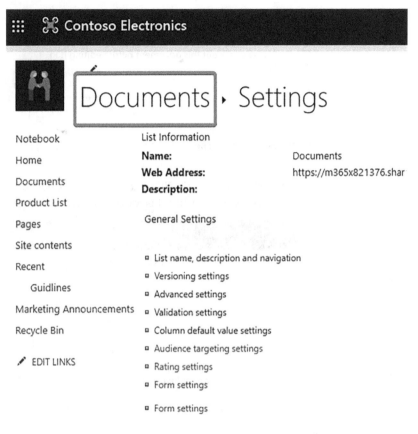

Figure 5.32: Selecting the library name from the Settings page

7. Click any document to open it.

8. If your document opened in the browser, you will notice a new **Edit Document** menu option in the top-right corner of the screen, as shown in the following screenshot:

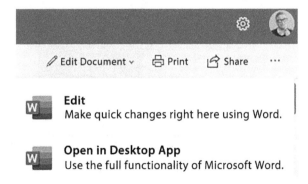

Figure 5.33: An Edit Document menu now appears if checkout is activated

9. Click **Edit** and notice that Office Online now requires you to check out the document before editing it:

Microsoft Word

 Please check out this document before editing it in Word.

Open in Reading View

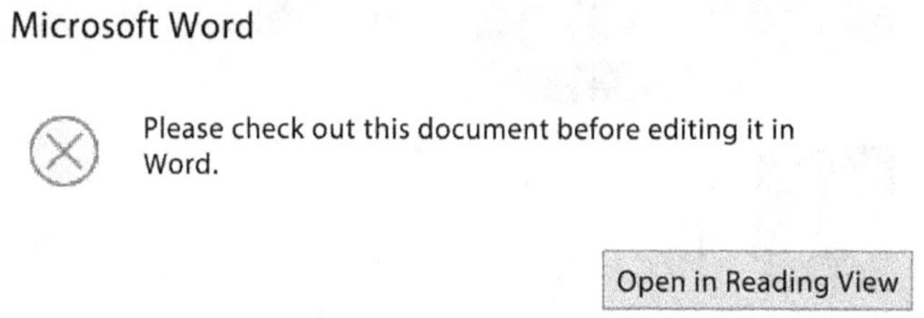

Figure 5.34: Popup for checking out appears when selecting Edit

This prompt will look different in different types of Office documents. For example, at the time of writing, it looks like this for PowerPoint presentations:

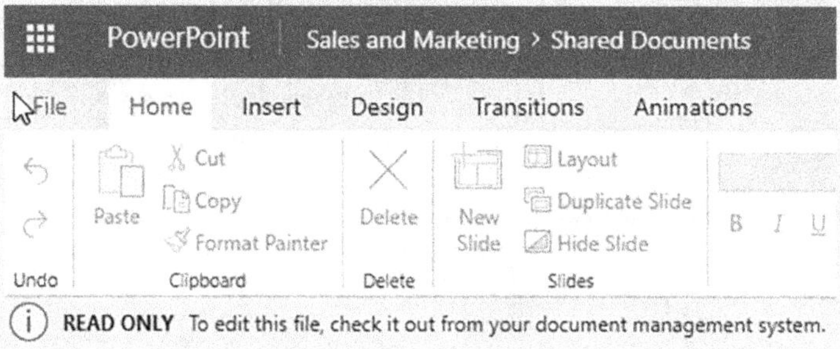

Figure 5.35: Prompt for checking out when using PowerPoint

10. Close the browser tab containing the document and go back to the library.
11. Click the ellipses next to the document name.
12. Click **More** and then **Check out**, as shown in the following screenshot:

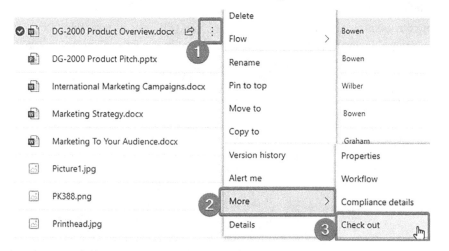

Figure 5.36: Navigation to check out a document

13. Click on the document to open it again in a new browser window.

14. Notice that the **Edit Document** option no longer appears, and you are now able to directly make changes to it.

15. Close the browser tab to go back to the library once you have made the required changes to your document.

16. In the library view, click the ellipses next to the document name again and then click **More**.

17. You can now click **Discard check out** to undo your changes or click **Check in** to save your changes to the document, as shown in the following screenshot:

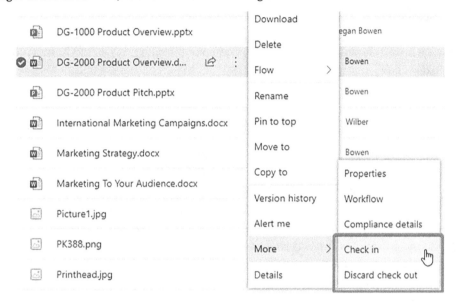

Figure 5.37: Options to discard or save changes to a document

18. Clicking **Check in** opens a window that lets you enter check-in comments, as shown in the following screenshot:

Figure 5.38: Adding a comment when saving changes to a document

Check-in comments are optional but are highly recommended. These comments should meaningfully describe the changes that you've made. Users with access to the document can then view these comments using the document version history and subsequently understand the changes that were made to the document throughout its life cycle.

19. Then, click **Check in** again on the comments screen to save your changes and make them visible to others.

You just saw how to enable document checkout for your library. You also saw how to work with documents in a library that requires you to check them out before they can be edited in a browser. The process is a little different for documents that open in the client. We will look at that process as part of the next section.

How it works...

Requiring document checkout is not usually recommended due to the following reasons:

- **You cannot co-author:** Checking out a document locks it for your exclusive editing and no one else can make changes to it unless it's checked in again. For this reason, co-authoring is not possible on documents in a library that requires document checkout.

- **Additional steps are required to create and edit files:** For libraries that require checkout, additional steps, such as checking out the documents and then checking them back in, are needed for the documents to be created and for the changes to be visible to others. These additional steps are usually a deterrent to user adoption.

- **People forget to check in:** It is not uncommon for users to forget to check in their changes. At other times, users accidentally check out the wrong documents for various reasons. This leaves stale checked-out documents in these libraries. Someone with appropriate access then needs to go back and either discard these documents (which results in the users losing their changes) or contact individuals to check in their documents. It can become cumbersome and time-consuming for library owners to do that.

It makes sense to require checking out in these situations:

- **Large viewers and very few collaborators:** Requiring checkout inherently allows the document author to make and save changes to it without making those changes visible to the rest of the viewers of the file. Others continue to see the previously checked-in document. This is useful in scenarios where you have very few people authoring the documents in that library but a large audience viewing them. Examples of these libraries are organization policy documents, guides, expense form templates, and other Excel templates.

- **Required metadata:** If you have libraries that require metadata to be entered, enforcing the Check-out/check-in process ensures that the metadata is filled in. If checkout is not required and the users save the document without entering the mandatory metadata, SharePoint will provide an indicator that the metadata is missing but will still allow the users to save such documents. If, however, Check-out/check-in is enabled on that library, SharePoint will prevent users from checking in the documents unless all the metadata required is entered.

Other versioning settings

Versioning settings additionally let you control the following options for your SharePoint lists and libraries:

- **Content Approval:** This setting allows you to control whether new documents or revisions to existing documents in the library should undergo content approval or review before they become visible to other users. This is a useful feature if you would like your documents to be reviewed and/or approved before they are visible to a broader group of visitors to your site or library. An **Approval Status** column is added to the library once content approval is enabled for it. When a new document is uploaded or changes to an existing document are submitted for such a library, the status of the document is changed to **Pending**. Only users that have the authority to approve documents (typically users having the **Design** or **Full Control** permission to the actual document) can view newly added documents or view changes to existing documents at that point. These approvers can then approve or reject the changes and the **Approval Status** column for the document is updated accordingly. Upon approval, the changes in the document become visible to regular users. You can read more about content approval in this support article here: `https://packt.link/require-approval`.

- **Document Version History:** The different options within this setting allow you to specify whether a copy of the document is maintained each time it is edited. Versioning is turned off for lists by default, but you can turn it on. For libraries, versioning is always on and cannot be turned off. In addition to enabling major versions (1, 2, 3...) you can also enable minor versions (1.0, 1.1, 1.2 ...). Minor versions are typically only used along with content approval and in publishing scenarios where you would like to check in your draft (minor) changes from time to time. This also allows content approvers to review the changes before they are published as a major version and become visible to everyone that has access to the item. In addition to enabling major versions (and optionally minor versions), you can also set a limit on the number of versions that SharePoint should keep.

 Limiting the number of versions is useful for older/on-premises versions of SharePoint. This was necessitated by the fact that SharePoint used to store duplicate copies of a document for every single version created, and this put a huge burden on the underlying on-premises infrastructure, depending on the number and size of the documents and libraries. SharePoint Online (and newer on-premises versions), however, save the original document in its entirety and then only store the changes from that point on. This is much more efficient and, as a result, limiting document versions now is not as necessary.

Once versioning is enabled, SharePoint maintains an audit trail of all the edits that were made to your list item or document. You can use the ellipses next to a list item or a document to view all the changes that were previously made to that item by date and time. If checkout was required for the library, this screen will also show you any check-in comments that your co-workers might have entered to describe the changes made to the document as part of that check-in.

As shown in the following screenshot, you can also click on a particular date and time entry to view, restore, or delete a historical version of the item at that point in time:

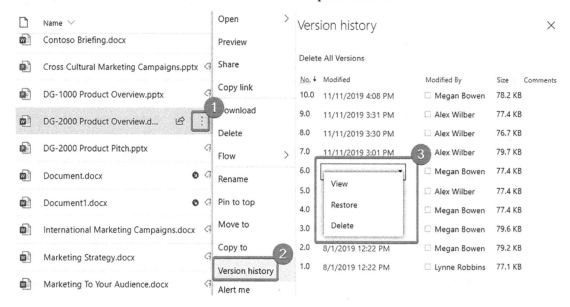

Figure 5.39: Reviewing version history for a file

- **Draft Item Security:** This setting allows you to specify who can see document drafts in your library. This setting is only available if minor (draft) versions are enabled in your library or if you have required content approvals for items in your list or library. You would typically keep this option set to the default value, which only allows the document author, approvers, and library owners to see the draft (minor) versions of the documents.

- **Require Check out:** As we have seen, you can use this setting to specify whether users need to check out documents before they can make changes to them. We saw this setting in great detail in the preceding recipe.

There's more...

In this section, we will discuss the effect of requiring checkout and enabling versioning on co-authoring and opening documents in the client.

Checkout process for documents that open in the client

The preceding recipe described the steps to check out and open documents in a browser. This experience is a little different when you open your documents directly in the desktop client or app. You will see a message at the top of the client app if your library requires documents to be checked out and you open a document from such a library in the corresponding client app:

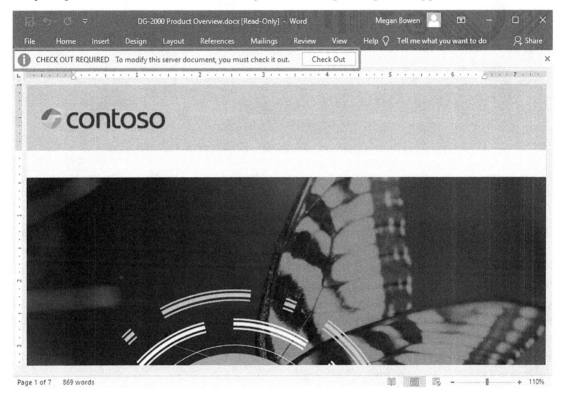

Figure 5.40: Checking out while using a desktop app

You can then click **Check Out** and make changes to your document as usual. Since the document was opened from a SharePoint Online document library, your changes to it will automatically be saved to the library. You will, however, need to check in the document for your changes to be visible to others. To do so, follow these steps:

1. Click the **File** menu and then **Info**.
2. Click **Check In** to initiate the check-in process.
3. Enter the check-in comments describing the changes you've made.

4. Click **OK** to check in your changes to the document, as shown in the following screenshot:

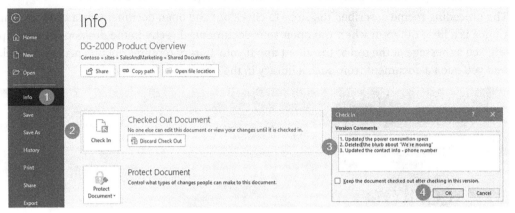

Figure 5.41: Navigation for checking in any changes to a document

This will then check in the document and make your changes visible to others in the organization.

Co-authoring and versioning settings

When checkout is not required in a library and two or more users are working with the same document from that library, SharePoint will keep synchronizing and saving the changes being concurrently made by the users. This **Save** operation occurs frequently (within a matter of seconds). Each time, SharePoint will save a version of the document and record the name of the person who made the changes when the **Save** operation occurred. **AutoSave** is, however, disabled when document checkout is required. Consequently, SharePoint will only save the draft versions when you explicitly click the **Save** button in the corresponding app. It will also only publish the final version of the document that was last checked in by the user instead of saving multiple versions for each **Save** operation when the document was checked out to the user editing it.

See also

- The *Viewing and editing documents in the browser* recipe in this chapter
- The *Viewing and editing documents in the client* recipe in this chapter
- The *Viewing and changing list settings* recipe in *Chapter 4, Lists and Libraries in SharePoint Online*
- The *Viewing and changing list permissions* recipe in *Chapter 4, Lists and Libraries in SharePoint Online*

Learn more on Discord

To join the Discord community for this book – where you can share feedback, ask questions to the author, and learn about new releases – follow the QR code below:

`https://packt.link/powerusers`

6

OneDrive

OneDrive is a cloud-based storage solution for your files. In that sense, it has a lot of capabilities in common with libraries in SharePoint. The key difference between OneDrive and SharePoint libraries is that while libraries enable you to work on team (shared) documents, you would use OneDrive to typically work on documents and files that are private to you. It is your personal space for files that belong just to you and are not ready to be shared with a wider team. Beyond this, there are a few other key differences between the two, which we will cover in later sections of this chapter, but for the most part, your OneDrive area is a simplified document library that you own. You can add, update, and delete files or folders in your OneDrive area as you would in any other document library. You can then share these files with others in your organization as well as those external to your organization (if your organization permits it), and in the process of doing so, grant them viewing or editing rights to these files.

 If you started with a file in OneDrive that is now ready to be shared with a wider audience, you can easily *move* it to a library on a SharePoint site or to Teams using the **Move to** feature.

As with any other file in a SharePoint Online library, you can view and edit your OneDrive files from a multitude of mobile and desktop devices. OneDrive also comes with a **client app** that you can install on your devices. This app (also referred to as the **OneDrive sync** app) maintains on-demand copies of your files for offline viewing and editing. It also ensures that any updates you make to these files locally on your device (mobile or desktop) are replicated to your online OneDrive storage area and to any other devices that run the app. The app also lets you share files with your co-workers from any device without you having to visit OneDrive online on Microsoft 365.

OneDrive comes in two different forms:

• **OneDrive for personal use:** You get personal (non-work) online storage when you set up a free or paid Microsoft home or personal account. You can use your personal OneDrive to store documents, photos, videos, and other files in the cloud and share them with your friends and family.

You can get started with a free account, which gives you limited free space (5 GB at the time of writing). It lets you and your family, or friends, view and edit various file types on the cloud. This also includes co-authoring capabilities for Microsoft Office documents. You can also install the OneDrive – Personal sync app to sync your files and work with them on your favorite devices (including mobile/cellular devices).

- **OneDrive for business use:** This is an online storage area offered through your **work or school account**. You get 1 TB of storage for individual use by default, but your organization can adjust it. Your account and certain account policies, such as external sharing, are managed by your organization. If permitted by your organization, you can additionally install the OneDrive app to sync files onto your favorite devices and work with them.

You can, potentially, have access to both versions of OneDrive—through your work or school and through your personal Microsoft account. You can install both versions of the sync client in parallel on the same device and concurrently work with both work and personal documents.

The recipes in this chapter will show you how to work with the files in OneDrive provided by your school or work account, although most of the recipes will also apply to your personal OneDrive account. We will also learn how to use the OneDrive app to locally sync your files and how to share them with others within and outside your organization.

In this chapter, we will cover the following recipes:

- Uploading a file to OneDrive
- Syncing files and folders
- Sharing a file

Uploading a file to OneDrive

Like we saw in earlier chapters on SharePoint, saving files online also makes sharing easier as it lets you share direct links to your file, rather than having to send over copies of the file each time. This enables you to maintain a single version of your file. You, and others that the file is shared with, can continue to make changes to that one single copy of that file, and everyone can easily see these changes as they happen.

In *Chapter 5, Document Management in SharePoint Online*, you learned how to browse to a SharePoint document library and create a new file or upload an existing file to it. In this recipe, you will learn how to browse to your OneDrive account and upload an existing file to it.

Getting ready

There are no special requirements for accessing OneDrive. As long as you have access to SharePoint Online, you will also have access to OneDrive.

How to do it...

To upload a file to OneDrive, take the following steps:

1. Browse to `https://office.com` or any other page in your organization's Microsoft 365 tenant. If you are not already logged in, you may be asked to sign in with your work credentials.

2. Once you sign in, click the app launcher in the top-left corner of the page and then click **One-Drive.** The following screenshot shows you what this looks like from the SharePoint Online home page:

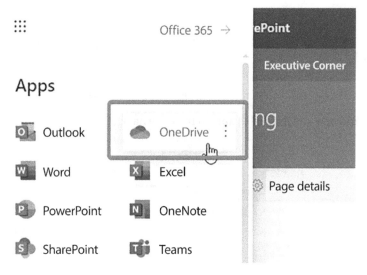

Figure 6.1: Opening the OneDrive home page

3. You will then be taken to your OneDrive home page, which shows you:

   • Files which may be relevant to you.

   • Recent files which were authored by or shared with you (across your organization's SharePoint sites, Teams, or OneDrive).

- Recent SharePoint lists accessed by you.

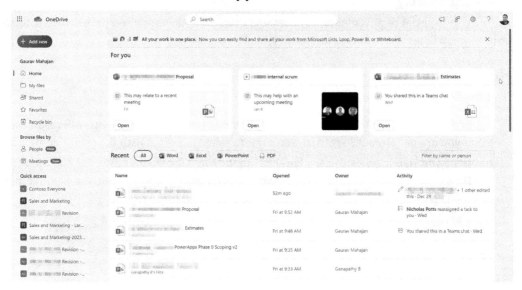

Figure 6.2: Recent lists

4. Click **Add new** and then **Files upload** from the navigation menu towards the top left of the page:

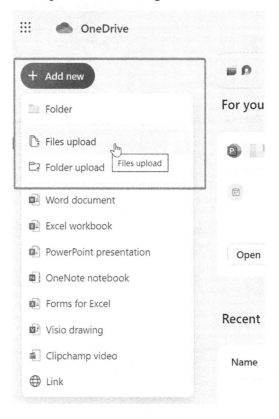

Figure 6.3: Uploading files in OneDrive

> Just like a regular document library in SharePoint, you can simultaneously select and upload multiple files and folders to your OneDrive area with this option. You can also choose the **Folder upload** option from the **Add new** menu to upload an entire folder and its contents instead of uploading a single file.

5. You will receive an on-screen notification confirming that the file was uploaded to your One-Drive My files. Clicking the link will take you to the **My files** area of OneDrive.

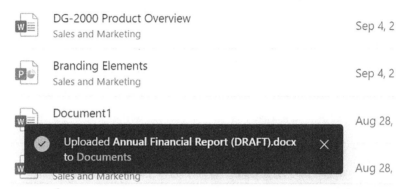

Figure 6.4: Notification for an uploaded file

That's it! You just learned how to browse to your OneDrive and upload a file to it.

How it works...

Saving your file to OneDrive and, in broader terms, saving it to the cloud, lets you access it from anywhere. Doing so also makes it easy for you to share these files with your colleagues. In addition, you can sync these files to your device using the OneDrive app and work with them offline as and when needed. We will see how to do that in the *Syncing files and folders* recipe later in this chapter.

File and folder operations

Your OneDrive home page is a simplified view of a document library (which you own). Most of the actions that you can perform in SharePoint document libraries can be performed here too. We discussed most of these actions in the following chapters:

- *Chapter 2, Introduction to SharePoint Online*
- *Chapter 5, Document Management in SharePoint Online*

Similar to those actions, you can perform the following actions in your OneDrive area:

- Create new files or folders
- Upload existing files or folders

You can now apply colors to the folders in your OneDrive (and also folders in SharePoint document libraries):

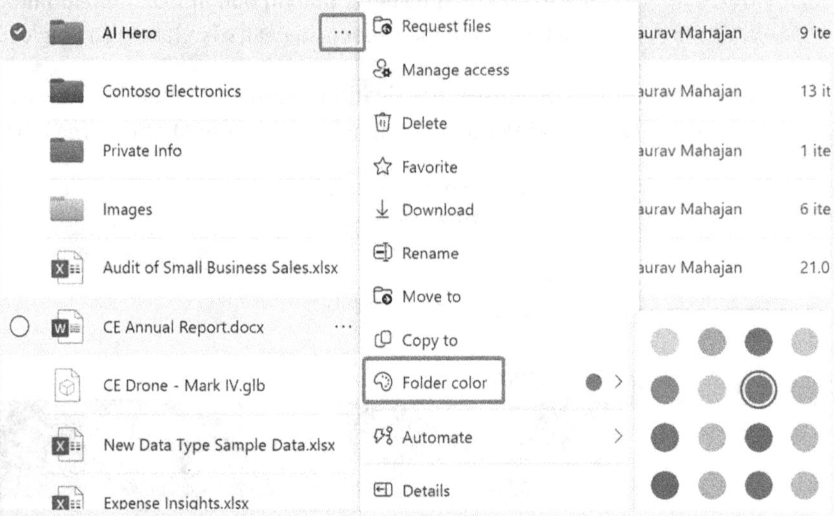

Figure 6.5: Coloring files

This helps in visually classifying or identifying your folders. For example, you may want to color code your personal folder with a unique color and those for one or more clients with a different color. When you copy or move folders, folder colors travel with them. When you share folders with other users, they also see the folder colors that you set.

- Save Microsoft Office documents and other supported document types directly to OneDrive using the **Save As** dialog:

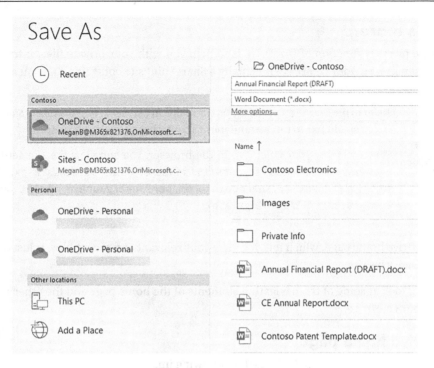

Figure 6.6: Saving a file in OneDrive

- View and edit existing files in your OneDrive
- Delete files or folders
- Move or copy files and folders between OneDrive and SharePoint
- Share files or folders with others

In addition to using the online browser-based interface, you can also perform these actions using the OneDrive app. We will describe this in more detail in the *Syncing files and folders* and *Sharing a file* recipes later in this chapter.

You can upload any file type to your OneDrive, but the maximum file size should not exceed 250 GB (at the time of writing). You can also view/preview hundreds of file types in the browser. The *Viewing and editing documents in the browser* recipe in *Chapter 5, Document Management in SharePoint Online*, discussed the file types that are supported for viewing and editing in Microsoft 365.

If you are using a mobile device, you can use the OneDrive app to scan a document, whiteboard, or business card directly to your OneDrive account, as well as to upload existing photos, videos, or files from it. Go to `https://packt.link/OneDrive-mobile` to find out how to do that.

There's more...

While the primary function of OneDrive is to help you with your private files, it truly is more than just a single library. Your OneDrive is actually a SharePoint site collection that you are the owner of.

 Refer to the *Creating a modern team site* recipe in Chapter 2, *Introduction to SharePoint Online*, if you would like to understand more about what site collections are.

When viewing your OneDrive in the browser, you can view the site settings page by replacing the part after_layouts/15/ in the URL with `settings.aspx`. (For example, `https://tenant-my.sharepoint.com/personal/gauravm_tenant_onmicrosoft_com/_layouts/15/settings.aspx`)

Your OneDrive home page, which lets you view your relevant and recent files, is just one of the pages on your OneDrive site.

Next, we'll look at some of the navigation elements of the home page and the other pages which are part of your OneDrive.

OneDrive home page

Your OneDrive home page will look like the following image:

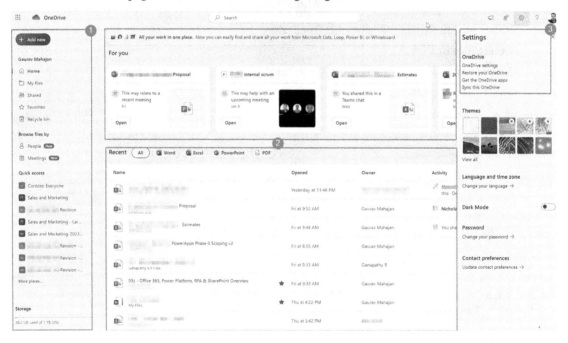

Figure 6.7: OneDrive Home page layout

Let's go over the various sections from the screenshot above starting with the links in section 1:

- **Add new:** Clicking this button allows you to add or upload new or existing files and folders. We read about this function earlier, in the *How to do it...* section of this recipe.
- **My files:** The **My files** page enables you to interact and work with your private files. In addition to viewing, uploading, and downloading your files from this page, you can also perform other standard document library functions such as (but not limited to) moving or copying files and sharing them with others. You can also **Favorite** (or **Unfavorite**) a file by clicking the ☆ icon next to it, as shown below:

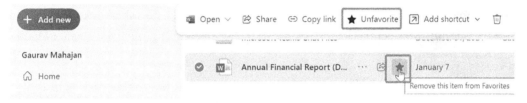

Figure 6.8: Favoriting a file

- Doing so results in the file additionally showing on the **Favorites** page in your OneDrive (discussed in more detail below)
- **Shared:** Here, you can view the OneDrive files that others have shared with you or those which you have shared with others:

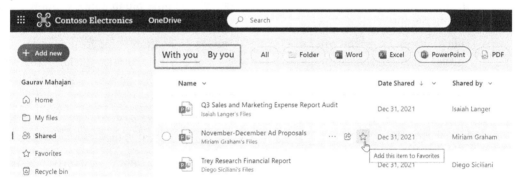

Figure 6.9: Shared files

- You can also carry out limited actions such as opening/downloading the file, further sharing it, or marking it as favorite.
- **Favorites:** You can view all your favorite files in one place here. You can carry out further limited actions from here, such as viewing the file, opening the original file location, sharing it or unfavoriting it (which removes the file from the **Favorites** view).
- **Recycle bin:** Click this tab to show your recently deleted OneDrive files. From here, you can select a file and permanently delete it or restore it to your OneDrive. Files stay in the recycle bin for a total of 93 days. Please refer to the *Deleting and restoring a file* recipe in *Chapter 2, Introduction to SharePoint Online,* for more details on the recycle bin.

- **Browse files by:** The links in this section allow you to view shared files by people or files shared in meetings. Clicking the **People** link will show you the most recent files shared between you and that person, as shown in the image below:

Figure 6.10: Browsing files by People

- You can further click the person's name to see a few of all files shared between you and them.

- Clicking the **Meetings** link will show your past meetings in which documents where shared:

Figure 6.11: Past meetings

- Clicking the meeting name will show you all files that were shared in that meeting, including the meeting recording. Clicking the filename will open the file in a new window (assuming the file supports online viewing).

- **Quick access:** Here, you will see a listing of the top eight SharePoint document libraries that you use the most. You can pin libraries so they always show in this list. Clicking **More libraries** toward the bottom of the list will take you to a page where you can see an expanded list of your most frequented libraries.

- **Storage:** This section shows your allocated and used storage space. You can click on the hyper-linked used storage space to see all your OneDrive files sorted in descending order of file size.

Note that we discussed section **2** of *Figure 6.7* earlier, in step 2 of the *"How to do"* it section of the recipe.

Section 3 of *Figure 6.7* shows you the OneDrive settings that you would see when you click the gear (🔧) icon towards the top-right corner of the page, and then click **OneDrive settings**:

- **OneDrive settings | Notification:** Clicking the OneDrive settings link brings you to the OneDrive **Notification Settings** page. This page lets you view and change your notification settings. The notifications you can manage from here are self-explanatory, so we will not go over them here.

- **OneDrive settings** à **More Settings:** Some settings on this page are either legacy settings or far too advanced for the scope of this book. There is, however, one setting that's worth men-tioning here:

- **Run sharing report**: Clicking on this link generates a report that lists all the files or folders that you have shared, who you have shared them with, and what permissions they have on each file or folder. It then places a copy of this report in a folder of your choice in your OneDrive. The following screenshot shows an example of the information that is generated in this report:

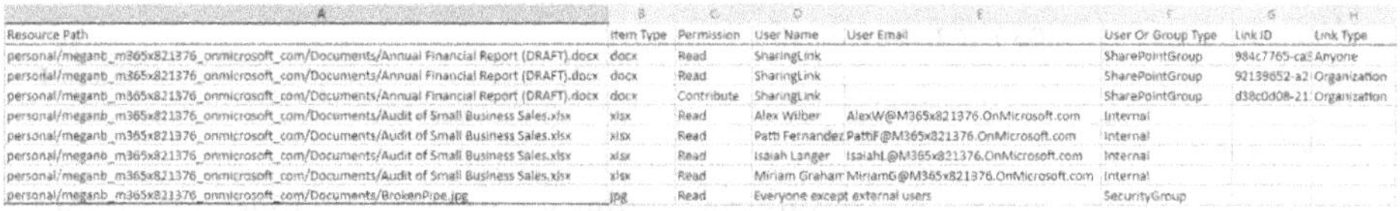

Resource Path	Item Type	Permission	User Name	User Email	User Or Group Type	Link ID	Link Type
personal/meganb_m365x821376_onmicrosoft_com/Documents/Annual Financial Report (DRAFT).docx	docx	Read	SharingLink		SharePointGroup	984c7765-ca	Anyone
personal/meganb_m365x821376_onmicrosoft_com/Documents/Annual Financial Report (DRAFT).docx	docx	Read	SharingLink		SharePointGroup	92139652-a2	Organization
personal/meganb_m365x821376_onmicrosoft_com/Documents/Annual Financial Report (DRAFT).docx	docx	Contribute	SharingLink		SharePointGroup	d38c0d08-21	Organization
personal/meganb_m365x821376_onmicrosoft_com/Documents/Audit of Small Business Sales.xlsx	xlsx	Read	Alex Wilber	AlexW@M365x821376.OnMicrosoft.com	Internal		
personal/meganb_m365x821376_onmicrosoft_com/Documents/Audit of Small Business Sales.xlsx	xlsx	Read	Patti Fernandez	PattiF@M365x821376.OnMicrosoft.com	Internal		
personal/meganb_m365x821376_onmicrosoft_com/Documents/Audit of Small Business Sales.xlsx	xlsx	Read	Isaiah Langer	IsaiahL@M365x821376.OnMicrosoft.com	Internal		
personal/meganb_m365x821376_onmicrosoft_com/Documents/Audit of Small Business Sales.xlsx	xlsx	Read	Miriam Graham	MiriamG@M365x821376.OnMicrosoft.com	Internal		
personal/meganb_m365x821376_onmicrosoft_com/Documents/BrokenPipe.jpg	jpg	Read	Everyone except external users		SecurityGroup		

Figure 6.12: Sharing report information

- **Restore your OneDrive**: The OneDrive app synchronizes files from your devices to OneDrive online (and vice versa). If the files on your device become corrupted—for example, by malware or a virus—you can use this feature to restore your OneDrive files. You can read more about this feature here: `https://packt.link/OneDrive-restore`.
- **Get the OneDrive apps**: Clicking this link takes you to the OneDrive sync app download page. We will learn more about the OneDrive sync app in the next recipe, **Syncing files and folders**.
- **Sync this OneDrive**: Clicking this link uses the OneDrive sync app to sync OneDrive with your computer. We will learn more about OneDrive sync in the next recipe, **Syncing files and folders**.

See also

- The *Creating a modern team site* recipe in *Chapter 2, Introduction to SharePoint Online*
- The *Uploading an existing document to the library* recipe in *Chapter 2, Introduction to SharePoint Online*
- The *Deleting and restoring a file* recipe in *Chapter 2, Introduction to SharePoint Online*
- The *Viewing and editing documents in the browser* recipe in *Chapter 5, Document Management in SharePoint Online*
- The *Moving and copying documents* recipe in *Chapter 5, Document Management in SharePoint Online*
- *Chapter 15, Microsoft Delve*
- The *Sharing a file* recipe in this chapter

Syncing files and folders

OneDrive online comes with the OneDrive app, which can be installed on a multitude of devices. The OneDrive app lets you work with your files locally, as you would with any other file on your computer or mobile.

In this recipe, we will look at how to sync your OneDrive online files to your local computer.

Getting ready

You should have the OneDrive sync client installed on your machine or have appropriate permissions to be able to install it. The following steps assume that you are using Windows as your OS. While the underlying concepts are the same, the installation steps for OneDrive, which we have described below for Windows, are different for macOS. Refer to `https://packt.link/OneDrive-mac` for the installation and configuration steps for macOS.

How to do it...

You can use the OneDrive sync app to sync either your OneDrive files and/or your SharePoint files locally to your computer.

To sync files from your OneDrive account, take the following steps:

1. Browse to OneDrive in the Microsoft 365 portal.

2. Click the **Sync this OneDrive** option in the **Settings** menu, as shown here:

Figure 6.13: Sync option

3. You will now be prompted to launch OneDrive on your computer. You will also receive the following message, indicating that OneDrive is launching on your computer. The message also provides a link to download OneDrive if you haven't already done so:

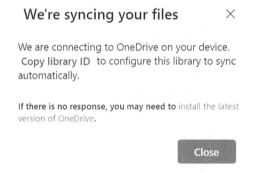

Figure 6.14: Syncing message when launching OneDrive

4. If this is your first time signing in, follow these steps:

    •   When prompted, enter your credentials in the OneDrive app:

Figure 6.15: Login page

•   Next, you will be prompted to select a location for OneDrive to store synced files. You can keep the default location suggested by OneDrive or change it if needed.

•   You will then be prompted for Office to remember your sign-in information for other apps as well. Click **OK** at this step.

•   The next screen will ask if you would like to use OneDrive to back up your files. It's usually a good idea to do so. You can select the folders you'd like to back up and click **Start backup**, or click **I'll do it later** to skip setting up the back up for now. You can always set this up later through the settings screen of the OneDrive sync app.

•   Next, the setup wizard will take you through a few information screens and will also prompt you to get the mobile app. You may want to set up the mobile app if you'd like to access OneDrive files on the go on your mobile devices.

•   You will then be prompted to open the newly installed OneDrive app.

•   OneDrive will now create a local sync folder and will start to sync your files.

5. Once the app is installed, clicking the **Sync** option from OneDrive in your browser will start the OneDrive app, if it isn't already running, and will also give you the option to open the local OneDrive sync folder.

 Unless you disable it, the OneDrive app will automatically start when your computer starts. This ensures that your local files always stay synced with the online files.

6. The OneDrive icon will now show up in the Windows taskbar. You can right-click on this icon to see the status of recent sync operations. This is as shown in the following screenshot:

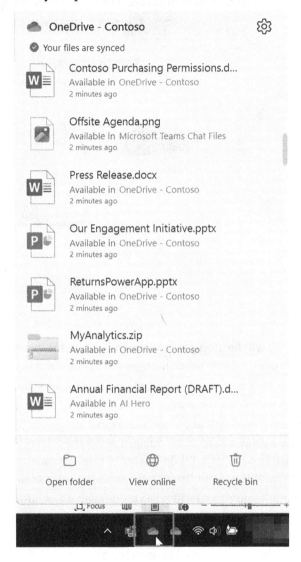

Figure 6.16: Checking sync status from the taskbar

 Note that if you have an account with more than one organization, or if you have a personal OneDrive account in addition to your organization's account, you will see a separate sync client for each of these accounts.

7. From here, you can also click on **Open folder** to open your OneDrive folder in Windows File Explorer. As the following screenshot shows, this folder shows all the files in your online OneDrive library:

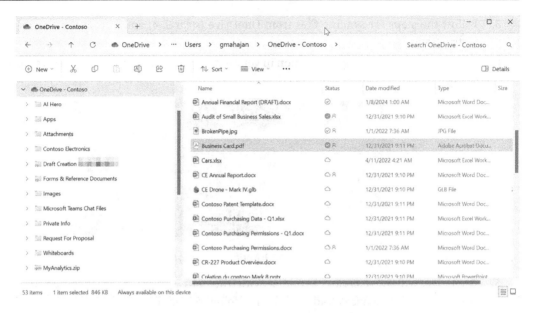

Figure 6.17: OneDrive visible in File Explorer

To sync the files and folders from a SharePoint library, take the following steps:

1. Browse to your SharePoint library.

2. Click the **Sync** option on the library's menu bar, as shown here:

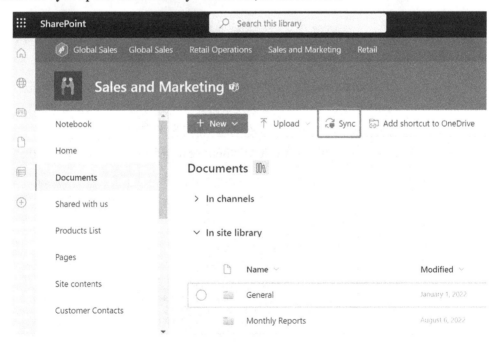

Figure 6.18: Sync option in a library

3. Follow the steps for syncing files from OneDrive (*steps 3, 4,* and *5* from the previous set of instructions).

4. You will see the following notification in your notification center once the sync is successfully set up:

Figure 6.19: Notification on sync setup

5. OneDrive will now create a folder with the name of your organization in the C:\ Users\<YourLoginName>\ folder or another folder of your choice, as shown here:

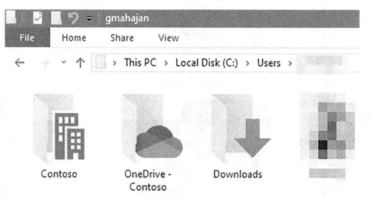

Figure 6.20: Name of OneDrive folder

6. As the following screenshot shows, it will then create a folder for each library that you sync:

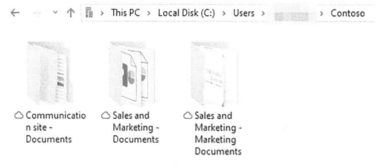

Figure 6.21: Folders created after syncing libraries

7. Opening or expanding the libraries in Windows Explorer will then show you a local representation of the online files and folders from that library:

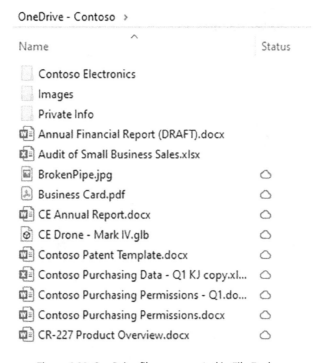

Figure 6.22: OneDrive files represented in File Explorer

Congratulations! You have just learned how to set up and configure the OneDrive sync locally. From this point on, you can work with the files locally on your computer.

How it works...

Once the OneDrive sync is set up, you can work on files in your local `OneDrive` folder, just as you would with files in any other folder on your computer. Any updates that you make to the files in your local `OneDrive` folder will also be automatically synced to your online OneDrive, and vice versa. You can add, view, edit, and delete files or folders locally as you normally would. You can also use the file explorer to organize your files within the local OneDrive folder. If you are connected to the internet, your changes will be copied over immediately to your online OneDrive and to other devices where you have OneDrive installed. If you are not connected to the internet while making these changes, OneDrive will continue to save the changes locally and sync them as soon as you get connected to the internet again. In the meantime, OneDrive will still let you work on the files and keep saving your changes locally.

 Once you have set up the sync client, you can easily move existing files from your computer over to OneDrive. To do so, simply right-click on the file(s), click **OneDrive**, then click **Move to OneDrive**. Doing so will move the files over to your local `OneDrive` folder and then automatically sync them over to OneDrive online.

The OneDrive app has various settings that enable you to control and manage your sync options.

OneDrive app settings

We are going to review the key OneDrive settings in this section.

Clicking the OneDrive icon and then clicking the gear icon (⚙) in the top-right corner shows the following options:

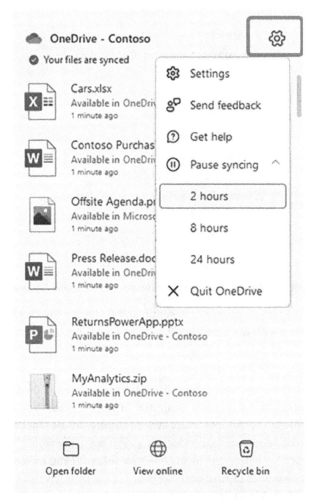

Figure 6.23: Opening OneDrive settings

We'll explain some of these options in the following list:

- **Settings:** This option opens the advanced settings for the OneDrive app. We will look at these settings shortly.
- **Pause syncing:** This enables you to pause the sync for **2**, **8**, or **24** hours. You can always resume the sync whenever you need to.

- **Quit OneDrive:** This closes the OneDrive sync client. Note that closing the sync client would mean that changes to your local OneDrive and SharePoint files will now be out of sync with the online files until the sync client is started again.

Clicking the **Settings** option from the preceding menu options opens the advanced settings dialog, which has the following tabs:

- **Sync and backup:** Most settings on this page are self-explanatory and you should leave them at their default selections. We will discuss some of the other key settings here:

    - **Backup:** The OneDrive sync client also enables you to back up your local files to the cloud. You can use this setting to select folders that you would like to back up to the cloud. It is recommended that you turn on this option so your local files are always backed up and available through the cloud in case there are issues with your computer.

      For personal OneDrive accounts, this is where you can also select whether you'd like to automatically save photos and videos to OneDrive when you connect a camera, phone, or any other device to your PC.

    - **Preferences:** You can also set additional preferences such as whether or not to start the OneDrive sync client when you sign in to Windows, whether the sync should pause if the computer is running on low battery, etc.

    - **Advanced settings – Files On-Demand:** The Files On-Demand feature allows access to all your cloud files locally while only downloading those files that you are actively working on. We will cover the Files On-Demand feature in greater detail in the next section, but it's worth noting here that the **Download all OneDrive files now** button in this setting allows you to pre-download all files on your OneDrive so they are all available to you even when you are offline. Please note that, depending on the number of files stored on your OneDrive and on the SharePoint Online libraries that you are syncing, this may cause significant local storage to be used on your device. It's therefore generally not recommended to pre-download all files unless you expect to be offline and need *all* files. You can always pre-download individual files that you may need if you are planning to be offline. We will cover this capability in more detail in the next section.

- **Account:** From this tab, you can:

    - Completely unlink your OneDrive account so the files are no longer synced with the current PC
    - Add a new account to sync to your PC
    - View a list of all libraries that you are (and are not) syncing

- For each library, you can then choose the folders that you would like to sync and also completely stop syncing that library on your PC:

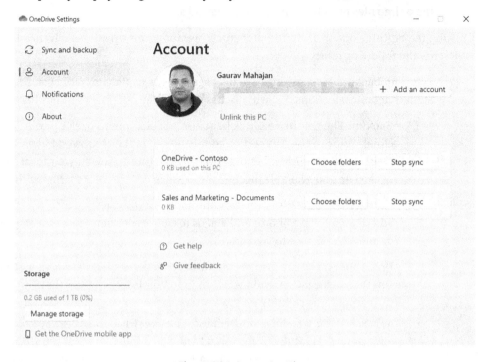

Figure 6.24: Account settings

- **Notifications:** The OneDrive sync client has a few built-in notifications. As an example, it can notify when a large number of files are deleted from the cloud. You can manage your notifications through the **Notifications** tab.

- **Manage storage:** Clicking this option opens your browser and takes you to the **Storage Metrics** page in your OneDrive. This page shows you a list of your OneDrive files and folders sorted in decreasing order of size. You can then use this information to delete large or unused files in case your OneDrive (online storage) is running out of space.

There's more...

In this section, we will first look at the **Add shortcut to OneDrive** feature, which is available for Share-Point document libraries.

We will then review the Files On-Demand feature of the OneDrive sync client. This feature enables you to download only those SharePoint and OneDrive files that you are currently working on, instead of synchronizing or downloading all the online files and folders from your OneDrive and SharePoint libraries at once.

Finally, we will look at why the sync app can sometimes fail to sync files, and how to identify and fix such sync issues.

Add a shortcut to OneDrive

When you sync a library or folder, it is synchronized in a separate folder on your local machine. This folder is different from your regular OneDrive folder and is usually the name of your organization as defined in your Office 365 tenant. In the screenshot below, you can see the two unique folders – one that is the name of your organization and contains a synchronized version of the **Documents** library from the **Sales and Marketing** site, and one that is a synced replica of the files and folders of your personal OneDrive library:

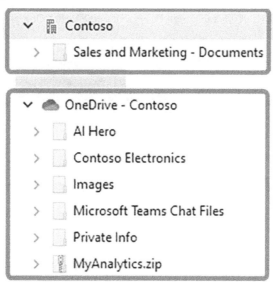

Figure 6.25: OneDrive represented in the File Explorer navigation bar

This can get confusing at times. This is where the **Add shortcut to OneDrive** menu option for the document libraries comes in handy:

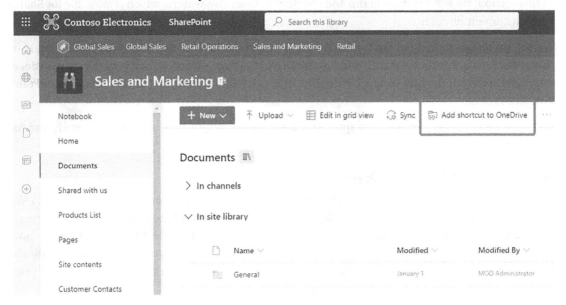

Figure 6.26: Add shortcut to OneDrive button

Clicking this menu within a library, or in a folder within a library, creates a shortcut for the library or folder within your OneDrive. This shortcut appears in your OneDrive online like so:

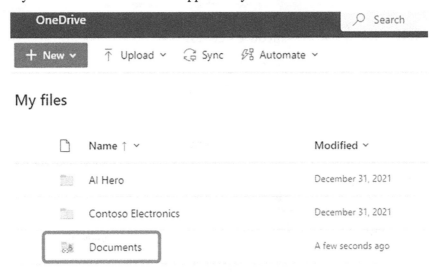

Figure 6.27: Shortcut appearing in OneDrive

It appears locally within the OneDrive synced folder on your computer as follows:

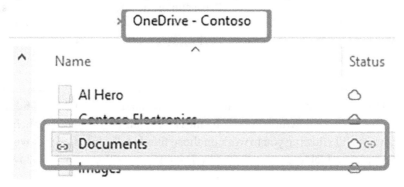

Figure 6.28: Shortcut appearing in File Explorer

This capability makes it convenient to access your online files in one place by giving you the ability to access them all from within your OneDrive.

You can read more about this capability and how to work with it here: `https://packt.link/OneDrive-shortcut`.

Please note that trying to sync a library and adding it as a shortcut to OneDrive can lead to sync issues. You can read more about these sync issues and how to resolve them at `https://packt.link/OneDrive-sync-error-1` and `https://packt.link/OneDrive-sync-error-2`.

Files On-Demand

The Files On-Demand feature lets you work with the files and folders in the cloud just like another file or folder on your PC, without pre-downloading all those files and folders beforehand. In doing so, it shows the sync status of the files using one of these icons:

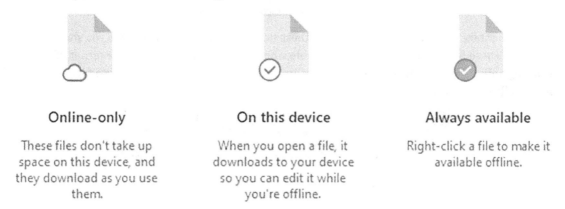

Figure 6.29: Explanation of sync status icons

You might not have the latest OneDrive app or the latest Windows 10 updates if you are unable to see the Files On-Demand feature. Please review the instructions at `https://packt.link/OneDrive-OnDemand` to look at potential reasons and also ensure you have the latest updates.

When you first set up the OneDrive sync for a library, OneDrive will only replicate the folders in that library or those from your OneDrive online. It will not download the actual files and will only create placeholders for them. By not downloading *all* the files from your online library, it helps save space on your computer, while still allowing you to work on those files locally, just as if they were other files on your device. These files and folders are indicated by a cloud icon, as shown in the following screenshot:

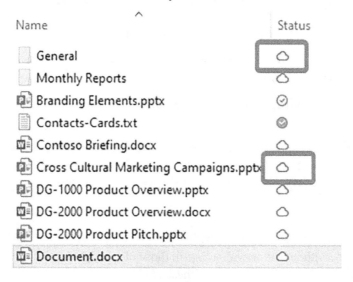

Figure 6.30: Sync status icons in File Explorer

So they don't take up space on your computer, these files are only downloaded when you start working on them. These files are therefore only available when you are connected to the internet. If you are working offline (that is, you are not connected to the internet), trying to open these files will result in the following error:

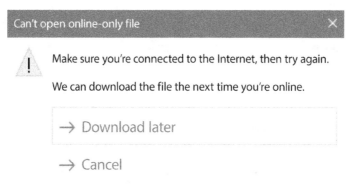

Figure 6.31: Error message when opening files while offline

Clicking **Download later** will download the file to your computer once you are online (and connected to the internet) again.

Once you open an online-only file on your device, the OneDrive app automatically downloads it before opening it locally. These files are indicated by a circle with a checkmark in it:

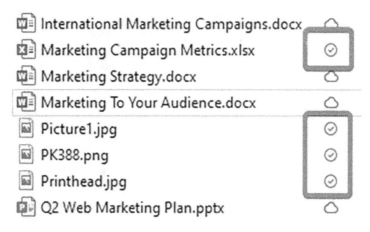

Figure 6.32: Icon for a downloaded OneDrive file

You can open these files at any time, even if you are not connected to the internet. OneDrive will then sync your changes to your online OneDrive area or to the corresponding SharePoint library when you next connect to the internet. Once you are done with your changes and you don't need to access the file locally—or if you'd like to remove the files from your local storage altogether—you can right-click on the OneDrive file or folder in question and then click **Free up space**. As the following screenshot shows, doing so will remove these local files and change their status to online-only, indicated by the cloud icon. Compare the icons in this screenshot to the status icons for these files shown earlier:

Figure 6.33: Icon for an online-only OneDrive file

Finally, you can make sure that a file (or all the files in a folder) is always available on your computer, even when you are offline. To do so, right-click on the file or folder and then click **Always keep on this device**. Doing so will change the status icon to a circle with a checkmark in it, as shown in the following screenshot:

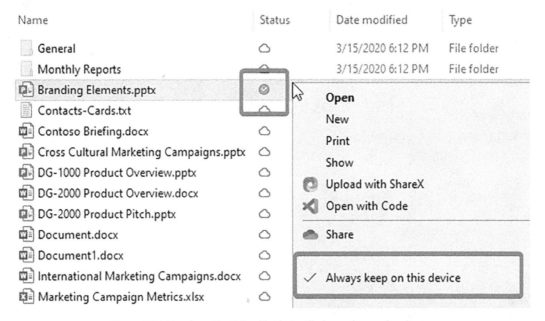

Figure 6.34: Icon for a OneDrive file that will always have a local copy

As mentioned earlier, you can always click **Free up space** to remove the local copies of these files or folders.

Note that the status icons and the OneDrive context menu shown in the previous screenshot will only appear in the OneDrive folders on your local device. Also, they will only show up when the OneDrive sync client is running.

Sync issues

The OneDrive sync app is very robust and has come a long way from when it was first introduced. One of the key gotchas of the sync client concerns filenames and invalid characters. Also, you may run into file lock issues and sync conflicts due to the nature of what the sync client does. You may find the following articles useful if you run into issues like this or if you would like to read more about the file naming conventions and restrictions:

*   Invalid filenames and file types in OneDrive and SharePoint: `https://packt.link/OneDrive-invalid-files`
*   Fix OneDrive sync problems: `https://packt.link/OneDrive-sync-issues`

Sharing a file

We saw how to share documents in the *Sharing a document* recipe in *Chapter 2, Introduction to SharePoint Online*. Sharing files or folders from OneDrive works in the same way. The one minor exception is that your organization can set up different sharing restrictions on the files stored in OneDrive versus those stored in SharePoint Online. For example, your organization may have turned off anonymous link sharing (where signing in is not required to view a shared document) for your SharePoint sites but may have enabled it for OneDrive.

In this recipe, we will use the OneDrive client to share a document from a locally synced OneDrive folder on our computer.

Getting ready

To share files directly from your computer, your organization should have enabled OneDrive and you should have the sync client installed on your machine. Other than that, there are no special requirements for sharing a file through OneDrive.

How to do it...

To share a file or folder from your computer, take the following steps:

1. Make sure the OneDrive sync client is running and then go to your local OneDrive folder.

2. Right-click on the file or folder that you would like to share and then click **OneDrive | Share**, as shown in the following screenshot:

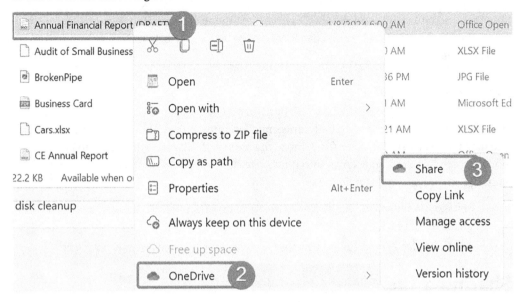

Figure 6.35: Option to share a file

3. This will open the OneDrive sharing dialog box with the default sharing option selected. As the following screenshot shows, the **People you specify can edit** option was shown for me, by default:

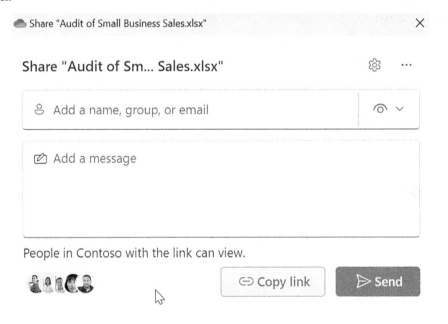

Figure 6.36: Sharing options

Note that the default sharing option that is presented to you is controlled by your organization. In the *Sharing a document* recipe in *Chapter 2, Introduction to Share-Point Online,* we saw the various other sharing options and how to switch to one of the other options.

4. As we saw in the *Sharing a document* recipe in *Chapter 2, Introduction to SharePoint Online,* we can select the people we want to share the document with. There is also an option to enter a message. After this, click **Send** to share the document with them. The person will receive an email containing a link to the document.

That's it! You have just learned how to directly share a link to a document stored on your OneDrive Business area from the OneDrive synced folder on your local machine.

How it works...

The sharing options that you will see when sharing from the OneDrive client will be the same as those that you will see from OneDrive online. The one advantage of directly sharing the files from your device is that you can share the link through the various apps installed on your machine, as shown in the screenshot below. Of course, if you are sharing a link this way, you will need to ensure that the person receiving the link is the intended recipient of the link and should have access to the file or folder that you are sharing with them.

You can also similarly share a document that's in your OneDrive area from within the document editing app that you are working on:

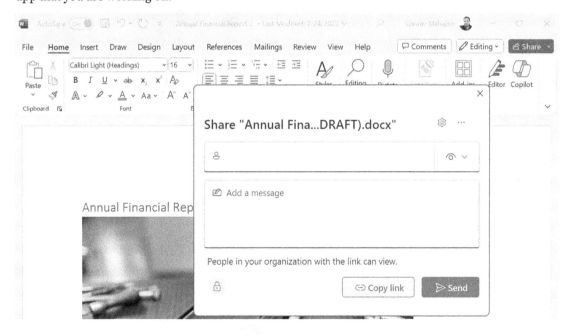

Figure 6.37: Sharing an open document

There's more...

We saw how to check document permissions in SharePoint Online in the *View existing permissions* section of the *Sharing a document* recipe in *Chapter 2, Introduction to SharePoint Online*. When you do that, the document information pane will also show you all the links that were used to grant access to the document and who they provide access to. You can use those steps to view existing permissions on a file stored on your OneDrive account.

If you are working on a OneDrive or SharePoint Online document from your local `OneDrive` synced folder, you can view the links for providing access right from the **Share** screen, which we discussed in the previous section. This is described in more detail in the section to follow.

Links granting access

To view the existing links that grant access to other individuals from OneDrive online, click the three dots to the right of the document and then click **Manage access**, as shown below:

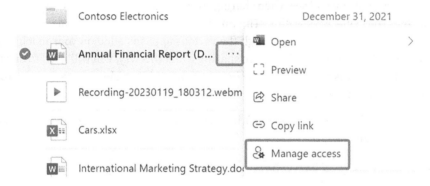

Figure 6.38: Managing OneDrive file access

To view the same thing from within the OneDrive folder on your computer, open the **Share** dialog and then simply view the list towards the bottom of the screen, as shown below:

Figure 6.39: Shared with section when sharing a file

You can mouse over each individual to see their name. You can also click anywhere in this list to see a detailed **Manage access** view, listing the access details along with the details of sharing links granting access to the document or folder, as shown here:

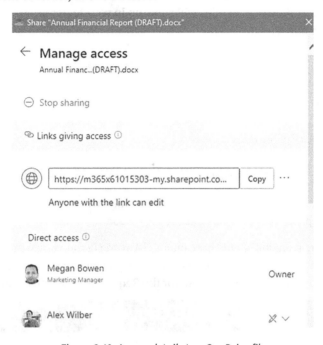

Figure 6.40: Access details to a OneDrive file

Please note that this screen will not show you any users that have access to the document through inherited permissions (if the document inherits permissions from the parent library). You will need to view the permissions of that document by browsing to the corresponding library in SharePoint Online. You can then view the permissions that users may have on a document by accessing the parent library. Please refer to the *Permission inheritance* topic in the *Determining and revoking permissions in a site* recipe of *Chapter 3, Modern Sites in SharePoint Online*.

Requesting files

As the name suggests, you can use this feature to request files from other users. The feature allows you to create a shareable link for a folder in OneDrive. You can then send the link to others so they can upload files to it.

People receiving the link will only be able to upload new files to it. They will not be able to see or edit existing files, even if they previously uploaded them. When uploading files, they will be asked to enter their first name and last name, and the filenames will automatically be prefixed with the full name that they enter. Additionally, the files will show up in your folder as modified/created by **Guest Contributor**, as shown below:

Figure 6.41: File details when using the Request files feature

The whole experience, both from the perspective of the link owner and those who receive the link, is documented here: `https://packt.link/requesting-files`.

Please note that your organization should have enabled **Anyone** (anonymous) links with **View**, **Edit**, and **Upload** permission for this feature to work. Also note that you will need to select a folder (and not just browse to it) in your OneDrive, as shown below, for the **Request files** option to appear in the menu bar:

Figure 6.42: Option to enable the Request files feature

This link provides concise guidance on what to look for if you are not seeing the **Request files** option even after selecting the appropriate folder in your OneDrive: `https://packt.link/enable-request-files`.

See also

- The *Syncing files and folders* recipe in this chapter
- The *Sharing a document* recipe in *Chapter 2, Introduction to SharePoint Online*
- The *Determining and revoking permissions in a site* recipe in *Chapter 3, Modern Sites in SharePoint Online*
- The *Changing list permissions* recipe in *Chapter 4, Lists and Libraries in SharePoint Online*

Unlock this book's exclusive benefits now

This book comes with additional benefits designed to elevate your learning experience.

Note: Have your purchase invoice ready before you begin. https://www.packtpub.com/unlock/9781803243177

7

Microsoft Teams

Microsoft Teams is your hub for collaboration in Microsoft 365. While it provides a chat-based workspace that lets you have instant threaded communication, video chats, and meetings with your peers, it also provides a collaboration space to work together and share information. Teams' deep integration with SharePoint and Microsoft 365 groups can change the way your team members communicate, collaborate, and interact with others. The collaboration experience is further enriched by the integration capabilities that Teams provides with other applications, such as Trello or GitHub.

Those of you who are familiar with Skype for Business (Microsoft's instant communication application) might wonder what the difference is between Skype for Business and Teams. One of the key aspects of Teams is that, unlike Skype for Business, conversations within Teams are threaded around a specific topic. So, conversations always have a context. Besides conversations, Teams also brings together other Microsoft 365 collaboration services, such as groups, Planner, OneDrive, and SharePoint. Teams also supports connectors to numerous third-party applications, such as Trello, GitHub, Evernote, SurveyMonkey, and so on.

In this chapter, you will learn about the following:

- Installing Teams
- Creating a new team
- Adding a member
- Joining a team
- Leaving a team
- Deleting a team
- Creating channels and tabs
- Initiating conversations via posts
- Scheduling a meeting
- Sharing files
- Searching within Teams
- Adding a connector
- Using Approvals in Teams

- Create a channel calendar tab
- Creating custom registration forms for Teams meetings
- Using breakout rooms in Teams meetings

Let's first learn about installing Teams.

Installing Teams

Teams can be accessed from both the web browser (which doesn't require any installation) and the desktop app (which requires an installation). There are some benefits to installing the Windows client as some of the features are not supported on the web (although the web client is catching up fast with its app counterpart). One key difference between the two versions is that the web version requires you to be logged in to your Office account to receive notifications. The Teams client, on the other hand, runs in the background, even while you are working on a different application. So, the user receives notifications about team activities and individual messages. Once installed, new updates are applied automatically to the Teams client. It checks for updates every time the client is launched.

In this section, we will learn how to install the Teams app.

Getting ready

To access the Teams app, you need the appropriate Microsoft 365 license plan as described in *Chapter 1, Overview of Microsoft 365*.

Microsoft also provides a Commercial Cloud Trial offer for existing Microsoft 365 users in your organization for 6 months without charge. They can try the product for 1 year without being licensed for Teams.

How to do it...

To install Teams, follow these instructions:

1. Go to www.office.com.
2. Sign in with your work account as described in *Chapter 1, Overview of Microsoft 365*.
3. Click on **Teams** (shown in the following screenshot):

Figure 7.1: Installing Teams

4. You will be prompted to download the desktop version by a pop-up screen, as in the following screenshot:

Figure 7.2: Desktop vs web

5. Click the **Get the Windows app** button to get the client version of Teams.

This will download the client application installer for you. Running the installer will guide you through the installation process and install Teams for you. You can then sign in to the Teams desktop app by using your organization credentials.

If you are using the free version of Teams, you can log in using your Live account.

 If you choose to stay on the web app, you can download the app later by clicking on the **Get App** icon in the lower left-hand pane of your Teams web application interface.

How it works...

Although Teams has a web and client version, the user experience on the web and desktop applications is strikingly similar. The ability to join video calls and share your screen is supported on both the desktop app and the web version (only Edge and Chrome are supported at the moment). However, some features, such as "Allow Control" (to remotely control another user's desktop) and the ability to host "live events," are only available on the desktop version.

Figure 7.3: Download Teams desktop app

Let us look at the layout of the Teams app.

Teams top panel

The top panel in the Teams interface provides the following options:

Figure 7.4: Top panel

1. Teams introduced its new experience while this book was been written. A toggle switch is now available to switch between the modern and classic experience, although it will eventually be removed.

2. Clicking the search bar next to the magnifying glass allows you to perform a search and invoke commands (explained in the *Searching within Teams* recipe in this chapter). In the latest update, Teams has introduced the ability to add multiple organizations within your Team's client, allowing you to switch between them without the need to sign out.

3. Clicking the profile picture provides additional settings, such as:

    •   **Setting availability** (Available, Busy, etc.)

    •   **Change Org:** The Org icon allows you to change organization: you will see other organizations in this section if you are invited to collaborate with external teams outside of your organization

    •   **Setting a status message** (for example, I am working from home today)

    •   **Accessing Saved messages** (discussed in the *Initiating conversations via posts* recipe in this chapter)

- Updating **General Settings** such as: choosing a Teams skin color; setting default audio devices for Team calls; managing notifications (discussed in the *Creating channels and tabs* recipe in this chapter); setting keyboard shortcuts for common Teams tasks, etc.
- Teams left panel

The panel on the left lets you navigate through various features within Teams.

Figure 7.5: Left panel

Please note that some feature icons might be hidden under the **...** icon. Let's look at some of these features in more detail.

Activity

Clicking on the **Activity** tab takes you to the activity feed. This feed rolls up notifications related to all your team channels and team conversations and one-on-one chats or calls. A notification appears in your activity feed whenever someone mentions you or a team that you're a part of, or if they like your post, message or call you, or add you to a team or make you a team owner.

Additionally, under **Activity** | **Feed** | **My Activity**, you will see all the messages that **you** posted on any of your Team channels.

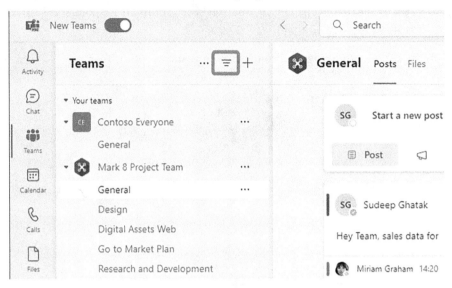

Figure 7.6: Filter feed

Clicking the *filter* icon next to the **Feed** heading displays a text box that lets you type free text, thereby filtering the search results:

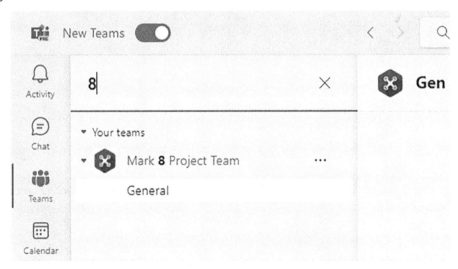

Figure 7.7: Add filter

You can also click on the ... icon to manage your teams.

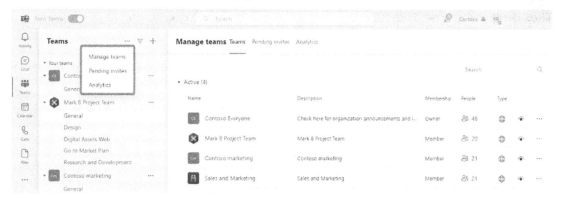

Figure 7.8: Manage your teams

Chat

The **Chat** tab lets you initiate a chat with an individual or a group. You can have threaded conversations with one or more people. You can also share files by uploading the files in the chat window or just by dragging them to the conversation text window. The files are automatically uploaded to OneDrive and participants receive a link to access them:

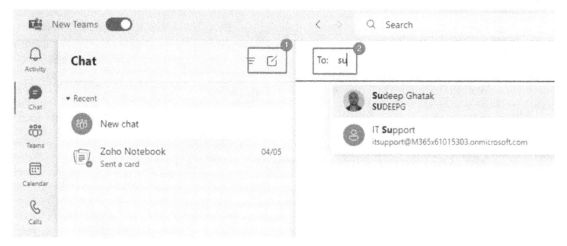

Figure 7.9: Teams chat interface

You can initiate a chat by clicking on the *Compose* (1) icon. A text box appears (2) where you can specify the name(s) of the people you would like to chat with.

Teams

The **Teams** tab displays all the teams that you are part of. It also lets you join or create a team:

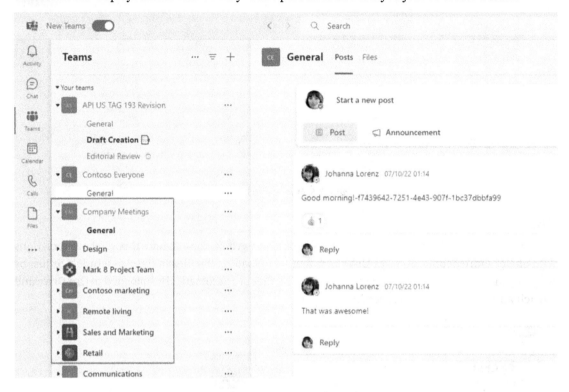

Figure 7.10: Teams and channels

Every team that you create has a default **General** channel to start with. Channels let you create focus areas, such as a specific topic, department, or project. We'll learn about channels shortly.

If you are a team owner, you can add more channels:

Figure 7.11: Image showing channels within a team

Each channel gets its own area for posts and a storage place for channel-specific files in SharePoint:

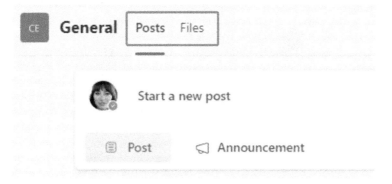

Figure 7.12: Components of a Teams channel

We will learn about channels in the *Creating channels and tabs* recipe in this chapter.

Calendar

The **Calendar** option lets you schedule team meetings or audio/video calls with an individual or team. Read more about the Calendar in the *Scheduling a meeting* recipe.

Calls

The **Call** option lets you make audio/video calls with an individual or team. Clicking on this tab, takes you to the section that lets you view your call list:

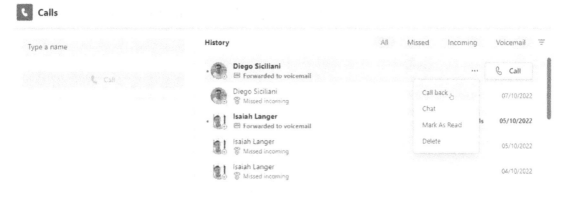

Figure 7.13: Calls on Teams

If your organization has PSTN (**Public Switched Telephone Network**) enabled, you will also see a dial pad within Teams:

Figure 7.14: Teams Call (PSTN)

You can type the name of the person you want to call and then press the **Call** button:

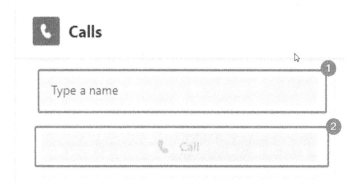

Figure 7.15: Calling Teams contacts

Teams also support voicemails. People can leave a voicemail for you if you are unable to attend the call. The good thing about voicemails is that they even generate a transcript of the message. So, you can choose to read the message instead of listening to it. This is especially handy when someone leaves you a voicemail while you are in a meeting. Instead of attending the call, you can glance through the transcript of the voicemail.

Read more about calls in the *Scheduling a meeting* recipe.

Files

Finally, the **Files** option displays all the files that you have access to or files that have been shared with you in Office 365. The location of the file is mentioned under the file name. The file can be stored in SharePoint (1) or someone's OneDrive account.

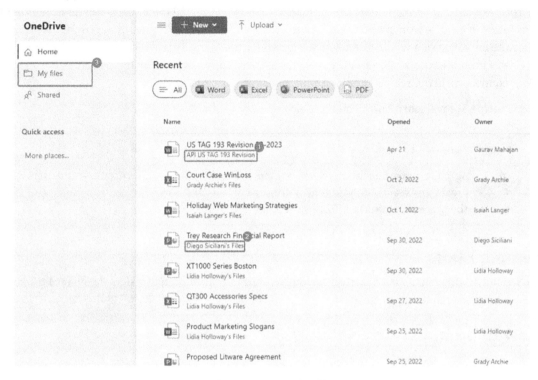

Figure 7.16: Accessing files

You can access your OneDrive files by clicking on the OneDrive link on the left (3). You can move or copy your files from OneDrive to Teams using the context menu (the three dots at the end of each line).

There's more...

Microsoft Teams also comes with a free version that can be used for chats, file sharing, and video calling. The features that it offers have been listed on the Office website. You can access this at: `https://packt.link/teams-free`.

Microsoft Teams supports keyboard shortcuts and might be handy for those who prefer the keyboard. You can find Teams keyboard shortcuts for Windows and Mac listed in the following link: `https://packt.link/teams-shortcuts`.

Next, we'll learn about one of the most important Teams recipes that explains how you can create a team.

See also

- Adopt Microsoft Teams | Microsoft Learn: `https://packt.link/adopt-Microsoft-Teams-landing-page`

- Admin training resources – Microsoft Teams | Microsoft Learn: `https://packt.link/IT-admin-readiness`

Creating a new team

Microsoft Teams lets team members achieve more together when all their chats, meetings, files, and apps reside in a single workspace. Creating a team does a lot in the background. It provisions a SharePoint site for you, along with a Microsoft 365 group for the team. Teams lets you connect with other services within Microsoft 365, as well as with third-party apps (via connectors). We shall learn more about connectors in the recipe titled *Adding a connector*.

In this recipe, we will learn how to create a new team.

>
>
> **Note**
>
> As of the time when this book was written, the new Teams app does not allow end users to create new teams. Only administrators can provision teams. The following steps outline the process in the classic Teams version.

Getting ready

You should be able to create a new team as long as your organization has assigned you a valid Teams license and has enabled team creation.

How to do it...

Follow these steps to create a new team:

1. Click on the **Join or create a team** option:

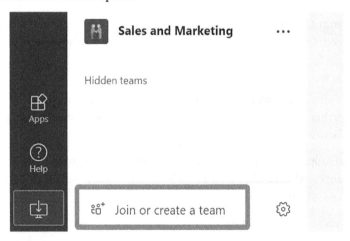

Figure 7.17: Creating a team

2. Clicking **Join or create a team** takes you to the screen where you can join one of the existing teams, join a team with a code, search for an existing team to join, or create a new team.

3. If you **Create a new team**, you can choose to create a new team (which creates a Microsoft 365 group in the background) or connect the team to an existing Microsoft 365 group. Those of you who are already using Microsoft 365 Groups can use the latter option to connect your existing group to Teams:

 Creating a Microsoft 365 group does not create a team; however, creating a team creates a group. The Microsoft 365 group created as a result of a team doesn't appear in Outlook by default. Administrators will need to run a script if this feature is required. Learn more about Microsoft 365 Groups in *Chapter 16, Microsoft 365 Groups*.

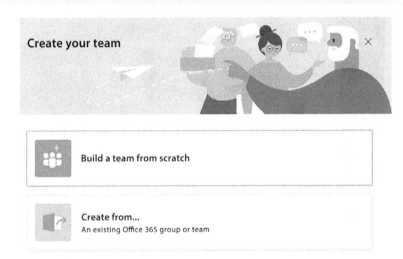

Figure 7.18: Options available while creating teams

4. You will then be asked whether you want to create a private, public, or organization-wide team.
5. Give your team a name.

Now, you have created your own team.

How it works...

We just learned how to create a new team from scratch. The other option lets you convert an existing Microsoft 365 group into a team. As it turns out, Microsoft 365 Groups was released before Microsoft Teams. So, this option allows you to upgrade an existing Office 365 group (that was created before Teams was released) to Teams. We will discuss this more in the next section.

Based on its privacy, a team can be of the following types:

*   A **private team**: This is a restricted area that is only accessible to the team members.
*   A **public team**: This team is available to join for everyone in the organization.
*   An **organization-wide team**: This adds all of the organization's staff to a team. Only global administrators can create organization-wide teams. You will automatically be added to an organization-wide team unless your administrator has explicitly disabled your Teams account.

There's more...

The following key considerations should be kept in mind while creating teams.

When you specify the team name while creating a team, Microsoft 365 doesn't validate whether a team with the same name already exists. It will instead let you create another one with the same name, as shown in the following screenshot:

Figure 7.19: Teams with same names

The new team with the same name then appears in the Teams interface.

This poses a challenge because a SharePoint site is created for each team and you cannot have two SharePoint sites with the same URL. To assign a separate storage space, Microsoft 365 adds a random number next to the team name when provisioning the SharePoint site, which can then result in a lot of confusion. As an example, it created the following site for the second Team from the screenshot above: `https://m365x263078.sharepoint.com/sites/Sales774/Shared%20Documents`.

It is, therefore, recommended that you check for an existing team before creating one using the search option on the team creation page, as shown here:

Figure 7.20: Check for existing team

Team owners can assign an email address to each team channel. The email address cannot be changed or modified, is assigned at random, and appears in your organization's global address list. This feature has some benefits, which we will see in the recipe on *Creating channels*.

Microsoft Teams templates

Microsoft Teams templates offer a convenient way to establish teams with preconfigured settings, channels, and applications. They streamline the process of creating collaboration spaces tailored to diverse business needs and projects. For instance, you can leverage templates to form teams dedicated to event management, project coordination, or crisis response.

Microsoft Teams provides a variety of template options, including those designed by Microsoft for specific industries like education, healthcare, retail, and government. Additionally, there are generic templates suitable for a wide range of purposes, such as ideation, content development, or employee training. Should the need arise, organizations can craft custom templates aligned with their unique requirements and preferences.

To utilize Microsoft Teams templates, the user must possess the requisite permissions, typically granted by the administrator.

See also

- Use organization-wide teams in Microsoft Teams - Microsoft Teams: `https://packt.link/create-an-org-wide-team`
- Manage large teams – Microsoft Teams: `https://packt.link/best-practices-large-groups`
- Create a template from an existing team in Microsoft Teams - Microsoft Teams: `https://packt.link/create-template-from-existing-team`
- The *Adding a member* recipe in this chapter *Chapter 16, Microsoft 365 Groups*

Now that you have created a team, let's learn about adding members to it.

Adding a member

You can add new members to an existing team. They can belong to the same organization or can be added as a guest from another organization. A team can hold up to 5,000 people.

Members of a team can have one of the following roles:

- **Owner:** The team owner manages the settings for the team. The owner can do the following:

    - Add and remove members
    - Add guests
    - Change team settings
    - Restore deleted files or older versions

     A team can have multiple owners.

- **Member:** Members are added to a team by the owner. Members can do the following:

    - Post messages
    - View, upload, and change files
    - Schedule team meetings

- **Guest:** Guests are people outside your organization. They can only be invited by the team owner. They can:

    - Post messages
    - Share files with the team

Follow the instructions provided in the next section to add a member to a team.

Getting ready

Members can be added to a team by the team owner. Only an owner can promote another member to the **Owner** role.

How to do it...

To add a new member:

1. Select **Teams** from the left-hand pane.
2. Click on the ... link next to the team name.
3. This brings up a context menu with an **Add member** option.
4. Type the name of the person you would like to add.

5. Change the role of the member to **Owner** (if you have owner privileges).

The team members section will look as follows:

Figure 7.21: Team members

How it works...

The new member automatically gets access to all the related Microsoft 365 services, such as SharePoint, Planner, and Microsoft 365 groups. The new member receives an introductory email after being added.

You and other members of your Team are notified via the **General** tab about new members being added to your team:

What a member or a guest can or cannot do is set by the team owner through the **Teams and channel settings:**

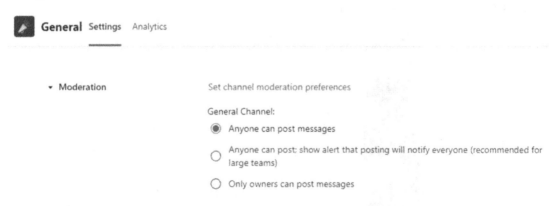

Figure 7.22: Managing team permissions

You can request to **Join a Team** even if you were not specifically added to it by an owner. We'll see how to join a team in the next topic.

See also

- The *Joining a team* recipe in this chapter
- The *Leaving a team* recipe in this chapter
- Chat, teams, channels, & apps in Microsoft Teams – Microsoft Teams: `https://packt.link/deploy-chat-Teams-channels`
- Manage Teams with policies – Microsoft Teams | Microsoft Learn: `https://packt.link/manage-Teams-with-policies`

Joining a team

You can join an existing team by either using the **Join** option (in the case of public teams) or asking the owner to add you as a member (in the case of private teams). This recipe will show you how to join a new team.

> **Note**
>
> As of the time when this book was written, the new Teams app does not allow end users to join new teams. Only Team owners or admins can add other members or owners. The following steps outline the process in the classic Teams version.

Getting ready

You are added to an organization-wide team as soon as you are added to your organization's Microsoft 365 tenant. For public and private teams, you need to take the following steps.

How to do it...

To join a team, do the following:

1. Select **Teams** from the left-hand pane.

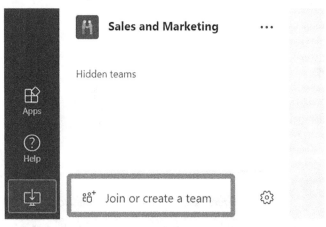

Figure 7.23: Joining an existing team

2. To join a public team, click on the **Join or create a team** option.

3. You should see all the publicly available teams.

4. Click on the **Join team** option to join the team.

5. To join private teams, the team owner will have to either add you as a member or send you a team code. A team code can be generated by going to **Team | Settings | Team code**.

6. Click the **...** next to the team name, then go to **Manage team | Settings | Expand Team code | Generate**.

 Guest users won't be able to join a private team using a code. They need to be added explicitly by the owner.

How it works...

After joining a team, you can participate in team conversations. You can also view conversations that have taken place in the past. When you are part of a team, you can access all the channels within that team. Once you have joined it, the team starts to appear in the left-hand navigation pane along with the other teams you are part of.

There's more..

External teams in Microsoft Teams are groups that include participants from outside your organization, such as partners, vendors, or clients.

External teams in Microsoft Teams are valuable for various reasons:

- **Collaboration with partners**: You can work closely with external partners, vendors, or clients without the need for them to be part of your organization.

- **Secure communication**: Using external teams provides a secure environment for sharing information, documents, and messages with external parties, ensuring data privacy.

- **Efficiency**: External teams streamline cross-organizational collaboration, enhancing efficiency and reducing the need for emails or other communication tools.

- **Project collaboration**: They are ideal for project-based or short-term collaborations, allowing easy onboarding and offboarding of external participants.

- **Maintaining organizational boundaries**: You can maintain control over your internal teams and resources while extending collaboration outside your organization's boundaries.

To join an external team, you can either accept an invitation from the team owner through an email link, or enter a provided team code. Once joined, you gain access to the team's channels and resources, enabling secure collaboration and communication with external parties while respecting organizational boundaries and permissions.

See also

- The *Leaving a team* recipe in this chapter
- The *Adding a member* recipe in this chapter

Now that we know how to join a team, let's see how you can leave a team that you are a member of.

Leaving a team

If you think you no longer need to contribute to a team or you find that a team is no longer relevant to you, you can leave the team. To leave a team, follow the steps provided in the next section.

Note

As of the time when this book was written, the new Teams app does not allow end users to leave a team they are part of. Only team owners or admins can remove other members or owners. The following steps outline the process in the classic Teams version.

Getting ready

You do not need special permission to leave a private or public team.

You cannot leave an organization-wide team on your own. You will need to ask the administrator to remove you.

How to do it...

To leave a team:

1. Select **Teams** from the left-hand side pane.
2. Click on ... next to the name of the team you want to leave.
3. Select the **Leave the team** option from the context menu, as shown here:

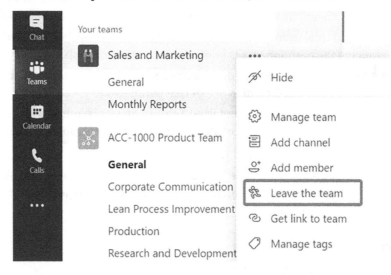

Figure 7.24: Leaving a team

How it works...

When you click **Leave the team,** all the permissions associated with that team and its channels are revoked. You also lose access to the underlying SharePoint site and all the content within it.

See also

- The *Deleting a team* recipe in this chapter
- The *Joining a team* recipe in this chapter

If there is a team that you provisioned, you can delete it by following the next recipe.

Deleting a team

In Teams, it is possible for owners to delete specific teams if they deem it necessary. It is a good practice to inform the members beforehand so that any contents (files and conversations) can be moved/archived elsewhere. Within 30 days, a deleted team can be recovered by recovering the Microsoft 365 group that gets deleted along with it. Please note that there is also an option available to *Archive* a team instead of deleting it. Archiving adds a temporary freeze on the content of the team. It can be unarchived at any point.

> **Note**
>
> As of the time when this book was written, the new Teams app does not allow end users to delete teams. Only admins can delete a team from the admin center. The following steps outline the process in the classic Teams version.

Getting ready

You need to be the owner to delete a team. You can delete a team via the Outlook client, Outlook Web Access, or the Outlook mobile app.

How to do it...

To delete a team, do the following:

1. Click on ... next to the name of the team you want to delete.

2. Select the **Delete the team** option from the context menu, as shown:

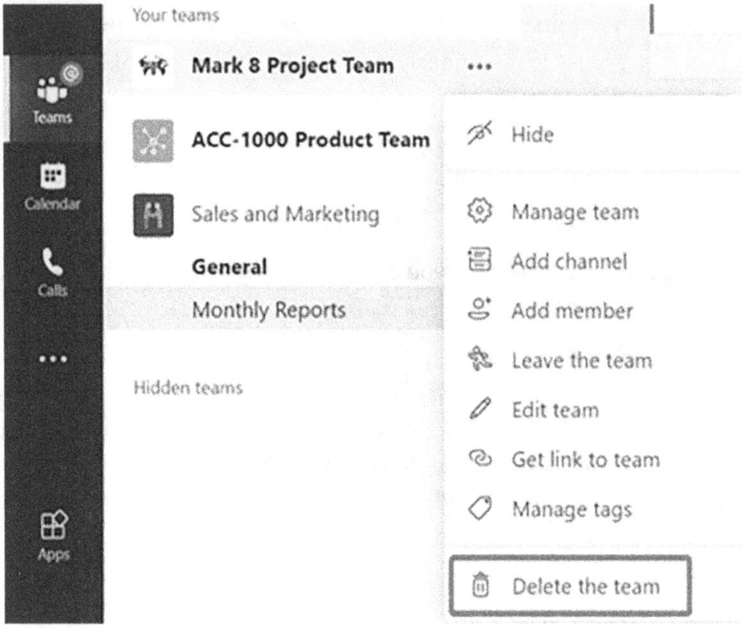

Figure 7.25: Deleting a team

How it works...

By deleting a team, you lose all its associated components, such as the team mailbox, calendar, SharePoint site, notebook, Planner tasks, and so on.

The team owner or administrator can restore a deleted team within 30 days.

See also

- The *Leaving a team* recipe in this chapter
- The *Joining a team* recipe in this chapter

In our next recipe, we are going to learn about creating channels and tabs in a team that you are a member of.

Creating channels and tabs

Channels are dedicated spaces that keep conversations and files around a topic together. Every team comes with a default channel named **General**, but additional channels can be added. Every team supports up to 200 channels. All team conversations happen within a specific channel. The following section explains how you can create new channels and tabs.

Note

As of the time when this book was written, the new Teams app does not allow end users to create new channels. Only admins can create a channel within an existing Team. The following steps outline the process in the classic Teams version.

Getting ready

Team owner can create new channels. The owner decides if members can create channels and tabs.

How to do it...

To add a channel:

1. Select **Teams** from the left-hand pane.
2. Click on **...** next to the name of the team you want to add a channel to.
3. Select the **Add channel** option from the context menu, as shown:

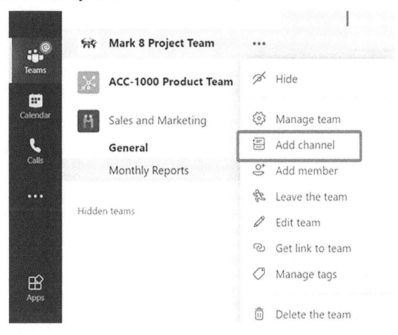

Figure 7.26: Add channel

4. Provide a channel name and set the **Privacy** option.

Adding a channel adds two tabs to the channel—one for conversations and the other for shared files.

Besides the standard apps, a channel lets you enhance the Teams experience by connecting other Microsoft 365 or third-party applications. You can use connectors for scenarios that include the following:

• Managing team backlog items in Trello

- Posting messages in your team channel using Power Automate
- Enhancing team conversations using actionable cards

To add additional tabs, do the following:

1. Click on the + symbol next to the **Files** tab.
2. Choose an app from the list or search for it, as shown here:

Figure 7.27: Channel tabs

3. Provide the details required for the specific app and click **Save**.

How it works...

Creating a channel provides you with a dedicated conversation area and a place to store all your files. Channels are public or private. All public channels in a team share a common SharePoint document library in a team site.

However, creating a private channel assigns you with a separate SharePoint site collection altogether. Owners or members of the private channel are the only ones who can access the channel.

Private channels appear with a lock icon (🔒) in front of the channel name.

Tabs in the channel let you connect to both Microsoft 365 as well as to connect to other third-party apps to your team. There are two types of tabs:

Static tabs provide a personalized experience to everyone (such as a tab for your personal notes in the channel).

Configurable tabs need you to provide additional configuration information while adding the app, such as the following:

- To add a Power BI dashboard, you need to specify the workspace name.
- To add an Excel app, you need to provide the worksheet name.

Tabs offer interactive web content to the user without them having to leave the team's interface.

Showing or hiding teams and channels

Keep your list of teams and channels tidy and relevant by hiding any teams or channels you don't want to see. Just click on **...** beside the team/channel name and select **Show** or **Hide**:

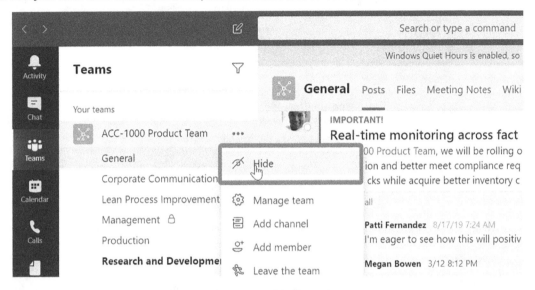

Figure 7.28: Hide channel

Hiding a team will remove it from your list of teams, but you can always access or show it again by expanding the **Hidden teams** section towards the bottom of the teams list. If you know you're a member of a team but you can't see it, you can scroll down to this section, click the ellipsis next to the team, and then click **Show** to move it to the **Your teams** section.

Managing notifications

There are, broadly, three types of notifications that you receive in Teams.

- **A banner:** This alert pops up on your device (on desktop, your web browser, or mobile) even when you are using another application:

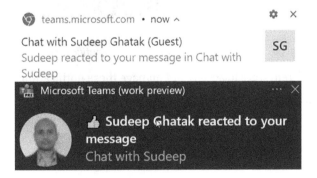

Figure 7.29: Banner notification

- **In the feed**: A badge notification appears on the icon:

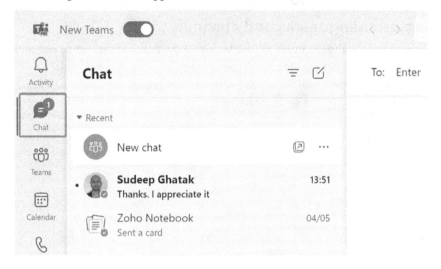

Figure 7.30: Feed notification

- **An email**: A notification arrives in your inbox:

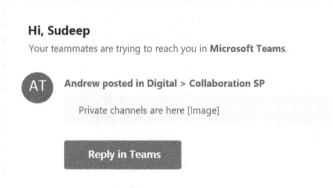

Figure 7.31: Email notification

There are lots of different ways to access and manage these notifications in Teams.

A good place to start is via the notification settings.

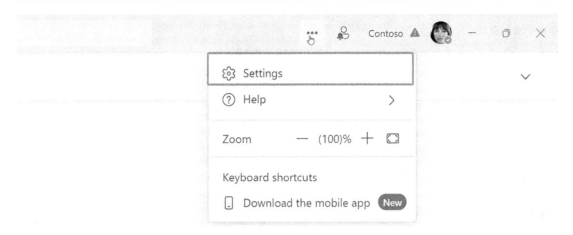

Figure 7.32: Notification settings

This is where you can turn your notifications (and their associated sounds) on and off and select how you would like them to display. There are lots of things you can turn on and off, so you can either set it up to your liking or just stick with the default:

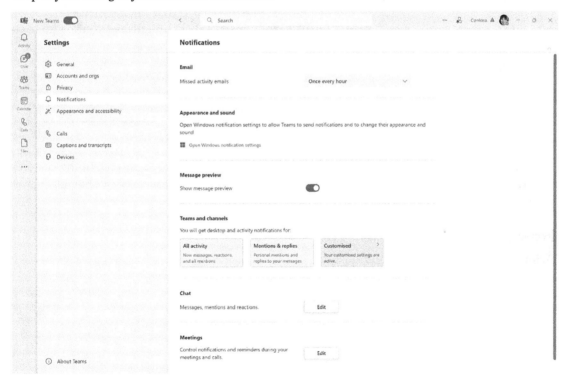

Figure 7.33: Notification settings

If you receive too many notifications, you can also reduce them by hiding a channel. Hidden channels will only show up in your list if a message is marked important or when someone @**mentions** you or the channel.

See also

- The *Initiating conversations via posts* recipe in this chapter
- The *Sharing files* recipe in this chapter
- IT Admins – Private channels in Microsoft Teams – Microsoft Teams: `https://packt.link/private-channels`
- Shared channels in Microsoft Teams – Microsoft Teams: `https://packt.link/shared-channels`

Channels are a medium of having conversations with other members of the team. We shall learn about conversations in our next recipe.

Initiating conversations via posts

Posts or conversations can be described as group chats where everyone in the team participates. Conversations are in a team channel. They can be viewed by all members of the team. Teams attempts to reduce reliance on the more formal and conventional mode of communication—email. The following section provides steps for how to initiate a conversation.

Teams is great for conversations with your teammates:

- Conversations are persistent—your conversation history sticks around and you can go back to it later.
- You can share files with offline participants.
- You can add GIFs and memes.
- The conversations are searchable—search for files, content, or people.

Getting ready

We mentioned earlier that every team can have one or more channels. The **Post** tab in the channel displays team conversations and other channel activity. All team members can view channel conversations and participate in them.

How to do it...

To initiate a conversation:

1. Select **Teams** from the left-hand side pane.
2. Click on **...** next to the name of the team that you want to post in.
3. Select a channel. You will see all the channel activity in the conversation area.
4. For a new post, click on the button shown below.

Figure 7.34: Post button

5. Type your message in the text box that appears:

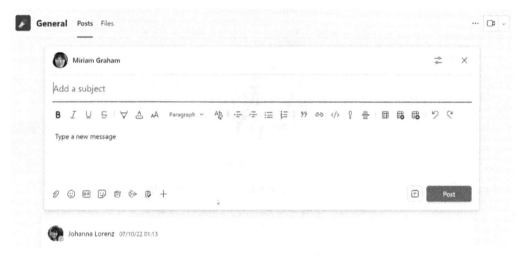

Figure 7.35: Starting new conversation

Conversations support @mentions, emojis, attachments, and video calling.

6. Press **Enter** or the ▷ symbol.

7. To edit a message, click on the **...** symbol and choose the **Edit** option.

The ⎗ option lets you save a message. You can search for saved messages later.

You can upvote a conversation by clicking on the like button.

How it works...

The most recent conversations are displayed at the top, while older messages can be accessed by scrolling down.

The options available under the text box are configurable and can be switched on or off by your administrator. This can be done through the team's admin center.

Using @mentions is a way of notifying an individual or team of a message (shown in the following screenshot). When mentioned, the individual or team will receive a notification in their Microsoft Teams client. Using the **Reply** button will keep messages in the same conversation thread:

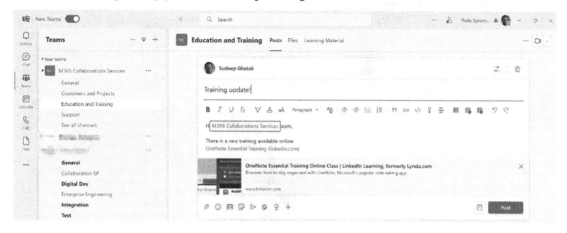

Figure 7.36: Team mentions

A channel appears in bold if there are new, unread conversations in the channel:

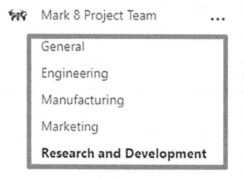

Figure 7.37: Active channel

There's more...

The comment box in the Teams chat is more than just a text box. It is your connection to other Microsoft 365 applications such as Power Automate, Viva Learning, and Loop components. The following paragraph covers these capabilities:

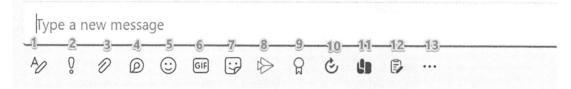

Figure 7.38: Message box capabilities

1. This icon lets you add text formatting such as font color, font size, ordered lists, etc. With this option selected, pressing the **Enter** key adds a new line.

2. You can mark your message as important by clicking this icon

3. This icon lets you attach files with your message. These can be uploaded from your device or OneDrive

4. Clicking this icon lets you add Loop components (ordered lists, paragraphs, etc.) that can be co-authored by team members collaboratively. These components can be accessed from within other Microsoft 365 apps.

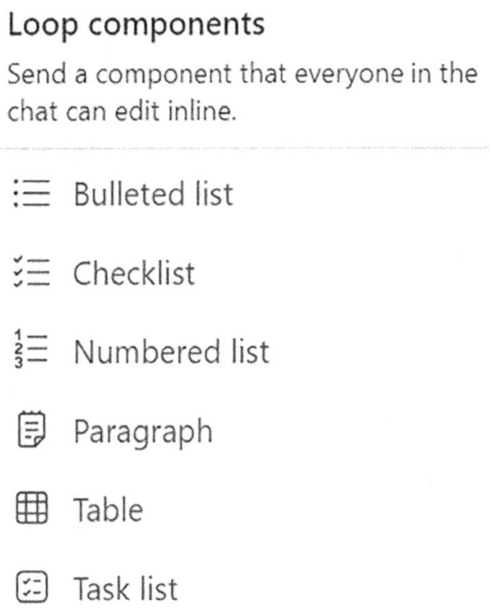

Loop components

Send a component that everyone in the chat can edit inline.

:≡ Bulleted list

✓≡ Checklist

¹₃≡ Numbered list

📄 Paragraph

⊞ Table

☑ Task list

Figure 7.39: Adding Loop components

5. You can also add emojis to your conversation.

6. This icon lets you insert GIFs from a set of available GIF files.

7. You can insert stickers using this option.

8. You can insert a Microsoft stream video by clicking this icon.

9. This icon lets you send a praise to your team or colleague.

10. Power Automate workflows can be triggered from within Teams using this option. You can build custom approvals flows or use inbuilt e-signature workflows on your Teams documents.

11. You can insert a link to a Viva Learning course by clicking on this icon.

12. The update option lets you track progress on an ongoing or upcoming project. There are several templates you can choose from:

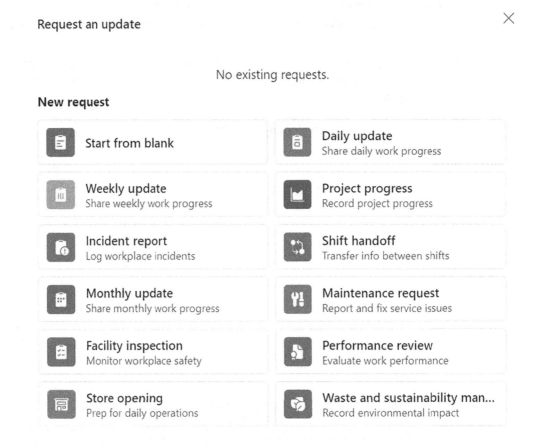

Figure 7.40: Update templates

Besides conversations, Teams also supports one-to-one and group chats. These chats can be initiated from the chat icon in the top pane (see **(1)** in the following screenshot). You can type the name of the individual(s) you would like to chat with (see **(2)** in the following screenshot). Your conversations are only seen by the participants of the chat. Any files that you share in these chats will be saved in OneDrive and shared with the participants:

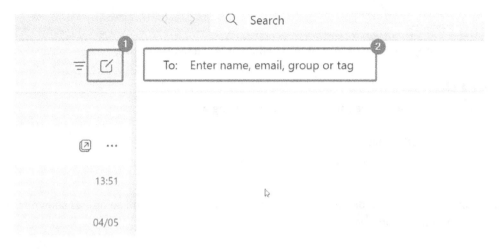

Figure 7.41: One to one chats

See also

- What is Teams Phone – Microsoft Teams | Microsoft Learn: `https://packt.link/what-is-Teams-phone`
- The *Sharing files* recipe in this chapter
- The *Adding a connector* recipe in this chapter

Now let's look at another key feature of Teams: meetings.

Scheduling a meeting

Microsoft Teams lets you organize team meetings or have one-off audio/video calls with your colleagues.

There are four meeting types that you can use with Teams based on the context:

- **Scheduled meetings:** When you want to schedule meeting at a future date with an individual or colleagues.
- **Meet in a channel:** When you need to hold an open meeting in your team, create a meeting in a channel.
- **Instant meetings:** When you want to convert your ongoing conversation into a desktop sharing session
- **Teams live events:** When you want to broadcast video and meeting content to a large online audience.

To schedule a meeting in Teams, follow the steps in the next section.

Getting ready

You do not need any special permission to schedule or join a team meeting.

How to do it...

You can set up the various meeting types in the following ways:

Scheduled meetings

1. Select **Meetings** from the left-hand side pane.
2. Click on **+ New meeting**.
3. Provide the required details (such as a title, the participants, and so on), as shown in the following screenshot:

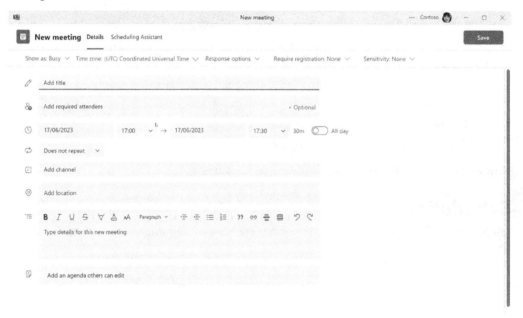

Figure 7.42: Meeting details

4. Click **Schedule**.

You have now scheduled a meeting.

Meet in a channel

1. Select **Meetings** from the left-hand side pane.
2. Click on **+ New meeting**.
3. Provide the required details as shown in the **Scheduled meetings** section above.
4. Select a channel as shown in the following screenshot:

Figure 7.43: Channel Meeting

5. Click **Schedule.**

Another way to initiate conversation is using the **Meet now** option that we will learn in the next section.

Meet now

Meet now option is used for unplanned meetings that you want to initiate right away. You can initiate a Meet now meeting by following the steps below:

1. Go to your team's channel (**1**).

2. Go to your team's channel **Posts** (**2**).

3. Click on **Reply** (**3**) and then click on the video camera (**4**) icon:

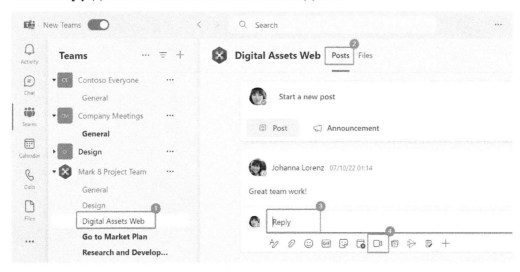

Figure 7.44: Reply with Meeting

4. Specify the title of the meeting, turn video **on** or **off**, and click **Meet now**.

Live events

1. Select **Meetings** from the left-hand side pane.
2. Click on **+ New meeting**.
3. Click on **Live event**.
4. Add presenters, and assign them a producer or presenter role:

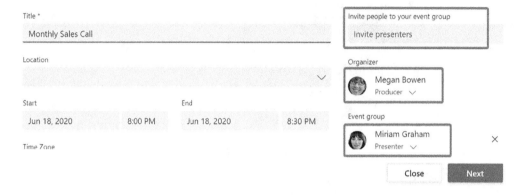

Figure 7.45: Adding presenters

5. Define the scope of the live event, you can run it across the company or within a selected group:

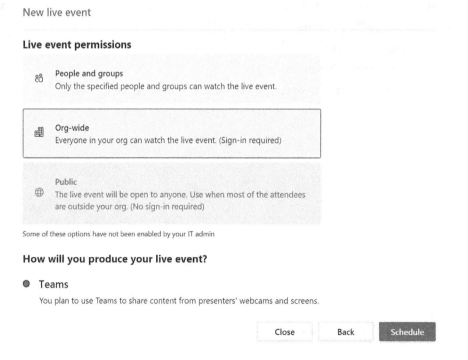

Figure 7.46: Live event permissions

6. Click **Schedule**.

How it works...

All meeting types (except live meetings) provide an interactive experience to the attendees. The team's meeting interface displays a control pane when you move your mouse in the meeting interface:

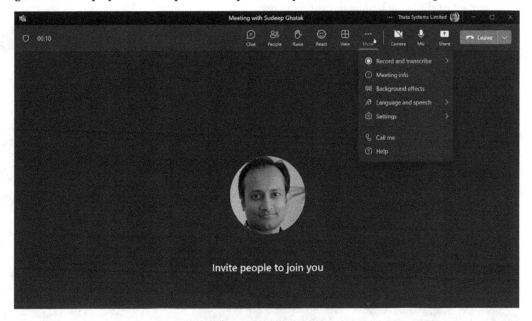

Figure 7.47: Panel options

These options give us an insight into what features are available in a Teams meeting.

If you record a meeting, the transcript will automatically appear in Microsoft Stream (refer to the chapter on Microsoft Stream in the *Appendix*) and can be shared with others who missed the meeting. A searchable transcript of the recording is also generated:

Figure 7.48: Microsoft Stream

Teams has various capabilities to enhance the calling experience in meetings.

Live captions

The live captions feature adds real-time captions to a conversation for anyone who wants to use them, which helps make meetings more inclusive and effective. The feature is useful for people with a hearing impairment or differing language proficiencies:

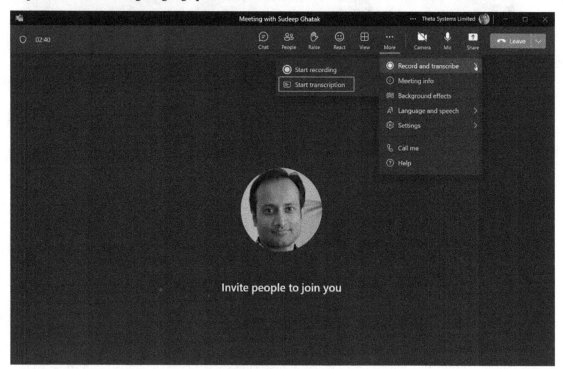

Figure 7.49: Live captions

Once it is turned on, the function will transcribe what anyone says and display it as a live caption at the lower-left side of the meeting screen.

Custom backgrounds

This feature lets you add a custom background while keeping your face in focus. It is a useful feature to use when you are in a public place or working from home. There are many custom background images provided by default.

The one highlighted in the following screenshot lets you blur your background:

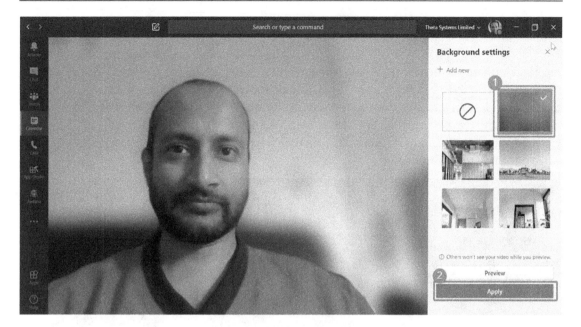

Figure 7.50: Teams background settings

You can take this even further by using a photo of your office with your company branding or simply use an image to add some humor:

Figure 7.51: Custom background image

Avatars

Avatars in Microsoft Teams offer the ability for users to connect and display their presence in Teams meetings without the need to enable their cameras. It presents a viable alternative to the existing binary choice between having video on or off. Avatars for Teams grants you the valuable opportunity to take a break from the camera while maintaining the ability to collaborate efficiently. This feature allows for increased participation in conversations, accommodating those who require a break from video fatigue, individuals joining from different time zones, or those who simply prefer keeping their video off for personal comfort.

Figure 7.52: Avatars in Teams

There's more...

Those of you who prefer using Outlook to schedule meetings can use the Teams add-in that gets installed when you install Teams:

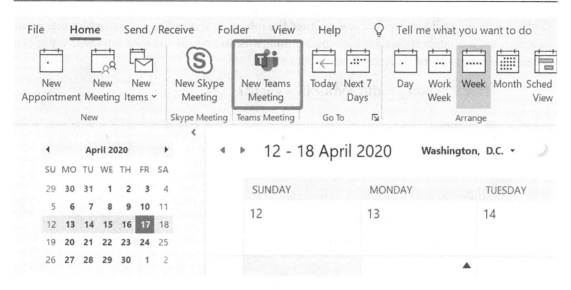

Figure 7.53: Teams add-in

This option lets you leverage Outlook's familiar scheduling window. A link to the Teams meeting is inserted automatically in the invite and the meeting location is set to Microsoft Teams Meeting:

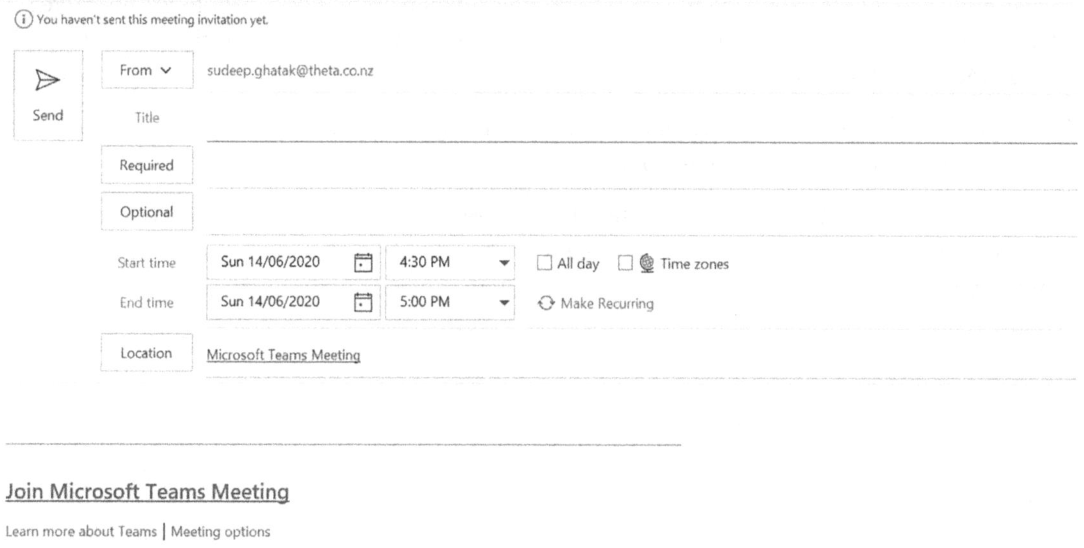

Figure 7.54: Teams meeting

Microsoft Teams also comes with a special meeting type called **Live event** that lets you stream a video or content to a large audience. You can schedule and run a live event using the Teams client.

When you schedule a live event, you are assigned the role of producer. You can add additional event presenters or co-producers. Besides the meeting time, meeting venue, and meeting agenda, you can choose some other special options as shown below:

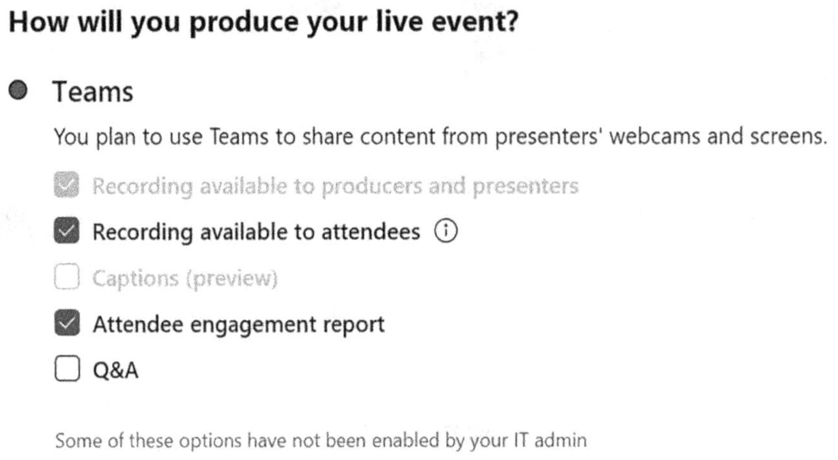

How will you produce your live event?

● Teams

You plan to use Teams to share content from presenters' webcams and screens.

☑ Recording available to producers and presenters

☑ Recording available to attendees ⓘ

☐ Captions (preview)

☑ Attendee engagement report

☐ Q&A

Some of these options have not been enabled by your IT admin

Figure 7.55: Live event options

The **Q&A** feature is very useful when you are running a webinar and don't want to get distracted by attendees talking in the background. Attendees are all muted; they can ask questions, which appear on the producer's dashboard.

The questions that are asked are not visible to others until the producer chooses to publish them. The producer can publish or delete a question.

The producer controls the streaming content that appears on the screen of live attendees. You can share your desktop, application, or a video feed with the attendees. You can even live stream a video or YouTube clip by turning on the option to share system audio:

Figure 7.56: Live event sharing

You can run a live event from Microsoft Stream as well (refer to the section on Microsoft Stream in the *Appendix*). You can turn on captions for the event and share a video with subtitles later. The transcription can be updated manually too.

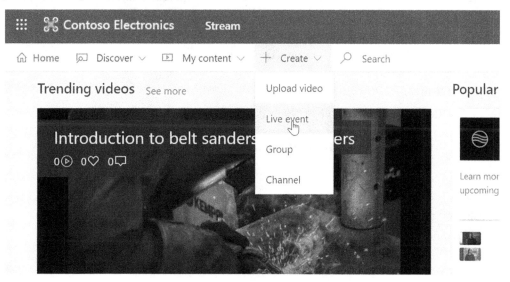

Figure 7.57: Live event from Stream

You can also use Teams for webinars to host online events for up to 1,000 attendees. Teams webinars provide the tools to schedule webinar events, manage attendee registration, run an interactive presentation, and analyze attendee data for effective follow-up.

Teams for townhalls, an added feature, allows you to host and deliver large-scale, internal events to create connections across your organization. You can use Teams for townhalls to host various types of events, such as company-wide town halls, all hands, global team meetings, internal broadcasts, fireside chats, and more. Teams for townhalls provide a one-to-many format with advanced production capabilities and a structured approach for attendee engagement. You can also customize the registration form, the email invites, and the event branding for your townhalls.

See also

- Plan for Teams webinars – Microsoft Teams | Microsoft Learn: `https://packt.link/plan-webinars`
- Plan for Teams town halls – Microsoft Teams | Microsoft Learn: `https://packt.link/plan-town-halls`
- Meeting themes for Teams meetings – Microsoft Teams | Microsoft Learn: `https://packt.link/meeting-themes`

Sharing files

Teams provides an extremely simple collaboration platform to exchange files with colleagues and teams. Files in public teams can be accessed by everyone. Private teams only provide access to team members. Teams lets you share files within each channel.

The next section explains the different ways that files can be uploaded to Teams.

Getting ready

All members of a team can upload files to any channel they wish to.

How to do it...

There are multiple ways of adding files to your team channel, which we will explore in detail.

Sharing files via the Upload button

To upload files within teams:

1. Select **Teams** from the left-hand pane.
2. Click on a channel.
3. Go to the **Files** tab (as shown):

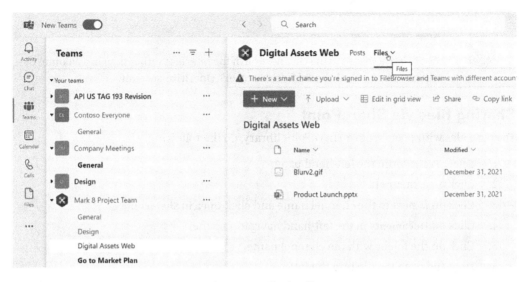

Figure 7.58: Sharing files

4.   Click on **Upload**.

Select the file you want to upload. The file is stored in the team's channel and is accessible to all team members.

Sharing files via conversations

To share files with peers in a conversation:

1.   Select **Teams** from the left-hand pane.
2.   Click on a channel.
3.   Drag and drop a file into the conversation area, as shown in the following screenshot:

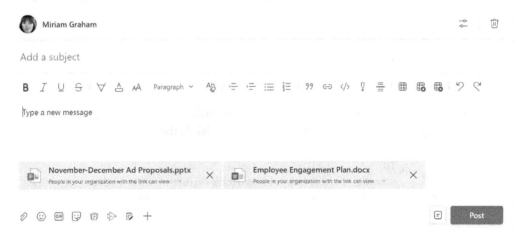

Figure 7.59: Dropping a file in the chat

> **Note**
>
> The files are shared in the chat portion of the interface rather than in a channel post, they will be stored in and shared from the user's OneDrive account.

Sharing files via SharePoint

To share files with peers from a SharePoint library, do the following:

1. Select **Teams** from the left-hand pane.
2. Click on a channel.
3. Click on **...** next to the channel name and click **Open in SharePoint**.
4. Click on **Documents** in the left-hand navigation panel.
5. Click on the folder with the channel name.
6. Drag and drop the file into the folder:

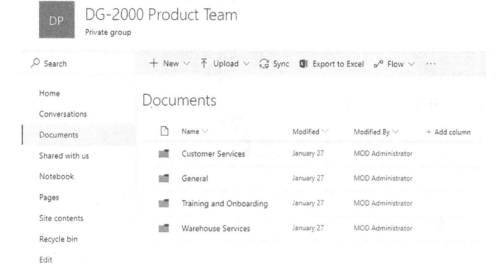

Figure 7.60: Dropping a file in the folder

7. Once you are in SharePoint, you can add additional libraries to manage the team's files. However, only the files in the **Documents** library are visible through Teams.

> Note that if you create your own folder structure within a document library, *it does not appear* as a channel within Teams; it only flows from Teams into SharePoint.

How it works...

Files are stored in the **Documents** library inside a folder with the same name as the channel name.

Files that are shared in the conversation area are uploaded to the **Documents** library automatically.

The uploaded files can be copied, moved, or even shared across multiple channels (instead of creating copies of the same files) by using the **Get link** option and then pasting the link in another team or channel.

There is a **File** option in the left-hand side navigation panel, as shown in the following screenshot:

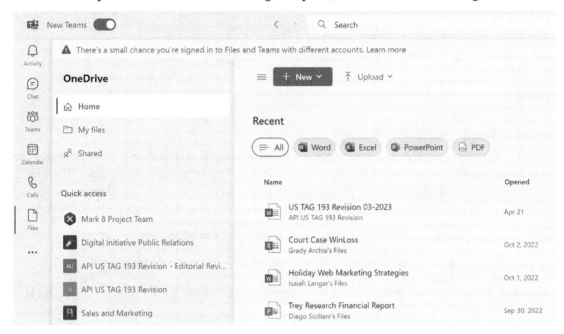

Figure 7.61: Team files

There is also a **File** option in each channel:

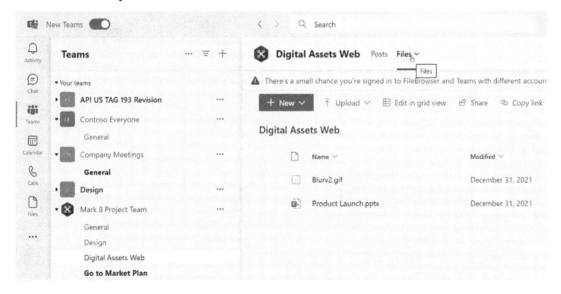

Figure 7.62: Channel files

The difference is that the option in the left-hand navigation panel displays all the files that you have access to or the ones that have been shared with you by a colleague from within SharePoint, OneDrive, and Teams, whereas the option under the channel area displays only the files shared within that channel.

See also

- The *Initiating conversations via posts* recipe in this chapter
- The *Creating channels recipe* in this chapter
- The *Scheduling a meeting* recipe in this chapter

All content within Teams is searchable via the search/command bar; we shall learn about it in the next recipe.

Searching within Teams

When you are a member of a vast number of teams, finding specific information you need can become a challenge. That is where the search functionality within Teams comes to the rescue. The search function lets you search for people, conversations/messages, and documents, as well as the contents of documents. The search box provided in Teams' interface serves as both a search and a command box.

To search for messages, people, or files, follow the instructions provided in the next section.

Getting ready

The search feature within Teams is available to everyone. However, you can only search for content you have access to.

How to do it...

To search for a message, person, or file:

1. Type the word or phrase you are searching for in the search box. In this example, we will search for the word everyone. The search results are grouped under three topics—**Messages**, **People**, and **Files**:

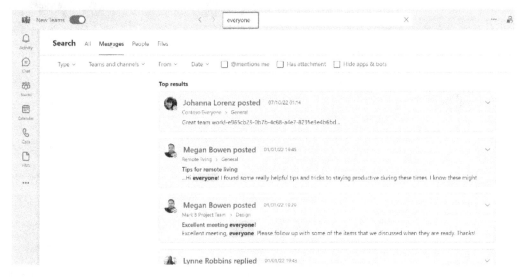

Figure 7.63: Teams search

2. Clicking on a search result will reveal the contents of the result.

3. You can use the filter option to narrow down your search results:

Figure 7.64: Teams filter

4. The search box (in classic Teams) also serves as a command box if you type / in the search box. The Microsoft Teams interface brings up a list of all the available commands and what each command does:

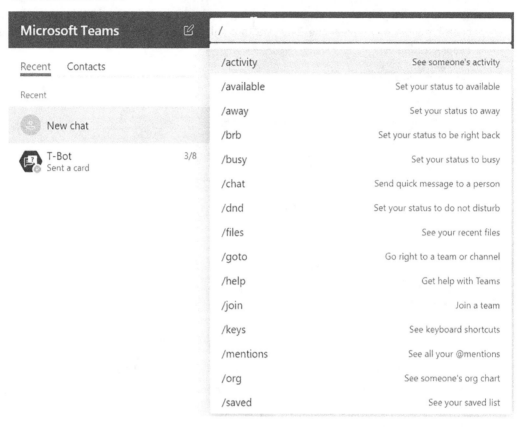

Figure 7.65: Teams command bar

How it works...

Using Teams, you can search for messages, people, and files.

Searching for messages and conversations within teams

You can search for a keyword across all the channels and teams you have access to. The keyword you entered is highlighted in the search results, along with a preview of the message. Clicking on a preview reveals the entire thread in the main area. You can filter the search results further by specifying a start and end date or specifying a specific team or channel.

Searching for people in your Microsoft 365 tenant

You can search for your colleagues from within the Teams interface:

Figure 7.66: Searching for people

You can initiate a chat with your colleague using the Teams command box. Simply type /chat followed by the name of the person:

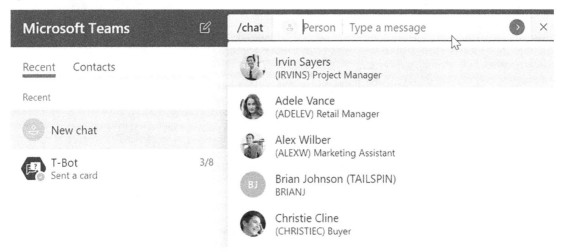

Figure 7.67: Initiate chat with individuals or group

Searching for files within Teams and other Microsoft 365 locations

The /files search feature searches for files across Microsoft 365, including OneDrive and SharePoint. Just typing /files reveals all your recent files. The list is filtered as you type the filename:

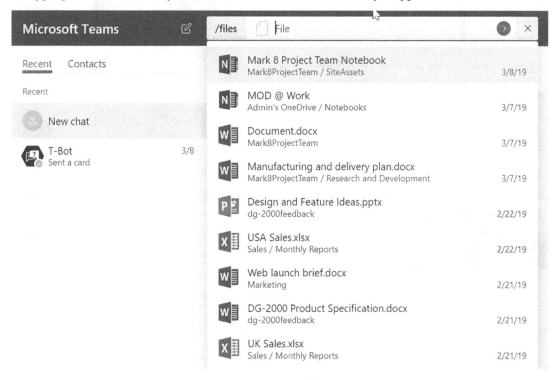

Figure 7.68: Searching for files

See also

- The *Initiating conversations via posts* recipe in this chapter
- The *Scheduling a meeting* recipe in this chapter
- The *Sharing files* recipe in this chapter
- Use Content Search in Microsoft Teams | Microsoft Learn: https://packt.link/ediscovery-content-search
- Search for telephone numbers for users – Microsoft Teams | Microsoft Learn: https://packt.link/search-for-phone-numbers

The power of Teams is enhanced by its ability to integrate with other applications. This is achieved by using connectors. We will learn about connectors in the next recipe.

Adding a connector

One of the highly effective features of Teams is the ability to add connectors to other applications inside a channel. Connectors let Teams communicate with an external application. So, you can do things such as manage your GitHub project from within Teams or track your team's progress within Trello.

Trello is a popular web-based Kanban-style task management application.

This is different from adding a tab to a Teams channel. Adding a tab would just render the application within the Teams interface, but it would not actually talk to Teams specifically. However, adding a connector allows you to send or push information from one application to another.

The next section provides steps to integrate other applications with Teams.

 Note

As of the time when this book was written, the new Teams app does not allow end users to add connectors. Only admins can add connectors within an existing team. The following steps outline the process in the classic Teams version.

Getting ready

You need to be a team owner to add a connector.

How to do it...

To add an external connector:

1. Select a team using the navigation bar on the left.
2. Select the channel you want to add the connector to.
3. Click on the ... symbol, as shown, and select **Connectors**:

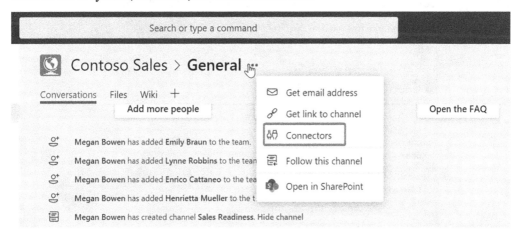

Figure 7.69: Adding connectors

4. The next screen will display all the available applications that can be connected to Teams. You can use the filters on the left to narrow down the list:

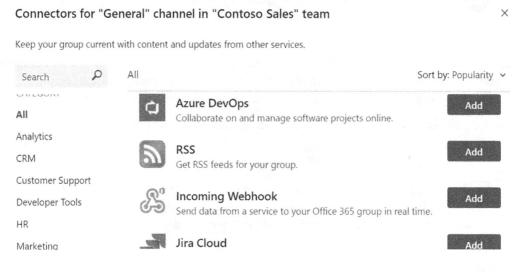

Figure 7.70: Searching for available connectors

5. Click **Add** and follow the application-specific instructions.

How it works...

Depending on what app you add, you might see subsequent screens that take you through a setup process. For instance, if you add a connector to GitHub, it will ask you to log in with your GitHub credentials and then it will pull your GitHub information through:

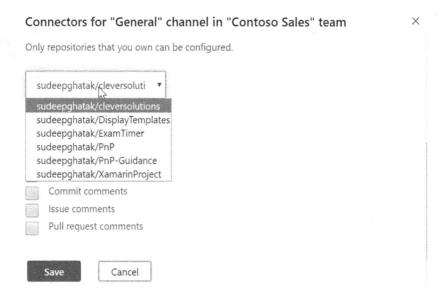

Figure 7.71: GitHub connector

So, now, we don't need to have access to GitHub to track progress. We can track progress right from within a Teams channel conversation area:

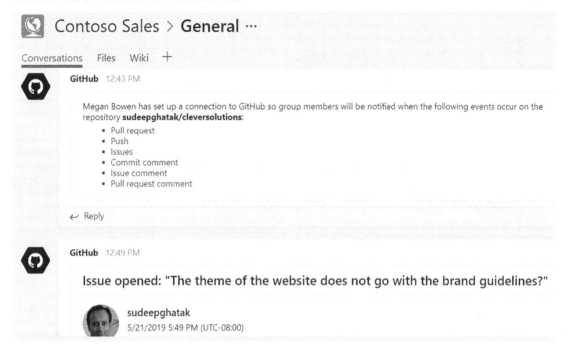

Figure 7.72: Using Azure DevOps connector within Teams

There's more...

You can use connectors to create actionable cards in Teams, which lets you perform actions in the external application without having to leave the Teams interface. You can read about actionable cards here: `https://packt.link/adaptive-cards`.

See also

• The *Creating channels and tabs* recipe in this chapter

Let's now learn how you can use Microsoft Teams to help facilitate approval business processes in your organization.

Using approvals in Teams

This recipe details the steps involved for setting up an approval in Teams and working it through the approval process to an end result.

Getting ready

Anyone with policy-granted permissions to use the Approvals app in Teams (allowed by default) can create approvals. A Teams Administrator would have to explicitly block the Approvals app via permission policy assigned to a user in order for it to not be available for that user.

How to do it...

1. From a new channel conversation or reply, select the **Approvals** icon from beneath the text box:

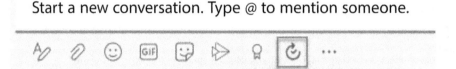

Figure 7.73: Approvals icon below a channel conversation or reply box

2. In the resulting dialog, leave **Request type** as **Basic**, add a request name, approver(s), and any relevant details your approvers need to know. You can also choose whether a single approver or all approvers' responses are required to qualify as approval:

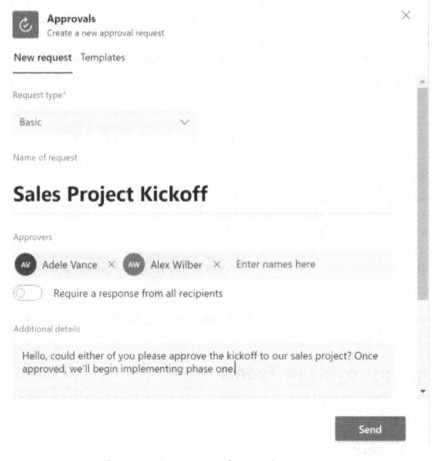

Figure 7.74: A new approval request in progress

3. Optionally, scroll down in the dialog to attach a document and customize responses:

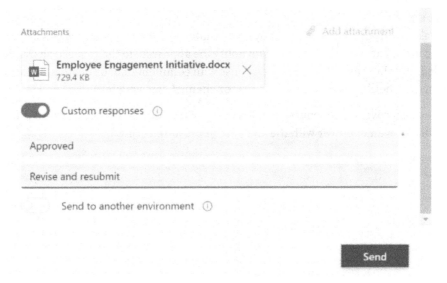

Figure 7.75: An approval request being configured with custom response options

4. When you're satisfied with the approval, click **Send** to notify approver(s) and request their response(s).

5. If your team members haven't used Approvals in your team before, you'll get a prompt your first time to accept the privacy policy and terms and conditions for using Power Automate (which supports the Approvals app). Click **Continue** if you agree.

6. The Approvals app will post to the channel conversation with the details of the requested approval. All team members can see these details and monitor its current status:

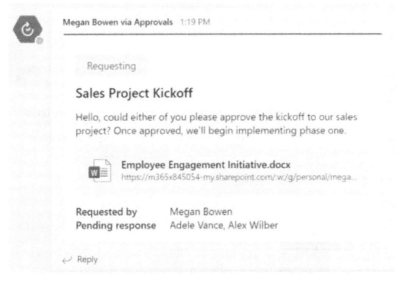

Figure 7.76: A Teams post by the Approvals app with the request details

How it works...

Posting a new approval in a Teams chat or channel conversation creates an approval process in the Approvals app. Approvals is powered by Power Automate, so the process is actually an approval flow running in the background. The flow will notify the approvers in the request, share the details you've provided, and allow them to submit a response with comment that, ultimately, updates in the original location (whether it was requested in a chat or channel conversation).

If you're an approver of the request, you'll see response options on the same post shown in *step 6* (since **Megan Bowen** is an approver with the ability to approve/reject):

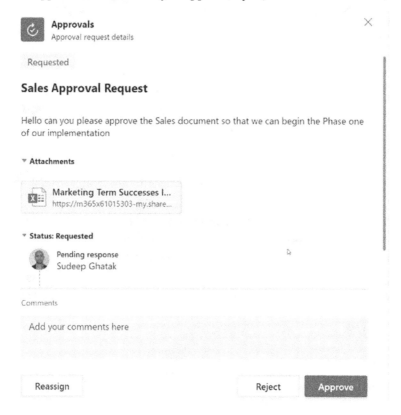

Figure 7.77: An approver's perspective on a new request with response options visible

Approvers also get a Teams activity notification when an approval is requested:

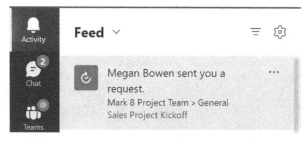

Figure 7.78: Activity notification for a pending approval

Approvers can also use the Approvals app in Teams to review all requested approvals and work through them in one place:

Figure 7.79: Approvals dashboard in Teams

Once a request is approved, the original location (a channel conversation post in this case) is updated so all team members can see the status. Requester and approvers also have a history in the Approvals app they can refer to:

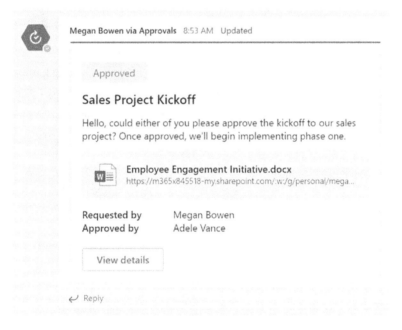

Figure 7.80: A completed approval showing an approved response

There's more...

Approvals can also be used in one-on-one and group chats. No matter where approvals are initiated (chats or channel conversations), you can find a history of all sent and received approvals and their current status by navigating to the **Approvals app** via the Teams left-hand navigation (app bar). Simply click on the ellipsis and click on the app, searching for it if necessary.

The Approvals app has two tabs along the top to help you navigate from the requests you've been sent as an approver, as well as those you've sent as a requestor. If you were to look at the **Sent** tab for the approval we created in this recipe, you'd see the following:

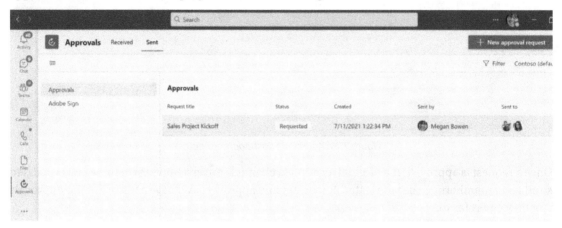

Figure 7.81: The Approvals app dashboard showing sent approvals

You can also pin the Approvals app to the app bar so it will stay there as you navigate to other apps within Teams. Simply right-click the **Approvals** app once it's visible on the app bar and choose **Pin**.

From the Approvals app, Teams administrators and team owners are also able to customize the templates available in the entire organization, or in their specific teams respectively. This way, users can do more than a generic approval. To customize templates, you can go to the **Approvals** app in Teams, select the **...** next to **New approval request**, then **Manage templates**:

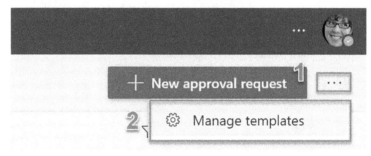

Figure 7.82: Template location next to the New approval request button

Then select the team for which you want to add a new template, followed by **New template**:

Figure 7.83: New template button in Template management

Choose from a large selection of templates from which you can start, or choose to create a new approval template from scratch:

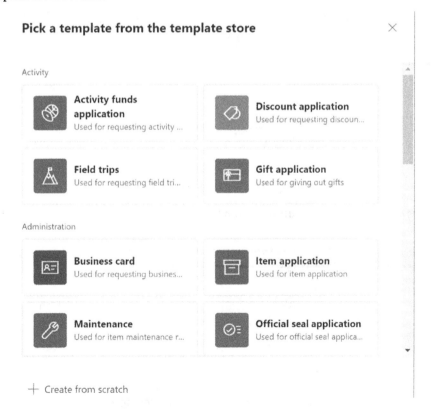

Figure 7.84: Available templates in the template store

Depending on the template chosen, you can then customize the fields (like form fields) and arrange them how you like. As you work through the wizard, you'll have an opportunity to not only change fields but also specify specific approvers for a process so users can't simply choose their own. This standardizes processes and simplifies things for your users. In the following screenshot, you can see the screen from which you are able to specify approvers for this particular new template:

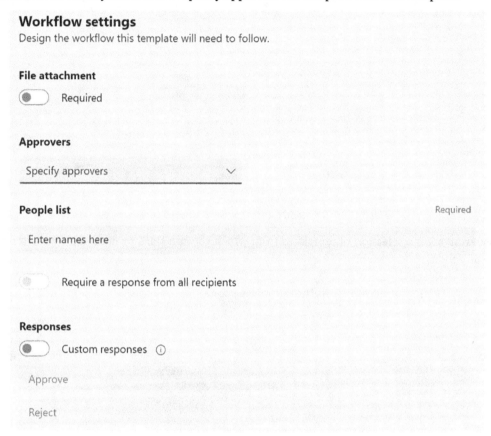

Figure 7.85: Approval workflow settings for a template

You can always edit this template again later from the same place (**Approvals > Manage templates | Select team**):

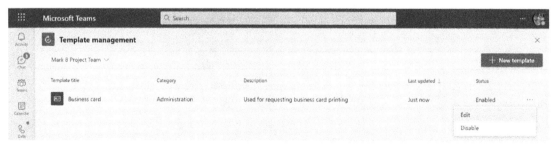

Figure 7.86: Custom templates in the Template management screen

Finally, users will now be able to use this new template whenever they add an approval to a channel conversation in that team. They'll just need to select **Templates** from the **Approvals** dialog, followed by the template of choice:

Figure 7.87: Choosing a business card template for an actual approval request

By using Approvals in Teams, your team will be able to reduce its reliance on paper form processes and perhaps even simply some manually built digital form processes and their associated approvals.

See also

- Approvals app now available on Microsoft Teams: `https://packt.link/Approvals-app`
- Approvals in Microsoft Teams – Power Automate: `https://packt.link/native-approvals`

Now that we know how to implement approval processes in Teams, let's look at how our team can create, share, and execute events easily within each channel.

Create a channel calendar tab

Each Teams channel has tabs for **Posts**, **Files**, and **Wiki** by default. Each channel can have additional tabs, including the channel calendar tab, which embeds the group calendar from Outlook and shows that channel's meetings and events. This recipe will share the steps involved in adding a team's shared calendar as a channel calendar tab in a particular channel.

Getting ready

You will need to be a team owner or team member with permissions to add tabs to channels in your team to be able to complete the steps in this recipe.

How to do it...

1. Navigate to the specific team channel to which you'd like to add the channel calendar. In this recipe, we'll use the **General** channel of the **Design** team.
2. Select the + to the right of the existing channel tabs along the top of the channel to add a new tab.

3. Search for or find and select **Channel calendar:**

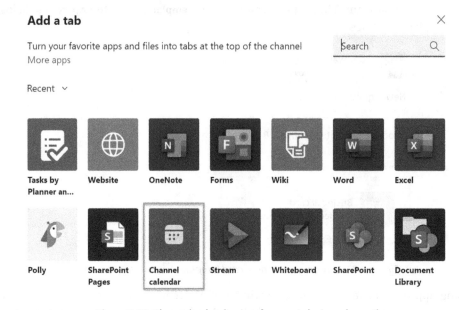

Figure 7.88: Channel calendar app for new tabs in a channel

4. Choose **Add:**

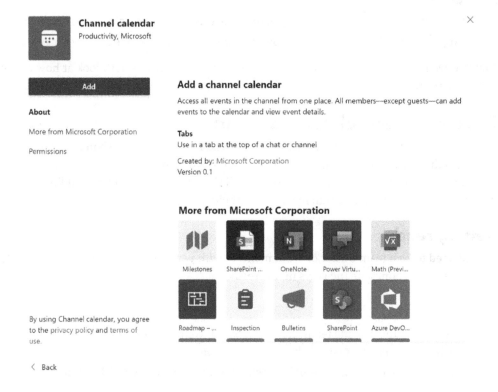

Figure 7.89: Channel calendar app information

5. Enter a name for the new tab (**Channel Calendar** is default) and click **Add** when ready:

Figure 7.90: Naming the tab for a channel calendar

6. Your channel now shows the calendar for your team/group, specifically filtered to events for its hosting channel. In this case, we see the Design team's group calendar filtered to the events for the **General** channel:

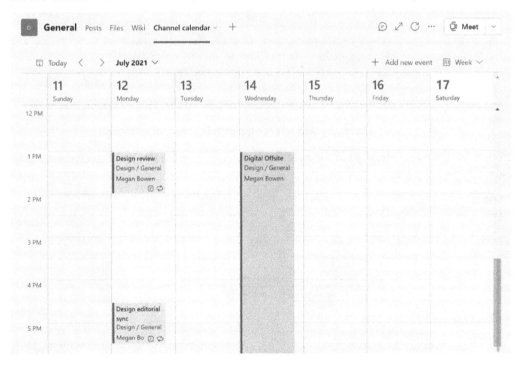

Figure 7.91: A channel calendar embedded as a tab in a channel

How it works

Each team in Microsoft Teams is supported by a Microsoft 365 group. That Microsoft 365 group comes with an Outlook shared inbox and calendar.

Each channel in a team can have its own meetings. When you schedule a meeting and invite a channel, the recordings, chats, etc. are all stored/accessible via that channel. The channel calendar allows you to show these events in a calendar view for ease of access and navigation. You can now easily navigate previous and upcoming events and all of their resources such as chats, recordings, attendance reports, and more without having to search the **Posts** tab at length.

There's more...

Once you've added the Teams channel calendar tab to a channel, you can use it to not only view events but to add more. When you add an event to a channel calendar, it automatically inserts that channel as an invited channel in the new event to save you time and keep you focus in the current context.

To add an event via the channel calendar, click **Add new event** in the upper right:

Figure 7.92: Add new event button in a channel calendar

Notice the new event already has the specific channel inserted in the event so all team members will certainly get an invite:

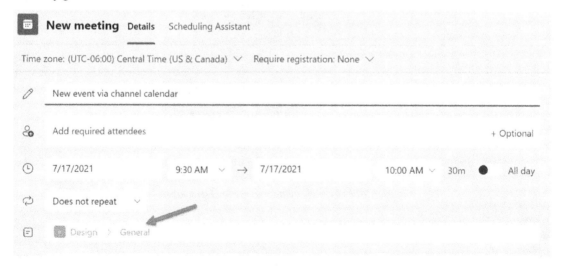

Figure 7.93: Channel meeting location/channel specification

See also

- See all your meetings in Teams: `https://packt.link/see-meetings`

Next, let's learn how we can gather pre-event information by requiring registration for a meeting or webinar.

Creating custom registration forms for Teams meetings

Custom registration forms can be added to any Teams meeting or webinar so that your attendees have a more formal process of signing up to attend your event. You'll also be able to capture additional attendee details, opinions, etc. in advance of the meeting through using this method. In this recipe, we'll go through the steps required to add and configure a custom registration form for a Teams meeting.

Getting ready

You'll need to be the meeting organizer/creator to create the custom registration form. Your settings for who can complete the registration form may also be limited if your admin has restricted external access in your organization.

How to do it...

1. Click **Calendar** in the left-hand pane:

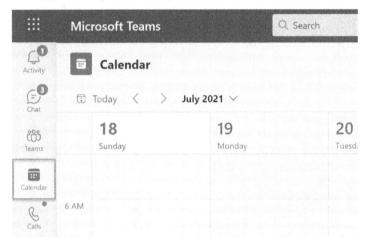

Figure 7.94: Calendar app in Teams

2. Find and open the meeting or webinar details for which you want to create a custom registration form:

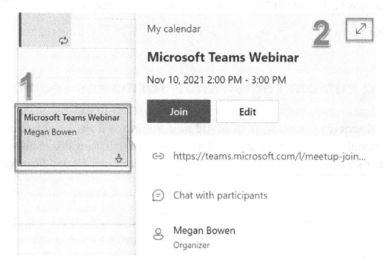

Figure 7.95: An expanded event details dialog

3. Select **Require registration**, then choose the audience for this event (who can register for the meeting or webinar). In this example, we'll choose **For everyone** so people outside our company can register to attend as well:

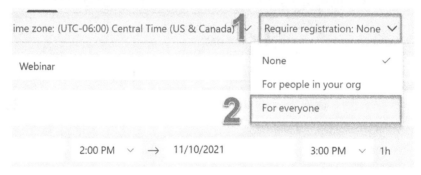

Figure 7.96: Registration requirement options for an event

4. In the dialog that pops up, select **View registration form**:

5. From here you can upload a banner image for the registration form, add or change event details (that those registering will see), and add speaker details:

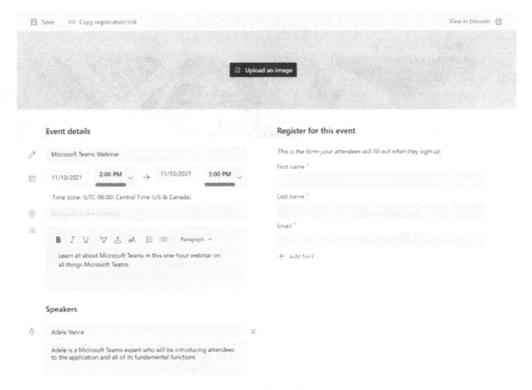

Figure 7.97: A custom registration form in edit mode

6. Under the **Register for this event** column of the form, you can click **Add field** to add additional fields to survey attendees on their interests, opinions, job function, existing knowledge, etc. prior to the event. As you add these additional registration form fields, you can check a box for each to require it as well:

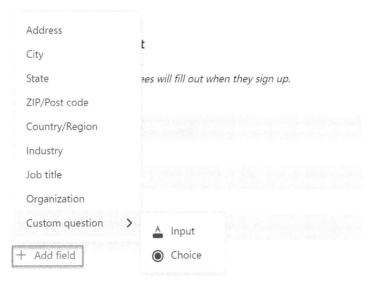

Figure 7.98: Adding registration fields

7.   When you're satisfied with the registration form, click **Save** in the upper left corner:

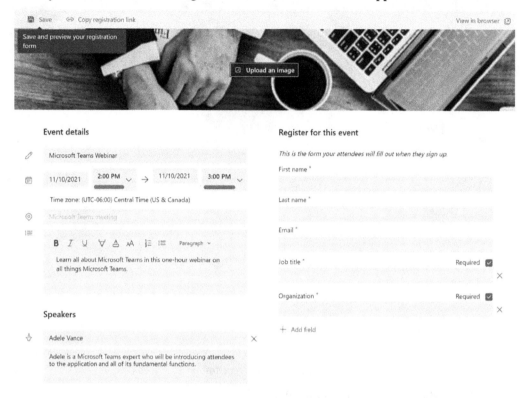

Figure 7.99: Custom registration form fully configured before a save

8.   You'll now see a preview of your registration form. You can choose to **Edit** it again, or **View in browser**. But if you're satisfied with the way it appears, you can return to your Teams event details:

Figure 7.100: Final custom registration form preview

9. You can share the form with potential attendees by selecting **Copy registration link** either in event details as shown in the following screenshot, or from the registration form's edit page as seen in the previous screenshot. Then include that link in any Teams chats, SharePoint event pages, mailing list blasts, social media posts, etc. to promote your event and get attendees to register:

Figure 7.101: Copy registration link option in an event with a custom registration form

How it works...

The custom registration form is available for meetings and webinars using Microsoft Teams. It allows you to build a web-based registration form for attendees (whether exclusively within your company, or a combination of internal and external). Meeting and webinar organizers can use this to better plan for the event, as well as to collect information about the audience such as industry, years in the profession, interest levels in various agenda items, etc.

There's more...

As people are registering to attend your meeting or webinar, the meeting organizers can access the automatically generated and updated registration report at any point. This can be found in the event details and is labelled **Registration** as seen in the following screenshot. The registration report is an Excel worksheet with one registration per row, and your registration form fields across the columns:

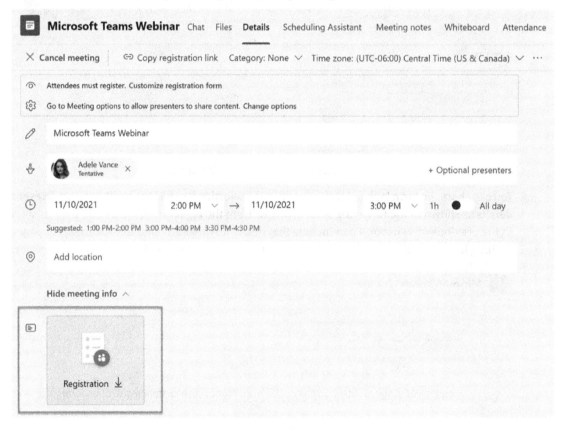

Figure 7.102: Registration report download location

Just as with live events, your webinars and meetings with custom registration forms should be treated differently than a normal meeting. Be sure not to share the **Join** links with any attendees of registration-required events. Attendees should only use the **Copy registration link** option you share with them:

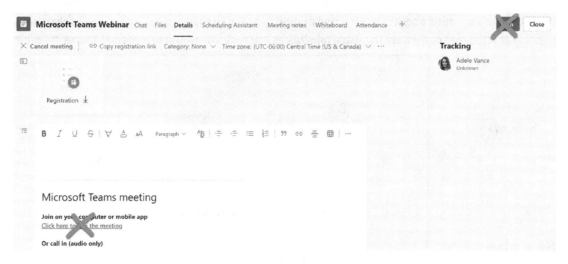

Figure 7.103: Join meeting links in event details

You can share the **Join** link (or invite attendees or forward the Outlook invite) with presenters and organizers only.

If you need to edit the registration form at a later time (after initial creation), open the event details from your Teams calendar (*step 2*) and choose **Customize registration form**:

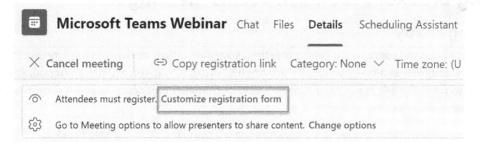

Figure 7.104: Customize registration form link in an event

You'll then need to choose edit as the form will first be displayed in preview mode:

Figure 7.105: Edit link location for a custom registration form

If you change your mind about requiring registration, you can change **Require registration** back to **None**, then invite attendees or forward the usual **Join** link as you typically would in a normal Teams meeting:

Figure 7.106: Require registration options for an event

See also

*   How to schedule a Microsoft Teams webinar: `https://packt.link/schedule-a-Teams-webinar`
*   Schedule a Teams meeting with registration: `https://packt.link/schedule-a-Teams-meeting`

Now that we know more about the pre-meeting setup, let's explore a popular intra-meeting feature you can use to help facilitate Teams meetings: breakout rooms.

Using breakout rooms in Teams meetings

Getting ready

To manage breakout rooms for a Teams meeting, you must either be the meeting organizer or must have been assigned as a co-organizer by the original organizer. If you are not an organizer or co-organizer, you will not see the breakout rooms icon or management settings and will only be able to participate as an attendee.

In addition to being an organizer or co-organizer, you'll only be able to manage breakout rooms using the Teams desktop app (you won't find the ability in the Teams web or mobile apps).

How to do it...

1. Join the Teams meeting for which you'll be managing breakout rooms as an organizer or co-organizer.

2. Click the **Breakout rooms** icon next to the **Reaction/Raise hand** icon:

Figure 7.107: Breakout rooms button location in a meeting

3. Change the number of rooms to the desired number, and then choose if you want attendees automatically distributed evenly into that number of rooms or if you'll be manually assigning attendees as they join. For this recipe, we'll choose 3 rooms and automatic assignment:

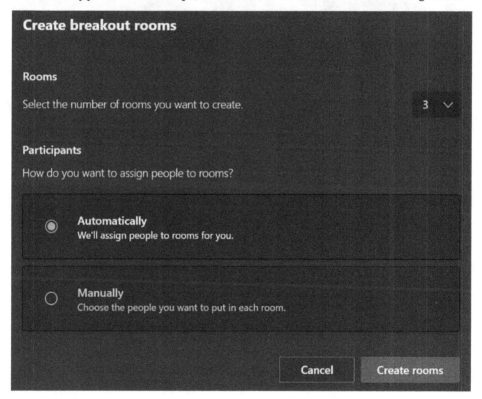

Figure 7.108: Breakout rooms configuration screen for participant assignment

4. Click **Create rooms**.

5.   Once created, you may wish to configure a timer for the rooms. Click the **...** at the top of the
     Breakout rooms panel and choose **Rooms** settings:

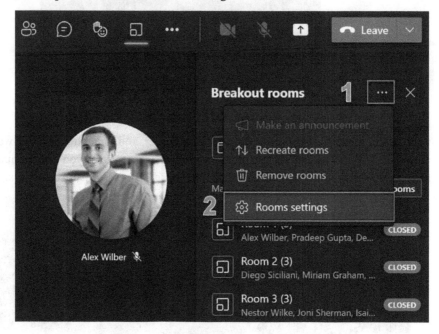

Figure 7.109: Rooms setting location for breakout rooms

6.   Make any room setting changes such as specifying a time limit (to end rooms after a specific pe-
     riod), whether participants are automatically moved or have to move themselves, and whether
     participants can return to the main room before breakout rooms are officially stopped. When
     you're satisfied with your selections, choose the < to the left of **Settings**:

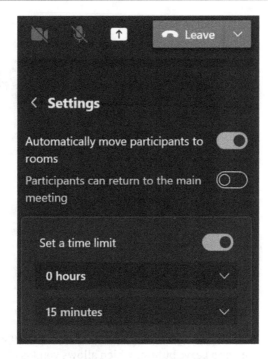

Figure 7.110: Room settings for breakout rooms

7. Once back on the breakout rooms' main panel, you'll see the ability to **Start rooms** (send attendees to their designated breakout rooms) or **Add room** if you determine you'll need another. Click **Start rooms** to begin the breakout rooms:

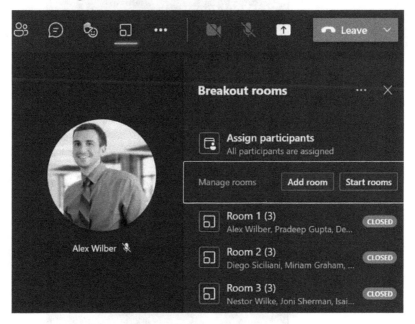

Figure 7.111: Start rooms link for breakout rooms

8. As organizer, you may wish to join one of the now-open rooms. Use the **...** next to an open room to join it:

Figure 7.112: Join room link for a breakout room during a meeting

Your breakout room will open in a new window. You'll notice a timer if you set a time limit for the rooms as well as a **Leave** button, which allows you (as organizer) to return to the main meeting only. Click **Leave** when ready to return to the main room.

You can reassign a participant to a different room manually by selecting the room they're in, selecting their name, choosing **Assign,** and then choosing their new room:

Figure 7.113: Breakout room assignment/reassignment location during a meeting

9. During your breakout room sessions, you may wish to make an announcement to all rooms (such as remaining time, sharing links or prompts, etc.). Announcements appear in each of the rooms' chat panels. You can make an announcement by choosing the **...** then **Make an announcement**:

Figure 7.114: Announcement capability for breakout rooms administration

10. When you're finished with breakout rooms, you can end them (or end them early if a time limit is running) by choosing **Close rooms**:

Figure 7.115: Close rooms button for breakout rooms during a meeting

11. All rooms are now ended, and participants will automatically rejoin the main meeting. When the main meeting is over as well, you can use the dropdown arrow next to **Leave** to **End meeting** for all.

How it works...

Breakout rooms allow meeting organizers to plan for larger meetings where the agenda items could benefit from attendees breaking into smaller groups for more focused discussions, but ultimately returning to the main meeting.

Some organizers may use breakout rooms professionally, such as when committees need to collaborate for a period of time before returning to the larger group. Others may choose to use breakout rooms for less formal purposes such as virtual trivia or other activities in which questions are shared in the main meeting, then trivia teams split out into their breakout rooms to submit answers before returning to the main meeting when answers will be shared and winners announced.

No matter the purpose, these breakout rooms allow for less hassle than setting up separate meeting and requiring attendees to manage multiple links. We, as organizers, can instead send a single link and manage their "presence" ourselves.

Technically, when a participant is in a breakout room it's as though they've joined another meeting and placed the main meeting on hold. When they return, they leave the second room (breakout room) and reconnect to the main meeting.

There's more...

Breakout rooms also have their own settings where instead of automatic attendee assignment, you can manually assign attendees to specific rooms (such as committee members or trivia teams).

Automatic may be more useful if you simply need an even distribution of attendees across the number of rooms you've specified. But manual can be handy when you know specific people need to collaborate, or perhaps you have a designated moderator per room.

To set up manual assignment, you'd choose **Manually** in *step 3* instead. After creating the rooms, you can then click **Assign participants**:

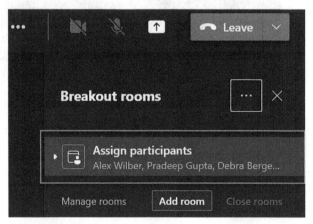

Figure 7.116: Assign participants option during a meeting

Then you'll select the attendees to group together, choose **Assign**, then the room to which they'll breakout:

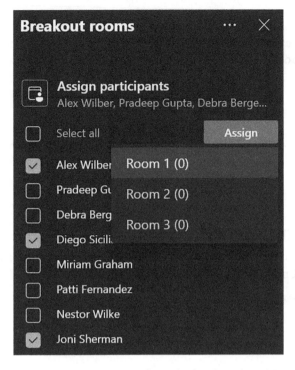

Figure 7.117: Room assignment for multiple selected participants

You can also configure a timer for breakout rooms so that automatically after 15 minutes, for example, your attendees are brought back to the main room. In these scenarios they'll see a timer in their individual breakout rooms and are given a 5-minute warning before they're returned to the main room.

You may also wish to rename breakout rooms. Instead of Room 1, Room 2, etc. you may wish to name them after committee names, strategic initiatives, etc. To do this, you'll select the **...** next to the room and choose **Rename room**:

Figure 7.118: Rename room option for a breakout room

Attendees cannot currently choose their own breakout rooms, and you cannot configure breakout rooms and manual assignments prior to joining the meeting.

See also

- Using breakout rooms in Teams: `https://packt.link/using-breakout-rooms`

Learn more on Discord

To join the Discord community for this book – where you can share feedback, ask questions to the author, and learn about new releases – follow the QR code below:

`https://packt.link/powerusers`

8

Power Automate (Microsoft Flow)

Power Automate (formerly Microsoft Flow) was launched as Microsoft's lightweight workflow engine for end users, developers, and IT professionals. It lets you build personal automated workflows using a wide range of services, without having to learn any code. There are hundreds of templates available to build flows that talk to Dropbox, Twitter, Viva Engage, Facebook, Dynamics 365, and other services. This makes building flows quicker and easier.

So, what do you use the Power Automate service for?

The clue is in the name, "Power" and "Automate." "Power" refers to the fact that it is meant to be used by Power users as part of the Power Platform, and "Automate" indicates that the service lets us program the automation of a manual business process.

In this chapter, we will learn how to use Power Automate by working through the following topics:

- Introducing flows
- Creating a flow using a template
- Editing a flow
- Testing a flow
- Exporting a flow
- Importing a flow
- Adding owners to a flow
- Sharing your flow
- Creating a solution
- Creating a flow in a SharePoint library
- Creating a business process flow

First, we will learn about the simple elements involved in making a workflow in Power Automate, and then we will look at the **process builder**, which helps visualize the steps a workflow will follow. Then, we will cover the landing page where we will design our first flow. After covering how to distribute, add co-owners, and share our flow, we will then go through some more advanced concepts such as solutions and business process flows. For now, let's look at the basics.

Technical requirements

Let's briefly look at the paid plans available for Power Automate, before exploring the initial concepts of a flow and the landing page where we will create a flow. Power Automate is available with two plans (not considering RPA plans):

Power Automate per user plan	This plan lets a user with rights run an unlimited number of flows (within service limits) with the full capabilities of Power Automate, including standard and premium connectors, based on their unique needs for a monthly fixed cost for each user.
Power Automate per flow plan	This plan lets your organization implement flows for a specific team, a department, or an entire organization without having to license each user separately.

Table 8.1: Power Automate per user and per flow plans

You can check the pricing of these plans at `https://packt.link/Power-Automate-pricing`.

Introducing flows

We have mentioned that flows are the *automation of a manual business process*. More specifically, Power Automate lets you design a workflow comprising a sequence of **tasks** and **conditions**. These tasks can be achieved using **connectors**.

 There are over 500 connectors available at the time of writing this chapter. New connectors are listed here as they are added: `https://packt.link/connectors`.

To help keep track of all the connectors being used for tasks and conditions, Power Automate provides a rich user interface that allows you to build a **process map**. The process map is a tool that shows the inputs, actions, and outputs of a process in a graphical format, step by step:

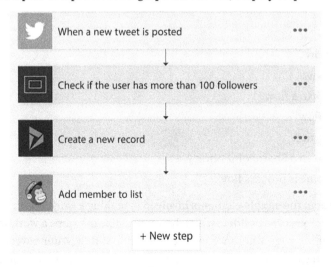

Figure 8.1: Sequential actions in Power Automate

We can see that after the flow is triggered, it works through a series of steps that are laid out one after the other. With the process map, we can clearly see what conditions lead to what tasks, and which connectors are being used.

Now we will look at the flow landing page, where we will design our first flow.

Flow landing page

This section explains how the flow designer is structured. On your left, you have the following links:

- **Home:** The **Home** page displays the featured flow templates available for you to use grouped by category. You can even search for flows by use case:

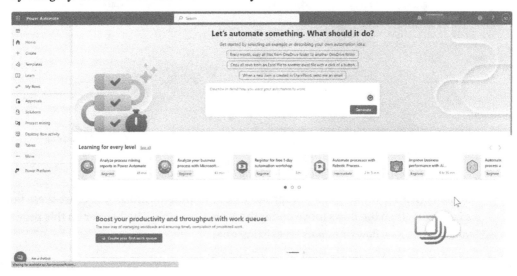

Figure 8.2: Power Automate Home page

🔍 **Quick tip:** Need to see a high-resolution version of this image? Open this book in the next-gen Packt Reader or view it in the PDF/ePub copy.

🔒 **The next-gen Packt Reader** and a **free PDF/ePub copy** of this book are included with your purchase. Unlock them by scanning the QR code below or visiting `https://www.packtpub.com/unlock/9781803243177`.

- **Action items:** All your approval tasks (across every flow) will appear under the **Approvals** section. You can approve or reject them by providing comments. All your past approval actions can be seen under the **History** tab:

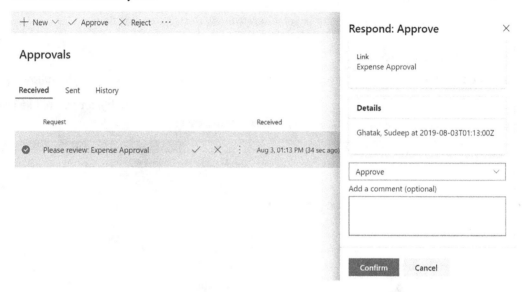

Figure 8.3: Actioning Power Automate approvals

- **My flows:** The flows that you build appear under the **My flows** link. If you share these flows with a colleague, then the flows move under the **Team flows** link. The banner on this page also lets you create a **New flow** or **Import** an existing one:

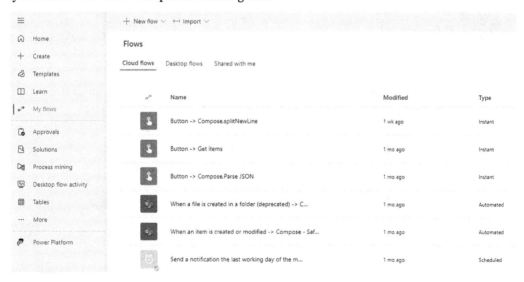

Figure 8.4: My flows

- **Business process flows:** These are flows built using Dataverse. You can think of Dataverse as a storage option for your business data. Dataverse stores data within entities, unlike databases, which store data in tables. Dataverse manages data as well as the entity schema, so you can focus only on the business process (which you can build using Power Automate).

- **UI flows:** These let you record and play back user interface actions (clicks, keyboard input, and so on) for applications that don't have APIs available. UI flows have a **record** feature that lets you perform your manual actions and save them as a part of the flow.

- **Templates:** As the name suggests, this page displays a list of flow templates to choose from.

- **Connectors:** The connectors in Power Automate provide you with access to the functionality of other Microsoft 365 services (SharePoint, OneDrive) or third-party services (Dropbox, MailChimp, and so on). A list of available connectors can be seen at `https://packt.link/ Power-Automate-connectors`.

- **Data:** The **Data** link provides access to Dataverse entities as described previously. It also enables you to pull data from your on-premises environment through **gateways**.

- **AI Builder:** AI Builder lets you leverage Microsoft's artificial intelligence features, such as text recognition, outcome prediction, and so on, to build AI models.

- **Solutions:** Hosting flows in a solution makes it easier to move them and all their components from one environment to another. You can add multiple flows in a single solution.

Now that we have seen the landing page where we can create a flow, we will begin our first recipe, where we will go through the actual process of making one.

Creating a flow using a template

If you have an idea for a flow, there's a good chance that someone already thought about it before you. So, before building a new flow from scratch, look for an existing template. This will save you a lot of time since the template will come with actions and a process flow that can then be modified or extended. It will also serve as a quick-start guide and a learning tool. Just as you can use flows created by others, you can submit your own flows to the flow store. Your flow will appear on the gallery page if it successfully goes through the approval process.

Getting ready

You can sign up for a free Power Automate account at `https://flow.microsoft.com`. It has a free plan as well as business plans. Power Automate comes with most Microsoft 365 licensing plans. Refer to the Microsoft Licensing guide for more details. You can download it from `https://packt.link/ PP-licensing-guide`. The free plan is good for prototypes. You can sign up for a business plan once you are ready to go live.

The free plan lets you run a limited number of flows until it expires. The free plan lets you create unlimited flows, but you only get 750 runs per month and checks happen every 15 minutes.

How to do it...

1. Log in to `https://office.com` using your Microsoft 365 account.
2. Click on **Power Automate** from the list of apps.

3. On the Power Automate landing page, scroll to the end of the page to access the starter templates. If you can't see what you are looking for, click on **See more templates** and use the search bar to find more templates:

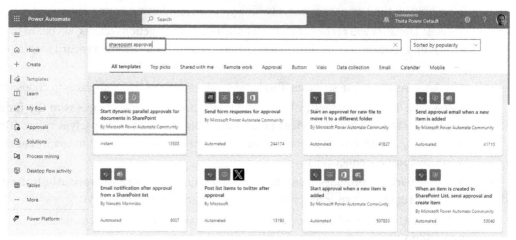

Figure 8.5: Looking for the right template for use

4. Select a template that looks the most like what you are looking for. We'll pick the first one in the preceding list.

5. The next job is to provide credentials for all these connectors, as shown in the following screenshot:

Figure 8.6: Power Automate connections

6. You will then be taken to the Power Automate designer screen, as shown in the following screenshot:

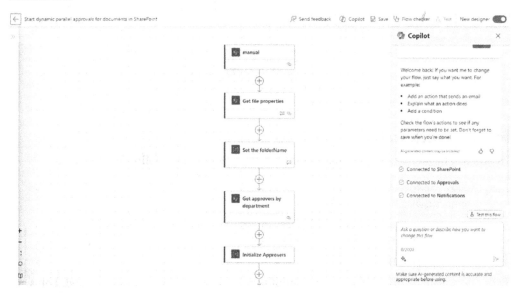

Figure 8.7: Power Automate designer

7. You can customize the flow as per your requirements at this stage and click on **Save** in the top-right corner once you are done:

Figure 8.8: Saving your flow

8. Click on the field at the top left to change the name of the flow:

Figure 8.9: Giving your flow a name

Congrats! You just built your first flow.

How it works...

In order to master Power Automate, you need to understand the following concepts:

*   Flow components
*   Flow history
*   Flow details

Flow components

Every flow is made of a trigger, a number of actions, and any connections needed. Let's go through each of these components.

Trigger: Every flow starts with a trigger. A trigger is a condition that initiates the flow. In the preceding example, creating a list item in SharePoint acted as a trigger, which means that the flow will run every time a new item is created.

You can create three main types of triggers:

- **Automated:** A flow triggered automatically by an event, such as creating a new item in Share-Point or receiving an email in your inbox.
- **Instant:** A flow triggered manually by a button.
- **Scheduled:** A flow that runs once or as a recurring action at a specific time.

Triggers have a setting called **trigger conditions**, which let you specify one or more expressions that must be true for the trigger to fire—for example, if you have a trigger on an item update event, then the flow will run every time the item is updated. But if you want to refine the trigger condition so that the flow only gets triggered when a particular column (let's say the **Status** column) in the list has a specific value (for example, **To Process**), then you can achieve this by adding a trigger condition:

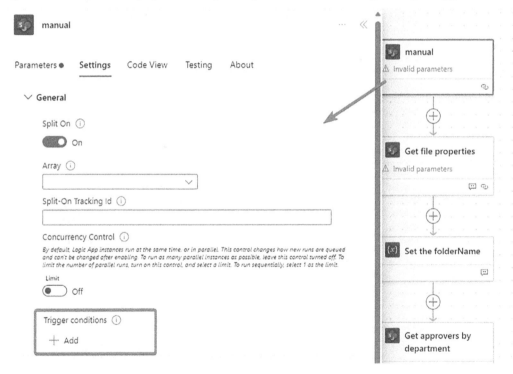

Figure 8.10: Adding a trigger condition

Action: A trigger is followed by one or more actions. An action could be a query, create, update, insert, or delete operation. The following are some examples of actions:

- Creating a new list item
- Moving a file from OneDrive
- Sending an email notification

To add an action, click on the + icon:

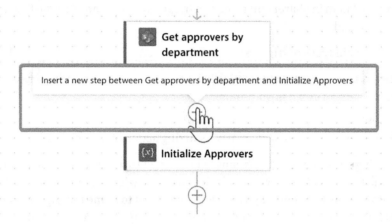

Figure 8.11: Adding a new flow step

This reveals all the actions that you can add to your Power Automate workflow.

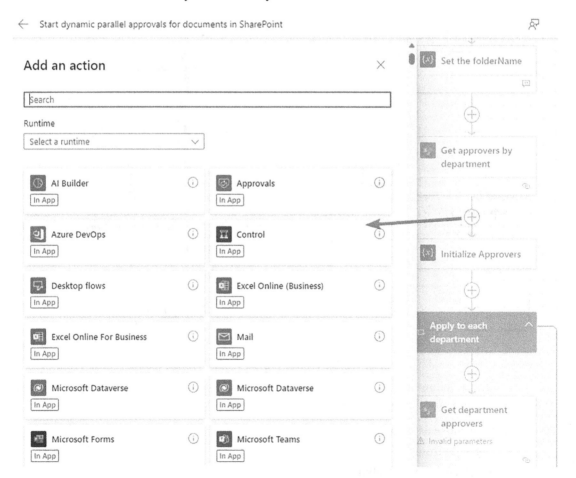

Figure 8.12: Available Power Automate actions

To find out more about an action, click on the info icon to the right.

Connections: Connections let you interact with data from other systems. To establish a connection, you need to specify the credentials with which to log in to the application you are connecting to.

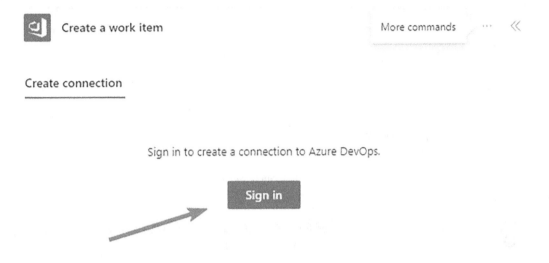

Figure 8.13: Create a flow connection

Flow history

A run history shows you each instance of execution of a given flow, or in other words, every time the trigger condition is met:

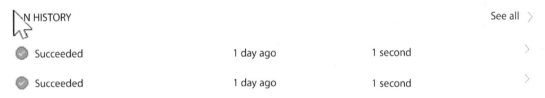

Figure 8.14: Looking through the run history

If you click on a specific run, the flow expands and displays the actions that were executed, along with the time it took to run each action:

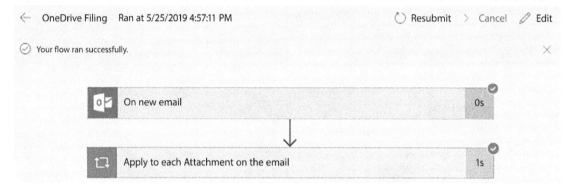

← OneDrive Filing   Ran at 5/25/2019 4:57:11 PM   ⟳ Resubmit   › Cancel   ✎ Edit

⊘ Your flow ran successfully.   ✕

| | On new email | 0s |
| | Apply to each Attachment on the email | 1s |

Figure 8.15: Successful run

 The run history is maintained for 30 days. If you want to use this information for auditing purposes, save the information in SharePoint or another data store.

Flow properties

You can update the flow properties from the context menu against the flow name. The flow properties let you modify the properties of a flow, such as the following:

- **Edit:** Lets you open the flow in designer mode
- **Share:** Add other owners to the flow
- **Save as:** Lets you create a copy of the flow
- **Send a copy:** Allows you to share a copy of this flow with others so that they can build their own version of the flow
- **Export:** Lets you save the flow as a package. It can then be imported to another tenant
- **Run history:** Lets you view all the flow execution instances
- **Analytics:** Lets you see the metrics related to the flow
- **Turn Off:** Disables the flow
- **Delete:** Deletes your flow

There's more...

The newly announced AI features within Power automate now let you Automate a specific task using natural language.

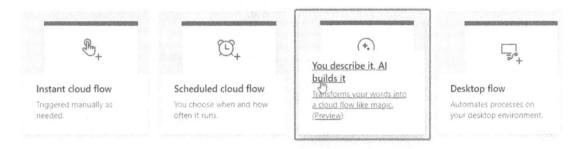

Figure 8.16: Option for creating a flow using natural language

The flow builder suggests the actions you can use and the sequence in which they need to be executed. Even if it doesn't build your flow from end to end, it drastically reduces the development time. It also flattens the learning curve.

When you build a flow, you are added as the owner automatically. The flow then runs in the context of your user account. This isn't a bad practice, but requires you to make the following considerations:

- If you have used **Send email** actions in your flow, recipients will receive emails from the user who published the flow
- If your flow is updating SharePoint list items, the **Modified By** field will display the flow owner's name
- Your flows will stop running if the user's account gets deleted or disabled
- The flow will only be able to perform tasks that the user is authorized for

User accounts can be used for simple scenarios but should be avoided for complex business processes. You should use a **service account** in such cases. A service account is just a regular Microsoft 365 account that is not associated with a staff member. However, you need to keep the following points in mind while using a service account:

1. You need to assign a Flow license to the service account.
2. The service account should be given the most limited access that it needs to perform its job.
3. Service accounts shouldn't be added to privileged groups or other security groups.
4. Set the password to **never expire**. If the password expires, your business process will error out.
5. Do not set **Multi-Factor Authentication** on service accounts.

 User accounts are meant to be used by the specific user for whom the account is created. A service account, on the other hand, doesn't belong to a specific user, rather it is meant for a specific service, such as a flow.

See also

- The *Editing a flow* recipe in this chapter
- The *Testing your flow* recipe in this chapter

- Browse Templates | Microsoft Power Automate: `https://packt.link/Power-Automate-templates`

Having created our first flow, let's see how we can edit one that already exists.

Editing a flow

You can update the flows that you have created. These flows appear under the **My flows** tab on the flow landing screen. Other flows that have been shared with you can be seen in the **Team flows** area.

Getting ready

You need to be a flow owner to edit it.

How to do it...

1. Log in to `https://office.com` using your Microsoft 365 account.
2. Click on **Flow**. This takes you to the landing page.
3. Choose the flow you want to modify or click **Edit**:

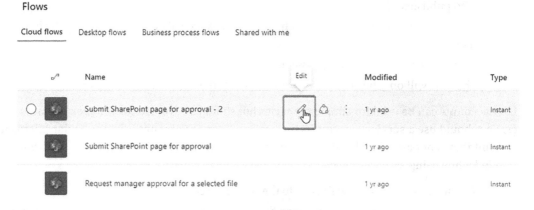

Figure 8.17: Editing your flow

4. Edit the flow by clicking on the **Edit** link in the top right-hand corner.
5. Make changes to the flow and click **Save**.

How it works...

A newer version of the flow is created every time you make a change. Currently, there is no way of going back to an older version. If you would like to save multiple versions of the flow, then you can do so by exporting the flow before making a change and saving the package in a version control system, such as VSTS or GitHub.

See also

- The *Creating a flow using a template* recipe in this chapter
- The *Testing your flow* recipe in this chapter

- The *Creating a flow on a SharePoint library* recipe in this chapter
- Get started with Power Automate – Training | Microsoft Learn: `https://packt.link/get-started-with-flows`

Is the flow that you just built up to the mark? Does it handle all possible scenarios? To answer these questions, you need to test your flow. Let's see how that's done.

Testing a flow

Every solution that we build needs to be validated against a set of test cases to ensure that it does what it was created to deliver. Power Automate offers a very good platform to test the flow logic. The testing process runs the business logic, so you shouldn't test flows on your production (live) system. The flow user interface (as demonstrated in the *How to do it...* section) can be used to observe inputs and outputs, as well as to investigate errors.

Presently, the feature only lets you test the last five flow runs.

Getting ready

Only the flow owner can test the flows, which means that you will need to be added as a co-owner if you want to test the flow.

How to do it...

1. Go to the Power Automate landing page.
2. Select the flow that you want to test and click **Edit**.
3. Click on **Test** in the top right-hand corner to test the flow:

Figure 8.18: Testing a flow

4. This will reveal a panel on the right with some options:

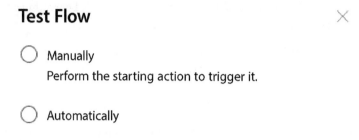

Figure 8.19: Adding a test trigger

5. Choose the appropriate option from the list. This list might look different depending on the type of trigger that is chosen. Here are the ways to provide a trigger:

   - **Manually**: Use this option if you want to trigger the flow manually or on a schedule. It lets you initiate the flow instantly.
   - **Automatically**: This option lets you test a flow using the same trigger inputs as the previous one. You can only use this option if the flow has been run before. This is a useful feature because you don't have to create data in your source system to kick off your flow.

How it works...

To ensure that your flows run as expected, perform the trigger, and then review the inputs and outputs that each step in your flow generates.

After the flow has run, you can investigate the flow by looking at the flow output in the center of the page.

The actions that succeed have a green check, whereas the ones that fail have a red cross:

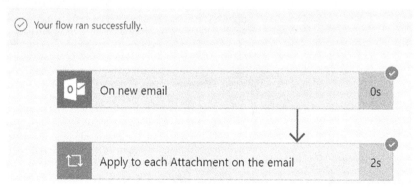

Figure 8.20: Successful flow run

Clicking the action (or trigger) reveals more information:

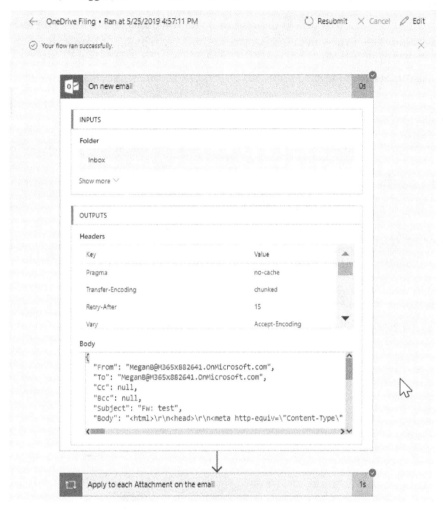

Figure 8.21: Investigating the flow output

This view lets you investigate the input and output values. In the case of an error, the error information is displayed.

See also

- The *Creating a flow using a template* recipe in this chapter
- The *Editing a flow* recipe in this chapter
- Testing strategy for a Power Automate project – Power Automate | Microsoft Learn: `https://packt.link/testing-strategy`

Now that we have tested our flow, we will turn our attention to how to distribute it. This will involve exporting and importing a flow, as well as adding owners with edit access and sharing it with others. In the next recipe, we will learn how to migrate flows across environments.

Exporting a flow

Exporting and importing a flow allows the reusability of the package and its deployment from one environment to another environment. A flow can be saved as a template, along with the dependencies used by the flow and all associated metadata, so that it can be reproduced in another Microsoft 365 tenant. This feature is useful in the absence of a version-control mechanism within a flow.

Flows can also be moved from one environment to another, using solutions, but we'll discuss solutions in the *Creating a solution* recipe.

If you want to migrate a *single* flow, then the **Import/Export** options are useful features to employ.

Getting ready

You need to be a flow owner to save a flow as a template.

How to do it...

1. Log in to `https://office.com` using your Microsoft 365 account.

2. Choose the flow you want to export.

3. Go to **Export | Package (.zip)** under the **More** link in the top right-hand corner, as shown in the following screenshot:

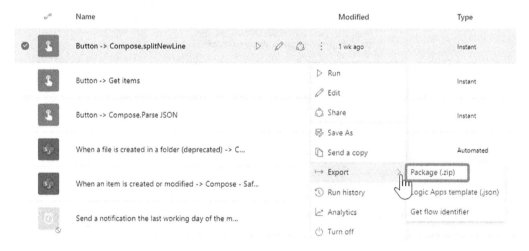

Figure 8.22: Exporting a flow as package

4. Give the package a name and click **Export | Package:**

Figure 8.23: Exported flow metadata

The flow will be downloaded as a ZIP file in the default download folder of your browser.

How it works...

The exported flow file can be saved in two formats: `.zip` and `.json`. A zipped version is perhaps the most widely used and user-friendly way to export flows. A JSON file is the coded version of the flow logic and is useful when migrating the flow logic to a separate platform, such as Logic Apps.

 JSON, short for JavaScript Object Notation, is a standard text-based format for representing structured data (just like XML) that is universally accepted for representing data.

See also

- The *Importing a flow* recipe in this chapter
- The *Creating a flow on a SharePoint library* recipe in this chapter
- Learn how to export solution-aware flows – Power Automate | Microsoft Learn: `https://packt.link/export-flow-solution`

In the next recipe, we'll see how you can import the flow we just exported.

Importing a flow

A flow package contains the logic of the flow as well as information about the connectors. It can therefore be imported into a new, separate environment, preserving the flow logic; however, the connection information needs to be updated according to the environment it is imported into.

Getting ready

Everyone within an organization can import a flow and publish it.

How to do it...

To import a flow, follow the following steps:

1. Go to the Power Automate landing page.
2. Click on **Import,** specify the location of the saved template, and click **Import.**
3. Specify whether you would like to update an existing flow by selecting **Update,** or create a new flow instead:

Figure 8.24: Importing a flow

4. When the flow is imported into a new environment, the connections must be reconfigured by clicking on the **Select during import** link:

Figure 8.25: Exported flow connections

5. This brings up a panel on the right that lets you create a connection or choose an existing connection:

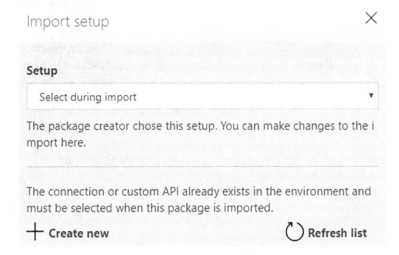

Figure 8.26: Reconfiguring the connections

6. You can save the flow after the connections have been configured.

How it works...

Please ensure that you don't have another flow with the same name in your environment when choosing **Update** in the import setup. This operation will overwrite your existing flow, which can't be retrieved once this is done.

> One of the limitations of the flow import process is that you cannot import a solution into an environment in which the solution already exists. You can use the **Save as** option if you wish to clone a flow.

See also

- The *Creating a flow using a template* recipe in this chapter
- The *Exporting a flow* recipe in this chapter
- The *Creating a flow on a SharePoint library* recipe in this chapter
- Import a solution – Power Automate | Microsoft Learn: `https://packt.link/import-flow-solution`

In the next recipe, we'll learn how to grant somebody edit access on a flow.

Adding owners to a flow

Owners can edit and save existing flows. By default, the creator of the flow is added as an owner.

While you could build personal flows to automate some of your personal work (such as monitoring your emails or OneDrive), it is always advisable to have more than one owner if you are designing the flow to achieve a common objective or business process. A flow that has more than one owner is called a **team flow**.

Besides editing the flow, an owner can also do the following:

- View the history of a given flow
- Edit the properties of a flow
- Modify an action or condition
- Manage owners
- Delete a flow

Getting ready

Owners must have a Power Automate plan to create a team flow (you can look at the options at `https://packt.link/pricing`). Only an owner of a flow can add other owners.

How to do it...

1. Go to the Power Automate landing page.
2. Go to the **Owners** section in the bottom right-hand corner of the screen and click **Add an owner**.
3. You should be able to add any individual from the organization or user group.
4. A pop-up screen will appear, explaining the permissions that the owner will have regarding the connections inside the flow. Click **OK**.

The new owner is added!

How it works...

When you add a new person as an owner of the flow, they will receive a notification and the flow will start appearing on their landing page under **Team flows**:

Figure 8.27: Adding a co-owner to your flow

As a co-owner, you can also add SharePoint lists to a flow so that everyone who has editing access to the list automatically gets editing access to the flow:

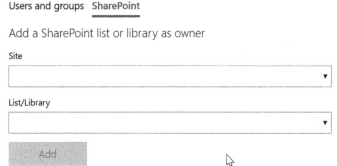

Figure 8.28: Adding owners for manual flows

 Owners will be able to use services in a flow, but they won't be able to modify the credentials for a connection created by another owner.

Power Automate enables you to share flows with your colleagues either by adding them as co-owners or (for manual flows only) run-only users.

See also

- The *Creating a flow using a template* recipe in this chapter
- The *Editing a flow* recipe in this chapter
- The *Creating a flow on a SharePoint library* recipe in this chapter

Next, we'll learn how you can share a flow that you designed with your colleagues.

Sharing your flow

Sharing a flow lets your colleagues manage your flow. This ensures the flow can be managed even if the creator of the flow leaves the organization. The flows that have been shared with you will appear under the **Shared with me** tab.

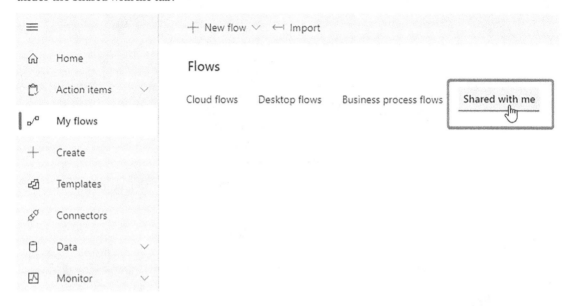

Figure 8.29: Team flows (flows shared with others)

Getting ready

To work through this recipe, you should have a valid Power Automate license, and you need to be an owner of the flow that you wish to share.

How to do it...

To share a flow, follow these steps:

1. Select the flow you want to share.
2. Click on the **Share** option in the command bar, or choose the **Share** option from the context menu.
3. You will be presented with a screen that lets you specify the people you want to share the flow with.

Owners

Adding another owner allows others to edit, update and delete this flow. All owners can also access the run history and add or remove other owners.

Learn more

Users and groups SharePoint

Add a user or group as owner

Enter names, emails, or user groups

Sudeep Ghatak
sudeep@sudeepghatakdemos.onmicrosoft.com

Ashish Ghatak
ashish@sudeepghatakdemos.onmicrosoft.com

Embedded connections

Everyone listed as an owner will have access to all these connections and will only be able to use them in this flow.

Learn more

Connections in use

Connections listed are actively being used in this flow. Manage connections

sudeep@sudeepghatakdemos.onmicrosoft.com
SharePoint   ✕

Figure 8.30: Sharing a flow

4. You will receive a warning that describes the permissions that the recipients will be granted as part of the sharing process:

Connections Used

Owners of the flow will have full access to all connections in the flow and the content within the connected accounts. Owners are not required to add connections to their own accounts, and can take any actions in existing connections and their content.

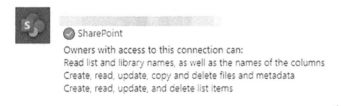

SharePoint
Owners with access to this connection can:
Read list and library names, as well as the names of the columns
Create, read, update, copy and delete files and metadata
Create, read, update, and delete list items

Only add owners to a flow if you wish to share full access to all connections and the content within them. If you want to have someone else edit a flow offline without granting access to connections, you can export your flow. Learn more

OK   Cancel

Figure 8.31: Reviewing flow connections

How it works...

When a flow is shared, the new owner receives an email notification. The notification has a link that takes the new owner to the flow.

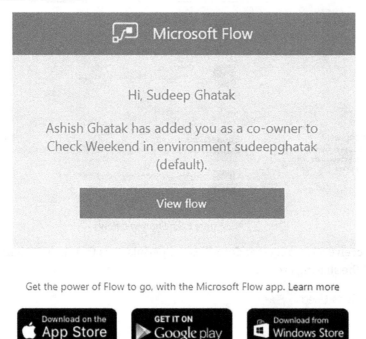

Figure 8.32: Confirmation message

The flow owners also receive notifications when the flow is modified or if the flow fails at any point. The owners also can view the flow history and delete the flow.

 It is recommended that the owners add error handling within their flow instead of relying on the flow error notification.

Please refer to the article at `https://packt.link/error-handling` to learn more about error handling within flows.

Connections

Some flow actions require you to first establish a connection (for example, SharePoint actions and Office 365 Mail actions). The connection determines what credentials will be used when transactions are carried out with the external system.

SharePoint users must have Edit permissions for the site or be a member of the Members or Owners groups of the site to run flows in SharePoint.

You can configure multiple connections for an action (by using the **+Add new connection** option) but only 1 connection can be used. The other connections appear under the **Other connections** section.

Instant/manual flows

The flows with a manual trigger and those using the **On item being selected** trigger have an additional sharing option called **Run only users.** Users that are granted the **Run only** permissions can run/trigger the flow but cannot modify it.

You can add **Run only users** by using the **Edit** option. Here, you have the ability to:

• Add a single user or group
• Add a SharePoint list (everyone who has contribute access to the SharePoint list will get access)

You can also specify whether the flow will use the connection that you have configured or the credentials of the **run-only** user:

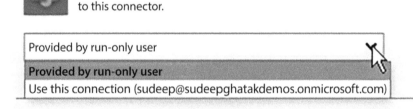

Figure 8.33: Specify who has rights to run the flow

There's more...

You can also share a flow with another colleague without sharing the original copy of the flow. This is done by using the **Send a copy** option. The user receives a template of your flow and will need to configure the connections themselves.

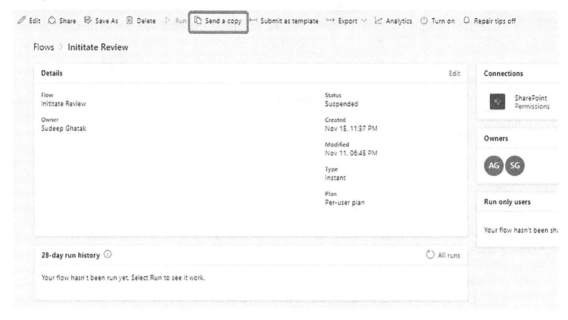

Figure 8.34: Sending a copy of the flow

The flow will be available under the **Templates** section of your flow landing page.

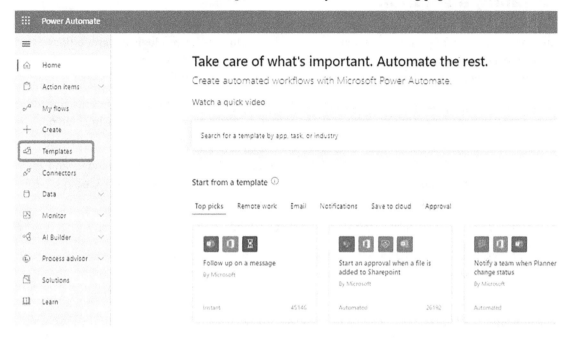

Figure 8.35: Flow templates

See also

- The *Creating a flow using a template* recipe in this chapter
- The *Editing a flow* recipe in this chapter
- Share a cloud flow – Power Automate | Microsoft Learn: `https://packt.link/create-team-flows`

Now, we will go into some deeper concepts of flow creation. Let's start by talking about **solutions**.

Creating a solution

As you might have noticed, when you build flows under **My flows**, they all appear one below the other, and there is no way of grouping related flows together. Solutions let you logically group the related flows into a single container. So, if your application has multiple flows, you can bundle them all into a solution container, which simplifies navigating and managing these flows.

Solutions provide the **Application Lifecycle Management** (**ALM**) capability for Power Apps and Power Automate. Solutions let you bundle related flows (and apps) within a single deployable unit and migrate them from one environment to another.

Solutions are created within environments. An environment is a place to store, manage, and share your organization's business data, Power Apps, and flows. They also act as secure spaces to separate apps that may have different roles, security requirements, or target audiences.

The following are some scenarios where you could consider different environments:

- Creating separate environments for test and production versions of your apps
- Isolating the apps and flows to specific teams or departments in your company
- Creating separate environments for different global branches of your company

Creating and managing environments for Power Platform is beyond the scope of this book, because environment creation is an admin task. You can read more about creating environments for Power Platform at: `https://packt.link/environments-overview`.

Getting ready

To create solutions, you must have Dataverse in your Microsoft 365 environment, an environment with version 9.1.0.267 or later. You can check the version you are using on the **Environments** page of the Power Platform admin center.

How to do it...

To create a solution, go through the following steps:

1. Go to your **Power Automate** home page.
2. Choose an environment you want to create the solution in.

3. The solution will get created in the default environment unless a specific environment is chosen from the environment selector.

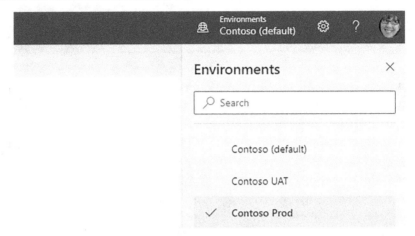

Figure 8.36: Environment selector

4. Select **Solutions** from the left pane. You'll see all the solutions available in your environment:

Figure 8.37: Power Platform Solutions

5. Click on **+ New solution** to create a solution.

6. Provide a display name, name (only letters, numbers, and underscores), publisher, and version number, as shown in the following screenshot:

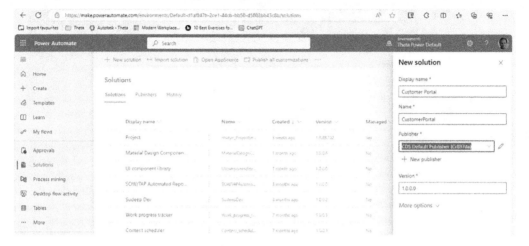

Figure 8.38: Creating a solution

7. Click on **Create**.

8. Now click on the solution you just created. You will be taken to a page that displays the components of the solution.

9. Click **New** to add a new component (for which you can choose from **Flow**, **App**, **Entity**, and so on):

Figure 8.39: Adding components to a solution

Your solution is ready to be exported, along with its components.

How it works...

Solutions provide you with a convenient and efficient way of grouping multiple resources (apps, flows, entities, reports, and so on) together. This method lets **independent software vendors** (ISVs) deploy their solutions on Microsoft AppSource. Creating solutions lets you deploy your components in another environment without having to go through the pain of exporting each individual component and then importing it in.

You can export a solution by navigating to the **Solutions** page and selecting the **Export** option from the context menu, as shown in the following screenshot. Your components need to be published before the solution can be exported:

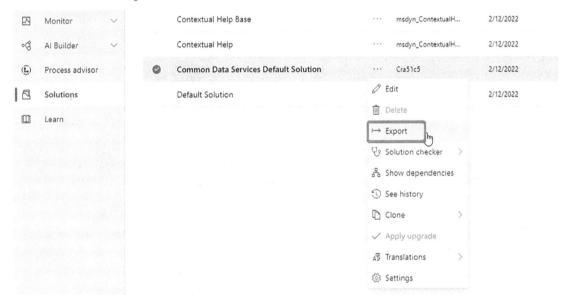

Figure 8.40: Exporting a solution

 Please note that only currently unmanaged solutions can be exported.

Clicking **Export** launches a wizard that takes you through the exporting process. You need to specify the version number and export type during the process:

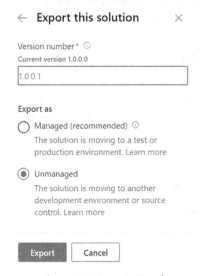

Figure 8.41: Export wizard

Choose the **Unmanaged** option if you are exporting solutions for a development environment. For production or UAT environments, export them as **Managed** solutions.

 You cannot edit components in a managed solution, or import a managed solution, if an unmanaged solution already exists in the same environment.

Once you have selected the right managed/unmanaged option based on the environment the solution is for, and then exported the solution, you can then move it to a different environment (or even a separate tenant) by importing it. The **Import** option is available on the **Solutions** page:

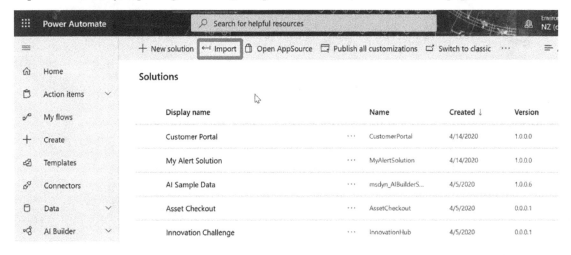

Figure 8.42: Importing a solution

The import process takes you through a series of steps, as shown in the following screenshots (before running the solution, fix the flow connections):

1. Upload the solution package
2. Cross-check the solution package details
3. Confirm solution deployment
4. The import status bar

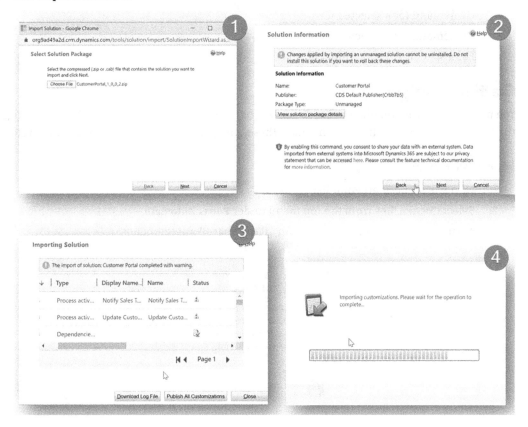

Figure 8.43: Import process stages

See also

- The *Importing a flow* recipe in this chapter
- The *Exporting a flow* recipe in this chapter
- Overview of solution-aware flows – Power Automate | Microsoft Learn: `https://packt.link/overview-solution-flows`

Our next recipe will continue with advanced flow building concepts by looking at flows that interact with SharePoint lists or libraries.

Creating a flow in a SharePoint library

Power Automate is integrated with SharePoint. The Power Automate option appears against every SharePoint list and library. This lets you set up SharePoint-specific triggers right from within the SharePoint list or library. You can use Power Automate to build your custom events, such as the addition of a document, metadata updates, and so on. Within SharePoint, you can run a flow with the following scopes:

- On demand for a selected file
- On demand for a selected list item
- For a specific folder within a library

Getting ready

You need to have a SharePoint license to access SharePoint Online. You also require editing rights for the list to add a flow to it. If you do not have these, please get in touch with your administrator.

How to do it...

1. Navigate to the SharePoint list (or library).
2. Select **Create a flow** from the top menu under **Power Automate**.
3. A panel will appear on the right with all the SharePoint templates:

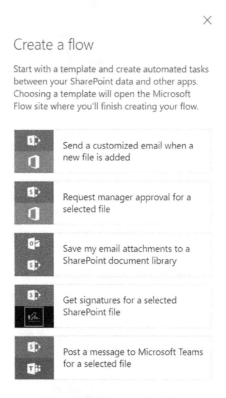

Figure 8.44: Choose a template

4. Select a template and build a flow as we described before.

How it works...

Selecting a template takes you to the flow designer page. The template provides a basic outline that serves as a good starting point. The flow creation logic is the same as described earlier.

See also

- The *Creating a flow using a template* recipe in this chapter
- The *Editing a flow* recipe in this chapter

Now that we have learned about flows that work with SharePoint libraries, we will finish our coverage of Power Automate with a slightly different type of flow.

Creating a business process flow

Business process flows in Power Automate are significantly different from a normal flow. Business process flows are intended to walk users through a particular process stage by stage to make sure that the process – such as handling support issues, onboarding employees, or processing requests – is handled consistently and thoroughly.

Getting ready

To build business process flows, you require a per-user license for Power Apps or Power Automate, or a Dynamics 365 license plan that encompasses usage rights for business process flows. Additionally, it is essential to have a table linked to the business process flow. If the business process flow is not associated with an existing table, it is necessary to create a new table before initiating the flow.

How to do it...

In this recipe, we'll create a business process flow that requests a new position to be posted:

1. Go to Power Automate (`flow.microsoft.com`) and log in if you're not already. Make sure the environment shown in the upper-right corner is the environment in which you intend to build this business process flow.

2. Navigate in to the solution in which the business process flow is needed. Click on **New -> Automation -> Process,** then **Business process flow:**

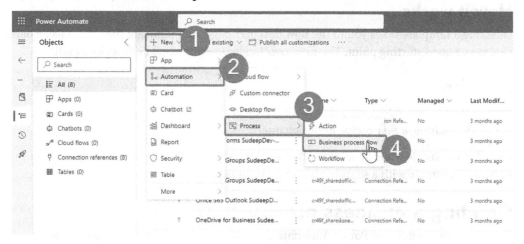

Figure 8.45: Business process flow option when creating flows in Power Automate

3. Name the flow New Position Request, leave the name as **newpositionrequest,** and choose **None** for table. This automatically creates a new table in Dataverse for your new process. Click **Create:**

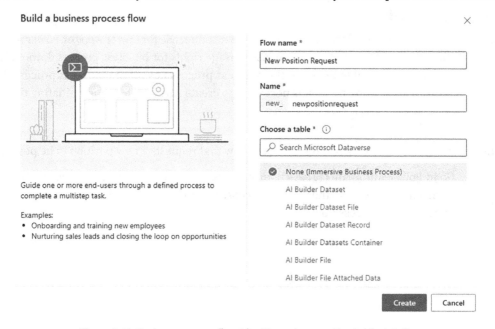

Figure 8.46: Business process flow identity and supporting table details

4. Select the name of your new process or the pencil icon next to it to open the editor.

5. Select the default stage (**1**), and rename it (**2**), then select **Click to add fields and forms:**

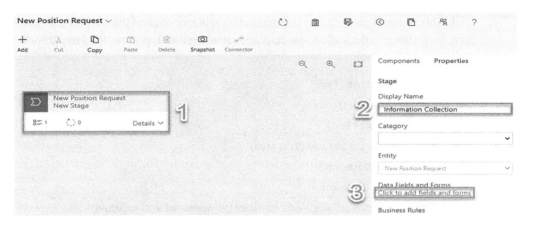

Figure 8.47: Stage properties

6. Select **Update** (rotating arrow and checkmark at the top) to save your change.

7. In a separate tab or window, go to Power Apps (`make.powerapps.com`), select **Data | Tables**, then the name of your new table **New Position Request**:

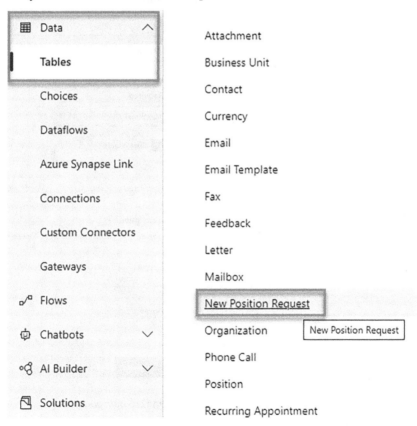

Figure 8.48: Table selection

8. Click **Add column** to create a new column in this table for each of the following items. For each item, name the column and choose its corresponding data type (specified in parentheses next to the column's name):

    •   `Position title` (**Text**)
    •   `Department` (**Text**)
    •   `Salary range` (**Text**)
    •   `Position description` (**Text area**)
    •   `Open date` (**Date only**)
    •   `Close date` (**Date only**)
    •   Approval status (**choice** – add choices for **Approved** and **Rejected**)

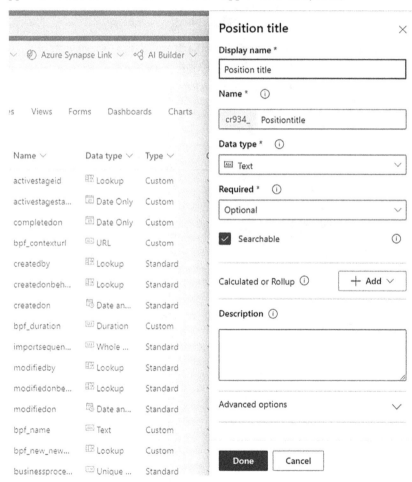

Figure 8.49: Table column creation panel

9. Click **Save Table** in the lower-right corner.
10. Return to the business process flow tab or window and refresh your window. Locate the **Information Collection** stage, then select **Details** to expand it.

11. Select **Data Step #1** and rename it to Position title. Select **Position title** (the field you created earlier) for **Data Field,** and check the box to make the field **Required:**

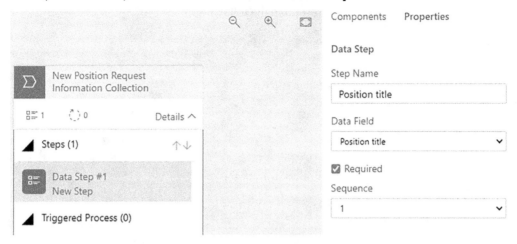

Figure 8.50: Data step properties

12. Click **Apply.**

13. Select **Components** from the top of the right panel, then drag **Data Step** underneath **Position title** in the **Information Collection** stage:

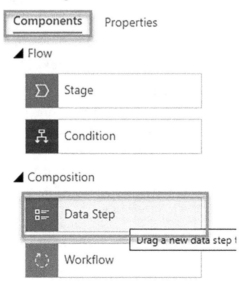

Figure 8.51: New Data Step addition

14. Name the new data step Department, select **Department** for **Data Field,** and click **Apply.** Repeat *steps 11-12* for each of the fields you created in *step 8, except for Approval status.* When you're finished, your stage should resemble the following:

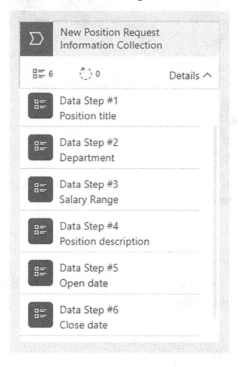

Figure 8.52: Completed stage with 6 data steps

15. Click **Update** (rotating arrow and checkmark icon at the top) to save.

16. Select the **Components** tab from the right panel and drag a new **Stage** to the right of **Information Collection** on top of the plus sign that appears when dragging.

17. Select the new stage, and rename it in the **Properties** panel to Approval for posting. Click **Apply.**

18. Select **Data Step #1** inside the stage and rename it to Approval status and set **Data Field** to **Approval status.** Check the box to require this. Click **Apply.**

19. Click **Update** one more time to save your work.

How it works...

We've just built a business process flow that will help us collect information along a visual path where all participants can see the progress of the overall process as they work through their parts of it. We could further enhance this by adding conditions, logic, and additional workflows to automate as much as we could reasonably do. We could also customize the form that appears on the page as users work through the process.

You may be wondering why we had to add table columns outside Power Automate. Currently, if you choose to edit data fields from Power Automate, it uses the classic UI. That's why we go to a separate tab or window and edit the table via Power Apps – to utilize the modern UI.

When users complete your form, it'll save their input to the table that was created automatically for this flow – specifically into the columns you added to it. We can then expand on this recipe to add notifications based on approval status.

Seen here is a new position request at the final stage of its completion. We can see the person completing it is about to approve it and click **Finish**:

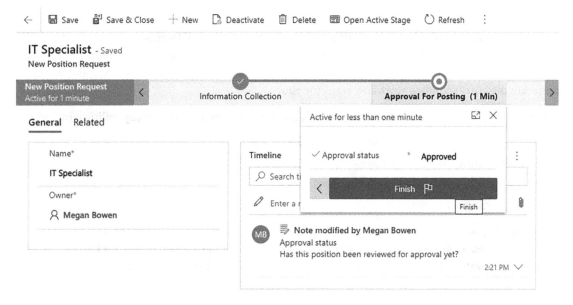

Figure 8.53: User experience working on a business process flow

If we check our table in Dataverse, we can confirm the item is there and updated with **Approval status**:

Figure 8.54: Dataverse table view of a business process flow in process

Since our data is in Dataverse, we can also use it throughout Microsoft 365 in other apps, flows, etc. For example, perhaps we build a regular automated flow that watches for column changes in the **Approval status** column and performs actions based on its value. If you don't want people to have to launch the process from Power Automate, you may wish to embed this business process flow as part of a Power Apps model-driven application.

See also

- Create or edit a business process flow: `https://packt.link/create-business-process-flow`
- Advanced concepts to improve business process flows in Power Automate: `https://packt.link/advanced-business-process-flows`

Copilot in Power Automate

Power Automate's Copilot is an innovative AI-driven feature designed to enhance your experience in creating and modifying Power Automate workflows by enabling a more conversational approach. It allows you to articulate your workflow requirements using natural language, and Copilot will then generate the corresponding workflow steps for you.

While Copilot is still in its development stage, it already possesses a range of capabilities, including:

1. Initiating the creation of new workflows from scratch.
2. Facilitating the editing of existing workflows.
3. Responding to queries regarding workflows.
4. Providing recommendations for optimizing workflows.

To get started, you can describe your desired workflow in a few words or sentences. For example, you can say, "I need a workflow that notifies me via email when a new task arrives in Planner." Copilot will then generate the corresponding workflow for this task, and you can make further adjustments as needed.

Furthermore, Copilot can assist you in more intricate tasks such as debugging workflows and identifying the appropriate actions and connectors to utilize. For instance, you can inquire, "How can I send an email with an attachment?" or "Which connector should I employ to connect with Salesforce?"

Copilot proves to be a valuable tool that streamlines the process of creating and editing Power Automate workflows, potentially saving you time and effort. While it's still in development, it holds the potential to revolutionize how individuals automate their tasks.

Here are some practical examples of how Copilot can be utilized within Power Automate:

- Design a workflow that sends email notifications when new tasks are added to Planner.
- Create a workflow that automatically approves purchase orders below a specified amount.
- Develop a workflow that posts messages to a Microsoft Teams channel when new files are added to a SharePoint library.
- Establish a workflow that updates Salesforce records upon the creation of new leads in Dynamics 365.
- Construct a workflow that sends personalized birthday emails to your customers.

Despite being a work in progress, Copilot has the potential to make Power Automate more accessible to individuals of all skill levels.

Getting ready

At the time of writing this book, the feature is only available for users with the Office 365 environment in the United States region. Some additional requirements are:

- Browser language must be set to English (United States)
- You must have a Microsoft Dataverse database in your environment.
- AI Builder must be enabled for your environment to use the AI models or controls leveraging AI models.

This can be done by following these steps:

- Sign in to the Power Platform admin center.
- In the admin center, go to **Environments** | [select an environment] | **Settings** | **Product** | **Features**.
- On the **Features settings** page, under **AI Builder**, enable or disable AI Builder preview models.

How to do it

1. Go to the Power Automate home page and type `Save Outlook email attachments I receive to Onedrive if the subject of the email is Invoices` in the text box provided.

Figure 8.55: Copilot on the Power Automate home page

2.   Copilot will suggest one or more flow templates matching your needs. Click **Next**.

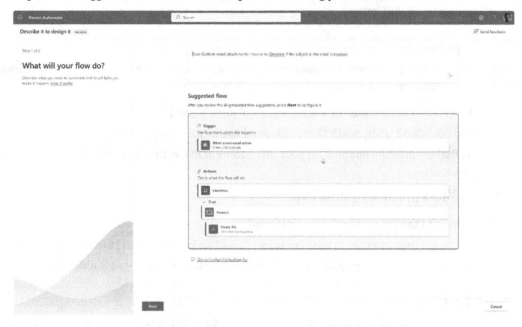

Figure 8.56: Flow templates from Copilot

3.   Provide the credentials required for the connection and click **Create flow**.

Figure 8.57: Creating a flow with Copilot

4. Copilot will take you to the Copilot designer. Here you can perform the remaining configurations to complete the flow.

Figure 8.58: Copilot designer

5. You can use **Dynamic content** or **Expression** to provide inputs to the action.

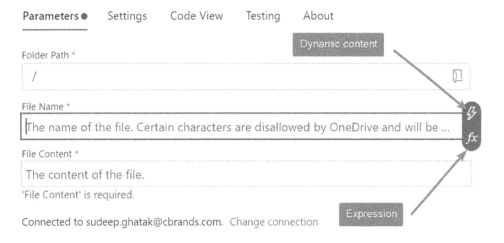

Figure 8.59: Adding expressions to a flow made with Copilot

6. Provide the following inputs to the **Create file** action.

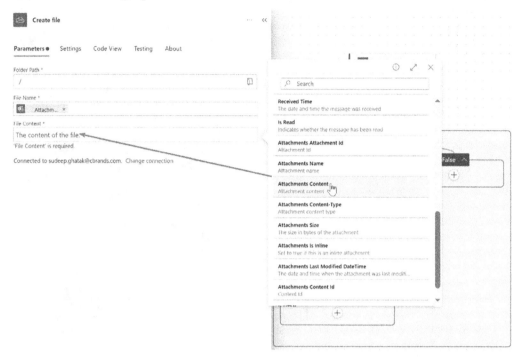

Figure 8.60: Adding inputs to an action

7. Ask Copilot to add a compose action to display the attachment name.

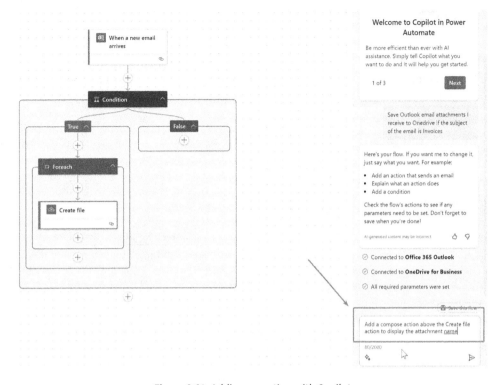

Figure 8.61: Adding an action with Copilot

8. Copilot will add the action with the requested content.

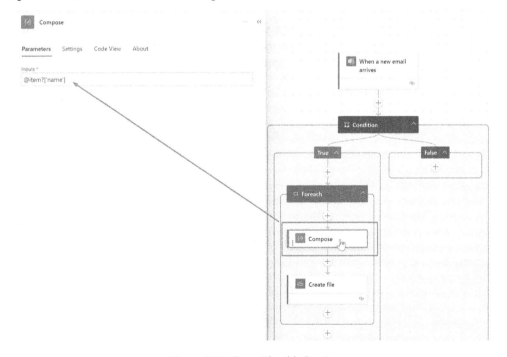

Figure 8.62: Flow with added action

9.   Click **Save** to complete the flow.

How it works

The Power Automate designer is the original designer that has been used to create and edit flows for many years. It is a powerful tool, but it can be complex to use, especially for beginners.

The Copilot designer is designed to be more accessible and easier to use than the Power Automate designer. It is still under development, but it has the potential to revolutionize the way that people automate their work.

Here is a table that summarizes the key differences between the Copilot designer and the Power Automate designer:

Feature	Copilot designer	Power Automate designer
Type	AI-powered	Traditional
Interface	Conversational	WYSIWYG
Learning curve	Lower	Higher
Power	Lower	Higher
Flexibility	Lower	Higher

Table 8.2: Comparing the Copilot and Power Automate designer experiences

The Copilot designer can be used for a variety of tasks, including:

Creating new flows from scratch

The Copilot designer can be used to create new flows from scratch simply by describing what you want your flow to do in natural language. For example, you could say "I want to create a flow that sends me an email when I receive a new task in Planner." Copilot will then generate a flow that performs this task, and you can edit the flow as needed.

Editing existing flows

The Copilot designer can also be used to edit existing flows. To do this, simply open the flow that you want to edit and then click the **Copilot** button in the top menu bar.

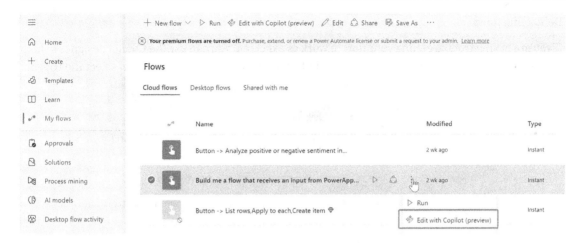

Figure 8.63: Editing flows with Copilot

Copilot will then generate a list of suggestions for improving the design of your flow. You can also ask Copilot questions about your flow, such as `Explain what this flow does` or `How can I make this flow more efficient?`

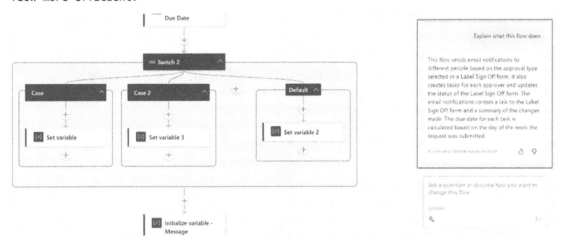

Figure 8.64: Learning about a flow by asking Copilot

Debugging flows

If you are having trouble getting your flow to work as expected, you can use the Copilot designer to help you debug it. To do this, simply click the **Test** button in the top menu bar and then select the trigger.

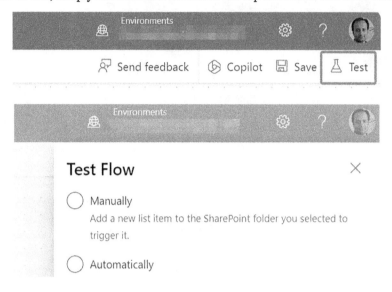

Figure 8.65: Flow testing

Copilot will then help you to identify the source of the problem and suggest solutions.

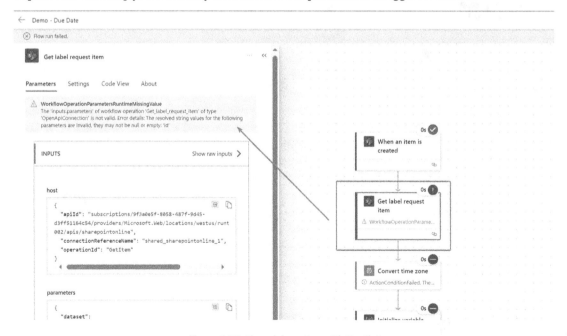

Figure 8.66: Flow debugging with Copilot

Learning more about Power Automate

If you are new to Power Automate, or if you want to learn more about a specific feature, you can use the Copilot designer to get help. To do this, simply click the **Copilot** button in the top menu bar and then select the **Learn more about Power Automate** option. Copilot will then provide you with links to relevant documentation and tutorials.

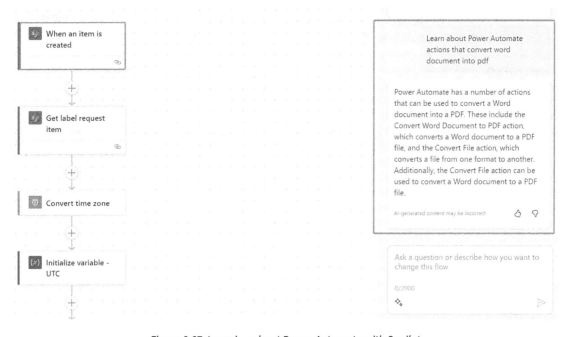

Figure 8.67: Learning about Power Automate with Copilot

Which designer should you use?

If you are new to Power Automate, or if you are looking for a way to create and edit flows more quickly and easily, then the Copilot designer is a good option to consider.

If you need to create complex flows, or if you need the full power and flexibility of the Power Automate designer, then you may want to stick with the traditional designer.

You can also use both designers together. For example, you could use the Copilot designer to get started on a new flow, and then switch to the traditional designer to finish the flow if needed.

Ultimately, the best designer for you will depend on your individual needs and preferences.

Benefits

The Copilot designer offers a number of benefits, including:

- Increased productivity: Copilot can help you create and edit flows more quickly and easily.
- Reduced errors: Copilot can help you to avoid making errors in your flows.
- Improved flow design: Copilot can provide you with suggestions for improving the design of your flows.
- Greater flexibility: Copilot can help you to create more flexible and adaptable flows.

Limitations

The Copilot designer is still under development, and it has a few limitations. For example, it may not be able to understand all natural language prompts, and it may not be able to generate flows for all tasks. However, Microsoft is actively working to improve the Copilot designer, and it is expected to become more powerful and versatile over time.

Overall, the Copilot designer is a promising new feature in Power Automate. It has the potential to make Power Automate more accessible and easier to use for everyone.

See also

- Get started with Copilot in cloud flows – Power Automate | Microsoft Learn: `https://packt.link/get-started-with-Copilot`
- Power Automate – Copilot for Power Automate | Microsoft Learn: `https://packt.link/Copilot-Power-Automate`
- FAQ for Copilot in cloud flows – Power Automate | Microsoft Learn: `https://packt.link/Copilot-cloud-flows-FAQ`
- Create a cloud flow from a description (preview) – Power Automate | Microsoft Learn: `https://packt.link/create-cloud-flow-from-description`

9

Creating Power Apps

Power Apps is essentially a form builder that you can use to build rich and powerful online forms for your business. With the help of Power Apps, you can build whole custom business applications that connect to your business data, whether it's stored on-premises or in cloud storage. Apps built using Power Apps provide a rich user interface that can run seamlessly in the browser or on mobile devices (phone or tablet).

These apps are built using Power Apps Studio. When building an app, you can choose between a web or mobile layout. With Power Apps on mobile, you can even leverage mobile device features such as GPS and the camera in the apps.

Power Apps is a low-code development platform designed primarily for end-users, but developers can take it to the next level; not only to create apps for end-users but also to build "design concepts." For now, it is enough for us to learn how to create apps at a beginner level.

The first thing to do is to decide what kind of app you want to create. Apps in Power Apps (more commonly referred to as "Power Apps") fall into two categories:

- **Canvas apps** are suited to simple processes and forms. They give you the independence to do pretty much anything you want to do. You can tailor the application to meet your business requirements.
- **Model-driven apps** are more suited to use cases where data drives your user interface, such as when you have different components in your Power Apps that are visible to different people based on the data that they have access to. For this, you need to configure the read/write permission to be granted based on the user's role. You can write a canvas app to achieve this; however, model-driven apps provide you with a framework to achieve this easily. Model-driven apps are built using Microsoft Dataverse as the data source.

Additionally, **Power Pages** lets you build websites that can be accessible to external, anonymous users such as customers. Although Power Pages now exists separately from Power Apps, it was previously known as *Power Apps Portals* and is still relevant when discussing Power Apps. We've included it here for comparative purposes, but it should be known that it is not strictly a type of Power App. Note that the pages are also built using the Microsoft Dataverse backend.

The notable differences between canvas apps, model-driven apps, and Power Pages are listed below:

Feature	Canvas apps	Model-driven apps	Power Pages
Target user base	Internal users	Internal users	Anonymous users
User interface	Offer more flexibility in terms of the user interface design	The forms are created automatically based on the data model that you choose and hence the flexibility with design is less	Internal and external users can perform data manipulation in Dataverse
Licensing	A Microsoft 365 Power Apps license is sufficient (if premium connectors are not used)	A Premium or Dynamics 365 license is required	A Premium or Dynamics 365 license is required for app creators, and additional licensing is required for anonymous users
Data sources	Support several data sources	Only support Dataverse	Only supports Dataverse
Version history	Manage version history	Do not support version control	Does not support version control
Teams compatibility	Can be embedded within Teams	Not compatible with Teams	Not compatible with Teams
Responsiveness	Not responsive out of the box	Responsive by design	Responsive by design
Offline capability	Limited	Yes	No
Development skills	Low code	No code	No code

Table 9.1: Different features across app types

Picking which internal app to create

Build a canvas app if you want to focus deeply on the design of the app. Canvas apps let you build pixel-perfect apps as per your requirements. Note that you must build the app by connecting to a data source that you already have.

Build a model-driven app if you want to build an app quickly using the default data models that Microsoft has provided and made available through Dataverse. You can perform limited customizations on such apps.

In this chapter, we will go through recipes that cover the following topics:

- Creating a template-based app
- Connecting to data sources
- Adding screens
- Creating a canvas app from a blank template
- Creating Power Apps from a SharePoint list/library
- Creating a Power Pages website using Power Apps
- Creating a model-driven app
- Using custom pages and the modern app designer

As we go through the contents of this chapter, we will cover the steps necessary to create a Power App for business users. We will begin with how to create an app from a template, where we will look at Power Apps Studio and the formulas we can use to design an app. We will start by building an app using a template already provided by Microsoft.

Creating a template-based app

Power Apps comes with prebuilt templates that let you create functional Power Apps without having to acquire a deep knowledge of Power Apps concepts. This provides you with an opportunity to get a deeper insight into the prebuilt apps and understand the concepts of data binding, data updates, validation, and so on. This way, you could reverse-engineer some of the applications that Microsoft and other vendors have developed and shared with the community. Go through this recipe to learn about creating apps using a template.

Getting ready

You need a Power Apps plan included in your Microsoft 365 subscription to build a Power App. Power Apps is available in two subscription models and a pay-as-you-go plan:

- **Per app per user:** Lets you run one application or one website using all the premium Power Apps features.
- **Per user:** User specific, a user enrolled on the plan can run as many apps as they like.
- **Pay-as-you-go:** Similar to the per-user plan, except it is based on the number of apps or websites run each month. Requires an Azure subscription.

 You can check the pricing of these plans at `https://packt.link/Power-Apps-pricing`.

How to do it...

To create an app, go through the following steps:

1. Log in to `Office.com` and click on **All Apps**.

2.   Choose **Power Apps** from the list of applications.

3.   You will be taken to the Power Apps landing page. Select the option to **Create** an app from the left navigation:

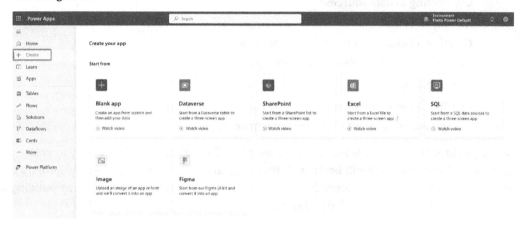

Figure 9.1: The Power Apps landing page

4.   Scroll down to the section displaying the templates. There are lots of templates to choose from. Select the one that is closest to your requirement:

Figure 9.2: Sample templates

5.   Give your app a name and choose the appropriate layout (**Phone** or **Tablet**). Click **Create**. In this case, we have selected the **Budget Tracker** template:

Budget Tracker

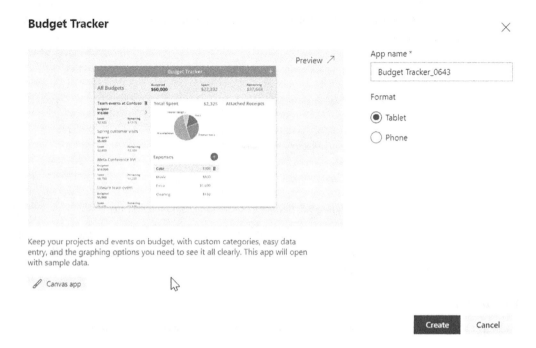

Figure 9.3: Selecting the Budget Tracker template

If this is the first time you are using Power Apps, you will be presented with a welcome message:

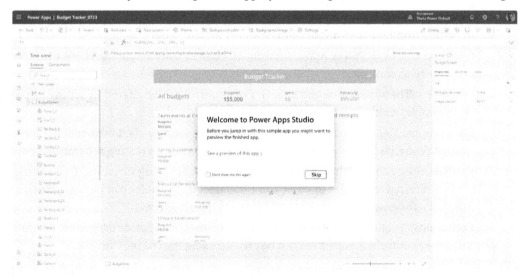

Figure 9.4: Power Apps Studio welcome message

6. The app gets loaded in Power Apps Studio. Press the play icon, as shown in *Figure 9.5*, to see the app in action:

Figure 9.5: Budget tracker made using a template

7. Now, if you are happy with the functionality of the app and want to share it with your colleagues or want to extend/change the app, click on **Make my own app**. Power Apps will then create a copy of the app that you can customize.

How it works...

To better understand Power Apps, we need to dive deeper into what Power Apps Studio can do.

Power Apps Studio

Let's start with the Power Apps Studio components:

*   **Screens:** Screens are the containers for Power Apps' different controls. The screen is simply the visual frontend of an application designed for user interaction.

*   **Controls:** To design Power Apps, different UI elements are required. These UI elements are also known as controls.

*   **Properties:** The appearance and behavior of a control can be altered by setting its properties – for example, width, height, text, and so on.

*   **Connections:** You can access the data in other data sources via a connection – for example, you can read data from SharePoint, SQL Server, or Excel by creating separate connections.

*   **Variables:** You can save the state of a control or its value using variables. These variables can then be referred to in rules or other conditional logic. Variables can be created using the Set function – for example, Set(x,34) will store 34 in variable x.

*   **Collections:** A collection stores data in tabular format. This is often used to act as a data source for gallery controls. A collection can be created using the Collect function.

Now let's learn how to navigate Power Apps Studio, numerically going through the areas marked in *Figure 9.6*:

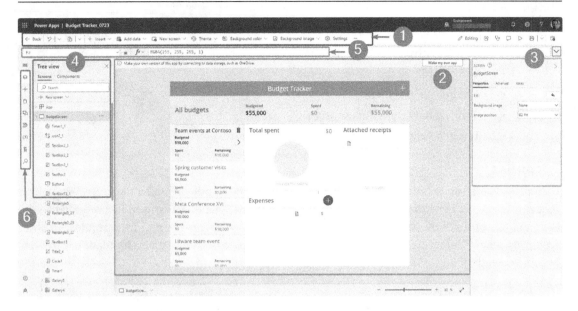

Figure 9.6: Power Apps Studio layout

1. The first section is the **menu bar**. We will look at the menu items later in this chapter.

2. The second section we have highlighted is the center panel, called the **canvas**. It is used to build the layout of the app. The controls can be placed and arranged in the layout. The center panel also lets you select a control by clicking on it, thereby accessing all the properties of the control in the properties panel.

3. The third section marked is the **property panel**, which lets you change the properties of the selected control, such as height, color, and so on.

> Please note that the properties of a control might vary based on the control type – for example, the label and text controls have a `Text` property whereas a pie chart control has an `Item Color Set` property.

4. The section on the left highlights the **Tree view**, where all the controls used in the app are displayed. You can select a control from here if the controls in the center panel are inaccessible (for example, if a control sits behind another control).

5. The section highlighted at the top of the screen is known as either the **formula bar** or the **property pane,** where a property is set with a given value. You can also specify conditional values, as shown in the following code:

```
If(Text(Value(ThisItem.Expense)) = "0", "$",  Text(Value(ThisItem.
Expense),"$#,##"))
```

6. The last section to look at is the **side bar**, which lets you perform the following tasks:

    •   Access controls that you place in the center panel

    •   Add controls in the center layout

    •   Add images and media

    •   Connect to various data sources

    •   Test and validate your app

Formulas

Formulas enable you to build engaging user experiences and handle complex logic. Not every form requires formulas. For instance, in scenarios where Power Apps is being used just to enhance the look and feel of the form (such as SharePoint list forms), you might not require formulas. In other scenarios, where the form requires validations, conditional logic, and data manipulation, formulas become essential.

 Find Microsoft's completed glossary of formulas at `https://packt.link/power-fx-formula-reference`

Some notable and frequently used formulas are as follows.

Collect, Clear, ClearCollect, Distinct

You will use these formulas a lot when working with collections. Collections let you store a single value, an item, or a table.

The `Collect` function lets you create a collection and assign it some data. This data could be fetched from a data source such as a SharePoint list or it could just be specified in the app itself:

```
Collect(CollectionName, data)
```

```
Collect(MovieCollection, {Name: "The Shawshank Redemption", Director: "Frank
Darabont"}, {Name: "The Godfather", Director: "Francis Ford Coppola"}, {Name:
"The Godfather: Part II", Director: "Francis Ford Coppola"})
```

The `Clear` function removes all entries from a collection and leaves an empty collection behind:

```
Clear(CollectionName)
```

The `ClearCollect` function removes items from the collection before adding new items:

```
ClearCollect(CollectionName, data)
```

The `Distinct` function removes the duplicate values of the column specified:

```
Distinct(MoviesCollection,LeadActor)
```

Concat, Concatenate

These formulas are used when working on string manipulation.

The `Concat` function is used to convert an array into a string. For example, `Concat(MovieCollection, ",")` will result in:

```
The Shawshank Redemption, The Godfather, The Godfather: Part II
```

The `Concatenate` function joins multiple strings into a single string:

```
Concatenate("The Shawshank Redemption", "The Godfather", "The Godfather: Part II")
```

CountRows, CountIf

These formulas are handy when you are dealing with collections and tables.

The `CountRows` function returns the numbers of records in a table:

```
CountRows(MovieTable)
```

The `CountIf` function returns the numbers of records in a table if the logical operator returns true:

```
CountIf(MovieTable, ReleaseYear = "2021")
```

DateAdd, DateDiff

These formulas are used when you are working with dates.

The `DateAdd` function adds days, months, years, etc. to any date:

```
DateAdd(Now(), 3, Hours)
```

The `DateDiff` function returns the difference between two dates in days, months, years, etc:

```
DateDiff (Now(), DateValue("01/05/2022",Hours)
```

Filter

This function returns the number of records from a table or collection that meet a condition:

```
Filter(MovieCollection, ReleaseYear = "2021")
```

ForAll

This function allows you to loop through each record in a collection:

```
ForAll(MovieCollection,
Collect(Movies2021,{
MoviewName: ThisRecord.Name,
Director: ThisRecord.Director
}))
```

Navigate

This function is used to go to another screen:

```
Navigate(Screen2)
```

Notify

The Notify function lets you send a notification success or error message on the Power Apps screen:

```
Notify("Record saves succefully",NotificationType.Success)
```

Launch

This function is used to launch a webpage in a browser:

```
Launch("http://www.google.com")
```

LookUp

This function returns a single record from a table or collection that meets a condition:

```
LookUp(MovieCollection, ID=5)
```

Param

Since a Power App is web-based, you can pass parameters using a query string as shown below:

```
https://appurl?Key1=3&Key2=6
```

The Param function then lets you extract the query string values from the URL using the formula as shown below:

```
Param("Key")
```

This will return a value of 3.

Patch

The Patch function is used to update specific fields in a data source:

```
Patch(Movies, LookUp(Movies,ID = 5) , {Director: "Francis Ford Coppola"})
```

Reset

The Reset function reverts the value of a control to its default value:

```
Reset(ControlName)
```

Set

The Set function is used to set a variable:

```
Set(VariableName,"Variable Value")
```

Text

The Text function converts a number or date value into a string with a specified format:

```
Text(Now(),"mm/dd/yyyy")
```

Saving and publishing

When you build a Power App, remember to save the app before closing the window. This can be done by clicking on **File | Save**. When you save the app, you will be asked to specify a name, as shown in the following screenshot:

Figure 9.7: Saving an app in Power Apps

You can save your app in the cloud or on your desktop as a .msapp file. While saving, click on **Settings** to specify the app settings, such as the orientation, icon, background, and so on:

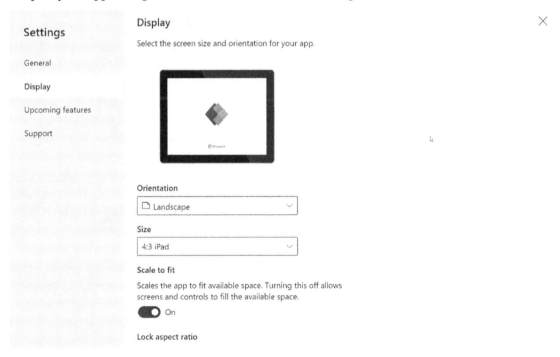

Figure 9.8: Power Apps settings

By default, your app will only be available to you and those who have edit permissions. You will need to share the app with others if they want to access it. We will learn more about sharing in the *Sharing an app* recipe in *Chapter 10, Applying Power Apps*.

When you make a change to an app that you had saved earlier, it needs to be saved and then published, as shown in *Figure 9.9*. The users will continue to see the last published version until you **Publish** your changes:

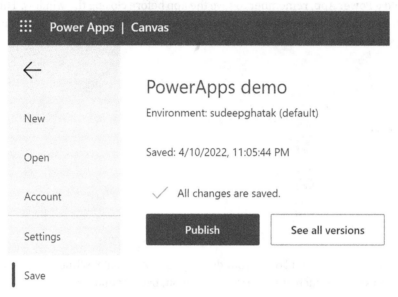

Figure 9.9: Publishing an app in Power Apps

Power Apps also has an autosave feature that enables you to save the app every two minutes. You can enable or disable the **Auto save** setting from **Settings** in the **File** menu.

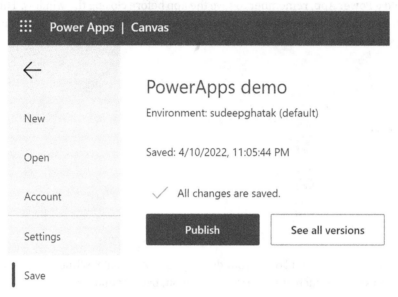

Figure 9.10: Autosaving an app

Versioning

Power Apps creates a new version every time you save the app. You can only have one published version of an app at a time. If you ever want to revert to an older version, click **Restore** from the context menu of the app version or from the top bar:

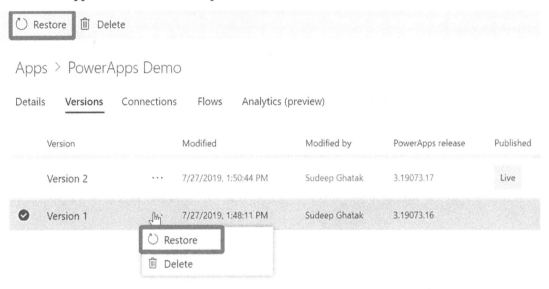

Figure 9.11: Restoring an app in Power Apps

See also

- The *Creating a canvas app from a blank template* recipe in this chapter
- The *Creating Power Apps from a SharePoint list/library* recipe in this chapter
- Get started with formulas in canvas apps – Power Apps | Microsoft Learn: `https://packt.link/canvas-apps-formulas`
- Understand behavior formulas for canvas apps – Power Apps | Microsoft Learn: `https://packt.link/canvas-apps-formula-behavior`

Connecting to data sources

Power Apps lets you build business applications that use data from line-of-business applications. Using Power Apps, you can build apps that work with local as well as connected data sources.

Connected data sources are external to Power Apps, such as Excel spreadsheets, SharePoint lists, OneDrive, Dropbox, and SQL Server.

Local data sources save the data in data tables within Power Apps. Collections are one such data source that gets stored within the Power App when the Power App is saved and published.

We will see how you can connect to data sources in this recipe.

Getting ready

You need a Power Apps plan included in your Microsoft 365 subscription in order to build a Power App. Download the `Cars.xlsx` file from the `Chapter 9` folder in the GitHub repository of this book at `https://packt.link/GitHub-repo` and save the file in your OneDrive.

How to do it...

To connect to a data source, take the following steps:

1. Open Power Apps Studio.
2. Click on **View** | **Data sources** to open the **Data sources** pane.
3. Click **Add data**.
4. Search for `OneDrive` and select it:

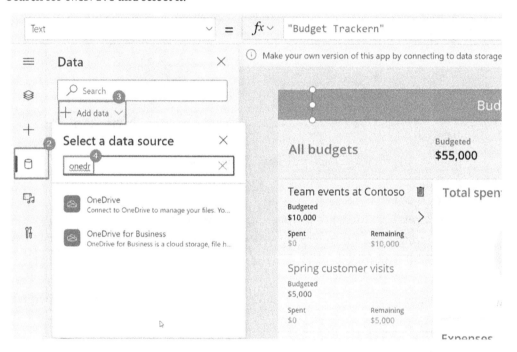

Figure 9.12: Connecting to data sources

5. Select the downloaded file from OneDrive and click on **Connect**.

Some connectors, such as Microsoft 365 Outlook, require no additional steps, and you can show data from them immediately. Other connectors prompt you to provide credentials, specify a particular set of data, or perform other steps – for example, SharePoint and SQL Server require additional information before you can use them. With Dataverse, you can change the environment before you select an entity.

How it works...

Connectors in Power Apps let you bring data from other systems. Some connectors provide data in the form of tables, some provide only actions, and some provide both. You can store all your connections by going to **Power Apps | Data | Connections**:

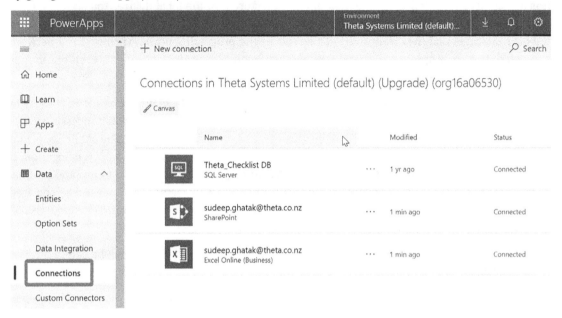

Figure 9.13: Data source connections

Let's look at the two different types of connections:

- **Data connections:** The data source connections that you make are used by some of the Power Apps controls, such as galleries, dropdowns, and checkboxes. Data connectors have an **Items** property that can be bound to the controls:

Figure 9.14: Querying data

- **Action connectors:** Action connectors perform an action instead of fetching data, like the `Office365.SendEmail()` action, which sends an email.

There's more...

It is a good practice to minimize the amount of data stored on the local device. You should always retrieve only the subset of the data required for your application and re-query the database only when the user indicates that they want more. This reduces the processing power, memory, and network bandwidth that your app needs, thereby reducing response times for your users, even on phones connected via a cellular network.

Power Apps supports features such as filtering, sorting, and so on. These functions enhance the user experience. The way that Power Apps achieves this is by delegating the task of data processing to the data source, instead of retrieving the data into the app and processing it locally. The challenge is that not every data source supports delegation, and not every Power App function supports delegation. If you're working with small datasets (fewer than 2,000 records), you can use any data source and formula because the app can process data locally if the formula can't be delegated. The limit can be changed from the Power Apps settings page by going to **File** | **Settings** | **Advanced Settings**. The default is 500 and the upper limit is 2,000 (at the time of writing this book).

Working with large datasets requires you to use data sources and formulas that can be delegated. The following tabular data sources support delegation:

- Dataverse
- SharePoint
- SQL Server

Go to Understand delegation in a canvas app (`https://packt.link/delegation-overview`) to find out more about the functions that support delegation.

You can write a custom connector of your own by following the documentation at *Create a custom connector from scratch* (`https://packt.link/custom-connector-from-scratch`).

See also

- The *Creating a template-based app* recipe in this chapter
- The *Adding screens* recipe in this chapter
- The *Creating a canvas app from a blank template* recipe in this chapter
- The *Creating Power Apps from a SharePoint list/library* recipe in this chapter
- Overview of connectors for canvas apps – Power Apps | Microsoft Learn: `https://packt.link/Power-Apps-connections-list`

Adding screens

A screen in Power Apps is an element that contains a set of controls. Power Apps lets you add as many screens as you like. It also supports navigation between screens based on the user's action. For instance, you could have a screen displaying a list of records, but when the user clicks on an item from within the list, it takes them to the details screen. There could be another screen that lets the user modify the list item. The transition between the screens is controlled by the **Navigate** function. In the next section, I will talk about adding screens to your canvas.

Getting ready

You need a Power Apps plan included in your Microsoft 365 subscription in order to build a Power App.

How to do it...

To add a screen, go through the following steps:

1. Open the app in Power Apps Studio.
2. From the **File** menu, click **Insert** and add a screen:

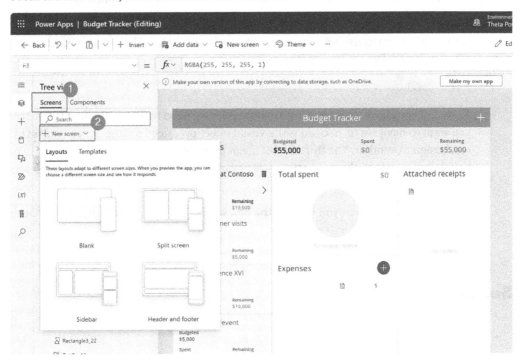

Figure 9.15: Adding a screen

How it works...

Screens act as the interface between the app and the user. There are various types of screens. Some common ones are as follows:

- **Blank:** As the name suggests, the screen does not contain any controls by default.
- **List:** This comes with a **Gallery** control that can be used to display a list of items.
- **Tutorial:** This screen comes with some drawing elements that can be used to provide guided navigation.
- **Success:** This screen can be used to display confirmation messages after an add, update, or delete operation.
- **Email:** This screen provides a template to compose an email.
- **Calendar:** The screen comes with a calendar control.

There's more...

Every app that performs get, create, update, add, and delete operations typically requires three screens. You can add more screens if you think this will improve the usability of your app. In order to switch between one screen and another, Power Apps provides two functions called `Navigate` and `Back`:

- `Navigate` lets you transition to another screen of your choice. The syntax of using the `Navigate` function is as follows:

```
Navigate(Screen,ScreenTransition,UpdateContext)
```

  As we can see above, there are three parameters we need to fill in. The first is the `Screen` that you want to navigate to. Second is the visual effect produced for the `ScreenTransition` from one screen to another. The third and *optional* parameter is for whether you want to pass additional parameters to the next screen—for example, `{Shade:Color.Green}` will set the `Shade` context variable to `Green`.

- The `Back` function takes you back to the last screen you navigated from. It only accepts one. optional variable: `ScreenTransition`:

```
Back(ScreenTransition)
```

See also

- The *Creating a template-based app* recipe in this chapter
- The *Connecting to data sources* recipe in this chapter
- The *Sharing a Power Apps* recipe in *Chapter 10, Applying Power Apps*
- The *Creating a canvas app from a blank template* recipe in this chapter
- The *Creating Power Apps from a SharePoint list/library* recipe in this chapter

Creating a canvas app from a blank template

Power Apps has several templates that give you a head start in creating an app; however, if you want to start from scratch, you can start with a blank template. The following example demonstrates how you can create an app from scratch. The app queries data from a spreadsheet in your OneDrive. This demonstration only focuses on the basics and doesn't go into detail about building a fully functional solution.

 It is recommended that you start with a template that closely resembles what you are trying to build. This will save you a lot of time and effort.

For this example, we will build an app that gets a list of cars from an Excel spreadsheet that is stored in OneDrive:

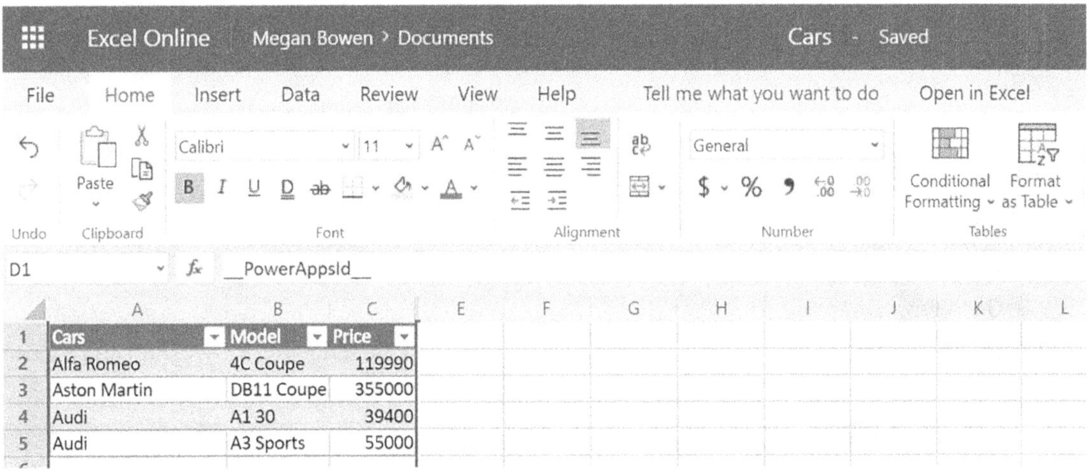

Figure 9.16: Sample data source

Although we can extend this app to add/update and delete records from the spreadsheet, our intention is to just introduce the users to the concept of a screen, a control, and a data connection.

Getting ready

You need a Power Apps plan included in your Microsoft 365 subscription to build a Power App.

Download the Cars.xlsx file from the Chapter 9 folder in the GitHub repository of this book at https://packt.link/GitHub-repo and save the file in your OneDrive.

If you are using a file of your choice, note that Power Apps supports Excel files that have data stored in tables. To learn more about Excel tables, refer to Overview of Excel Tables (https://packt.link/overview-of-Excel-tables).

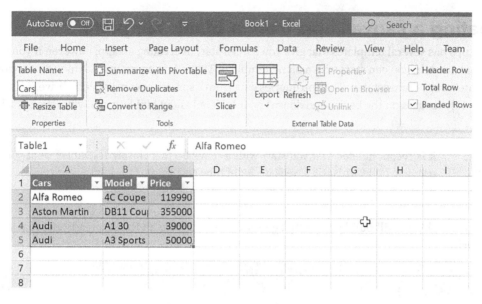

Figure 9.17: Creating a data table

How to do it...

To start building an app from scratch, go through the following steps:

1. Go to Office.com and log in with your organization's credentials.

2. Go to **Power Apps**.

3. Select the option to create a blank app (labeled with a *1* in the following screenshot) and choose the app type. For this example, we will use **Blank canvas app** (labeled with a *2*):

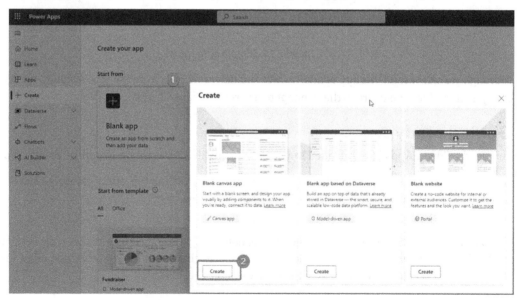

Figure 9.18: Blank canvas app

You will be taken to Power Apps Studio:

Welcome to Power Apps Studio

Here are a few ways to start building an app from a blank canvas.

Create a form >

Create a gallery >

☐ Don't show me this again   Skip

Figure 9.19: Welcome page for Power Apps Studio

4. Select the option to **Create a gallery.** A panel will appear on the right of your Power Apps Studio window. Search for, and select, **OneDrive**:

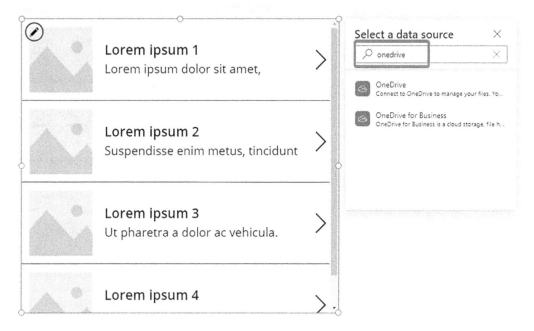

Figure 9.20: Establish connection

5. Now choose the Excel file (`Cars.xlsx` in our case) that you want to build the Power App with and select the table within it:

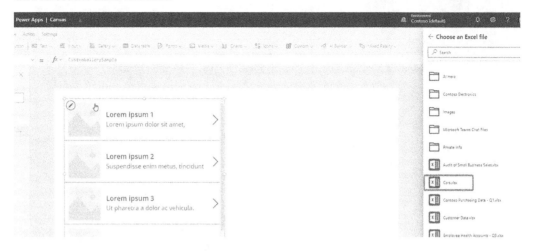

Figure 9.21: Select data source

6. From the right-hand pane, find the **Items** dropdown under **Properties** and select **Cars**:

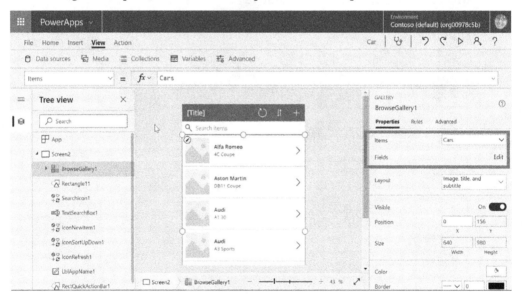

Figure 9.22: Gallery control

7. Click on the **Edit** link next to **Fields** and map the fields to the labels in the gallery:

Figure 9.23: Mapping items to gallery labels

8. Add an additional label control on the gallery by going to **Insert | Label**. Select the label and set the **Text** property to the formula, as shown in the following screenshot:

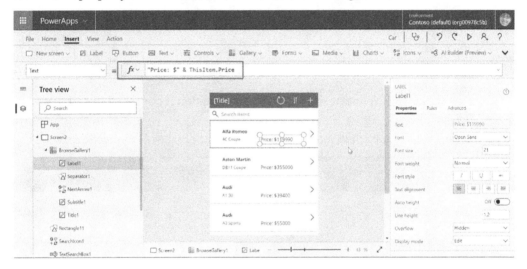

Figure 9.24: Setting the Text property of a label

9. A screen to display the data will now be ready. You can add additional screens to add/edit/ update operations.

10. Save the app by pressing *Ctrl + S* or through the **File** menu.

11. You will now be prompted to name the app, as shown in the following screenshot:

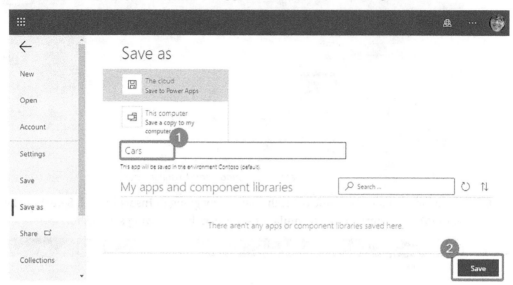

Figure 9.25: Saving the app

12. Publish the app. Note that you will not see this option if this is the first time you are saving the app.

13. Once you have published your app, you can then share it with your colleagues:

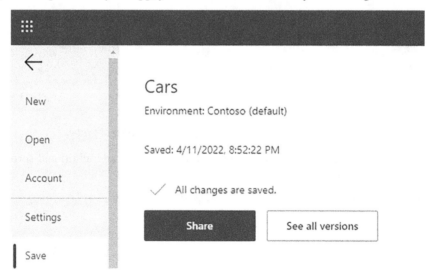

Figure 9.26: Sharing an app

How it works...

You can see your app in action by pressing the play button in the top-right corner, as shown in the following screenshot:

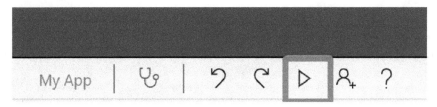

Figure 9.27: Preview mode

Your app will then launch on your device.

 Note that the play button should not be mistaken for a "preview" mode. There is no preview mode in Power Apps, except for the studio layout itself. If the form is submitted, then the data gets added, updated, or deleted in the underlying data source.

Whenever you save changes to a canvas app, only you and anyone else who has permission can see the changes. To make it available to everyone else, you need to publish the app. Every time you save the app, a new version is created. You can access the previous versions on the **Publish** screen:

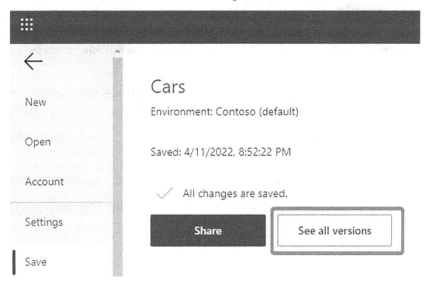

Figure 9.28: Version history

Those who do not have edit rights to the app can only access the last published version. The published version shows **Live** in the **Published** status column. You can restore an older version by clicking **Restore** in the drop-down context menu:

Figure 9.29: Restoring older version

There's more...

The app we built was a simple one. Most apps that you build will require an understanding of some core concepts, which we will look at in the following sections.

Power Apps events

Events occur when some sort of interaction takes place in the app. This could be a click of a button, the loading of a screen, the submission of a form, and so on. Some notable events in Power Apps are as follows:

- OnStart: The OnStart event is fired when the app loads. This is the first event that fires, and so it is used to prepare the app. The OnStart event is often used to do the following:

  - Set app variables.
  - Navigate to a specific screen within Power Apps.
  - Read values from a query string if Power Apps are accessed from the web.

  The OnStart property of Power Apps can be set by selecting the **App** object from the left pane:

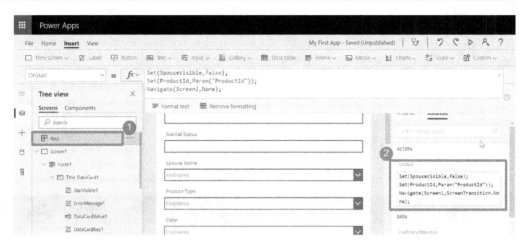

Figure 9.30: OnStart property

- **OnVisible**: The **OnVisible** event is fired when a user navigates to a screen. This function can be used to set screen-specific variables or prefill some field values.

- **OnSelect**: The **OnSelect** event fires when a control is clicked by the user. The event is usually used to handle button click events—for example, the **OnSelect** event of a **Save** button can be used to update the data store and refresh the screen:

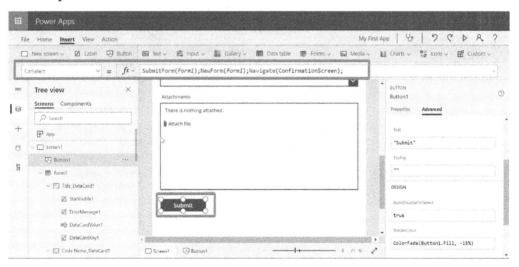

Figure 9.31: OnSelect property

Variables

You can create variables in Power Apps by using the **Set** function:

```
Syntax:
Set(variable_name,value)
```

Unlike languages where you perform a calculation and then store it in a variable, in Power Apps, the value of a variable can change based on the state of another control or variable—for example, when we want to hide the spouse name if the marital status of the employee is unmarried.

We can achieve this by setting the SpouseVisible variable to True if the user selects Married and False if they select another status:

```
Syntax:
Set(SpouseVisible,if(MaritalStatus.Selected.Value = "Married",false,true))
```

We then set the Visible property of the SpouseName field to the SpouseVariable variable:

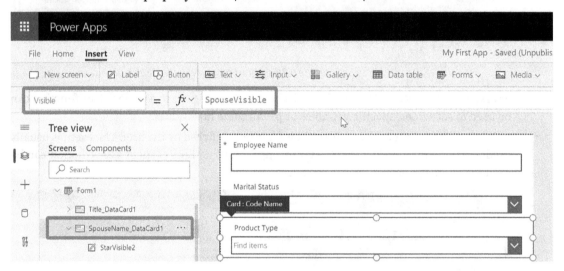

Figure 9.32: Working with variables

Power Apps continuously evaluates the variable based on the value in the **Marital Status** dropdown and changes the visibility of the SpouseName field.

There is a special variable in Power Apps that is known as the ContextVariable.

Context variables can hold several data types:

- A single value
- A record
- A table
- An object reference
- Any result from a formula

A context variable holds its value while the app is running. The context variable in one screen is local to that screen and its value is preserved even if the user navigates to a different screen. Once the app is closed, the context variable's value will be lost and must be set when the app is loaded again.

Functions

Power Apps supports lots of functions, some that perform string or date manipulation and others that perform mathematical calculations. One of the functions that needs a special mention is UpdateContext.

The UpdateContext function is used to create a context variable. You can set multiple context variables in one UpdateContext function using the following code:

```
Syntax:
UpdateContext({ ContextVariable1: Value1 [, ContextVariable2: Value2 [, ... ] ]
} )
```

Power Apps and AI

A recent capability that has been introduced to Power Apps is being able to build UI elements from a hand-drawn mockup or using a wireframe built on *Figma*.

Just imagine sitting with a customer and building some rough sketches while talking, and then simply importing the drawing to Power Apps using the **Create** option:

Figure 9.33: Building apps using hand-drawn sketches

This new feature lets you tag the components on your sketch and assign controls available within Power Apps:

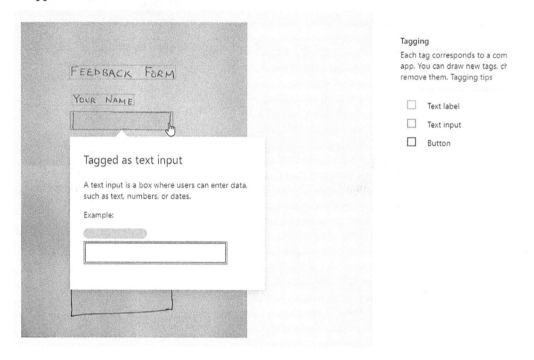

Figure 9.34: Tagging controls

And after just a few clicks, your app UI is ready. This feature looks very promising and works well for simple user interfaces.

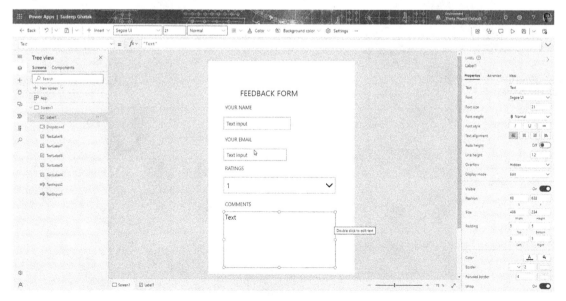

Figure 9.35: Wireframe inside the Power Apps canvas

Note

This feature saves some time if you are planning to design apps on a Dataverse backend, since it creates Dataverse tables for you when you go through the wizard. Keep in mind, though, that it doesn't currently support other data stores.

If you are familiar with the Figma prototyping tool, you can import your Figma designs using the **Figma** import option:

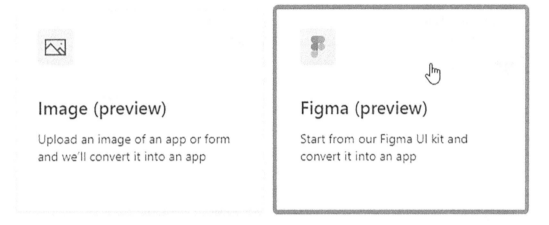

Figure 9.36: Figma wireframes

We will talk more on artificial intelligence in *Chapter 12, Overview of Copilot in Microsoft 365 and Power Platform*.

See also

- The *Sharing a Power Apps* recipe in *Chapter 10, Applying Power Apps*
- The *Copilot* recipe in *Chapter 10, Applying Power Apps*
- The *Creating Power Apps from a SharePoint list/library* recipe in this chapter
- Understand experimental, preview, and retired features in canvas apps: `https://packt.link/canvas-apps-experimental-features`

Creating Power Apps from a SharePoint list/library

A SharePoint list comes with in-built list forms that let users create or update records in the list. Power Apps gives you the ability to change the form-editing experience. Once the form is customized using Power Apps, it takes over the SharePoint item-editing experience.

The following are some use cases when you should consider using Power Apps:

- Including a logo on a form
- Hiding some list fields from the end-user

- Managing the conditional visibility of list fields
- Adding conditional formatting in the form-editing experience

 Custom forms for lists are only supported in generic lists for the time being. Custom list and library templates are currently not supported, including, but not limited to, lists such as *Announcements*, *Contacts*, and *Tasks*.

In document libraries, Power Apps only supports editing custom metadata. Editing or managing file(s) is not supported.

In the following example, we use a SharePoint list that maintains a list of customer contacts and change the add/update item experience using Power Apps:

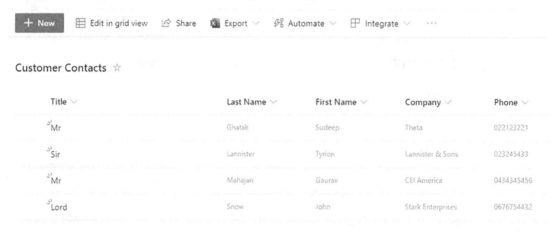

Figure 9.37: SharePoint list as data source

 Please note that not all SharePoint data types are supported in Power Apps. Check out `https://packt.link/Power-Apps-issues` for more details.

In this section of this chapter, we'll look at the steps to create an app from a SharePoint list.

Getting ready

People with SharePoint permissions to manage, design, or edit the associated list will be able to create Power Apps list forms.

How to do it...

There are two options available for creating Power Apps from within a SharePoint list, as shown in the following screenshot:

Figure 9.38: SharePoint integration

1. **Create an app:** This option lets you create a standalone application that can connect to other data sources. It can be accessed outside SharePoint, made available as a mobile app, and can be embedded inside a SharePoint site.
2. **Customize forms:** This option lets you replace the default SharePoint forms with the Power Apps forms; however, the app is tied to the SharePoint list and cannot be accessed outside the list.

We'll look at each option in the next two sections. Let's begin by looking into the **Customize forms** option.

Customize forms

To customize an existing SharePoint list form, go through the following steps:

1. Open the SharePoint site where the list resides.
2. Click on the **Customize forms** option from the context menu in the ribbon:

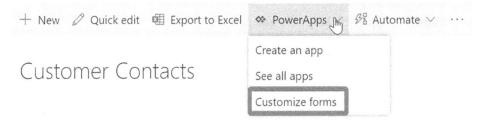

Figure 9.39: Customize list form

3. Power Apps Studio will load and a SharePoint edit form will be available for customization.

4. From the right pane, click **Edit fields** (labeled with a *1* in the following screenshot) to add or remove list fields from the form (labeled with a *2*). Let's get rid of the **Attachments** field because it is not relevant to our use case. We'll also move the **Company** field to the top:

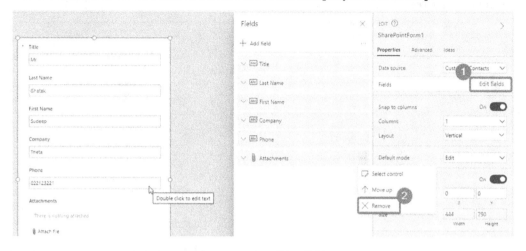

Figure 9.40: Specifying fields

5. To save and publish your changes, click on the **Back to SharePoint** link in the top left-hand corner:

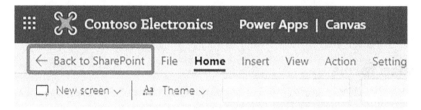

Figure 9.41: Saving a Power Apps list form

6. Save the app by pressing *Ctrl + S* or go to the **File** menu.
7. Publish the app by clicking **Save and publish**:

Save and publish your changes

Save your changes so you don't lose your work. To make changes visible to SharePoint users, choose 'Save and publish'.

Figure 9.42: Publishing to SharePoint

Your changes will now be visible when someone tries to add or update a list item:

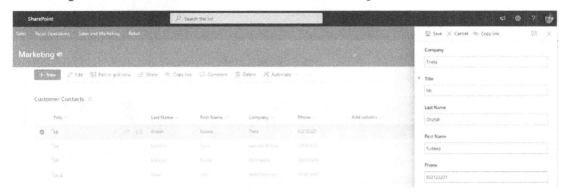

Figure 9.43: Testing a Power Apps list form

Now that we have learned how to customize a SharePoint form, let us look at the next option, **Create an app**.

Create an app

To create a standalone Power App connected to a SharePoint list, go through the following steps:

1. Open the SharePoint site where the list resides.
2. Click on the **Create an app** option from the context menu in the ribbon.
3. You will be asked to specify a name for your app. Click **Create** once you have chosen one:

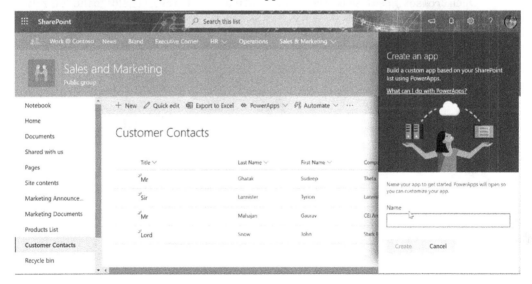

Figure 9.44: Standalone Power App using a SharePoint list as its data source

4. SharePoint builds a Power App for you based on the structure of the list. The app has three screens:

    •   **Browse**: Displays a list of items
    •   **Display**: Displays a single list item in read-only mode
    •   **Edit**: Displays a single list item in edit mode

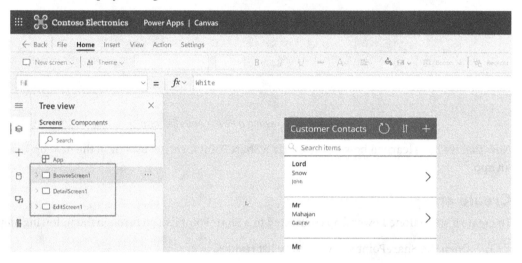

Figure 9.45: SharePoint builds an app with three screens

5. Open BrowseScreen1, select the gallery, and map the SharePoint fields to the controls in the gallery. SharePoint will have some fields selected by default, but you can change them from here:

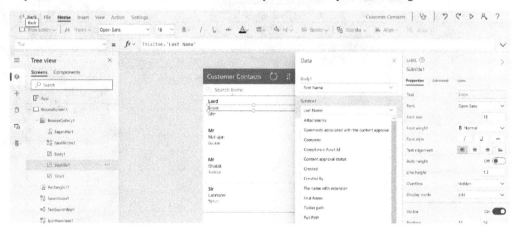

Figure 9.46: Browse screen

6. Open `DisplayScreen1` and select `DisplayForm1`. Configure the fields that you want to display on the form:

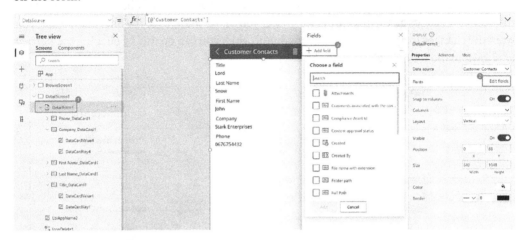

Figure 9.47: Display screen

7. Repeat *Step 6* for `EditForm1` in `EditScreen1`.

8. Save the app and publish it:

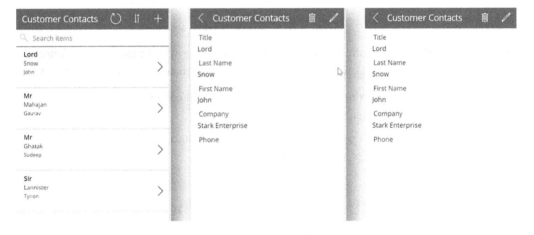

Figure 9.48: Power Apps screens in preview mode

How it works...

When you select the **Customize forms** option, Power Apps creates a SharePoint data source behind the scenes and does all the plumbing for you. If you make changes to the SharePoint list columns and want the changes to appear in Power Apps Studio, then you can do this by clicking the **Refresh** button, as shown in the following screenshot:

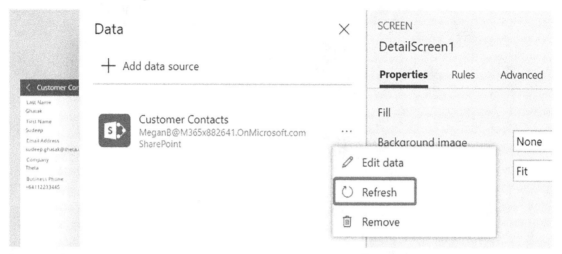

Figure 9.49: Refreshing the data source

Once you customize a SharePoint list form, Power Apps will take over the editing experience. If you want to revert to the default SharePoint list experience, then you can do that at any time from **List Settings**:

1. Select **List Settings** from the gear icon in the top-right corner.
2. Under **General Settings**, select **Form Settings**.
3. On the **Form Settings** page, select **Use the default SharePoint form**, and then select **Delete custom form**:

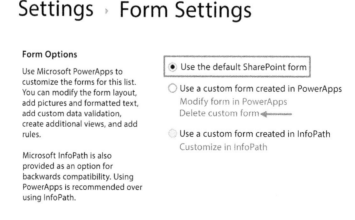

Figure 9.50: Specifying the SharePoint list form option

There's more...

Since SharePoint and Power Apps were built as two separate products, there are some limitations, some of which are as follows:

- Power Apps does not support all types of columns from SharePoint lists. The following list shows the kinds of columns that it does and doesn't support:

    - It supports single values for the **Choice** column.
    - It supports single values for the **Lookup** column.
    - It doesn't support **External Data**, **Rating**, and **Task Outcome** columns.
    - It doesn't support columns that have been configured to accept multiple values.

- Currently, Power Apps can only retrieve data from custom lists. It cannot use libraries on any other data stored in SharePoint.

See also

- The *Creating a template-based app* recipe in this chapter
- The *Connecting to data sources* recipe in this chapter
- The *Adding screens* recipe in this chapter
- The *Sharing a Power App* recipe in *Chapter 10, Applying Power Apps*
- The *Creating a canvas app from a blank template* recipe in this chapter

Creating a Power Pages website using Power Apps

In this recipe, we'll create a website using Power Pages that acts as an externally facing website for internal or external users who are accessing your environment's Dataverse database. You can choose whether to require authentication or not (making your data publicly or privately accessible).

Getting ready

Power Pages requires additional licensing. You'll need add-on licensing based on login capacity for authenticated users or page view capacity for unauthenticated users. Learn more about current pricing at `https://powerapps.microsoft.com/en-us/pricing/`. The first time you create a website, however, you can take advantage of a 30-day trial.

How to do it...

1. Sign in to Power Apps (`https://make.powerapps.com`).

2. Select **Create | Blank app | Power Pages website | Create** as shown in *Figure 9.51*. Alternatively, you can navigate to **Apps | New app | Website**:

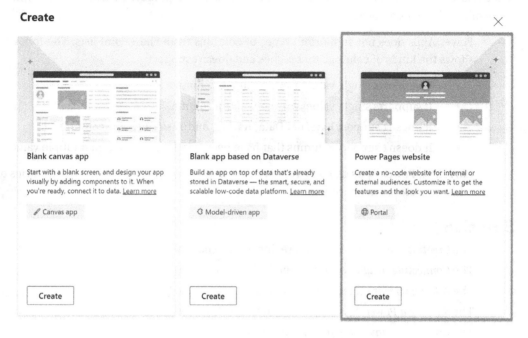

Figure 9.51: New website creation option within Power Apps

3. Name your website, choose a web address and language for it, and then select **Create**. Note that this may take several minutes to set up. Wait for the completion notification:

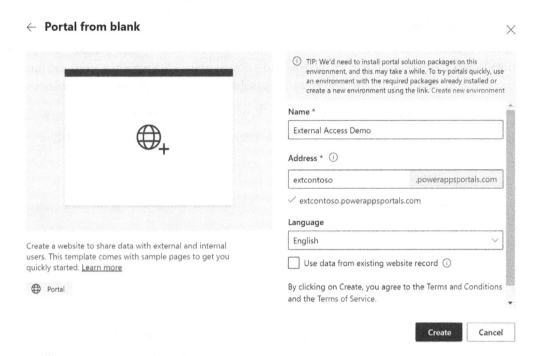

Figure 9.52: New blank website details panel in Power Apps

4. When you're ready, go to **Apps** and use the new website's ellipsis (**...**) to select **Edit**.

5. On the left navigation, you can choose from **Pages and navigation**, **Components**, **Themes**, **Page templates**, **Settings** (including data permissions), and **Progressive web app**. You can use several of these options to design various pages for your website and incorporate the data, apps, and charts your users can access.

You've now created your Power Pages website and can edit it to the desired result.

How it works...

Power Pages websites enable you to create digital assets that reflect your company's branding and provide data and app access to both internal and external users. With websites, users can interact with your Power BI, Power Automate, and Power Apps solutions from a single and simplified user interface.

You can format the pages of your site to have 1, 2, or 3 sections, laid out either individually or mixed.

For page contents, you can choose from several components to add, including the following:

- Text
- Image
- iFrame
- Form
- List
- Breadcrumb
- Power BI
- Chatbot

Your site's navigation menu is determined in the **Pages and navigation** panel, as shown in *Figure 9.53*. You can add subpages, move items around, hide pages such as "access denied" pages, and more:

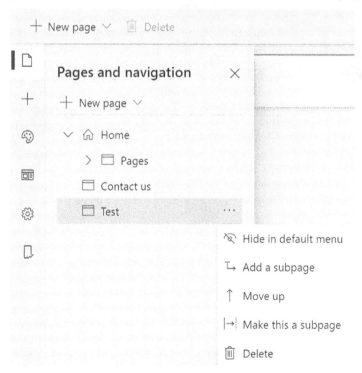

Figure 9.53: Pages and navigation panel of a Power Pages website

And because your website is live, there is no need to publish. Your changes are autosaved continually.

When you're ready to share your website, navigate to **Power Apps | Apps**, then select your new website and then **Share**. You'll be able to configure access here as shown in *Figure 9.54*:

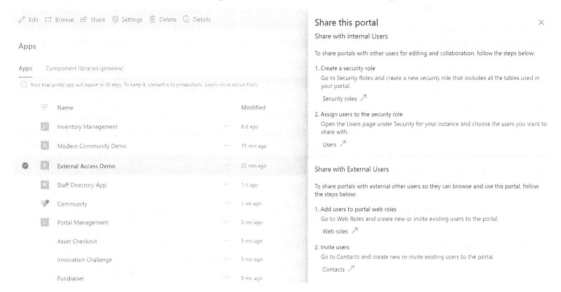

Figure 9.54: Website sharing panel for a selected Power Pages website

Notice that there are internal and external user instructions in the panel.

There's more...

Rather than start from blank, you can create a website from a template by signing in to Power Apps, selecting **Create**, and then scrolling to the bottom, where you'll find a **Modern Community** template you can use. This template is shown being edited in *Figure 9.55*:

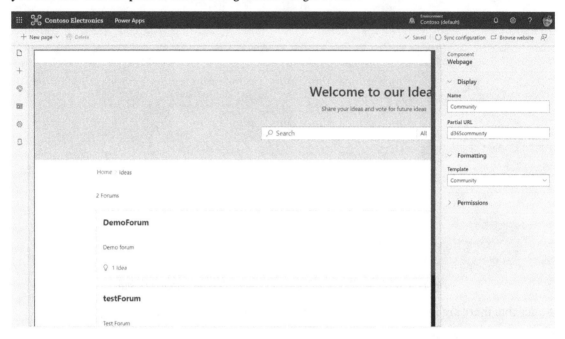

Figure 9.55: The Modern Community website template in Edit mode

This Modern Community template is a prebuilt forum template where people can share and vote on ideas.

We have focused on Power Pages' integration with Power Apps in this recipe, but you can also create sites directly within Power Pages. To do this, begin the recipe from `https://make.powerpages.microsoft.com` instead.

See also

- *Microsoft Power Pages is now generally available*: `https://packt.link/Power-Pages-generally-available`

Creating a model-driven app

In this recipe, you'll create a model-driven app. Model-driven apps allow you to add forms, views, charts, and dashboards to your Dataverse tables. This creates a user-friendly navigation interface for single or related tables in your environment. Microsoft recommends building model-driven apps from solutions, so this recipe will follow that guidance.

Getting ready

You'll need access to Power Apps and an environment in which you can publish a solution. You can either use default tables within the environment's Dataverse database or create new tables before creating your new app. In this recipe, we'll be using the default Accounts table.

How to do it...

1. Sign in to Power Apps (https://make.powerapps.com).
2. If you're not already in the environment in which you wish to create the model-driven app, switch environments to your preference. You can do this by selecting your current environment in the upper-right corner.
3. From the left-hand navigation menu, choose **Solutions** then **New solution**.
4. Provide a **Display name, Name, Publisher,** and **Version** if you wish it to be something other than 1.0.0.0:

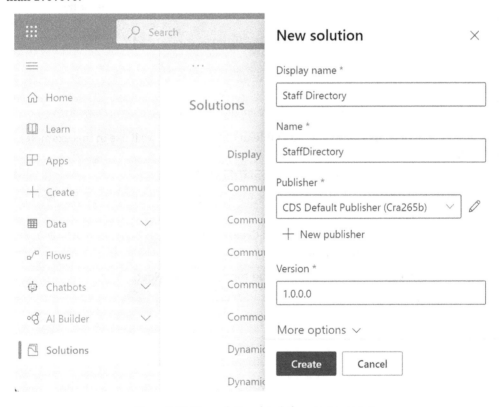

Figure 9.56: New solution details form in Power Apps

5. Click **Create**.
6. Select the name of your new solution once it appears.

7. Next, choose **Add existing**, then **Table**:

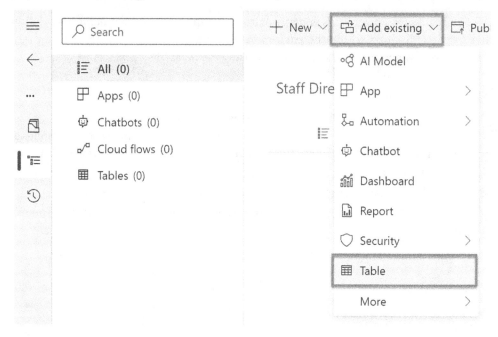

8. Select the **Account** table (a default table in Dataverse that we'll use in this example) then click **Next**.

9. Check the box to **Include all** components, then click **Add**.

10. Now that we have a solution with data, we're ready to create the app. Select **New** | **App** | **Model-driven app**.

11. Select the **Modern app designer**, then **Create**.

12. Name the app and click **Create**.

13. Select **New page** | **Table based view and form**, and then **Next**.

14. Select the **Account** table, then **Add**:

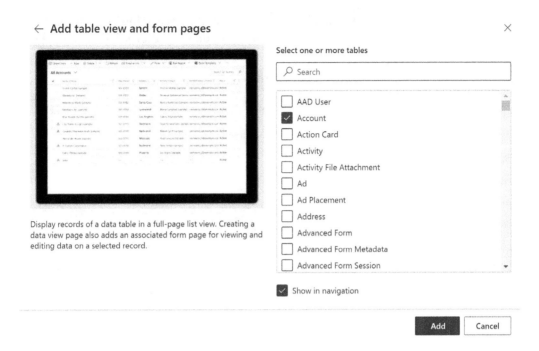

Figure 9.58: Adding the Account table from Dataverse to a model-driven app

15. Now expand **Account** from the left navigation and select **Account view**, then **Manage views:**

Figure 9.59: Manage views option found when Account view is selected

16. Select all of the views seen in *Figure 9.60* (**Account Advanced Find View, My Active Accounts, Active Accounts, All Accounts,** and **Account Lookup View**) then select **Save:**

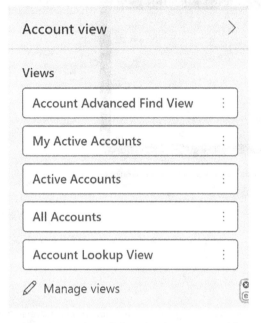

Figure 9.60: Selected views for the Account table

17. Select **Save** on the command bar in the upper-right corner.

18. Select **Publish** on the command bar in the upper-right corner.

19. You can test your new model-driven app by selecting **Play** or by navigating back to the Power Apps home screen and finding your app under **Apps**. If you have existing accounts, try selecting an account within your app's table so you can see how a user would navigate through the data. If you don't have an account yet, click **New** to add a new account to the table:

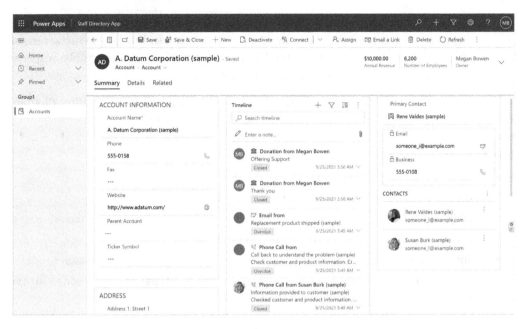

Figure 9.61: A specific account selected within the new model-driven app

You have now published a model-driven app.

How it works...

Model-driven apps use Dataverse databases, and each environment can have one database. The solution that you use for your model-driven app can contain tables from that Dataverse database, forms, views, Power Automate flows, apps, and more. This packaged solution makes it easy to move the entire solution and its dependencies from one environment to another (such as from a development environment to production).

Model-driven apps can also be accessed on mobile devices for on-the-go access to the rich data in your environment's Dataverse tables.

Canvas apps allow you to have more control over every element of the user interface, whereas model-driven apps are largely pre-configured for you. You're mostly deciding how to surface existing data and which components to include in the app. This helps ensure the app is accessible, responsive, and consistent with other model-driven apps in your environment.

To explore some sample model-driven apps, such as **Asset Checkout**, **Innovation Challenge**, and **Fundraiser**, visit `https://packt.link/sample-model-driven-apps`.

See also

- Model-driven apps: `https://packt.link/model-driven-apps`
- Design and build an app: `https://packt.link/app-building-steps`
- Build your first modern model-driven app: `https://packt.link/build-model-driven-app`
- Create a solution: `https://packt.link/create-PA-solution`
- Share a model-driven app: `https://packt.link/share-model-driven-app`
- Understand model-driven app components: `https://packt.link/model-driven-app-components`

Custom pages and the modern app designer

In this recipe, you'll learn how to use the modern app designer for Power Apps to create a custom page for a model-driven app.

Getting ready

You'll need access to Power Apps and edit permissions for an existing model-driven app to which you'd like to add a custom page.

How to do it...

1. Sign in to Power Apps (`https://make.powerapps.com`).
2. Select **Apps** from the left-hand navigation menu.

3. To open an existing model-driven app in the modern app designer, use the ellipsis (...) next to the app, then select **Edit in preview** from the **Edit** flyout menu, as shown in *Figure 9.62*:

Figure 9.62: Edit in preview option for an existing model-driven app

4. Select **+ Add page** from the top ribbon menu.
5. Select **Custom (preview)** for the page type, then **Next**, as shown in *Figure 9.63*:

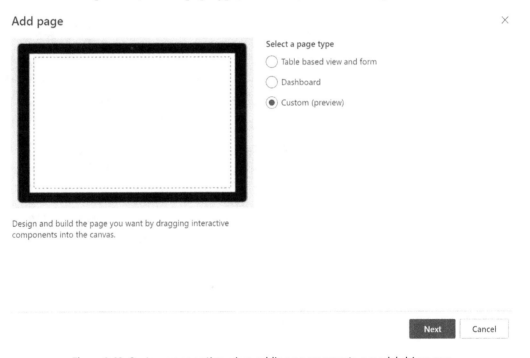

Figure 9.63: Custom page option when adding a new page to a model-driven app

6. From here, your editing experience is similar to editing a canvas app. Add components, such as galleries, text, labels, form fields, and more. *Figure 9.64* shows some components available to add to your blank page:

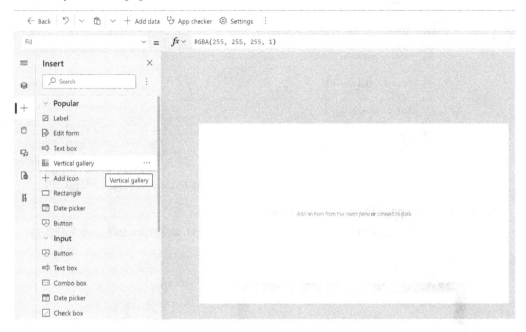

Figure 9.64: Popular components available for custom page insertion

7. After you've designed the page as you wish, select **Save** and then **Publish**.

8. Select **Back** to return to your model-driven app tab.

9. You can now use the custom page in your app and optionally place it in your navigation. *Figure 9.65* shows this new custom page in the **Pages** navigation panel of the model-driven app:

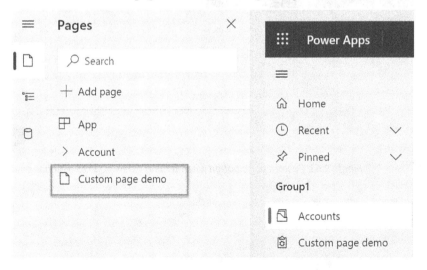

Figure 9.65: A custom page added to a model-driven app appearing in Pages

10. Republish your model-driven app to save your addition and make it available to users.

How it works...

To use the modern app designer, be sure to use the **Edit** flyout menu and choose **Edit in preview**. Otherwise **Edit** will be the classic editor and won't allow the sort of flexible editing required for actions such as adding custom pages.

Custom pages can be helpful to display additional data, collect data, etc. so you don't have to choose between just a canvas app and just a model-driven app. This gives you the flexibility to have canvas app-like components and user experiences within the more standardized model-driven app experience.

Once you've created your first custom page, you can add it to multiple apps in the future by choosing **+ Add page | Custom (preview) | Next | Use an existing custom page** as shown in *Figure 9.66*:

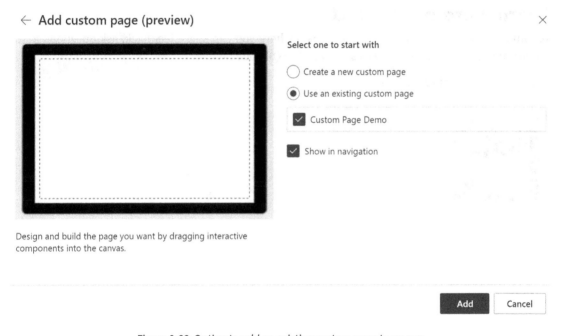

Figure 9.66: Option to add an existing custom page to an app

Developers may wish to explore more advanced topics such as pro-code additions and using PowerFx with their custom pages. This is a new feature in preview at the time of writing, so be sure to check the documentation in the *See also* section for the latest updates on these more advanced topics.

See also

- Model-driven app custom page overview: `https://packt.link/model-driven-app-custom-page-overview`

- Add a custom page to your model-driven app (preview): `https://packt.link/model-driven-app-custom-page-preview`

- Design a custom page for your model-driven app: `https://packt.link/design-page-for-model-driven-app`

- Using PowerFx in a custom page: `https://packt.link/Power-Fx-custom-page`

- Navigating to and from a custom page using client API: `https://packt.link/client-API-custom-pages`

- Code components for the custom page designer: `https://packt.link/custom-page-designer`

Learn more on Discord

To join the Discord community for this book – where you can share feedback, ask questions to the author, and learn about new releases – follow the QR code below:

`https://packt.link/powerusers`

10

Applying Power Apps

In the previous chapter, we learned how to create an app using Power Apps. Unwittingly, we also started to touch on the extensibility of Power Apps as it interacted with other tools and platforms. For example, model-driven apps use Dataverse as the groundwork to build up their capabilities, and Power Pages can be used as a website builder for external-facing functionality. However, we only looked at this connectivity of Power Apps with other services from the perspective of constructing an app. In this chapter, we will turn this on its head and start to look at how a completed app (known as a Power App) can be distributed across platforms and be applied nearly anywhere. We will also take a look at the newly released Microsoft Copilot.

Specifically, we will cover the following recipes:

- Sharing a Power App
- Embedding a Power App in Teams
- Embedding a Power App on a SharePoint page
- Creating a Power App using Dataverse for Teams
- Exporting a Power App
- Importing a Power App
- Copilot

With this knowledge, you should be able to apply an app to a vast number of scenarios. It's fun to think what could be done with a Power App that appears for user convenience directly on a Teams page or to imagine what a user might think seeing a new capability on a SharePoint page that handily simplifies their daily work. The spirit of this chapter is to think about the adoption of an app by making it convenient to find and begin using. We will begin this topic by learning how to share a Power App.

Sharing a Power App

Once the app is ready and published, you can share it with users so that they can run it. You could share the app with the entire organization if you want to, provided they have a valid Office 365 account. If you want certain users to make changes to your app, add them as owners. The following recipe talks about how you can share your app with your colleagues.

Getting ready

You need to be an owner of the app to share it with others.

How to do it...

1. Sign in to Power Apps, and then select **Apps** from the left-hand side menu.

2. Select the app that you want to share by clicking on it and selecting **Share** from the banner.

3. Alternatively, you could select the **Share** option from the context menu of the app:

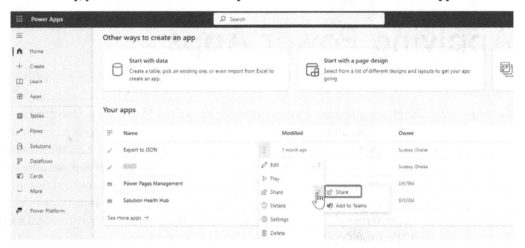

Figure 10.1: Sharing the app

4. Open the **Share** screen.

5. Start typing the name or alias of the users or security groups in Azure Active Directory (now known as **Entra ID**) that you want to share the app with. Check the **Send an email invitation to new users** checkbox to notify the users:

Figure 10.2: Broadcast app

 To allow your entire organization to run the app (but not modify or share it), type Everyone in the sharing panel. You can't share the app with people or groups outside your organization.

6. You can assign a co-owner by selecting the user and checking the **Co-owner** checkbox. These users will be able to edit the Power App:

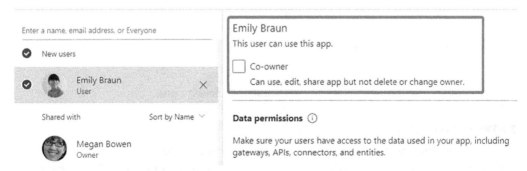

Figure 10.3: Specifying a co-owner

7. If you have built a model-driven app, then you need to go through some additional steps, as shown in the following screenshot:

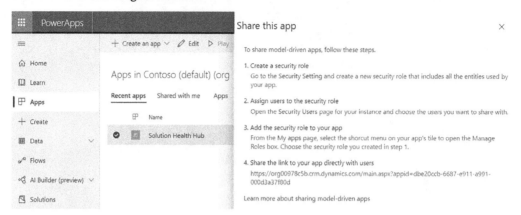

Figure 10.4: Configuring a model-driven app

 For more information about managing security for an entity, see `https://packt.link/entities`.

8. To stop sharing the app with a user or group, select the remove (**X**) icon next to the user or group:

Share Hello world

Add people as Users and Co-owners to your app. Make sure your data connections have been shared with all users.

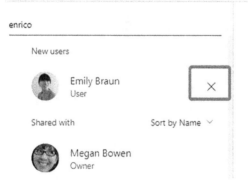

Figure 10.5: Removing a user

How it works...

If you checked the email invitation checkbox, then everyone with whom you shared the app can run it by selecting the link in the invitation. If a user selects the link on a mobile device, then the app opens in Power Apps Mobile.

If a user selects the link on a desktop computer, the app opens in a browser. Co-owners who receive an invitation get another link that opens the app for editing in Power Apps Studio.

 An experimental feature has been announced that enables real-time collaboration with others in both Canvas and Model-driven Apps. For more details, please check out the links provided in the *See also* section.

See also

- The *Creating a template-based app* recipe in *Chapter 9, Creating Power Apps*
- The *Connecting to data sources* recipe in *Chapter 9, Creating Power Apps*
- The *Adding screens* recipe in *Chapter 9, Creating Power Apps*
- The *Creating a canvas app from a blank template* recipe in *Chapter 9, Creating Power Apps*
- The *Creating Power Apps from a SharePoint list/library* recipe in *Chapter 9, Creating Power Apps*
- *Coauthoring in model-driven apps*, `https://learn.microsoft.com/en-us/power-apps/maker/model-driven-apps/coauthoring`
- *Coauthoring in canvas apps*, `https://powerusers.microsoft.com/t5/Power-Apps-Community-Blog/Co-authoring-in-Canvas-Power-Apps/ba-p/1526547`

Embedding a Power App in Teams

Embedding a Power App as a Teams channel tab makes it easier for your colleagues to access the app and use it more regularly. In this recipe, we'll embed a Power App as a channel tab to help create a single context in which our users can interact with the app and its related processes as well as navigate to other areas and resources in Teams.

Getting ready

You will need to be a member of a team with permission to add tabs to your desired channel as well as a Power App already built (though, alternately, you are able to create a new app from within Teams).

How to do it...

1. Navigate to the specific channel in Microsoft Teams to which you'd like to add your Power App.
2. Click the plus sign (+) to the right of that channel's existing tabs to add another:

Figure 10.6: Adding an app as a Teams tab

3.   Search for and select **Power Apps**:

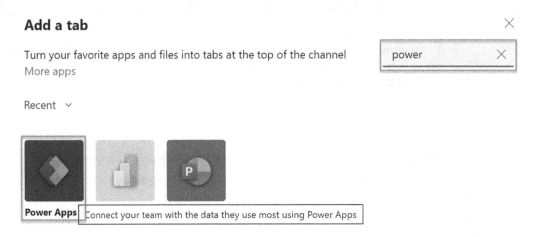

Figure 10.7: Selecting Power Apps to add an app to Teams

4.   Search for and select the name of the app you're embedding (and note the ability to navigate to **Power Apps** to create a new one). Once selected, choose **Save**:

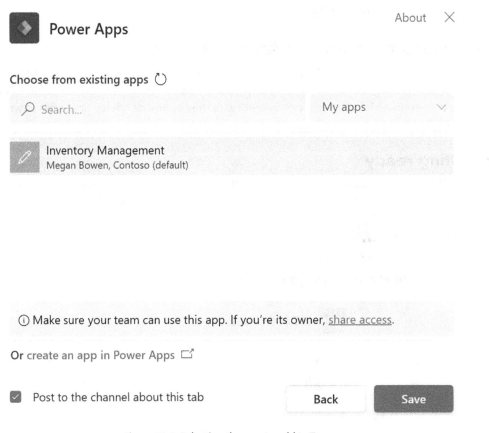

Figure 10.8: Selecting the app to add to Teams

How it works...

Once you've created an app in Power Apps and shared it and any relevant data connections with your site's users, you're ready to embed your app in Teams for convenience. Once the tab is added, the app is fully functional within the context of your channel:

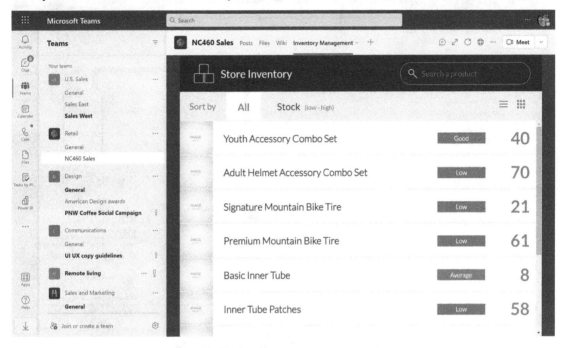

Figure 10.9: An app functioning inside Teams

There's more...

You may wish to rename the tab, depending on how you've named your app. By default, your tab name matches the app name. Click the arrow next to the existing name to rename your app's tab to something clearer and/or more concise:

Figure 10.10: Renaming the Teams tab for an embedded app

You can also add an app by clicking **Power Apps** on the left-hand navigation rail on Teams. Simply use the ellipsis in your menu, then search for and select **Power Apps**. This allows you to create new apps for your teams entirely within the context of Teams and has several templates to inspire you or get you started:

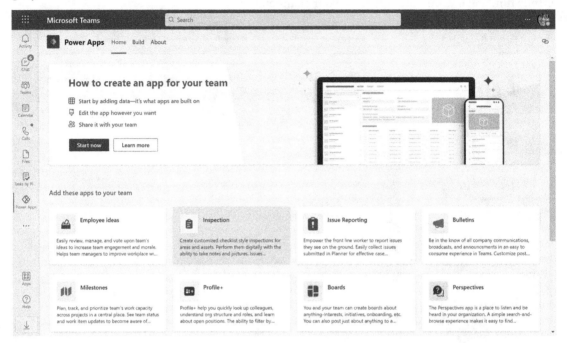

Figure 10.11: Adding an app with Power Apps on the left-hand menu

There is an alternative way to add an app to Teams but for your personal use (instead of your entire team). If embedding an app just for your own convenience, you can go to Power Apps (`https://make.powerapps.com`), choose **Apps** from the left-hand navigation menu, select the desired app, and choose **Add to Teams**:

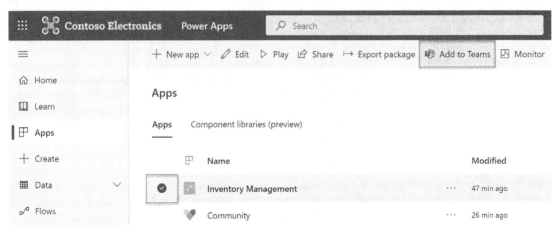

Figure 10.12: Adding an app to Teams for personal use

Then select **Add to Teams** (again, but from the right panel that appears), then **Add** (once inside Teams). This will add that specific app as a left-hand navigation option. Be sure to right-click and pin the app to keep it there (and not have to use the ellipsis menu to find it the next time you wish to use it again).

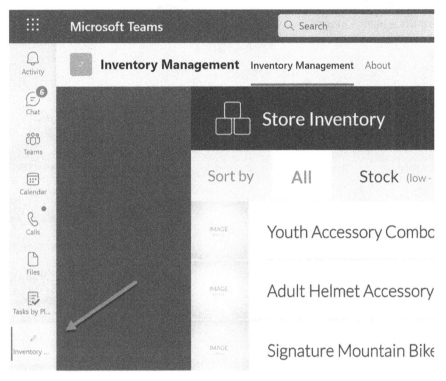

Figure 10.13: Pinning an app to the Teams navigation pane

See also

- Power Apps and Microsoft Teams integration: `https://packt.link/Power-Apps-and-Teams-integration`
- Embed a canvas app as a tab: `https://packt.link/embedded-Teams-tab`
- Embed an app in Teams: `https://packt.link/embedded-Teams-app`

Embedding a Power App on a SharePoint page

Embedding a Power App on a SharePoint page makes it easier for your colleagues to access the app and use it more regularly. In this recipe, we'll embed a Power App on a SharePoint page to help create a single context in which our users can interact with the app and its related processes, as well as navigate to other areas and resources on our site.

Getting ready

You will need a SharePoint site with edit permissions as well as a Power App that is already built.

How to do it...

1. Go to Power Apps (`https://make.powerapps.com`) and select **Apps** from the left-hand navigation menu.

2. Select the ellipsis (**...**) next to the app you would like to embed, then choose **Details**:

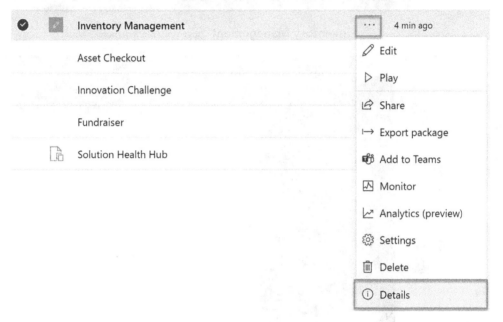

Figure 10.14: Going to Details for a selected app

3. Copy the **Web link** URL from **Details**:

Figure 10.15: Finding the web link of an app

4. Now go to the SharePoint page on which you'd like to embed this Power App.

5. Click **Edit** in the upper-right corner of the page to modify it.

6. Click the plus sign (+) in a section layout where you'd like to initially add the Power App – you can always move it later.

7. Search for and select the **Microsoft PowerApps** web part (without the space):

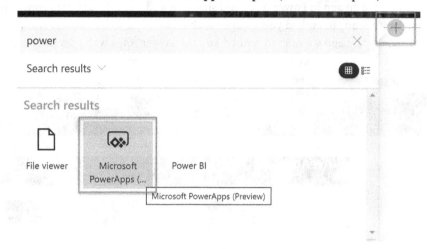

Figure 10.16: Adding a PowerApps web part to a SharePoint page

8. Paste the URL you've copied in the web part's **Properties** panel on the right. You'll see the app appear in the web part placeholder automatically after pasting:

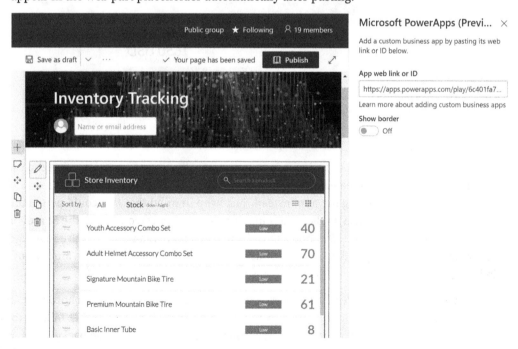

Figure 10.17: An embedded app visible on a SharePoint page

9. When finished with making modifications to the page, you can either select **Save as draft** (if you don't want users to see it yet) or **Publish** (when you're ready for users to begin using the embedded app).

How it works...

Once you've created an app in Power Apps and shared it and any relevant data connections with your site's users, you're ready to embed your app on a SharePoint page for convenience. We use the app's web link to specify the app we wish to embed and the Power Apps web part in SharePoint. Once the page is published, the app is fully functional within the context of your page:

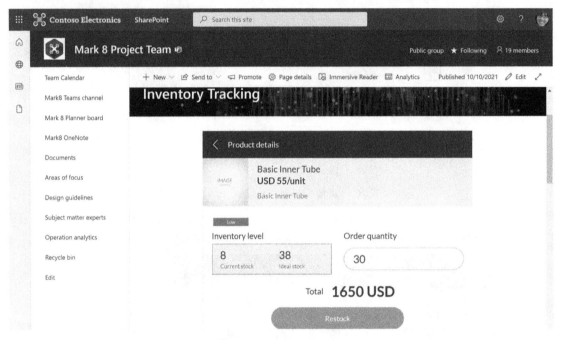

Figure 10.18: The embedded app is functional on a published SharePoint page

There's more...

If you find that the embedded experience is too compact, you might consider using the same web link you copied in *Step 3* to create a quick link on a SharePoint page that allows users to click into a full-screen experience of using the app instead. Just keep in mind that this could potentially disorient less familiar users because it takes them into a new user interface without the SharePoint site's navigation and general context. By choosing to embed an app in SharePoint, we're making it easier for users to access, create, and/or manage shared data, and we're reducing the amount of context switching taking place.

You may have also noticed in *Step 8* that there's an extra option available to show a border around your app. Compare the screenshot in the *How it works...* section to the screenshot that follows to see the difference. Since this particular app has a background that matches the page background, it seems to blend in with the page seamlessly without a border. With the border, however, our focus is drawn to a more specific area on the page that houses the app.

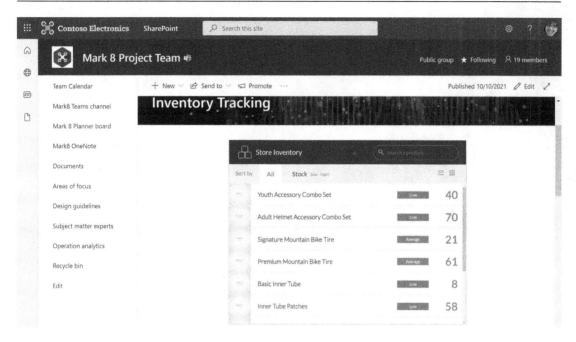

Figure 10.19: Using a border to focus on the part of the screen housing an app

See also

- Embed Power Apps on SharePoint pages: `https://packt.link/embed-apps-on-SP-pages`

Creating a Power App using Dataverse for Teams

Microsoft Dataverse for Teams provides the user with a built-in, low-code data platform to build apps and flows in Microsoft Teams using Power Apps and Power Automate.

Microsoft Dataverse for Teams, being built on Dataverse, offers benefits such as:

- Relational data storage
- Rich data type
- Enterprise-grade governance
- One-click solution deployment to the Microsoft Teams app store

Getting ready

You will need to be a member of a team to build Power Apps using Dataverse for Teams.

How to do it...

1. Open Teams. From the left pane, click the ellipsis (**...**):

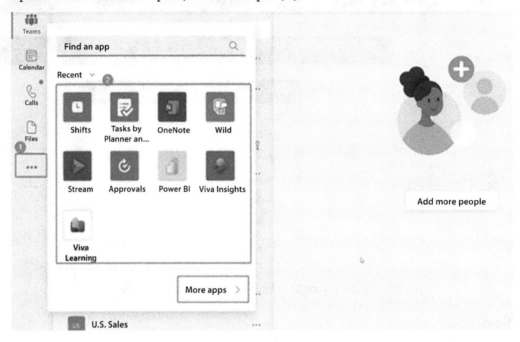

Figure 10.20: Adding Power Apps on Teams with the navigation pane

2. If you do not see Power Apps in your list of added apps, search for it by clicking on **More apps**:

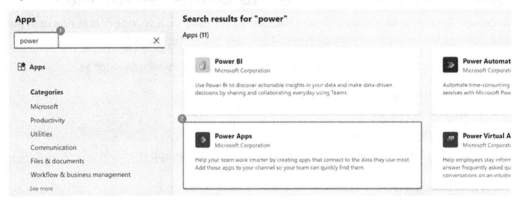

Figure 10.21: Searching for Power Apps

3. After selecting it, you will then have the option to add Power Apps to Teams:

Figure 10.22: Adding Power Apps to Teams

4. Select **Start now**:

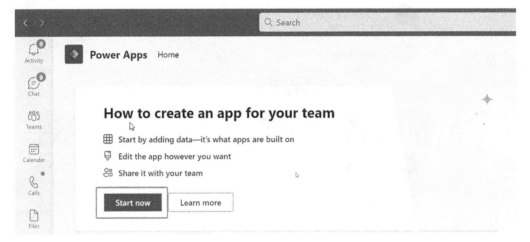

Figure 10.23: Beginning the process of adding an app on Teams

5. Select the team where you want to create the app:

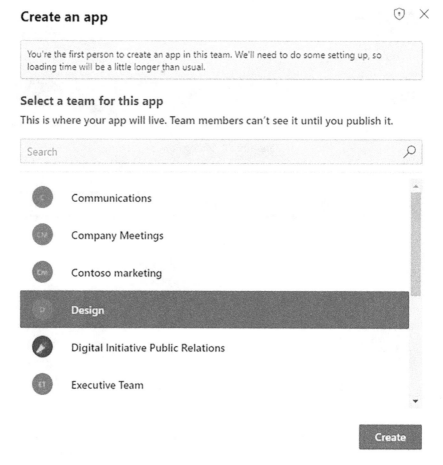

Figure 10.24: Choosing the team to which the app will be added

6. Click **Create** to provision a Dataverse for Teams environment in the team you selected.

7. You will be taken to the familiar Power Apps designer and prompted to specify a name for your app. Provide a name and click **Save**:

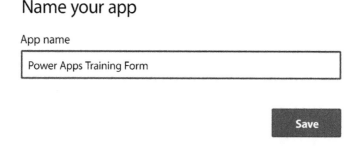

Figure 10.25: Naming an app on the Power Apps designer

8. Choose the option to build an app with data. You will be asked to choose an existing table or create a table of your own:

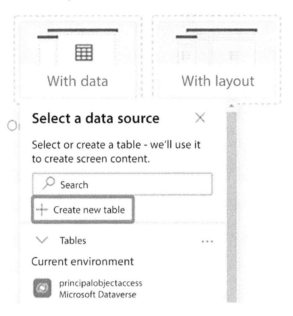

Figure 10.26: Choosing a table for building an app with data

Let's create our own table and call it `Power Apps Training Attendees` and click **Create**:

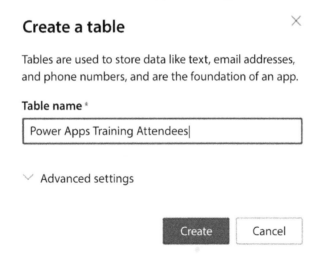

Figure 10.27: Naming a new table

9. The table designer lets you create your own schema. You can add columns of your choice and specify the data type. We will create two fields, as shown below, and click **Create**:

    *   `Email Address` (data type **Email**)
    *   `Contact Number` (data type **Phone**)

Power Apps Training Atten...

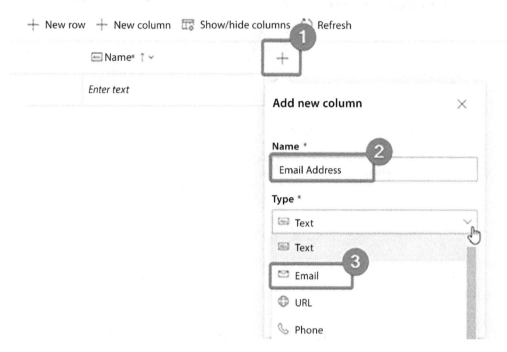

Figure 10.28: Three steps for adding a column, naming it, and specifying the data type

10. You can also add data using the table designer.

Power Apps Training Atten...

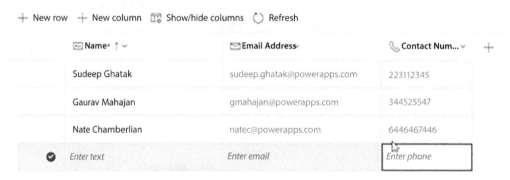

Figure 10.29: Adding data with the table designer

11. Click **Close** to save your table schema and data.

12. Your Power Apps form is ready and waiting to be published:

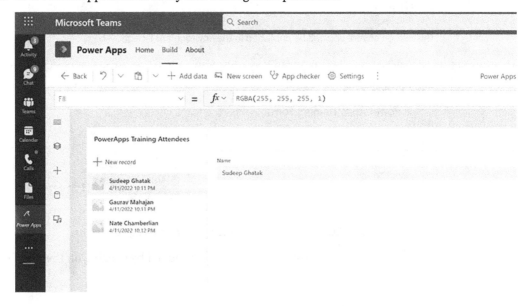

Figure 10.30: The Power Apps form prepared for publication

13. Publish this app by clicking on the **Publish to Teams** button in the upper-right corner of Power Apps Studio:

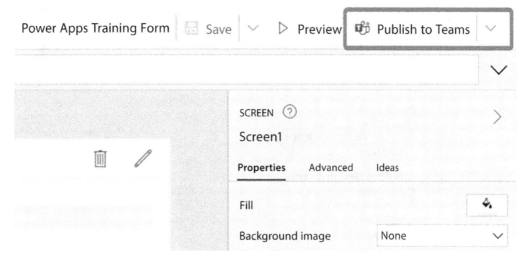

Figure 10.31: Publish to Teams option in the upper-right corner

14. You will be presented with a pop-up window. Click on **Next**:

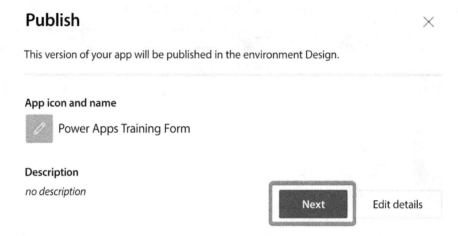

Figure 10.32: Pop-up window when publishing an app on Teams

15. Now select the channel where you want the app to be added by clicking on the plus (+) icon. Then click **Save and close**:

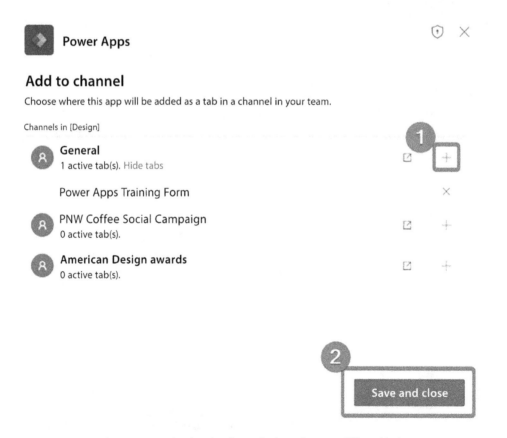

Figure 10.33: Selecting the channel where the app will be added

That's it. Your app gets added to the channel you selected:

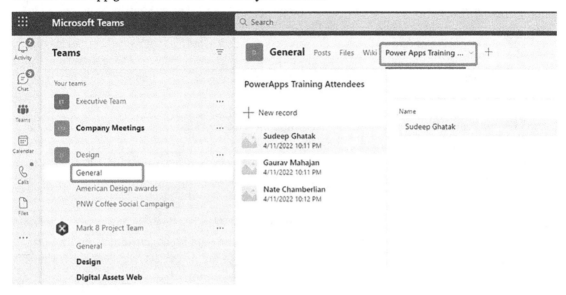

Figure 10.34: The app can be found on the selected channel

How it works...

While, in most cases, you might choose to use a SharePoint list when building a canvas app, it is not the ideal datastore when you are dealing with high volumes of data or building a complex solution that involves multiple tables. That is when you need a relational database like Dataverse for Teams. Here is a decision tree that can help you make the decision on whether to use Dataverse:

	Use SharePoint	**Use Dataverse**
Does your app require granular permissions?	No	Yes
Are you building a model-driven app?	No	Yes
Does your app deal with large data volumes (over 5,000 items)?	No	Yes
Are you likely to face delegation issues?	No	Yes
Does your app involve several tables or lists, each requiring separate add/update screens with search and sort functionality?	No	Yes

Table 10.1: Choosing between a SharePoint or Dataverse database

Power Apps have some delegable functions such as `Filter` or `Sort` that require you to apply a `Where` clause to reduce the number of items returned by the query. Applying this forces Power Apps to delegate the processing of data to the data source rather than moving the data to the app for processing locally. This can be a real problem if your SharePoint list has over 500 items. You can read more about delegation at the following link: `https://packt.link/delegation`

Dataverse for Teams provides you with a data model-focused design where you focus on building the data model (the tables, attributes, metadata, relationship, etc.); you do not need to worry about searching, sorting, filtering, business logic, and so on. These features are added automatically to your application by Power Apps. Not only this, but it also comes with support for files, images, and multiple related tables.

Dataverse for Teams is a lightweight version of Dataverse. It does not include all features that come with Dataverse, such as offline mobile support and advanced data types (customer, multiple transaction currencies, etc.). You can, however, upgrade Dataverse for Teams to leverage these features.

You can see a comparison between Dataverse and Dataverse for Teams at `https://packt.link/Dataverse4T`.

Please note that apps built on Dataverse for Teams are not accessible from `https://make.powerapps.com`.

Your apps can be accessed from the Teams interface by following the steps below:

1. Open Power Apps from Teams (assuming you followed the steps in the earlier recipe, *Embedding a Power App in Teams*):

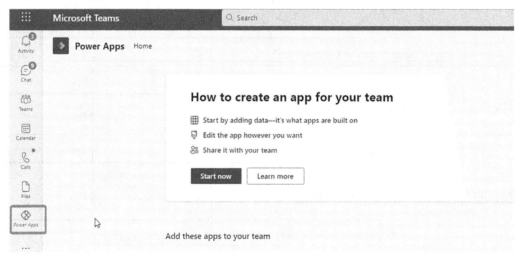

Figure 10.35: Locating Power Apps on the Teams navigation menu

2. You should see the apps that you have built and the teams they have been deployed to:

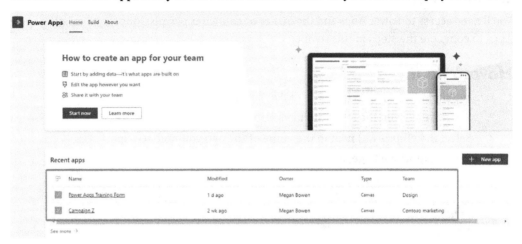

Figure 10.36: List of built apps with several information columns

3. To edit the app, click on **Build** from the top menu and select the team. You should see all apps that you have built for that team, along with the Dataverse tables. Click on the app or the table to edit/open it:

Figure 10.37: Three steps to start editing an app

See also

*   The *Creating a canvas app from a blank template* recipe in *Chapter 9, Creating Power Apps*
*   Microsoft Dataverse: `https://packt.link/dataverse`

Exporting a Power App

In this recipe, we'll export an app named `Inventory Management` to a `.zip` package. Exporting apps is a fairly simple process that makes it easy to later import that app's package into a different environment.

Getting ready

You'll need access to Power Apps and the owner or co-owner permissions for an existing app in Power Apps to complete the steps in this recipe.

How to do it...

1. Sign in to Power Apps (`https://make.powerapps.com`).

2. Select **Apps** from the left-hand navigation menu.

3. Select the ellipsis (**...**) next to the name of the app you wish to export.

4. Select **Export package,** as shown in *Figure 10.38*:

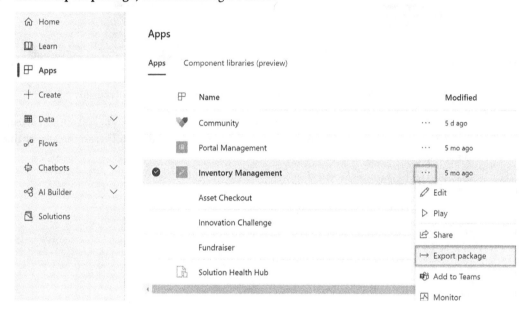

Figure 10.38: Export package option when viewing menu options for a particular app

5. Fill in the package details, including **Name**, **Environment**, and **Description**, as shown in *Figure 10.39*:

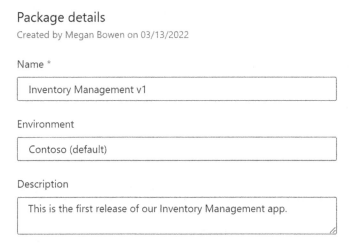

Package details
Created by Megan Bowen on 03/13/2022

Name *

Inventory Management v1

Environment

Contoso (default)

Description

This is the first release of our Inventory Management app.

Figure 10.39: Package details for an app being exported

6. Select the word or the wrench icon to choose **Update** (if the app already exists in the eventual target environment) or **Create as new** (if this is the first version of the app in the target environment):

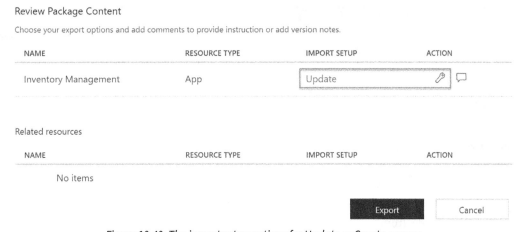

Review Package Content

Choose your export options and add comments to provide instruction or add version notes.

NAME	RESOURCE TYPE	IMPORT SETUP	ACTION
Inventory Management	App	Update	

Related resources

NAME	RESOURCE TYPE	IMPORT SETUP	ACTION
No items			

Export   Cancel

Figure 10.40: The import setup options for Update or Create as new

7. In this example, we've changed **Update** to **Create as new**.

8. If there are additional resources (such as Power Automate flows) in the **Related resources** section, repeat *Step 6* for each resource to specify whether that resource should be imported as new or an update.

9. Select **Export**.

10. The .zip file will automatically download when finished.

How it works...

Exported app packages include the app itself and any flows the app depends on. These can be imported into a different environment as brand new (app and flows) or an update to existing (if you're fixing bugs, releasing new functionality, etc.).

Custom connectors, connections, Dataverse customizations, and data gateways are not included in exported packages.

To export a package, you need to be the app's owner or co-owner. To later import a package, you'll need the **Environment maker** permission.

See also

• Export and import canvas app packages: https://packt.link/export-import-app

Importing a Power App

In this recipe, we'll import an app named Inventory Management to our environment. Importing apps is a fairly simple process that allows you to use an app somebody developed or fixed in a different environment than your own.

Getting ready

You'll need access to Power Apps and the **Environment maker** permission to complete the steps in this recipe.

How to do it...

1. Sign in to Power Apps (https://make.powerapps.com).

2. Select **Apps** from the left-hand navigation menu.

3. Select **Import canvas app**, as shown in *Figure 10.41*:

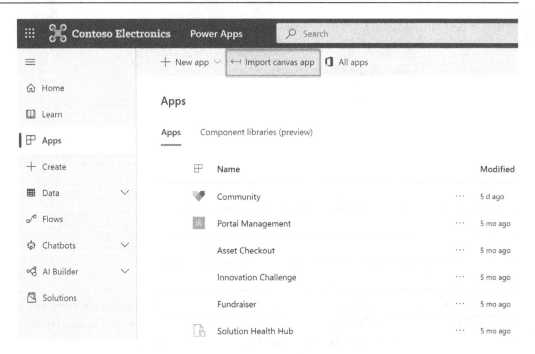

Figure 10.41: The Import canvas app option when viewing apps in Power Apps

4. Select **Update** or **Create as new**, or the wrench icon under **Action**, to change the import action if it is incorrect (i.e., if it says **Create as new**, but this app already exists in your environment and you just wish to update it). You can also rename the app here.

5. When all is correct, select **Import**, as shown in *Figure 10.42*:

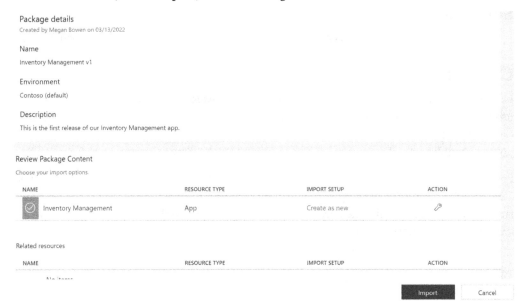

Figure 10.42: App details for an app package being imported

6. When finished, you'll get a confirmation message with a link to view the imported app, as shown in *Figure 10.43*. Click it to verify that the import was successful:

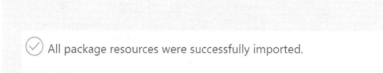

Figure 10.43: Successful app import message

How it works...

Just like when we looked at exporting, imported app packages include the app itself and any flows the app depends on. These can be imported into a different environment as brand new (app and flows) or an update to existing (if you're fixing bugs, releasing new functionality, etc.).

As we noted in the previous recipe, custom connectors, connections, Dataverse customizations, and data gateways are not included in imported packages.

Remember that, to export a package, you need to be the app's owner or co-owner. To later import a package as we did in this recipe, you'll need the **Environment maker** permission.

See also

• Export and import canvas app packages: `https://packt.link/export-import-app`

Copilot

In the present day, there is a growing need for app development tools that are both efficient and user-friendly. Fortunately, **Power Apps Copilot** has emerged to meet this demand. Harnessing the capabilities of artificial intelligence, Power Apps Copilot is poised to revolutionize the app development process, enabling developers to work faster and more intelligently than ever before.

Power Apps Copilot operates as a virtual assistant for app creators, offering them step-by-step guidance throughout the app development journey. Creators can communicate their instructions in plain language, and Copilot will take care of constructing the app and its underlying data infrastructure, streamlining the entire development process.

Power Apps Copilot is a feature (in preview at the time of writing this book) that uses artificial intelligence to help you build and customize Power Apps apps. It can build dataverse tables, based on user prompts, and answer questions about your app. Copilot is still under preview, but it has the potential to make Power Apps development more efficient and productive.

To enable Copilot, you need to have administrator access to your Power Platform environment. Once Copilot is enabled, you can add it to your apps as a control. The Copilot control can be used to ask questions about the data in your app, or to get help with building or customizing your app.

Getting ready

At the time of writing this book, the feature is only available for users with the Office 365 environment in the United States region. Some additional requirements are:

- The browser language must be set to English (United States).
- You must have a Microsoft Dataverse database in your environment.
- AI Builder must be enabled for your environment to use the AI models or controls leveraging AI models.

This can be done by following these steps:

1. Sign in to the Power Platform admin center.
2. In the admin center, go to **Environments** | [select an environment] | **Settings** | **Product** | **Features**.
3. On the **Features** settings page, under **AI Builder**, enable or disable AI Builder preview models:

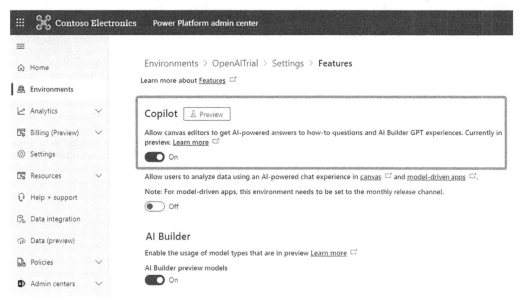

Figure 10.44: Feature settings

How to do it...

1. Sign in to Power Apps (https://make.powerapps.com).
2. Type what you are planning to build and press **Enter**. For this recipe, let's build a Visitor's log:

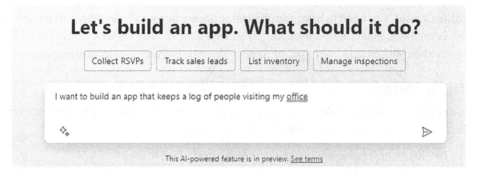

Figure 10.45: Copilot chatbot

3. Copilot builds a table structure that it deems fit for our app:

Figure 10.46: AI-generated table structure

4. You can modify the table using natural language in the chat interface on the right. For this example, we will type `Please remove the columns Date and Time. Add Start Time and End time instead`:

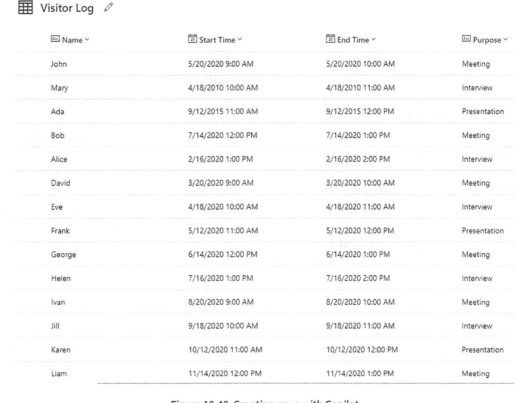

Figure 10.47: Modifying columns with Copilot

5. Now that we have the columns we need, let's create some more test data. Type Create 10 more rows for me:

⌨ Name ∨	📅 Start Time ∨	📅 End Time ∨	⌨ Purpose ∨
John	5/20/2020 9:00 AM	5/20/2020 10:00 AM	Meeting
Mary	4/18/2010 10:00 AM	4/18/2010 11:00 AM	Interview
Ada	9/12/2015 11:00 AM	9/12/2015 12:00 PM	Presentation
Bob	7/14/2020 12:00 PM	7/14/2020 1:00 PM	Meeting
Alice	2/16/2020 1:00 PM	2/16/2020 2:00 PM	Interview
David	3/20/2020 9:00 AM	3/20/2020 10:00 AM	Meeting
Eve	4/18/2020 10:00 AM	4/18/2020 11:00 AM	Interview
Frank	5/12/2020 11:00 AM	5/12/2020 12:00 PM	Presentation
George	6/14/2020 12:00 PM	6/14/2020 1:00 PM	Meeting
Helen	7/16/2020 1:00 PM	7/16/2020 2:00 PM	Interview
Ivan	8/20/2020 9:00 AM	8/20/2020 10:00 AM	Meeting
Jill	9/18/2020 10:00 AM	9/18/2020 11:00 AM	Interview
Karen	10/12/2020 11:00 AM	10/12/2020 12:00 PM	Presentation
Liam	11/14/2020 12:00 PM	11/14/2020 1:00 PM	Meeting

Figure 10.48: Creating rows with Copilot

6. Since the **Purpose** column has repeating values, let's change it to a choice column. Type Change the data type of Purpose column to Choice.

7. We are now ready to build our app. Click **Create App**.

8. We are now taken to the Power Apps designer gallery with a simple app with Read, Create, Update and Delete features built in:

Figure 10.49: Designer gallery

How it works...

Copilot is still under development at the time of writing this book, but it can already generate code for a variety of tasks, including the following.

Creating tables and columns

Once you have created your table and columns, you can use Copilot to help you populate the table with data. For example, you could say something like, "I want to add a row to the table with the following data: Name = John Doe, Age = 30, City = New York." Copilot will then generate code to add the row to the table.

You can also use Copilot to help you write formulas to manipulate the data in your table. For example, you could say something like, "I want to calculate the total age of all the people in the table." Copilot will then generate code to calculate the total age.

Copilot is a powerful tool that can help you build apps more quickly and easily. By using Copilot to create tables and columns, you can save time and effort.

Here are some additional tips for creating tables and columns using Copilot in Power Apps:

- Use descriptive names for your tables and columns. This will make it easier to understand your code and data.
- Use consistent data types for your columns. This will help to prevent errors when you are working with your data.
- Test your code after you have created it. This will help to ensure that it is working correctly.

Adding controls to a form

You can also use Copilot to help you configure the properties of the control. For example, you could say something like, "I want to set the text of the label to 'Name'." Copilot will then generate code to set the text of the label.

Here are some examples of how you can use Copilot to add controls to a form:

- "Add a text box to the form."
- "Add a label to the form with the text 'Name'."
- "Add a button to the form with the text 'Submit'."
- "Add a checkbox to the form with the text 'I agree to the terms and conditions'."
- "Add a drop-down list to the form with the items 'Red', 'Green', and 'Blue'."

Writing formulas

Type the formula you want to write. Copilot will suggest a list of formulas that match your query.

Select the formula you want to use. Copilot will generate code for the formula.

You can also use Copilot to help you troubleshoot formulas. For example, you could say something like, I'm getting an error when I try to calculate the total age of all the people in the table. Copilot will then generate code to help you debug the formula.

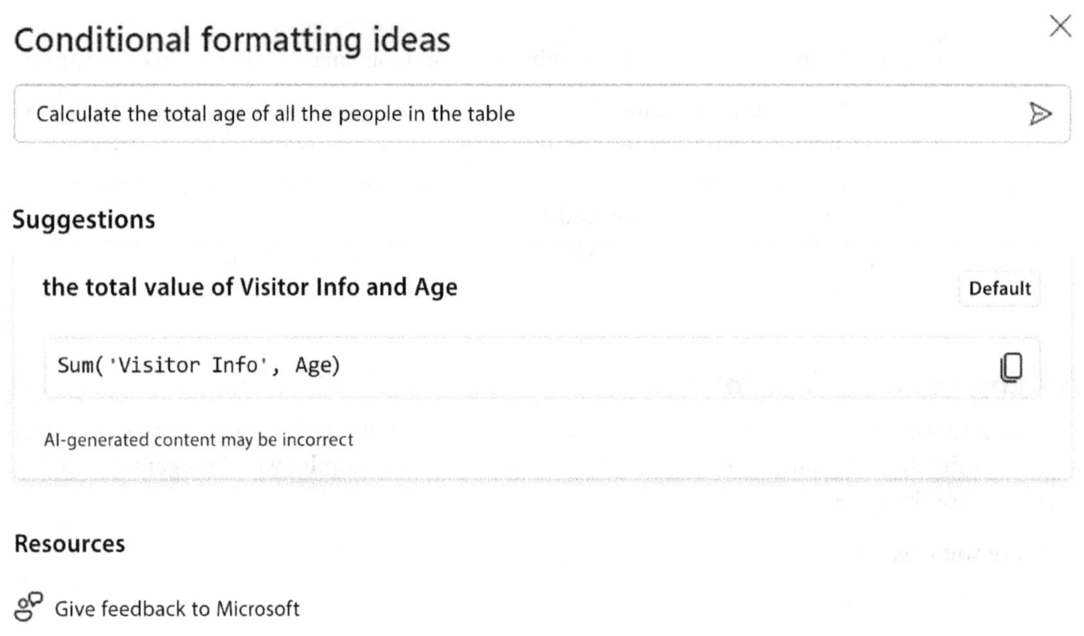

Conditional formatting ideas   ✕

Calculate the total age of all the people in the table   ▷

Suggestions

the total value of Visitor Info and Age   Default

```
Sum( 'Visitor Info', Age)
```

AI-generated content may be incorrect

Resources

⚭ Give feedback to Microsoft

Figure 10.50: Writing formulas with Copilot

Here are some examples of how you can use Copilot to write formulas:

-    `Calculate the total age of all the people in the table.`
-    `Calculate the average age of all the people in the table.`
-    `Calculate the number of people in the table who are over 18 years old.`
-    `Calculate the difference between the two dates.`
-    `Calculate the percentage of people in the table who are male.`

In summary, Copilot in Power Apps is an AI-powered feature that helps makers build and edit apps through conversation in natural language, and end users interact with apps and get insights about the data in them. It has the potential to revolutionize the way that apps are built and used, making it easier for makers and users alike.

11

Power BI

Business intelligence (BI) is all about connecting *business decision-making* to *facts about the business and its environment*. BI lets you take a deep dive into data in order to make better business decisions.

Microsoft Power BI is Microsoft's BI tool that helps you model, visualize, and share insights. It enables you to analyze information in more meaningful and intuitive ways.

Power BI is a tool for everyone. Decision-makers can use Power BI dashboards for making business decisions, while developers can use Power BI **application programming interfaces (APIs)** to push data into datasets and build data models.

You can build Power BI reports using Power BI Desktop. Power BI Desktop (`https://packt.link/Power-BI-Desktop`) is a free application that you can install right on your own computer.

While Power BI Desktop is a downloadable tool to build reports, the Power BI service is a cloud-based service that helps you share reports over the web and collaborate with your colleagues and teams with limited editing features.

If your organization is already using Microsoft 365, then you might already have an Enterprise plan that includes Power BI Pro. Power BI Pro is an individual user license that allows access to all content and capabilities in the Power BI service. Power BI Pro gives you features to collaborate and use work-spaces to share with other people, create apps, sign up for subscriptions, and so on.

If your organization has over 500 users using Power BI, you will need to move to a higher plan, which is the Power BI Premium plan. Power BI Premium allows organizations to better administer and manage the resources that are being used with Power BI.

This chapter provides you with a basic understanding of Power BI. There are several advanced concepts and topics that are not possible to be covered in a single chapter. This chapter should serve as a good starting point for end users or anyone who is new to Power BI.

In this chapter, we will learn about the following topics:

- Retrieving data
- Transforming data

- Modeling data
- Visualizing data
- Sharing a report, dashboard, or dataset
- Creating a dashboard
- Embedding a report on a SharePoint page

At the end of the chapter, we will discuss two important topics related to Power BI: Power BI's recent adoption of AI capabilities, and how Power BI relates to Microsoft Fabric. We'll see that Fabric can be used as an alternative to Power BI for data visualization, or it can be integrated with BI to handle backend data management while BI handles data visualization.

Note that it will be beyond our scope to properly show you how to use Fabric, and the AI capabilities of Power BI are new and rapidly changing. For those reasons we have decided to overview these topics without using recipes. This allows us to cover more features of Power Platform that we'd like to share with you across this book.

Technical requirements

Power BI Desktop is only supported on the Windows platform at the moment, on Windows 11, Windows 10, Windows 8.1 and Windows 8, as well as Windows Server 2022, Windows Server 2019, Windows Server 2016, Windows Server 2012 R2, and Windows Server 2012. It is available for both 32-bit (x86) and 64-bit (x64) platforms.

You can either download the standalone installer from the website or you can install it from the Windows Store as a Windows app.

Power BI reports can also be viewed on the mobile app (covered later, in *Chapter 26, Microsoft 365 on Mobile Devices*), which is available from the Windows, Android, and Apple stores.

 Please refer to the Power BI Desktop guide at `https://packt.link/Power-BI-Desktop`.

The examples used in this chapter have been demonstrated using Power BI Desktop. To share a report, create a dashboard, or embed a Power BI report towards the end of the chapter, you will need a Power BI Pro license. You can find information about licensing costs here: `https://packt.link/BI-pricing`.

Retrieving data

Retrieving is the process of fetching data from a location. Power BI has connectors to various data sources, ranging from text and **comma-separated values (CSV)** files to databases and web pages. Some common Power BI connectors are shown in the following screenshot:

Files

📗	Excel
▦	CSV
🗎	XML
🗐	Text
📁	Folder

Azure Services

- Microsoft Azure SQL Database
- Microsoft Azure SQL Data Warehouse
- Microsoft Azure Marketplace·
- Microsoft Azure HDInsight
- Microsoft Azure Blob Storage
- Microsoft Azure Table Storage
- ☆ Azure HDInsight Spark
- Microsoft Azure DocumentDB
- Microsoft Azure Data Lake Store

Databases

- SQL Server Database
- Access Database
- SQL Server Analysis Services Database
- Oracle Database
- IBM DB2 Database
- MySQL Database
- PostgreSQL Database
- Sybase Database
- Teradata Database
- SAP HANA Database

Other Sources

🌐	Web	🏧	appFigures
📑	SharePoint List	🐱	GitHub
	OData Feed		MailChimp
	Hadoop File (HDFS)		QuickBooks Online
	Active Directory	IQ	SweetIQ
	Microsoft Exchange		Twilio
	Dynamics CRM Online		Zendesk
f	Facebook		Marketo
	Google Analytics	☆	Spark
	Salesforce Objects		
	Salesforce Reports		
◇	ODBC		
◇	R Script		

Figure 11.1: List of common Power BI connectors

In this section, we will learn how to retrieve data from a CSV file.

Getting ready

Download the `Products_bikes.csv` file from the `Chapter 11` folder in the GitHub repository of this book: `https://packt.link/Power-BI-samples`.

You don't need any special permission to retrieve data from files such as text, CSV, or Excel files.

 If you are querying a secure data store, you might require additional permissions.

How to do it...

1. Open the Power BI Desktop tool.

2. Click on **Get Data** and select the **Text/CSV** option:

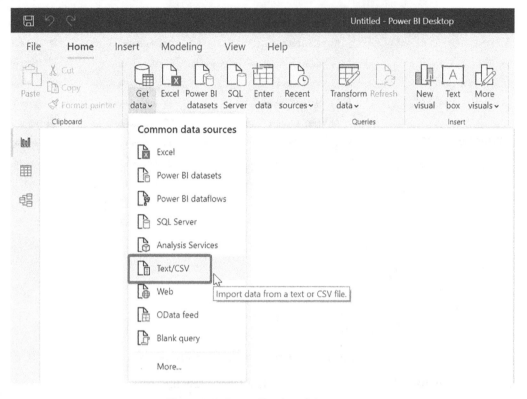

Figure 11.2: Connecting to a data source

3. Press **Connect**.
4. Browse to the location of the CSV file and open the `Products_bikes.csv` file.
5. Click **Load**.
6. Power BI Desktop will show a preview of the data. Click on **Load,** and the data gets loaded into the tool.

How it works...

After the data is imported, Power BI Desktop lets you analyze the data in three ways:

*   By using one of the visualizations on the imported data:

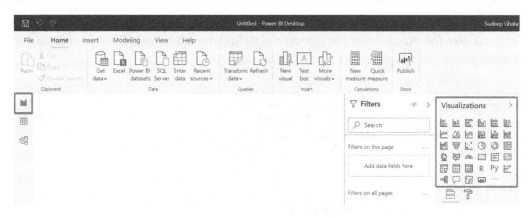

Figure 11.3: Visualizations section of the Power BI Desktop home page

- By looking at the raw data in tabular form:

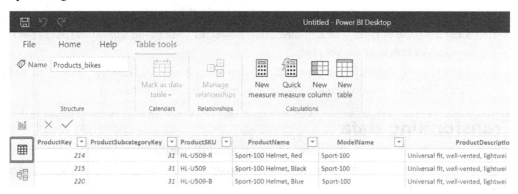

Table 11.4: Viewing data in a table

- By looking at the structure of the table and its relationship to other tables:

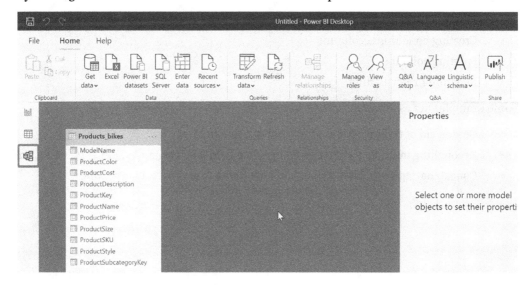

Figure 11.5: Table structure and relationships

If you import the data once, Power BI Desktop stores the data source details internally. So, if the data in the source file changes, you can just use the **Refresh** option in the **Queries** section to import the modified data.

 If you used credentials for a secure data store, they are not saved in the PBIX file itself, but are saved in the Power BI Desktop config. So, if you publish/share the PBIX file, the recipient cannot use your credentials—they need their own.

See also

- The *Transforming data* recipe in this chapter
- The *Modeling data* recipe in this chapter
- The *Visualizing data* recipe in this chapter
- The *Sharing a report, dashboard or dataset* recipe in this chapter
- Create a dataset from a SharePoint List - Power BI | Microsoft Learn: `https://packt.link/create-dataset-from-SP-list`
- Connect to datasets in the Power BI service from Power BI Desktop - Power BI | Microsoft Learn: `https://packt.link/Desktop-report-lifecycle-datasets`

Transforming data

Data transformation in Power BI involves the process of shaping and cleaning raw data from various sources into a structured format that can be easily analyzed and visualized. This could require simple or complex data manipulation, based on the nature of the data.

Some basic transformations include the following:

- Changing data types
- Filtering (rows and/or fields)
- Creating conditional columns
- Splitting columns
- Renaming/reformatting

Some examples are as follows:

- Getting rid of trailing spaces at the end of a text field
- Reconciling multiple formats saved in a date field (such as Jan-19, Jan 2019, 01-19, and so on)
- Concatenating **Title**, **First Name**, and **Last Name** to get the person's name

In most cases, the data that you retrieve from a data source is not in a format where it can be used as-is, and you might have to take some additional steps to clean it. The first step after retrieving data from a data store is to convert the data into a reusable, consistent format for a report. In the screenshot below, we can see a short list that needs to be cleaned before we can use it:

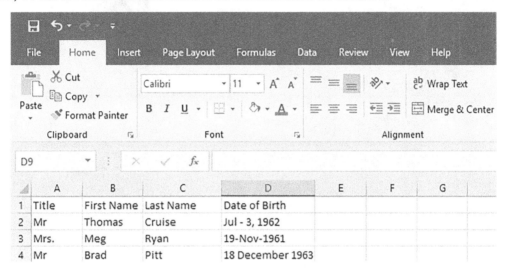

Figure 11.6: Data transformation example dataset

The first thing we need to do is get rid of the "." in the **Title** field where applicable. Depending on how we are using the data, we may also need to combine **First Name** and **Last Name** into one field. After this, we can see that the date format is inconsistent, so we will need to make it uniform if we are planning to use this data.

Getting ready

For this exercise, download the file `DOB.csv` from the `Chapter 11` folder in the GitHub repository of this book: `https://packt.link/Power-BI-samples`.

You don't need any special permission to perform data transformation on the data that has already been imported.

 You should have access to the data if you are querying a secure data store.

How to do it...

1. Connect to a data store and load the data; here we have used the table from the previous example:

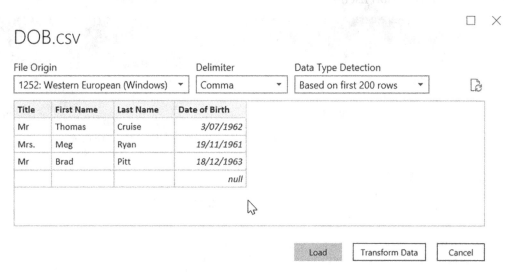

Figure 11.7: Loading data from CSV file

2. Once the dataset is loaded, click on **Transform data**:

Figure 11.8: Option to Transform data from the Home ribbon

3. You are now able to edit the imported data:

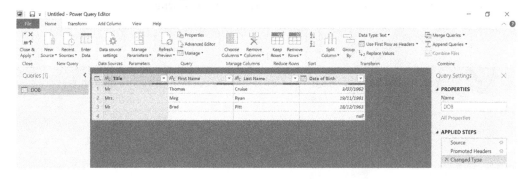

Figure 11.9: Applying transformation steps

Power BI Desktop has treated the first row in the DOB.csv file as a *header row*, and the data type of the **Date of Birth** column has automatically been changed to *Date*. Also, you'll note that all date fields now have a consistent date format. We'll explain this in the *How it works...* section.

4. Next, we need to remove the dot after **Mrs** to make the **Title** consistent with other records:

Figure 11.10: Using the Replace function

🔍 **Quick tip:** Need to see a high-resolution version of this image? Open this book in the next-gen Packt Reader or view it in the PDF/ePub copy.

🔒 **The next-gen Packt Reader** and a **free PDF/ePub copy** of this book are included with your purchase. Unlock them by scanning the QR code below or visiting https://www.packtpub.com/unlock/9781803243177.

5. The replace operation requires you to specify the text that needs to be changed, along with the replacement string. Replace the "." with an empty string.

6. Instead of having three name fields, we'll merge them all into one. To do this, select the three columns and click **Merge Columns**:

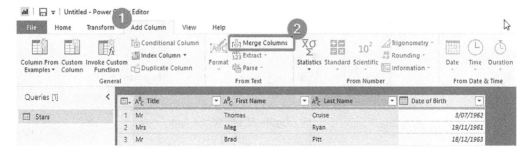

Figure 11.11: Merging three columns together

Note here that the order in which you select the columns will determine the order they are merged. That is, if you first selected **Last Name**, then held *Shift* and selected **First Name**, and finally **Title**, it would put the columns in the following order: *Last Name*, *First Name*, and *Title*.

7. Use **Space** as the separator between the three columns while merging:

Figure 11.12: Merge criteria

8. The merged column should now appear in the table:

Figure 11.13: Looking at the merged column

9. Finally, click on **Close & Apply** to close the transformation window and apply the transformations to the dataset:

Figure 11.14: Close & Apply

How it works...

Power BI Desktop can get involved as soon as you import data, as you saw in the preceding example. Three operations were applied to your dataset when it was loaded. They were as follows:

1. The first row got promoted to row header.
2. The data type of the **Date Of Birth** column was changed to **Date**.
3. The date format of all dates was set to dd/mm/yyyy.

 If you want to use a different date format, change the preferences from **File** | **Options and Settings** | **Options** | **Regional Settings**.

The way Power BI Desktop can do this is by applying a series of steps called **transformations**. The transformation we performed can be seen in the lower-right section of Power BI Desktop:

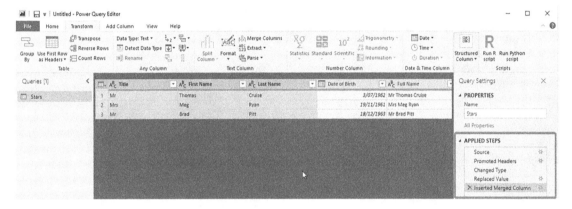

Figure 11.15: Transformation steps

As you witnessed in this example, the first three transformation operations were applied automatically for you. You can change the data type by clicking on the data type selector in the header and assigning a particular data type:

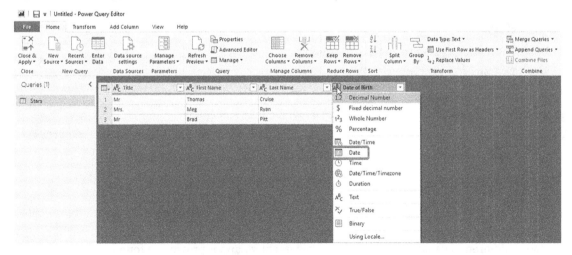

Figure 11.16: Data type changes

The beauty of transformation is that it eliminates the need to perform repetitive operations on data every time you connect to the data store. Power BI Desktop records all your transformation steps and then applies the steps sequentially every time you query the data store. In other words, you only need to spend time building the transformation steps once. From there on, Power BI Desktop manages the data cleansing operations for you.

You can see a preview of the data at each step, and you can insert, remove, or rearrange steps too. When you click **Apply** in the Power Query Editor, all the data goes through all the steps and then gets loaded to Power BI:

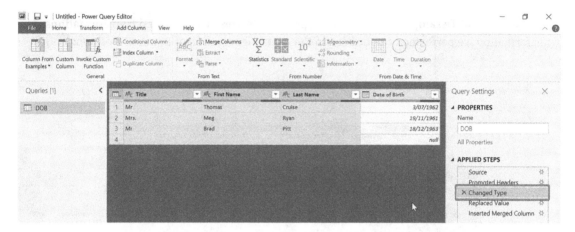

Figure 11.17: Going back to the previous transformation state

 You cannot undo the transformation actions once applied; however, deleting the action takes you back to the state before the transformation was applied.

See also

- The *Retrieving data* recipe in this chapter
- The *Modeling data* recipe in this chapter
- The *Visualizing data* recipe in this chapter
- The *Sharing a report/dashboard/database* recipe in this chapter
- Tutorial: Shape and combine data in Power BI Desktop - Power BI | Microsoft Learn: https://packt.link/Desktop-shape-and-combine-data

Modeling data

Data modeling in Power BI involves designing a structured representation of your data that enables efficient analysis, visualization, and reporting. A well-designed data model ensures that relationships between different data tables are accurately represented, and it provides a foundation for creating meaningful insights..

It is a crucial step in the data analysis process, as it provides a structured way to organize and understand complex data sets.

To understand modeling, you need to first grasp some key database terms:

- **Primary key:** The primary key of a relational table uniquely identifies each record in the table (refer to Customers.csv). A table can have only one primary key. Since a primary key is unique, it cannot be repeated in the same table. Take *Figure 11.20*, for example:

	A PK	B	C	D
1	Customer ID	Customer Name	Gender	Senior Citizen
2	EP-0001	Emily Pereira	female	1
3	DG-0002	Daniel Glossop	male	1
4	HF-0003	Howard Fontaine	male	1
5	LR-0004	Lessie Roby	female	0
6	RW-0005	Roberta Willis	female	1
7	JC-0006	Julia Cunha	female	1
8	DH-0007	Dennis Hunziker	male	1
9	EC-0008	Eduarda Cavalcanti	female	0
10	VC-0009	Vinicius Cardoso	male	1
11	AL-00010	Angelina Ling	female	0

Figure 11.18: Primary key in the Customer Info table

In the preceding example, by specifying the customer ID, I can uniquely identify a person. There can be two customers with the same name, but they will each have a unique customer ID.

- **Foreign key:** A database foreign key is a field in a relational table that matches the primary key column of another table (refer to Product_Sales.csv). See *Figure 11.19*, for example:

	A FK	B	C	D	E	F	G
1	Customer I	Customer Name	Order Date	Order ID	Postal Coc	Product IC	Quantity
2	EP-0001	Emily Pereira	4/10/2002	43	35801	102	3
3	DG-0002	Daniel Glossop	18/11/2003	34	99501	127	4
4	HF-0003	Howard Fontaine	28/01/2003	72	85001	18	1
5	LR-0004	Lessie Roby	25/05/2009	75	72201	103	5
6	RW-0005	Roberta Willis	6/10/2011	70	94203	119	2
7	JC-0006	Julia Cunha	14/06/2015	105	90001	90	3
8	DH-0007	Dennis Hunziker	22/10/2007	53	90209	28	4
9	EC-0008	Eduarda Cavalcanti	1/05/2006	59	80201	38	5
10	VC-0009	Vinicius Cardoso	10/07/2012	89	6101	2	2
11	AL-00010	Angelina Ling	15/08/2015	70	19901	91	3

Figure 11.19: Foreign key in the Sales Info table

The Customer ID column (used in the earlier example) becomes a foreign key when used in the sales table. The same person can buy two products, and hence the customer ID can appear multiple times on the sales table. Every foreign key value must always correspond to a primary key in another table.

- **Fact table:** A fact table stores quantitative information and is used for analysis and reporting. In our case, Sales Info is a fact table. If we compare a fact table to a dimension table, fact tables usually have information in the form of numeric data. This data can be modified quite easily, and that can be done by clubbing together and adding any number of rows. These tables typically have more rows and fewer columns because they store transactions.

- **Dimension table:** A dimension table is a collection of reference information about a business. In the preceding example, the Customer Info table will be a dimension table because it provides additional information about the customer. Similarly, we can have a Product Info dimension table (refer to `Products.csv`) with more information about the product being sold:

	A	B	C	D
1	Product ID	Product Name	Category	Sub-Category
2	1	Washington Berry Jui	Washington	Fruit Drinks
3	2	Washington Mango D	Washington	Fruit Drinks
4	3	Washington Strawber	Washington	Fruit Drinks
5	4	Washington Cream	Washington	Fruit Drinks
6	5	Washington Diet Sod	Washington	Fruit Drinks
7	6	Washington Cola	Washington	Fruit Drinks
8	7	Washington Diet Cola	Washington	Fruit Drinks
9	8	Washington Orange J	Washington	Fruit Drinks
10	9	Washington Cranberr	Washington	Fruit Drinks
11	10	Washington Apple Jui	Washington	Fruit Drinks

Figure 11.20: Product info in a dimension table

Dimension tables, compared to fact tables, tend to be shorter (because you can only have a given number of customers or products) but have many columns because they store metadata about the entity being stored, such as customer name, age, DOB, phone, address, email, and so on.

To look at these different key terms in action, let's create a sales report. To build a meaningful sales report, you will need to pull information from other supporting tables. For example, a Sales Info table will contain transactional information such as the date of sale, and the number of products sold. A Products Info table will store information such as the product category, product price, product color, discount, and so on. A Customer Info table will contain information such as customer name, city, and so on.

Power BI lets you combine information from the three tables, thus enabling you to view the report in multiple dimensions such as Sales by Region, Sales by Product Category, Sales by Year, and so on. In the following recipe, we will model our data using Power BI by defining the relationship between the product and sales data tables, which we will then proceed to visualize in the next recipe.

Getting ready

Download the following files from the `Chapter 11` folder in the GitHub repository of this book at `https://packt.link/Power-BI-samples`:

- `Customers.csv`
- `Locations.csv`
- `Product_Sales.csv`
- `Products.csv`

You don't need any special permission to perform data modeling once the data is imported.

How to do it...

1. After the transformations are applied, click on the 🔠 icon on the left-hand side of the screen. You will see all the data sources you have connected to:

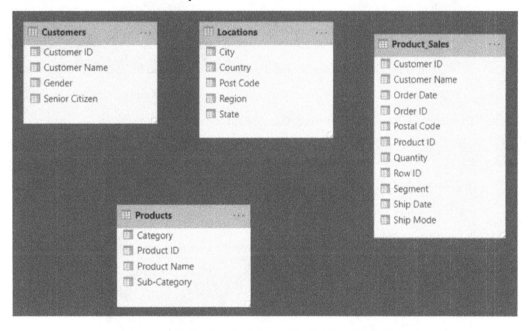

Figure 11.21: Visualize tables in the Relationship view

2. In some cases, Power BI Desktop will automatically determine the relationships based on the column names. If it doesn't, connect the columns manually by dragging the column from one table to another:

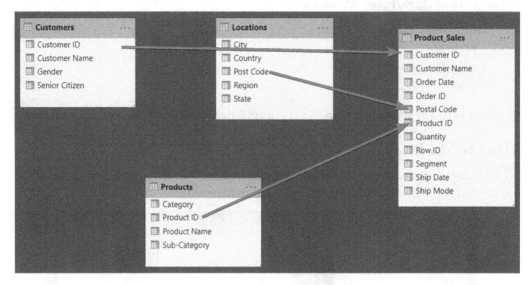

Figure 11.22: Apply column relationships

3. Once the columns are connected, your model is ready:

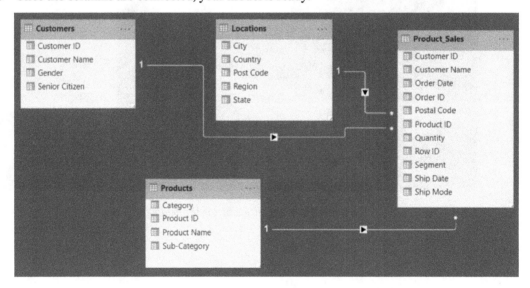

Figure 11.23: Verify relationship flows

How it works...

You might ask the question: *why do we need a model at all?*

A model signifies the relationship between the tables. This enables you to analyze the data by customer, location, product, or a combination of these. We will see this in action in our next recipe.

To better understand the concept of relationships, you need to understand two key terms: **Cardinality** and **Cross-filtering**.

Cardinality refers to the relationship between two tables based on the number of unique values in the column. It could be any of the following relationships:

- **One to many**: If the column is a primary key in one table and a foreign key in another table—for example, products and sales relationships
- **One to one**: If the column has a one-to-one mapping of data in both tables—for example, a person and driver license table relationship where there will be a unique record of a person against every driver's license number
- **Many to many**: When there is a possibility of multiple values in both columns—for example, a student and class relationship, where each student can take multiple classes, and each class can have multiple students enrolled

Cross-filtering is the ability to set a filter context on a table based on values in a related table. The cross-filter relationship can be one of the following:

- **Both**: Where data in one table can be filtered based on the data in another—for example, Sales and Store. A product could be sold in multiple stores; at the same time, a store could have multiple products.
- **Single**: This is a relationship where the filter direction is unidirectional—for example, a Product table versus a Sales table. A sale item will only correspond to a single product, but a product could be sold several times.

Power BI Desktop resolves cardinality and cross-filtering based on the column values in two tables. It also lets you change the cardinality and cross-filtering if you wish to.

 Assigning incorrect relationship parameters (cardinality and cross-filtering) will result in inaccurate visualizations, so a proper understanding of these concepts is necessary. We recommend watching Alberto Ferrari's presentation on Power BI relationships. The video can be found at: https://packt.link/BI-relationships.

For a more detailed view of your data relationships, you could try selecting the **Manage Relationships** option on the **Home** tab.

A pop-up screen will appear, listing all the relationships in a single view. From here, you can select **Autodetect** to find relationships in new or updated data. Select **Edit** in the **Manage Relationships** dialog to manually edit your relationships.

There's more...

Power BI modeling lets you do more than build relationships. It also lets you do the following:

- Perform custom calculations on existing tables.
- Define new metrics.
- Perform custom calculations for new metrics.

Before we jump into the visualizations, we should learn some additional concepts about modeling our data that will be useful in some situations—namely, calculated columns and measures.

Calculated columns

Sometimes, you need to make additional columns or measures within your model to create data for your visualizations. These are called **calculated columns**. You can create these columns using **Data Analysis Expressions** (DAX) formulas. For instance, if you have been provided the dimensions of a car in feet and inches, you could create a DAX formula to change them to their metric system equivalents (refer to `car_sales.csv`). DAX formulas look similar to the formulas used in Excel, such as the one shown here:

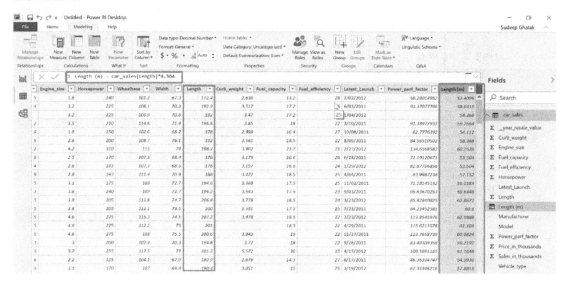

Figure 11.24: Using a DAX formula in Power BI Desktop

You might also need to create a calculated column to build a relationship between tables when no unique fields exist. To create uniqueness in data, you could hypothetically create a calculated column for phone numbers by combining column values for area codes and local numbers.

Calculated column values are stored in memory. They can cause performance issues if the dataset is too large. Hence, they should be used sparingly.

Measures

Measures are usually the numeric fields within a dataset that can be aggregated or used in other ways (such as average, minimum, and maximum) to derive meaning from your data—for example, total sales by state, or average sales by year. Measures are calculated at the time of the query and hence are not stored in the database. However, they use processing power to execute a query at the time of the request. Because measures are not stored in memory, they are generally faster but require more processing power. Hence, calculated columns and measures should be used judiciously.

You can create a measure in Power BI Desktop, as shown in the following screenshot. I am getting a forecast for the next year, based on the average number of cars sold this year:

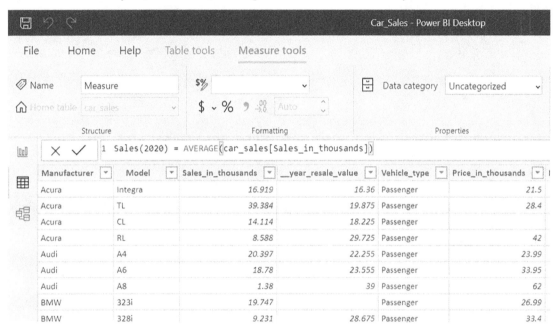

Figure 11.25: Using measures in a Car Sales table

Unlike calculated columns, they don't appear in the model next to other columns, but you can drag them to your visualization window in the **Report** tab, as shown in the following screenshot:

Figure 11.26: Including a measure in a visualization

Notice that the measures are context-aware. This means that if you drag the **Sales(2020)** field alone, it shows the average sales across all models, but when you place it along with the **Model** field, it represents the breakdown by each model:

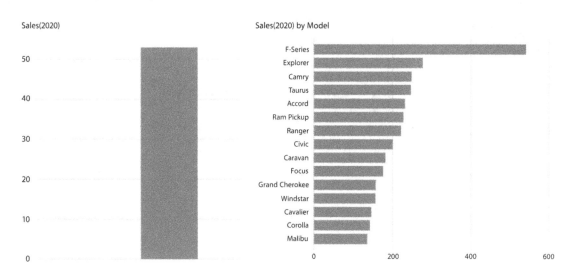

Figure 11.27: Using measures to break down data

See also

- The *Retrieving data* recipe in this chapter
- The *Transforming data* recipe in this chapter
- The *Visualizing data* recipe in this chapter
- The *Sharing a report, dashboard or dataset* recipe in this chapter
- Dataset modes in the Power BI service - Power BI | Microsoft Learn: `https://packt.link/service-dataset-modes`

Visualizing data

While modeling helps achieve the entity relationships and backend schema, data visualization refers to the process of representing data and information using visual elements like graphs, charts, and maps.

The end goal of any data-crunching exercise is to draw insights from your data. Power BI visualizations provide you with hundreds of visuals (some within Power BI Desktop; others from the marketplace). A Power BI report might consist of a single visual on the entire page, or it might have pages full of visuals.

There are many different visual types available directly from the Power BI **Visualizations** pane:

Figure 11.28: Visualization available with Power BI Desktop

And, for even more choice, visit the **MARKETPLACE**:

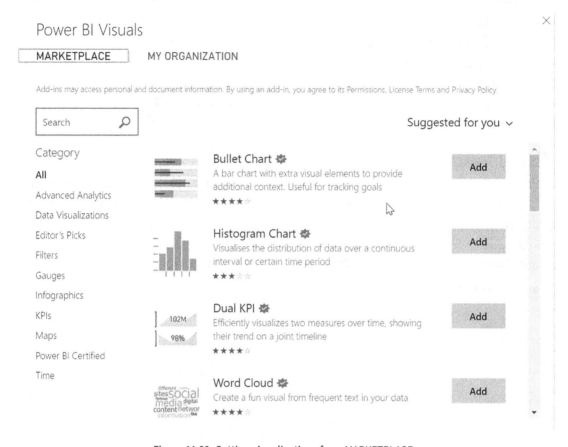

Figure 11.29: Getting visualizations from MARKETPLACE

 There is an upper limit to the number of fields you can add to any visual. The limit is 100 fields (including measures or columns). If your visual fails to load, try reducing the number of fields in your visualization.

A user can interact with a visual either as a designer or as a consumer.

A designer can add/edit or change visuals using Power BI Desktop. A consumer, on the other hand, can only look at the reports or dashboards shared with them. The consumer can interact with the visuals using filters and via natural language; they cannot make any major changes to the visualization.

In this recipe, we will create a demo report with data visualization.

Getting ready

Download the file `car_sales.csv` from the `Chapter 11` folder in the GitHub repository of this book: `https://packt.link/Power-BI-samples`

How to do it...

1. After you've completed the modeling of the dataset (refer to the *Modeling data* recipe earlier in this chapter), click on the ⩕ icon on the left-hand side of the screen to enter the report view.

2. From the right-hand **Visualizations** pane, pick a visual. We will use a line chart for this demo.

3. Pick the fields you want to display on the report.

4. Based on the field type, Power BI Desktop will place them under **Axis** or **Values**. You could also drag the fields as appropriate:

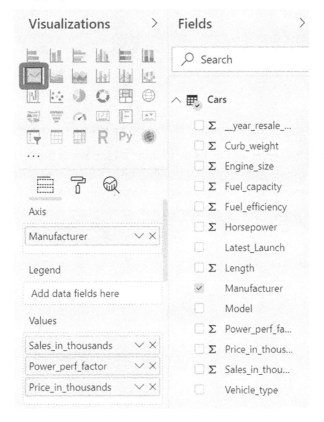

Figure 11.30: Adding visualization to report

5. As soon as the fields are selected, the report appears on the canvas. You can sort by graph on any of the selected fields to derive insights:

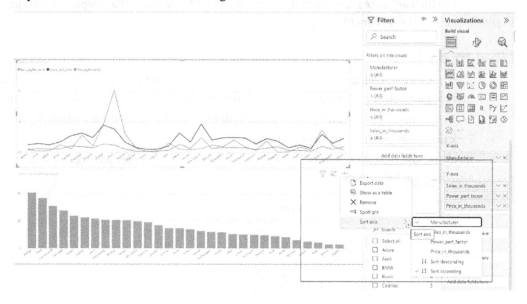

Figure 11.31: Applying sorting to a report

6. You can bring a visual into focus by clicking on the **Focus mode** option. This option displays the report in a full-page view. This is helpful when you have multiple reports on your page:

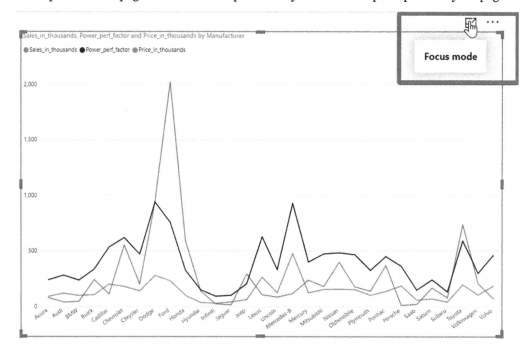

Figure 11.32: Using focus mode for a full-page view

7. To go back to your report, use the **Back to report** option:

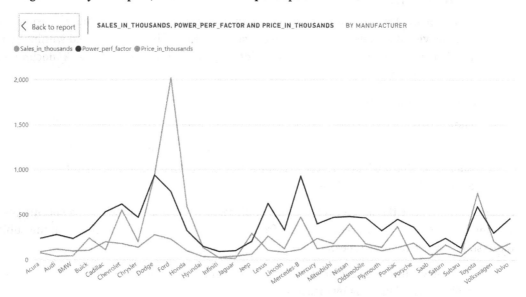

Figure 11.33: Closing the full-page view

8. Power BI Desktop generates a random report title based on the fields you have selected. You can change the **Title** by updating the **Title text** option:

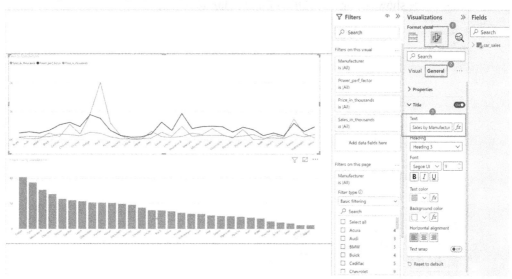

Figure 11.34: Changing the title of a report

9. You now have built your first report using Power BI Desktop.

How it works...

Visuals in Power BI Desktop can be changed by simply selecting the report and choosing another visual from the **visualizations gallery**. There are several visuals that are provided within the Power BI Desktop. You can read more about each individual visual on Microsoft's Power BI documentation page, at `https://packt.link/BI-visuals`.

A visualization has three property tabs:

- **Fields**: This tab lets you choose the fields for your visualization.
- **Format**: This tab lets you choose the data colors and labels for your dataset.
- **Analytics**: This tab lets you add additional lines to compare your data points against, such as a constant or an average line across your report.

Filters let you reduce the dataset you want to analyze. Say you want to focus on a specific year or a specific brand of car. Filters remove noise from the visual so that you can focus on the subject of interest. Filters are of three types:

- **Visual-level filters**: These only affect the selected visual but have more options, including **Top N** filtering and filtering by measure value.
- **Report-level filter**: This applies the filter on a specific visual without affecting the rest of the page.
- **Page-level filter**: This applies the filter on all the related visuals within the page. The following screenshot shows a page-level filter on the **Manufacturer** field:

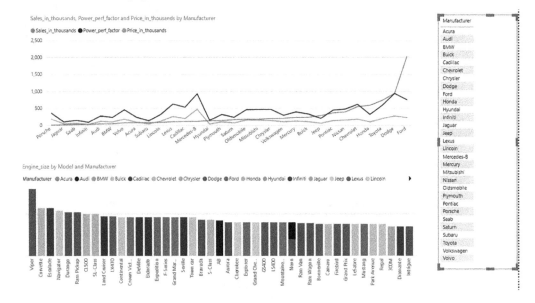

Figure 11.35: Filter types in Power BI

There's more...

Power BI has a powerful Q & A feature that can build charts by using natural language.

You can use this feature by dragging the **Ask A Question** button from the **Home** ribbon, as shown in the following screenshot:

Figure 11.36: Location and appearance of the Ask a Question button in Power BI

As soon as you drag this menu item on the canvas, Power BI suggests some probable questions based on the data. As you start typing, it even auto-selects a visual based on the data.

You can change the fields (highlighted with a yellow underline) to view the data in other ways (say, by model), as shown here:

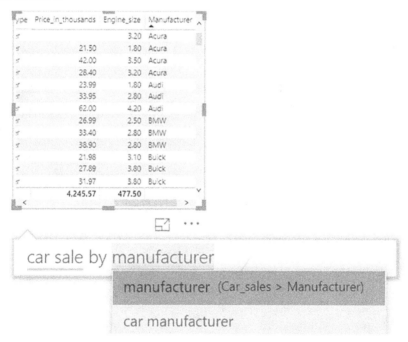

Figure 11.37: Auto suggestions generated by the Ask a Question AI

You get the same experience when you use the Q & A feature on the Power BI web experience.

See also

* The *Retrieving data* recipe in this chapter
* The *Transforming data* recipe in this chapter

- The *Modeling data* recipe in this chapter
- The *Sharing a report, dashboard or dataset* recipe in this chapter
- Create Power BI visuals using Python in Power BI Desktop - Power BI | Microsoft Learn: `https://packt.link/Desktop-Python-visuals`
- Learn which R packages are supported - Power BI | Microsoft Learn: `https://packt.link/service-R-packages-support`

Sharing a report, dashboard, or dataset

Microsoft 365 is a collaboration platform. The ability of users to build and share reports is a key factor. The Power BI service lets you share the charts and dashboards with your colleagues in several ways.

The **dashboard** feature is only available in the Power BI service. It is a non-interactive collection of visuals pinned from one or more existing reports. If you click on a report pinned into the dashboard, the Power BI service takes you to the individual report, which provides a richer and more interactive experience.

In this recipe, we will publish and share a report using the dashboard.

Getting ready

In order to share a report, you need to first publish it to your Microsoft 365 tenant. While Power BI Desktop is free, you need a Power BI license to share your report with your colleagues. If you have a Power BI Pro license, you should be able to publish your report to Microsoft 365:

Figure 11.38: Publishing a report to the Power BI service

You can publish the report to your Microsoft 365 workspace or to a workspace you have access to. After you publish the report, you can access it at `https://app.powerbi.com` and log in with your Microsoft 365 credentials:

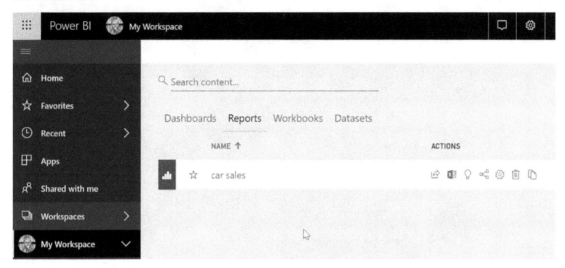

Figure 11.39: A published report in the Power BI Service

From the workspace, you can share the report with your colleagues. You need a Power BI Pro license to share your content, and those you share it with also require a Pro license, unless your organization has a Premium subscription. Read more about Premium subscriptions at: `https://packt.link/BI-premium`.

How to do it...

You can share a report in two ways:

1. In a list of **Dashboards** or **Reports**, or in an open dashboard or report, select **Share**:

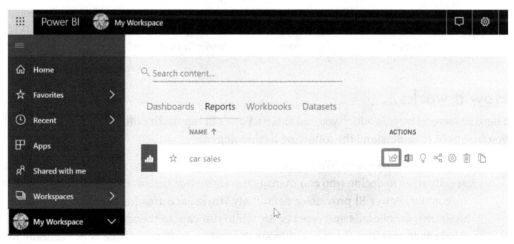

Figure 11.40: Sharing a report with colleagues

2. You can then specify the colleagues you want to share the report with. You could provide full email addresses for individuals, distribution groups, or security groups. Check the options as applicable:

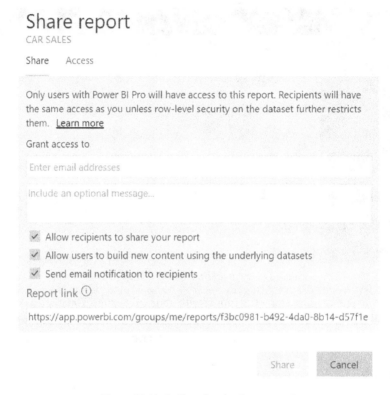

Figure 11.41: Options for sharing a report

 You can share with people whose addresses are outside your organization, but you'll see a warning. These external users must be added as guest users in your **Azure Active Directory** (**Azure AD** or **AAD**) if you want to share Power BI reports with them.

How it works...

There are several ways in which you can share a Power BI report. In order to choose the right platform, you first need to understand the following terminology:

-   **Share your workspace:** Workspaces provide a common area for your co-workers. You can specify roles to decide who can manage the entire workspace, edit its content, and distribute its content. Power BI provides a default **My Workspace** area for every user for them to store their own dashboards and reports. So, while you can, in theory, save the reports in your **My Workspace** area and share it with your co-workers, this workspace is not actually meant for collaboration. It is more like your personal space.

-   You should set up separate workspaces to work with your co-workers:

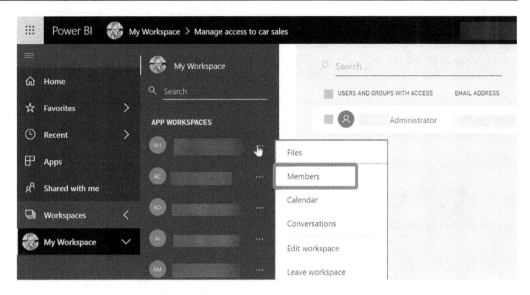

Figure 11.42: Workspaces in the Power BI Service

- **Share your dataset:** The dataset refers to the data that drives your visualization. We saw earlier how the data needs to go through transformation and modeling before it can be used within the report. You would obviously not want everyone to go through the same ordeal if they want to base their reports on the same data. So, while this option allows you to save time by sharing the cleansed data, on top of that, it also ensures that everyone is building their report based on a single version of the truth. You can share a dataset by clicking **Manage permissions**, as shown in the following screenshot:

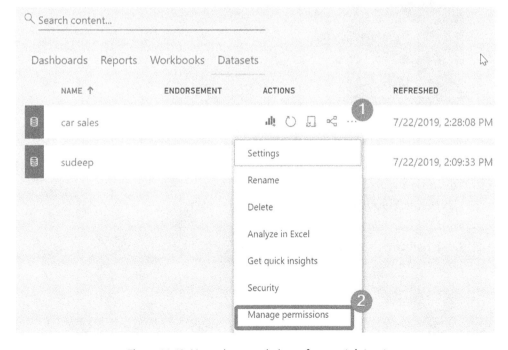

Figure 11.43: Managing permissions of a report dataset

Then, choose the people you would like to share with. You do not need to share reports with people who have access to the workspace already. They will be able to view the reports immediately in the workspace:

Figure 11.44: Sharing a report with an individual or group

- **Share your report or dashboard:** When you share a dashboard or report, recipients can view it and interact with it, but can't edit it:

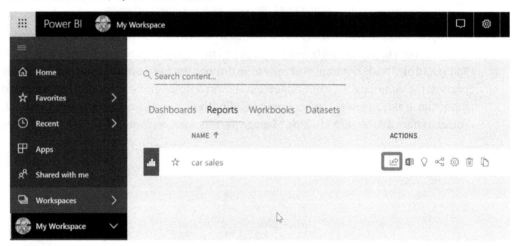

Figure 11.45: Sharing a report or dashboard that cannot be edited

See also

- The *Retrieving data* recipe in this chapter
- The *Transforming data* recipe in this chapter
- The *Modeling data* recipe in this chapter
- The *Visualizing data* recipe in this chapter

Create a dashboard

When you're first starting to use Power BI, you'll mostly be creating Power BI reports (these can be single or multi-page). Dashboards, however, allow us to combine visuals from across a number of separate reports to create a one-stop-shop for important metrics and data stories. In this recipe, we'll create a dashboard in Power BI that includes visuals from multiple reports.

Getting ready

You must have a license for Power BI and at least two separate reports already from which to pull visuals for your dashboard. These reports need to be in the same workspace (yours, or a group workspace).

How to do it...

1. Log in to the Power BI service (`https://app.powerbi.com/`).

2. Navigate to one of your existing reports from which you'd like to pin a visual to the new dashboard.

3. Hover your cursor over the visual you'd like to pin first, then select the **Pin visual** button as shown in *Figure 11.48*:

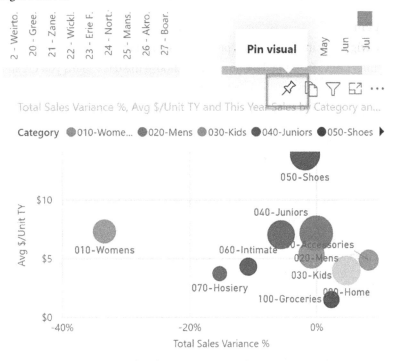

Figure 11.46: The Pin visual option for a specific report visualization.

4. Select **New dashboard** (if not already selected) and name your dashboard. In this example, the dashboard will be called `Sales Overview`:

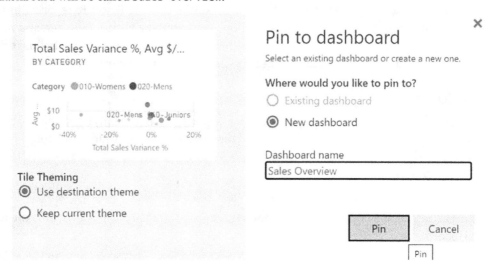

Figure 11.47: The dialog used when pinning a visual to a new dashboard

5. Select **Pin.**

6. Now navigate to another report, page, or visual you want to pin and repeat *step 3* to pin it.

7. This time, select **Existing dashboard** and choose the dashboard you created in *step 4*:

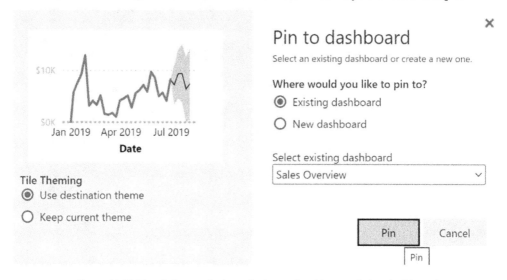

Figure 11.48: The dialog used when pinning a visual to an existing dashboard

8. Select **Pin**.

9. Find your dashboard by using the **Go to dashboard** pop-up option after pinning, or by using your left-hand navigation menu to find your new dashboard listed.

10. You should now see two visuals from different reports on your new dashboard. From here you can resize the tiles, share the dashboard, and much more:

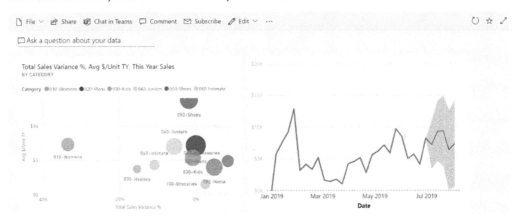

Figure 11.49: A dashboard showing two visuals from two separate reports

How it works...

Anyone with edit permissions for a report has the ability to pin visuals to a dashboard. Default access to the resulting dashboard depends on who already has access to the reports' workspace. You can, however, share reports and dashboards with additional people using the **Share** feature or by creating and publishing apps.

It's important that the reports you're using for visuals reside in the same workspace as the dashboard you want to create. For example, if you're working on reports in **My Workspace**, you can pin visuals from those reports to a dashboard you create that's also in **My Workspace**. But, if you're in a group's workspace, then the visuals you can pin must be from reports also in that group's workspace.

Any visuals you pin stay up-to-date following the same refresh schedules and actions taken on the underlying reports. For example, if you have a report with a scheduled refresh twice a day, the corresponding pinned visuals on your dashboard will also update twice a day.

There's more...

Rather than pin a single visual at a time, you also have the option to pin an entire report page to a dashboard. With the report page open, select the ellipsis (…) on the top menu and choose **Pin to a dashboard** as shown in *Figure 11.52*:

Figure 11.50: The option to pin an entire report page to a dashboard

After you've pinned visuals and created the initial dashboard, you can then resize visuals, ask questions of the combined underlying data, share the dashboard, and much more. When viewing the dashboard, for example, you can select **Edit** then add additional tiles (such as web content, images, text boxes, videos, or real-time data streams), change the dashboard's theme, or configure the dashboard's mobile layout. These options are shown in *Figure 11.53*:

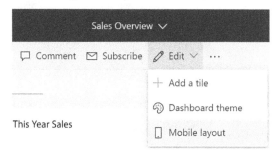

Figure 11.51: Edit abilities when viewing a dashboard that you have edit rights for

See also

- Create a Power BI dashboard from a report: `https://packt.link/BI-dashboard`
- Introduction to dashboards for Power BI designers: `https://packt.link/service-dashboard`

Embed a Power BI report on a SharePoint page

Power BI reports are excellent by themselves, but when combined with SharePoint pages, they have the potential to reach audiences more conveniently and be found within the context of related resources. Rather than share a link to a report that will open in a new window, this recipe will illustrate how you can embed an existing Power BI report directly onto a SharePoint page.

Getting ready

You must have a license for Power BI, a report already built, and editing rights on a SharePoint site to be able to complete the steps in this recipe.

How to do it...

1. Go to Power BI (`https://app.powerbi.com/`) and open the report you'd like to embed. Copy its URL from the browser bar:

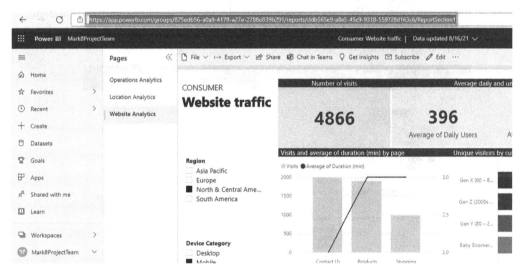

Figure 11.52: Web URL for a Power BI report

2. Now, navigate to the specific SharePoint site's page on which you'll be embedding a Power BI report and click **Edit** in the upper-right corner.

3. Click on the plus sign for whichever section of the page you want to add the Power BI web part to, then find and select the Power BI web part:

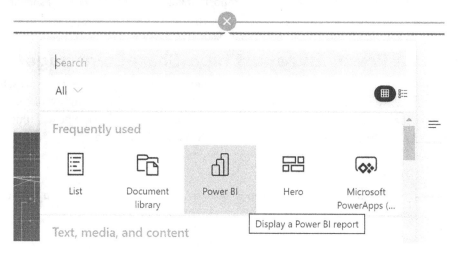

Figure 11.53: The Power BI web part for SharePoint pages and news

4. Paste the URL you copied in *step 1* into the first box in the web part's properties. Also, choose the specific page of the report you'd like embedded in the **Page name** dropdown. Be sure to deselect any components you don't want shown in the embedded report (such as additional report pages, editing options, etc.):

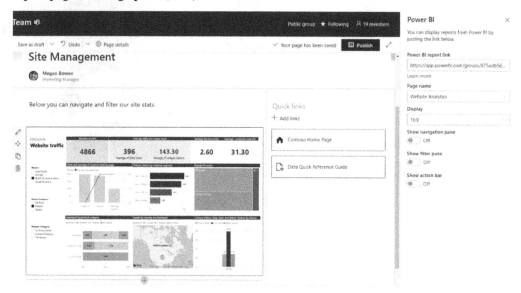

Figure 11.54: The properties panel for a Power BI web part

5. Once you have the report positioned where you'd like it, click **Publish** to save it and make it visible to your users.

How it works...

Once you've added a Power BI web part to a SharePoint page and specified the report's URL, your site's members and visitors will be able to use your Power BI report and interact with its filters and other components right within the context of the page alongside any other relevant links and resources.

Figure 11.55: A published SharePoint page with an embedded Power BI report

There's more...

One of your configurable options when using the Power BI web part is to show or hide navigation. If you choose to show it, you'll see the other pages in the report (when applicable) listed along the bottom or side of the report:

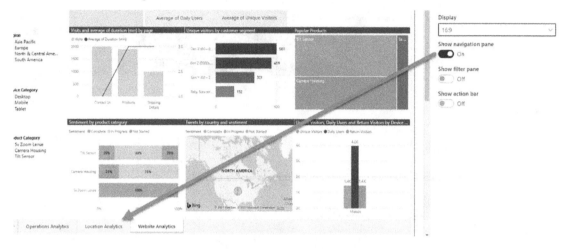

Figure 11.56: Navigation pane option in a Power BI web part's properties

If you choose to show the **Filters** pane, users will be able to use the report's collapsible **Filters** pane in addition to any slicers or other filter objects on the report itself:

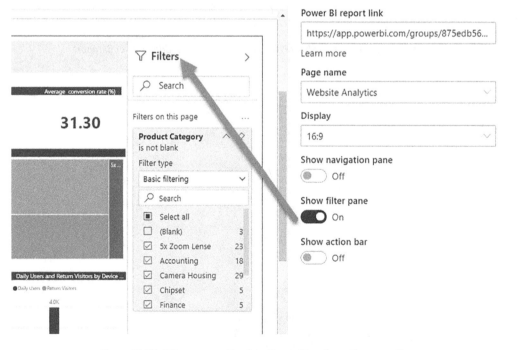

Figure 11.57: Filter pane option in a Power BI web part's properties

You can also choose to show the **action** bar, which allows users to perform a number of actions related to manipulating, sharing, and collaborating around the report. This also allows users the ability to open the report in Power BI for the full experience:

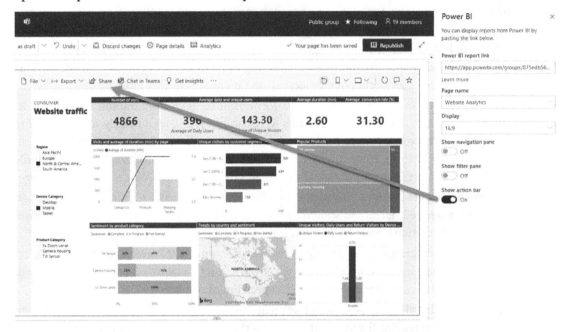

Figure 11.58: Action bar option in a Power BI web part's properties

See also

- Embed a report web part in SharePoint Online: `https://packt.link/embed-report-web-part-in-SP`

Power BI and AI

Recently, Power BI has received a host of AI-driven capabilities that enable customers to extract data from more sources and detect patterns in that data. This field is new and rapidly changing, so we will list some of the key features of Power BIs adoption of AI instead of exploring particular recipes with it. Some of the key topics to look out for when exploring Power BI's AI capabilities are the following:

- **AutoML (Automated Machine Learning)** combines Power BI with Azure Machine Learning. This feature allows you to create models that expect future tendencies and effects without needing a background in statistics.

- **AI visuals** such as Decomposition Tree aid users with dissecting complicated statistical relationships and understanding the drivers in the back of statistical traits.

- **Natural Language Query (NLQ)** helps users interact with information using natural language. Using NLQ in Power BI, this feature allows users to literally ask questions to Power BI, and Power BI responds with applicable visualizations and reports.

- Power BI's **Key Influencers visual** uncovers significant factors affecting a chosen metric. Through statistical analysis and visuals, it reveals correlations between influencing variables and the target metric, aiding data-driven decisions across sales, customer behavior, and more. However, it emphasizes correlation rather than causation, and (as always) accuracy relies on data quality.

- The **Anomaly detection** feature employs AI to identify unusual patterns or outliers in data. It helps users quickly spot irregularities, enabling timely attention to critical data points. This aids in mitigating risks, optimizing processes, and maintaining data integrity.

- **Power Query** is a major tool in Power Platform used for data preparation. Like Power BI, Power Query has much more to it than its AI capabilities, and could easily merit a book in itself (indeed, there are several books available about it). It's AI capabilities are focused on transforming data within Power Query Editor. Users define desired output values for new table columns, and Power Query automatically generates the appropriate logic for column creation.

- **Automated Insights** is a new statistics storyteller, using AI to craft narratives from data. Of course, AI-generated narratives should be used cautiously and properly investigated before being cited in decisions made by an organization.

- **Text Analytics** integrates with Azure Cognitive Services, enabling Power BI to examine textual content and create insights, which makes it a powerful tool for sentiment analysis. Along with image recognition, this broadens Power BI's spectrum of resources.

- **Image recognition** allows users to examine images and incorporate the extracted statistics into visualizations, increasing the scope of what material can be studied to gain insights.

Microsoft Fabric

Microsoft Fabric is an analytics platform that brings together all the data and analytics tools that organizations need. It is a cloud-based service that is part of the Microsoft Azure platform. Whereas Power BI is primarily a tool for data visualization, Fabric is typically seen as a solution for backend data management. That said, it does also have data visualization capabilities, so your organization should assess its features and determine whether you are better off integrating Fabric with Power BI, or only using one or the other.

Fabric itself is an integration of several Azure tools, including Azure Data Factory and Azure Synapse Analytics.

There are many benefits to using Microsoft Fabric, including:

- Using a unified platform instead of individual Azure tools provides a single place for data management.

- It is a cloud-based service, so it is scalable and easy to maintain.

- Thanks to incorporating many tools in the Azure family, it offers a wide range of functionality in data preparation, including (broadly speaking) data movement, data lakes, data engineering, and data integration.

- It is integrated with other Microsoft products and services, including Azure and Power BI itself.

To get started with Microsoft Fabric, you need to create an Azure account. Once you have an Azure account, you can enable Fabric in the Azure portal.

Once Fabric is enabled, you can start connecting to data sources and creating data pipelines, data models, and reports.

Since Fabric is not our main focus in this chapter, we will hold back from exploring data preparation in this chapter. Instead, we advice that you consult the many resources available to help you learn more about Microsoft Fabric, including online tutorials, documentation, and community forums.

Here are some examples of how Microsoft Fabric is being used by real-world customers:

- Ferguson, a distributor of plumbing supplies, is using Fabric to reduce the time it takes to generate business intelligence reports from 12 hours to just 30 minutes.
- ConocoPhillips, an oil and gas company, is using Fabric to improve the accuracy of its production forecasts by 10%.
- CVS Health is using Fabric to develop and deploy new AI-powered applications to improve patient care.

These are just a few examples of how Microsoft Fabric can be used to help organizations get more value from their data. If you are looking for an analytics platform that can help you manage and prepare your data, Microsoft Fabric is a great option to consider.

References

- Using Azure Databricks with Microsoft Fabric and OneLake | Microsoft Fabric Blog | Microsoft Fabric: `https://packt.link/Azure-databricks-with-Fabric`
- Introducing Microsoft Fabric: The data platform for the era of AI | Azure Blog | Microsoft Azure: `https://packt.link/introducing-Microsoft-Fabric`
- Data Analytics | Microsoft Fabric: `https://packt.link/Microsoft-Fabric`

Learn more on Discord

To join the Discord community for this book – where you can share feedback, ask questions to the author, and learn about new releases – follow the QR code below:

`https://packt.link/powerusers`

12

Overview of Copilot in Microsoft 365 and Power Platform

With the rising popularity of **artificial intelligence** (**AI**) tools such as ChatGPT, developed by OpenAI, it has become increasingly important to assess the applicability of AI tools in the context of business software. Microsoft's response to the success of ChatGPT is Microsoft Copilot, which will be the major focus of this chapter.

First, we will introduce the essential concepts of artificial intelligence, generative AI, and **Large Language Models** (**LLMs**). With that knowledge under our belts, we will explore Microsoft Copilot as part of the M365 ecosystem. Copilot can help accelerate the completion of everyday tasks on popular platforms such as Word, SharePoint, and Power Platform. We will also learn about Copilot's offerings as a chatbot, including Microsoft Copilot (Bing Chat) and Copilot for Microsoft 365.

This chapter will comprise the following topics:

- Introducing AI
- Copilot and AI in Microsoft 365
- Conversational AI chatbots
- Copilot in Microsoft 365 apps
- Copilot in Power Platform
- The future of Copilot

Note

Please note that, as of February 2024, Microsoft's adoption of AI has only just begun; the content referenced in this chapter is rapidly evolving at the time of publication. With that in mind, we have decided that a collection of recipes would be misleading. We recommend that you use this chapter as a foot in the door and learn through practice wherever possible. The people who will make the most of AI are those who are willing to adapt!

Introducing AI

Before we start touring the capabilities of Copilot, we should first go over some key words that you'll encounter when working with AI. Some of these may be obvious to you, but some are valuable concepts for improving how you use AI. We've listed these terminologies below:

- **AI**: Short for **artificial intelligence**, this is the field of computer science that aims to create machines and systems that can perform tasks that normally require human intelligence and creativity. AI is not a single technology, but a collection of methods and tools that can be applied to various domains and applications. Some of the biggest fields in the development of AI are **machine learning**, **computer vision**, **natural language processing**, **speech recognition**, and **robotics**. Conceptually, AI can also be classified into **narrow AI**, which is designed to perform a specific task, and **general AI**, which has the broader aim of being capable of understanding and performing any task that a human can.

- **LLMs**: In the field of AI, tools in Copilot's category are known as **LLMs**. This label refers to any deep learning algorithm that can recognize, summarize, translate, predict, and generate text and other content. At the moment, all the popular AI tools (think ChatGPT, Copilot, Claude, Bard, and so on; you could even count Cleverbot and Jabberwacky) are LLMs.

- **Prompts**: When you input a sentence into an LLM, you are providing a **prompt**, which details what you are instructing the LLM to do. On the surface, this is an incredibly simple statement – you can simply ask Copilot *"Make me a table comparing X and Y"* and it will do it – but to make the most of an LLM, you will need to learn what prompts are more effective at producing results.

  This study is known as **prompt engineering**. We recommend you investigate the young-yet-plentiful bounty of resources that explore effective prompt writing. We also recommend checking out **Copilot Lab**, which contains some guidance on prompt writing. We'll have a look at this later in the chapter.

Copilot can also be classed as a generative AI tool, which we will explore next.

What is generative AI?

The following list summarizes some of the key concepts about generative AI that are useful background information when learning what Copilot is and how it works:

- **Generative AI**: This is a branch of AI that focuses on creating new content or data from scratch, such as images, text, music, or code. Generative AI uses techniques such as **deep learning**, **neural networks**, and the aforementioned **natural language processing** to learn from existing data and generate novel and realistic outputs. In the context of Copilot, generative AI can be used for mundane tasks such as preparing data, creating tabular content, and creating Excel formulas.

- **GANs:** One of the most popular and powerful techniques in generative AI is using **generative adversarial networks,** or **GANs.** GANs are composed of two neural networks that compete with each other: a generator that tries to create fake data, and a discriminator that tries to distinguish between real and fake data. By training the generator and the discriminator together, GANs can produce high-quality and diverse data that resembles real data.

- **Hallucination:** Generative AI tools *hallucinate* when they provide inaccurate or illogical answers. If you spend some brief time online researching AI hallucination, you will see that this is a real and valid concern. Especially when prompted to perform a big task with little guidance, AI tools can sometimes provide incorrect answers. You should always look through the output of your LLM before, say, using it in a data model or a report.

- **Bias:** Bias refers to output errors caused by skewed training data. Biased models can produce inaccurate, offensive, or misleading predictions due to prioritizing irrelevant or misleading data traits over meaningful patterns.

- **Grounding:** Grounding is a term used for an approach to avoid inaccurate LLM results by providing more context for the tool to work with. Grounding entails adding use-case-specific, relevant information for the LLM to improve the output quality.

Prompt engineering and how we wrote this chapter

With the concepts of hallucination, bias, and grounding in mind, our advice for writing effective prompts is detailed in the following list:

1. **Provide narrow instructions:** Meaning we don't want to overwhelm Copilot by providing a complicated problem statement. Instead, we would break a multi-step problem into smaller chunks and have it solve one smaller problem at a time. This really is the secret to working with any AI. Even when building complicated machine learning algorithms, we break down the entire solution into smaller pipelines that solve one problem at a time.

2. **Write clear prompts:** Writing clear and descriptive prompts for Copilot is crucial for getting the most out of the AI-powered assistant. Clear prompts give Copilot adequate and useful parameters to generate a valuable response. They help you avoid common pitfalls, such as vague language, conflicting instructions, or inappropriate requests. Prompt engineering is the process of crafting effective prompts that enable AI models to generate responses based on given inputs. Prompt engineering can help you leverage the full potential of AI systems, by guiding them to generate relevant, accurate, and creative results. Here's a good one-pager from Microsoft as a reference for creating good prompts: `https://packt.link/prompt-advice-PDF`.

3. **Review and refine prompts:** You should adjust your prompts, re-prompt, and make updates to the responses generated by Copilot. Treating your use of Copilot as a conversation of continual re-prompting, not just one task, will help you understand what prompts work most effectively with Copilot. Once you gain more experience with Copilot, you'll get a better understanding of how to phrase your prompts and what details to include.

We can actually use this chapter as a case study for how to write grounded prompts that make the most of generative AI tools like Copilot.

Keeping in mind the above, here is a very brief summary of the steps we took to generate the chapter. Please note that since Copilot's capabilities were evolving at the time of writing (and so were ours), each step had to go through multiple iterations:

1. **Iterative table of contents (TOC) generation**: Following the principles mentioned earlier, we started small, by creating a TOC first:

    a. We provided the context of what we were doing and had Copilot create a level 1 TOC first.

    b. We then refined the level 1 TOC.

    c. We then used it to generate the level 2 TOC for each level 1 topic one at a time.

2. **Iterative content generation**: Once the TOC was generated, we went through each level 1 and level 2 topic one at a time and prompted Copilot to generate content for it. Each time, we took the following steps:

    a. We first provided context by sharing the entire TOC for each new building session (unless we had provided the context earlier in the session).

    b. We fed information on the specifics we wanted it to write through narratives or links to appropriate articles from Microsoft.

    c. We reviewed and refined the content a lot for conciseness, accuracy, specificity, and removing vagueness and redundancy.

3. While we used Copilot to gather and summarize the information for us, we added a lot of additional original content to it, such as (but not limited to) the following:

    a. Images showing real-world examples.

    b. The entire section on *Conversational AI chatbots* due to the spread and complexity of information in the section.

    c. Many similar sections and sub-sections throughout the chapter (such as this one).

In addition to the above, we had to refine the structure and content multiple times due to the fact that much of this was still being rolled out and refined by Microsoft itself at the time of writing. You can see from this use case that AI-generated text cannot be seen as a replacement for human writing or human effort; Copilot must be used in a conversation of continual grounding, re-prompting, and revising.

Again, we encourage you to learn through practice. Once you are more familiar with Copilot through this chapter, try out some of its capabilities. Once you start generating your own tables with Copilot, you'll quickly see for yourself how writing grounded prompts improves your results.

Now that we've had a 101 on AI, let's start looking at Copilot more specifically. We'll begin with a quick tour of its major developer.

What is OpenAI?

OpenAI is a research organization that was founded in 2015 by a group of prominent entrepreneurs, investors, and scientists, including Elon Musk, Peter Thiel, Reid Hoffman, and Sam Altman. OpenAI's goal is to create **artificial general intelligence** (**AGI**). As we saw earlier, general AI refers to the building of systems that can match or surpass human intelligence across any domain.

OpenAI publishes research papers, code, and data openly, encouraging collaboration and feedback from the global AI community. Some of the notable projects and achievements of OpenAI include:

- GPT-3, GPT-4: A deep learning model that can generate natural language text on various topics and tasks, such as writing essays, summarizing articles, composing emails, and answering questions

- DALL-E: A deep learning model that can generate images from natural language descriptions, such as "a cat wearing a bow tie" or "a skyscraper made of sushi"

- CLIP: A deep learning model that can learn from natural language and visual data and perform tasks such as image classification, object detection, and captioning

- Codex: A deep learning model that can generate and execute code from natural language commands such as "create a website that looks like Airbnb" or "make a game like Flappy Bird"

- OpenAI Scholars: A program that supports and mentors individuals from underrepresented groups in AI research and provides them with access to OpenAI resources and networks

- OpenAI Microscope: A collection of visualizations of the features and neurons of various deep learning models, such as GPT-3, DALL-E, and CLIP

- OpenAI Spinning Up: A free online course that teaches the basics of deep reinforcement learning, which is a branch of AI that deals with learning from trial and error and maximizing rewards

In 2019, Microsoft and OpenAI partnered together to advance AI research and democratize access to AI technologies. Azure, Microsoft's cloud platform, is the exclusive cloud provider for OpenAI. Azure supports OpenAI's workloads across research, products, and API services. With the connection of Azure OpenAI Service, Microsoft has the ability to tap into these services to enhance first- and third-party applications. These services securely drive Copilot's capabilities in the different Microsoft products and services, including Microsoft 365 and Power Platform.

Now, let's begin to look at the tool itself.

Copilot in Microsoft 365

Copilot is a new feature in Microsoft 365 that leverages generative AI to help you write documents, emails, presentations, and more. Copilot can suggest relevant content, formatting, and style based on your topic, audience, and purpose. Copilot can also help you find and cite reliable sources, check grammar and spelling, and optimize your SEO. For instance, when drafting an email, Copilot can suggest complete sentences based on the context of the conversation. Similarly, while working on a spreadsheet, it can provide insights into the data and suggest relevant charts.

Copilot works by analyzing your input and context and generating suggestions that you can accept, reject, or modify. Copilot can also learn from your feedback and preferences, and improve its suggestions over time. Copilot can help you save time, avoid errors, and create engaging and professional content.

Microsoft Copilot has found its way into a huge range of Microsoft software. As a result, it can be found in all sorts of different formats. Broadly speaking, Microsoft Copilot is available in the following forms:

- **Copilot in conversational AI chatbots:** Conversational AI chatbots mimic human conversation to provide you with the information you ask for. Chatbots can assist you with various tasks from summarizing information from internet resources to writing a poem to writing code. We will cover the capabilities of Microsoft's conversational chatbots and more in greater detail in the *Conversational AI chatbots* section.

- **Copilot in Microsoft 365 apps:** Copilot is integrated into various Microsoft 365 apps, including Word, Excel, PowerPoint, Outlook, Teams, Microsoft Loop, and Microsoft Whiteboard. In each of these apps, Copilot provides context-specific assistance. For example, in Word, it can help with grammar and style suggestions. In Excel, it can analyze data and suggest relevant charts. In Teams, it can assist with scheduling meetings and managing tasks. We will look at Copilot's capabilities in Microsoft 365 apps in greater detail in the *Copilot in Microsoft 365 apps* section later in this chapter.

- **Copilot in Power Platform:** Copilot in Microsoft Power Platform allows users of individual Power Platform workloads to build apps (including the data behind them), workflows (Power Automate), chat agents (Power Virtual Agents), dashboards (Power BI), and pages (Power Pages) just by describing what they need through multiple steps of conversation. Beyond this, you can also utilize Copilot and OpenAI's capabilities within your apps. We will review these topics in more detail in the *Copilot in Power Platform* section later in this chapter.

Before we dive deeper into the various Copilot capabilities, it is worth noting a few extremely useful resources:

- Copilot Lab (`https://packt.link/Copilot-Lab`): This site contains sample prompts, which teach us how to better prompt the different workload-specific Copilot offerings in Microsoft 365. The screenshot below shows some example prompts we can use to be prepared for or catch up on Teams meetings:

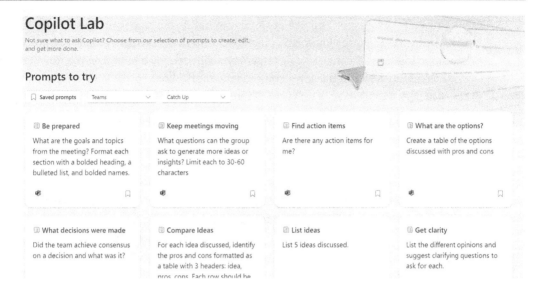

Figure 12.1: Copilot Lab

Also, here's a good support article from Microsoft explaining the best practices in writing prompts for Copilot: `https://packt.link/Copilot-prompts`.

- Microsoft adoption website (`https://packt.link/Copilot-adoption`): Microsoft's adoption website is the ultimate resource to learn about Copilot, how to prepare for it, and how to use it. It also links to many other useful Microsoft and community resources. It is highly recommended to aid you with your Copilot journey.

In the sections to follow, we will delve deeper into the workloads and prerequisites for each Microsoft 365 app and the Power Platform. Stay tuned to learn more about how Copilot is shaping the future of work.

Technical requirements

Before diving into Copilot, it's important to understand the general technical requirements for using it.

The following are the licensing requirements for each type of Copilot service. We'll learn more about these services in the *Copilot in Microsoft 365* section:

- Copilot for conversational AI chatbots: Licensing for conversational chatbots depends on the type of chatbot. We have covered the licensing requirements in the table titled *Differences between the various AI chatbots* in the *Conversational AI chatbots* section.

- Copilot in Microsoft 365 apps: You will require a valid Microsoft 365 subscription along with additional Copilot licensing to access Copilot's capabilities within various Microsoft 365 apps. You can refer to this link for the licensing requirements for Microsoft 365 Copilot: `https://packt.link/Copilot-for-Microsoft-365`.

- Copilot in Power Platform: The use of Copilot to build your apps (such as Power Automate, Power Apps, etc.) in Power Platform is included with the respective Power Platform license for the app. Additional licenses, however, are typically required to utilize or embed Copilot or OpenAI capabilities within the apps. You can read more about Power Platform licensing here: `https://packt.link/Power-Platform-licensing`.

Please note that these are general prerequisites and additional requirements may apply depending on the specific features of Copilot being used.

Conversational AI chatbots

We will now discuss the different generative AI chat platforms provided by Microsoft. These platforms include Microsoft Copilot (Bing Chat), Copilot for Microsoft 365 (Bing Enterprise Chat), and Copilot for Windows. Beneath the hood, each platform utilizes the capabilities of generative AI to enhance user experience and productivity but with slight differences. This section provides an understanding of how these chat platforms work and their unique features. It also highlights the differences between these platforms.

ChatGPT

Before we discuss the different conversational AI chatbots from Microsoft, it makes sense to introduce the biggest chatbot in AI right now, ChatGPT.

ChatGPT is an AI chatbot developed by OpenAI. It leverages deep learning techniques to produce human-like responses to natural language inputs. It's a member of the family of **generative pre-trained transformer (GPT)** models.

GPT is a type of AI model that utilizes machine learning techniques to produce human-like text. It is part of a larger family of models known as transformers, which use a mechanism called attention to dramatically improve the quality of the output. Explaining these models and mechanisms is beyond the scope of this book, but we encourage further reading. You can even ask ChatGPT to explain it!

Like any LLM, ChatGPT was trained on a vast amount of data, including books, articles, websites, and even social media. This allows it to create responses that make it seem like a friendly and intelligent robot.

ChatGPT is a versatile tool with a wide range of applications. It's mostly known for creating content and assisting with writing content (even code) and as an educational tool for retrieving information. There are even many content creators who use ChatGPT to generate entertaining scripts.

Microsoft Copilot

In the context of AI chatbots, Microsoft Copilot (also known as Bing Chat) is an AI-powered assistant that works with Microsoft's Bing search engine. It is powered by the same GPT-4 LLM that powers ChatGPT. Just like ChatGPT, the Copilot chatbot can answer simple and complex questions, assist with research, and provide summaries of articles, books, events, news, sports results, and so on.

However, beyond this, it also overcomes an important limitation of the free version of ChatGPT, which is its inability to provide answers based on real-time information. The way Microsoft Copilot works is that it first performs a gated real-time search (by gated we mean that it screens for things like profanity or malicious search results). It then passes these results along with a modified prompt to the GPT models for further processing and eventual generation of conversational responses, all within a matter of seconds.

Beyond that, you can also choose your conversational style with Bing Chat from one of the following options:

- Creative: This will create more imaginative and creative responses. It's tailored to writing or other creative tasks.
- Precise: We would use this conversational style for more concise and direct answers – this is tailored for obtaining historic information, solving mathematical problems, or generating responses for information that is readily available or can be derived.
- Balanced: This style can be used to obtain answers to everything in between the preceding. Examples where it can be used include trip planning or identifying product differences.

There are four ways to access Bing Chat:

- Using any web browser to browse to `https://copilot.microsoft.com` or `https://bing.com/chat`
- Browsing to `https://bing.com` and then clicking the **Chat** tab at the top

- Clicking the Copilot app from the app bar in Microsoft Edge:

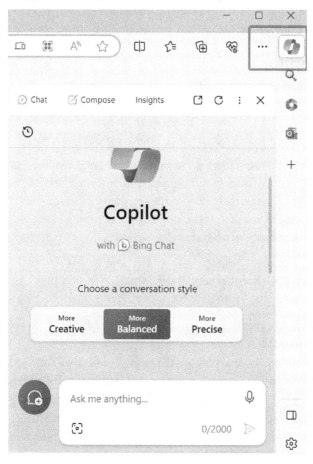

Figure 12.2: Copilot app on the app bar

- Using the Bing mobile app, *Chapter 26, Microsoft 365 on Mobile Devices*:

Figure 12.3: Bing mobile app

Copilot with commercial data protection

Copilot with commercial data protection (also known as Bing Chat Enterprise) is another form of Copilot as an AI chatbot. It provides all the benefits of Microsoft Copilot as well as the following:

- Your activity in Copilot with commercial data protection is not used or stored in any way.
- For this reason, session data is only maintained during the chat. All prompts and responses are discarded after the chat session. Further, your data is not used to train any data models.
- All models are stored in a private instance of Azure OpenAI and OpenAI does not have access to them.
- The content you share in Copilot with commercial data protection does not leave your organization's tenant. Further, Copilot with commercial data protection does not have access to your organization's data (emails, OneDrive, SharePoint, etc.).
- Your conversations and all related data are encrypted in transit.

Copilot with commercial data protection automatically replaces Microsoft Copilot for you as long as the following are true:

- It was enabled by your organization.
- You have an appropriate Microsoft 365 license assigned to you (Microsoft 365 E3, E5, Business Standard, Business Premium, or A3 or A5 for Faculty at the time of writing).
- You are signed in to the browser using your work account.

At that point, whether you browse to Microsoft Copilot through `https://bing.com` or `https://copilot.microsoft.com` or you browse to it using the Copilot app for Microsoft Edge, you are automatically shown Copilot with commercial data protection instead of Microsoft Copilot.

Copilot for Microsoft 365

Microsoft 365 Chat combines the power of AI with your work data to help you improve your everyday productivity and streamline some tasks. It has access to your organizational data through the Graph API. As we've come to expect from LLMs, Microsoft 365 Chat uses natural language interaction to help you to obtain insights. It's ideally used for drafting content, catching up on what you might have missed, and getting answers to specific work questions from your work content, such as chats, emails, and files.

A big advantage it provides is that it can help you leverage cross-app intelligence. However, unlike Copilot with commercial data protection or Microsoft Copilot, it does not have access to real-time external data. It is important to note that all data protection rules of Copilot with commercial data protection apply here as well and your data does not leave your tenant, nor is it used to train any AI models.

You can access Copilot for Microsoft 365 in several ways:

- Using any web browser to browse to `https://bing.com/chat`, `https://copilot.microsoft.com`, or `https://bing.com`, clicking the **Chat** tab at the top, and then clicking the **Work** tab:

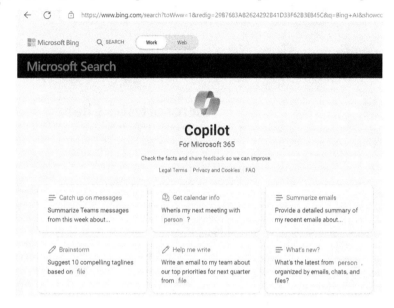

Figure 12.4: Reaching Copilot through the Chat and Work tabs

- Clicking the Copilot app from the **App** bar in Microsoft Edge and then clicking **Work**:

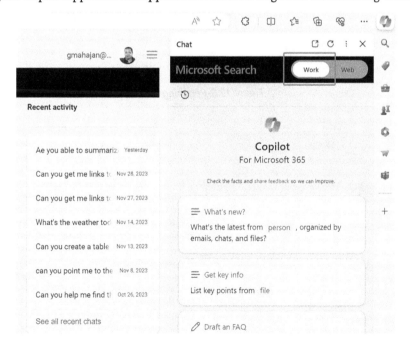

Figure 12.5: Reaching Copilot from the App bar

- Browsing to www.microsoft365.com and then clicking the **M365 Chat** app in the **App** bar to the left.
- Using Copilot in desktop and mobile versions of Microsoft Teams, as shown below:

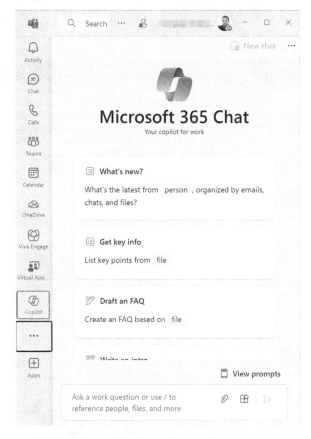

Figure 12.6: Reaching Copilot from Teams

Copilot in Windows

Copilot in Windows brings the Microsoft Copilot experience to your Windows 11 desktop (at the time of writing). The screenshot below shows a preview version of Windows Copilot:

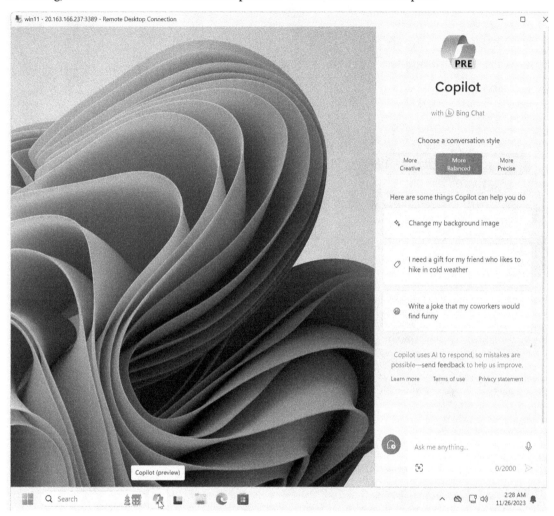

Figure 12.7: Windows Copilot in preview

As shown in the screenshot, Windows Copilot is represented by a **Copilot** button on the taskbar (when enabled). To launch it, simply click the taskbar button. Once launched, the interaction experience of Windows Copilot is the same as Microsoft Copilot on the web.

Beyond responding to your queries, Windows Copilot can also perform various tasks, from adjusting your PC's settings to organizing your windows with Snap Assist:

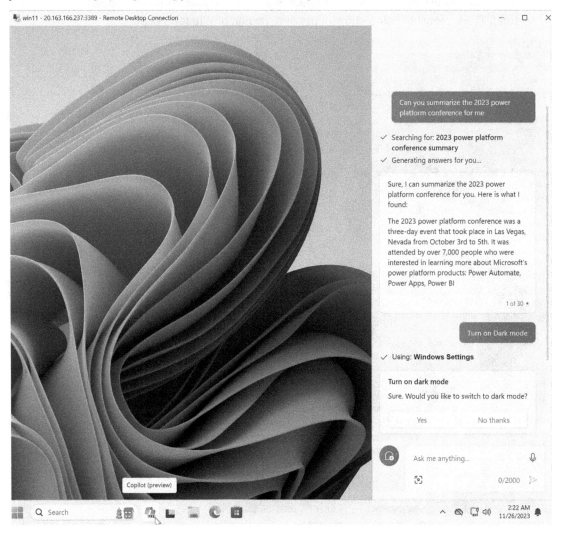

Figure 12.8: Writing prompts for Windows Copilot

Windows Copilot is a limited preview feature at the time of writing and is likely to change in the future. You can read more about it here: `https://packt.link/Copilot-AI-features`

Differences between the various AI chatbots

	ChatGPT	Copilot (Bing Chat)	Copilot with commercial data protection (Bing Chat Enterprise)/Windows Copilot	Copilot for Microsoft 365
Availability and licensing	Everyone – OpenAI signup required. Paid plans for enhanced capabilities	Everyone – signup not required	Only available to licensed M365 users with certain plans*	M365 license + Copilot for M365 license required
Access to real-time content from the internet?	Only with paid plans	Yes		
Can store information exchanged in conversations?	Yes	Yes	No	Yes
Can the stored information be used for training AI models?	Yes	Yes	No	No
Has automatic access to internal organization data (without being explicitly shared on chat)?	No	No	No	Yes
Can I directly share documents and ask the bot to summarize them?	No – but you can copy and paste the text	Yes, in the following scenarios: • 1. The document is shared anonymously and searchable through the internet. • 2. If it's a local PDF file, you can open the file in Microsoft Edge and click the **Ask Bing AI** toolbar button to get insights from the document. • 3. You can always copy-paste text from the document into the chat box and then ask the Chatbot to summarize it for you.		Yes, as long as the document is stored on M365 and you have access to it by means of permissions
*Available to Microsoft 365 E3, E5, Business Standard, Business Premium, or A3 or A5 for Faculty at the time of writing				

Table 12.1: Comparison of Copilot offerings

Based on the above, we can see these differences demonstrated by some example prompts.

Example 1:

- Prompt:

    - Can you please search the web to summarize announcements from the Oct 2023 power platform conference?

- Response by GPT-3 (the free version of ChatGPT):

    - I'm sorry, but I don't have the ability to provide real-time information.

- GPT-4 (paid version of ChatGPT), Copilot (Bing Chat), and Copilot with commercial data protection (Bing Chat Enterprise) / Windows Copilot provide a different response, since they have access to this data. They will comb the internet to get relevant results and then will generate an appropriate summary of announcements with appropriate attribution.

- Copilot for Microsoft 365 also fetches relevant information from the internet and will generate an appropriate summary of announcements with appropriate attribution.

Example 2:

- Prompt:

    - What's the weather today in Washington DC?

- ChatGPT will provide the same response as before:

    - I'm sorry, but I don't have the ability to provide real-time information

- GPT-4 (paid version of ChatGPT), Copilot (Bing Chat) and Copilot with commercial data protection (Bing Chat Enterprise) / Windows Copilot will retrieve the location-specific weather information and display it on the screen.

- Copilot for Microsoft 365, however, gives a different answer:

    - I'm sorry, but I am not able to provide weather information. I am a chatbot designed to help with Microsoft 365 related tasks and queries. Is there anything else I can help you with?

Here we can see that Copilot for Microsoft 365 has access to different data than Bing Chat. This makes sense, since it's intended for a different use.

Copilot in Microsoft 365 apps

Copilot is integrated into a huge variety of software offered by Microsoft 365. This means that you don't need to go online and interact with a chatbot to use Copilot – it can be accessed on the interface you are already working on. This helps a ton with convenience, and, as we'll see, it enables you to use Copilot for quick assistance while working on all sorts of projects, similar to how you use the spell-checker in Word to quickly check spelling and grammar.

In this section, we'll take a broad look at how you can use Copilot in Word, Excel, PowerPoint, Outlook, Teams, Loop, Whiteboard, OneNote, Stream, SharePoint, OneDrive, and Viva. We recommend that you pinpoint the software that interests you and jump ahead to that section.

Copilot in Word

Microsoft 365 has taken the leap of integrating Copilot in Word for document creation and editing. In this section, we'll take a bite-sized look at the core capabilities of Copilot in Word.

Drafting assistance

Copilot in Word redefines the drafting experience by generating first drafts, inspiring new ideas, and building upon existing content. It allows users to stay immersed in their creative process, facilitating seamless content creation.

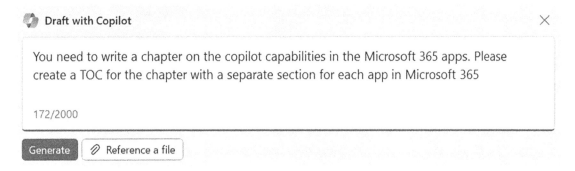

Figure 12.9: Example prompt for drafting content

Editing and rewriting

Copilot's editing prowess extends to rewriting text, including tonal adjustments, ensuring that the document's voice aligns with the desired style. Available on multiple platforms, it brings a high level of adaptability to diverse user needs.

Figure 12.10: Editing content with Copilot

Transforming content

Remarkably, Copilot can convert text into editable tables, showcasing its advanced formatting capabilities. This feature adds a significant layer of versatility in managing document layouts and information presentation.

Interactive insights and summaries

Copilot goes beyond traditional writing assistance. It interacts with users, answering questions about the document, generating concise summaries, and providing additional content or context as needed. This interactive dimension makes Copilot a valuable partner in document development.

As an example, imagine asking Copilot to summarize a meeting transcript, focusing on particular topics of interest. Or, maybe you'd benefit from a large annual report condensed into a few bullet points focused on sales or performance.

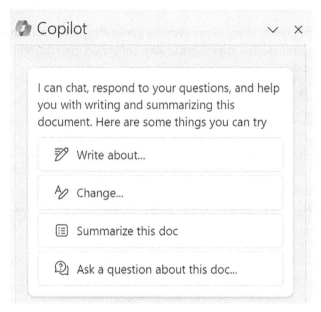

Figure 12.11: Inquiring with Copilot about a document

Additional capabilities

Beyond these core functions, Copilot brings a range of additional capabilities. It can integrate specific information from other documents, offer suggestions for content enhancement, and even generate content based on the context of existing material in the document.

Additional reading on Copilot in Word

- Copilot in Word: `https://packt.link/Copilot-in-Word`
- Draft and add content with Copilot in Word: `https://packt.link/draft-Word-content-with-Copilot`
- Transform your content with Copilot in Word: `https://packt.link/transform-Word-content-with-Copilot`
- Chat with Copilot about your Word document: `https://packt.link/Copilot-Word-chat`
- Create a summary of your document with Copilot: `https://packt.link/Copilot-Word-summary`
- Frequently asked questions about Copilot in Word: `https://packt.link/Copilot-in-Word-FAQ`

Copilot in Excel

Microsoft Excel, renowned for data analysis and visualization, becomes more intuitive and user-friendly with Copilot. This integration facilitates intelligent, context-aware suggestions to help users with data handling.

Intelligent data assistance

Copilot in Excel offers robust support in working with data. It intelligently suggests formulas, generates PivotTables, and recommends charts tailored to represent your data effectively. It streamlines tasks like formatting cells, creating tables, and managing worksheets, offering insights like summary statistics and trend analysis. Imagine describing a summarized view of your data and having the PivotTable work done for you in seconds. Or perhaps you'd like an existing spreadsheet to highlight anomalies in red conditionally without having to manually configure rules.

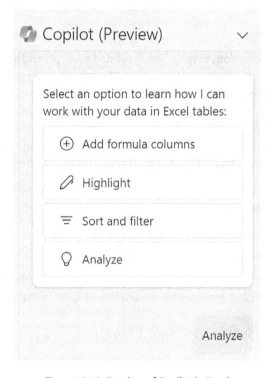

Figure 12.12: Preview of Copilot in Excel

Deep data exploration

Users are empowered to explore and understand their data better with Copilot. It extends capabilities beyond basic analysis, assisting in generating formula column suggestions, showcasing data through charts and PivotTables, and highlighting significant data portions.

Insight identification

Copilot's analytic prowess is evident in its ability to identify insights. It aids in recognizing trends, suggesting what-if scenarios, and crafting comprehensive dashboards, thereby enhancing decision-making processes based on data insights.

Efficient data management

Facilitating a focus on crucial data aspects, Copilot enables users to effortlessly highlight, sort, and filter data. This feature is pivotal in navigating through complex datasets and emphasizing key information.

Advanced formula generation

A standout feature of Copilot in Excel is its formula generation capability. It simplifies complex calculations by suggesting appropriate formula columns, making advanced data analysis accessible to a broader range of users.

Interactive user experience

Copilot encourages user interaction, responding to refined prompts and assisting in tasks like concise answer formulation and table generation from data. This interaction makes Copilot a potent tool for data analysis and visualization, accessible to a wide user base.

Accessibility and future prospects

Currently available to preview customers or in Teams with a work account, Copilot in Excel symbolizes a significant leap in accessible data analysis and visualization tools. Its future expansion to broader user access points promises even greater utility.

Additional reading on Copilot in Excel

- Copilot in Excel: `https://packt.link/Copilot-in-Excel`
- Get started with Copilot in Excel: `https://packt.link/get-started-with-Copilot-in-Excel`
- Identify insights with Copilot in Excel: `https://packt.link/Copilot-Excel-insights`
- Highlight, sort, and filter your data with Copilot in Excel: `https://packt.link/data-with-Copilot-in-Excel`
- Generate formula columns with Copilot in Excel: `https://packt.link/formulas-with-Copilot-in-Excel`

Copilot in PowerPoint

Microsoft PowerPoint, a staple for presentation creation, becomes even more dynamic and user-friendly with the integration of Copilot. This tool transforms the process of creating and editing presentations, making it more intuitive and efficient.

Intelligent presentation assistance

Copilot in PowerPoint offers intelligent assistance in creating and editing presentations. It provides context-aware suggestions, such as layout recommendations, formatting help, and advice on incorporating charts and images to enhance content.

It can also automatically create a presentation from a Word document.

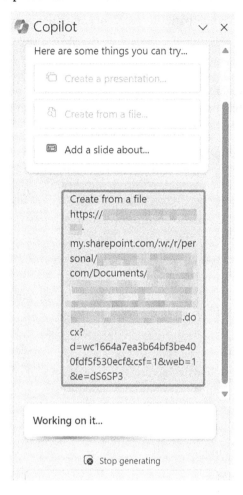

Figure 12.13: Creating a presentation with Copilot

Drafting and summarizing presentations

Copilot streamlines the creation of new presentations by generating drafts from given topics. This feature is invaluable when starting new projects, as it provides a structured outline. Additionally, Copilot can summarize lengthy presentations, highlighting key points for quick review.

Organizing presentations

An innovative aspect of Copilot is its ability to restructure presentations. It organizes slides into sections and adds section heading slides, with the option to undo changes if they don't meet the user's preference.

Enhancing presentation aesthetics

Copilot aids in building visually appealing presentations. It can generate slides or images, adding relevant visuals to make presentations more engaging.

Working with corporate templates

A notable feature is Copilot's compatibility with corporate templates. Users can create presentations that align with their organization's branding, enhancing the professional appearance of their work.

Mobile accessibility

Although specific details on mobile accessibility are not available as of the time of writing this book, Copilot's general adaptability suggests potential for mobile use, offering flexibility in reviewing and summarizing presentations on the go.

Additional reading on Copilot in PowerPoint

- Copilot in PowerPoint: `https://packt.link/Copilot-in-PowerPoint`
- Create a new presentation: `https://packt.link/creating-presentations-with-Copilot`
- Summarize your presentation with Copilot in PowerPoint: `https://packt.link/Copilot-presentation-summary`
- Organize this presentation with Copilot in PowerPoint: `https://packt.link/organizing-presentations-with-Copilot`
- Use your organization's branding with Copilot in PowerPoint: `https://packt.link/organization-branding-with-Copilot-in-PowerPoint`

Copilot in Outlook

Microsoft Outlook, a comprehensive personal information and communication manager many are well-familiar with, gains enhanced functionality with the integration of Copilot. This addition bolsters Outlook's capabilities as an email application and for personal management, making it more powerful and user-friendly.

Email drafting and management

Copilot in Outlook assists users in managing emails and schedules, offering intelligent context-based suggestions. It aids in drafting emails by suggesting complete sentences, correcting grammatical errors, and providing stylistic advice. This feature acts like a personal editor, enhancing the quality of email communication.

Email summarization and thread management

In addition to aiding in email creation, Copilot can summarize lengthy email threads, distilling them into concise summaries. This feature is invaluable for quickly understanding the key points of extended conversations.

Event planning with Copilot

Copilot in Outlook extends its utility to event planning. It assists in organizing and executing events by brainstorming and refining ideas, demonstrating its versatility beyond traditional email tasks.

Availability and access

Currently, Copilot is available exclusively in the new Outlook for Windows. Users interested in this feature should check their Outlook version and consult their IT administrators if necessary.

Additional reading on Copilot in Outlook

- Copilot in Outlook: `https://packt.link/Copilot-in-Outlook`
- Draft an email message with Copilot in Outlook: `https://packt.link/draft-email-with-Copilot-in-Outlook`
- Summarize an email thread with Copilot in Outlook: `https://packt.link/Copilot-Outlook-email-summary`
- How to plan a successful event with Copilot for Microsoft 365: `https://packt.link/plan-events-with-Copilot-for-Microsoft-365`

Copilot in Teams

Microsoft Teams, an essential tool for collaboration and communication within Microsoft 365, integrates Copilot to enhance its functionality. This integration aids in making team interactions more efficient and intuitive.

Effective meetings

Copilot in Microsoft Teams assists in real time during meetings by summarizing key discussion points, suggesting action items, and providing insights into who said what and where opinions differ.

Streamlined chat and channel communications

For chats and channels, Copilot helps users quickly catch up on the main points, action items, and decisions of ongoing conversations, without needing to scroll through long threads. This feature references information from a 30-day message history but does not include images, loop components, or files shared in the chat thread.

You can also use Copilot to help you write in a tone and manner that's most appropriate for the recipient and context of the message, such as making your message more concise or enthusiastic.

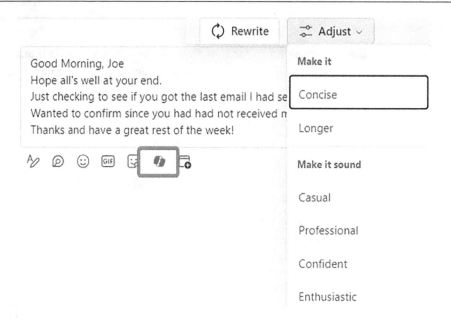

Figure 12.14: Editing tone with Copilot

Integration and accessibility

Copilot in Teams is integrated seamlessly with the Microsoft 365 suite, enhancing workflow efficiency across various applications. It is designed for a user-friendly experience and is accessible across different devices, ensuring flexibility in various working environments.

Additional reading on Copilot in Microsoft Teams

- Copilot in Microsoft Teams: `https://packt.link/Copilot-in-Teams`
- Get started with Copilot in Microsoft Teams meetings: `https://packt.link/get-started-with-Copilot-in-Teams`
- Use Copilot in Microsoft Teams chat and channels: `https://packt.link/Copilot-in-Teams-chat`
- Open Microsoft 365 Chat in Teams: `https://packt.link/Microsoft-365-chat-in-Teams`

Copilot in Microsoft Loop

Microsoft Loop is a dynamic application within the Microsoft 365 suite, designed to enhance team collaboration with a flexible and fluid canvas. It allows teams to co-create, collaborate, and stay in sync effectively.

Copilot integration in Loop

With Copilot integrated into Microsoft Loop, it becomes a more robust tool for team alignment and collaboration. Copilot assists in summarizing content on Microsoft Loop pages, enabling teams to quickly understand and engage with the collective work.

Here is how you will begin using Copilot in Loop:

To begin using Copilot in Loop, create a workspace (or edit an existing one), type "/", and select one of the options from the **Copilot** section of the menu. Then, choose from the suggested prompts including **Create**, **Brainstorm**, **Blueprint**, or **Describe**, or type your own prompt. After editing the prompt as needed, click the **Send** icon.

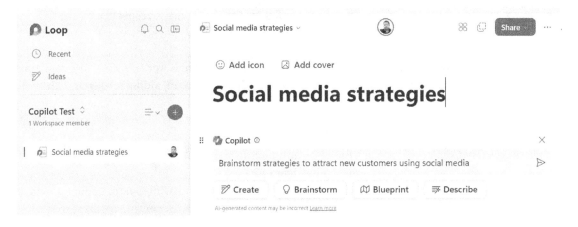

Figure 12.15: Suggest a caption here

Features and capabilities

Copilot in Loop can generate various types of content, including brainstorming ideas, planning events, and drafting content like newsletters or business plans.

Similar to other experiences of Copilot, it allows for the customization of content tone to suit different purposes and audiences.

Copilot in Loop facilitates real-time, multi-user editing, ensuring that all collaborators work with the latest information.

Copilot in Loop can also summarize and recap changes on Microsoft Loop pages, helping users stay updated and avoid duplication of work.

Limitations and languages supported

Copilot in Loop currently only recognizes content within its block and does not consider surrounding page content or linked content. As of the time of writing this book, it also only supports English, Spanish, Japanese, French, German, Portuguese, Italian, and Chinese Simplified, with plans to include more languages in the future.

Additional reading on Copilot in Microsoft Loop

- Copilot in Microsoft Loop: `https://packt.link/Copilot-in-Loop`
- Get started with Copilot for Microsoft 365 in Loop: `https://packt.link/get-started-with-Copilot-in-Loop`
- Edit results on a Loop page with Copilot for Microsoft 365 in Loop: `https://packt.link/edit-Loop-results-with-Copilot`
- Frequently asked questions about Copilot in Loop: `https://packt.link/Copilot-in-Loop-FAQ`

Copilot in Microsoft Whiteboard

Microsoft Whiteboard is a digital canvas that brings together people, content, and ideas. It offers a limitless surface for big ideas, enabling teams to collaborate in real time, irrespective of location.

Copilot integration in Whiteboard

Copilot in Whiteboard enhances the platform by suggesting new ideas and assisting in organizing content. It can automatically categorize all sticky notes on the whiteboard, aiding in idea organization and inspiration discovery.

In short, Copilot in Whiteboard has the following uses:

1. **Accessing Copilot:** Click the **Copilot** button next to the Whiteboard toolbar. In the Copilot menu, select options like Suggest or Categorize.
2. **Idea generation:** Use the **Suggest** feature to get started on a blank whiteboard. Copilot provides multiple suggestions based on your prompt, adding them as sticky notes, not text boxes.
3. **Idea organization:** To organize ideas, Copilot can cluster your ideas into categories based on their similarity. This feature only works with sticky notes.
4. **Content summarization:** Copilot can summarize complex whiteboards, creating a Loop component with a bullet-point summary that can be shared or edited as needed.

Availability and languages supported

Copilot in Whiteboard is accessible in the Whiteboard desktop app, web browser, iPad, and Teams client for users with a Microsoft 365 Copilot license.

Currently supported languages include English, Spanish, Japanese, French, German, Portuguese, Italian, and Chinese Simplified.

Additional reading on Copilot in Microsoft Whiteboard

- Copilot in Whiteboard: `https://packt.link/Copilot-in-Whiteboard`
- Welcome to Copilot in Whiteboard: `https://packt.link/welcome-to-Copilot-in-Whiteboard`
- Discover new ideas in Whiteboard with Copilot for Microsoft 365: `https://packt.link/ideas-with-Copilot-in-Whiteboard`
- Organize your ideas in Whiteboard with Copilot for Microsoft 365: `https://packt.link/organize-ideas-with-Copilot-in-Whiteboard`
- Summarize ideas in Whiteboard with Copilot for Microsoft 365: `https://packt.link/summarize-ideas-with-Copilot-in-Whiteboard`

Copilot in Microsoft OneNote

Microsoft 365 enhances the note-taking experience with the integration of Copilot in OneNote. This tool revolutionizes how users create, capture, organize, and recall information, making it an indispensable partner in various tasks.

Dynamic note creation

Copilot in OneNote excels in generating ideas, drafting plans, creating lists, and organizing information. It can transform text by summarizing, rewriting, formatting, and adding visual elements, ensuring notes are both informative and visually appealing.

Interactive summarization

A standout feature of Copilot in OneNote is its ability to summarize text selections, pages, or sections into concise, shareable formats, ideal for distilling complex information.

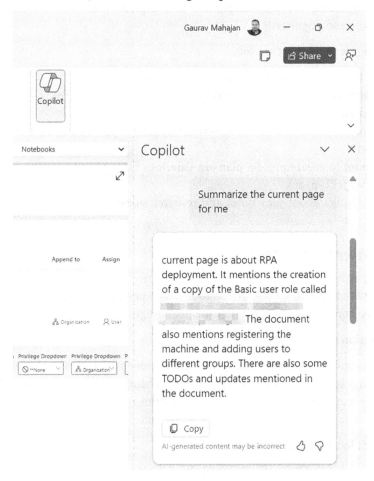

Figure 12.16: Getting a summary from Copilot

To-do list and plan design

Facilitating organization, Copilot effortlessly creates actionable to-do lists and plans for events, meetings, and other activities, ensuring users stay on top of their schedules.

Chat interaction

Copilot in OneNote provides a unique interactive experience, allowing users to chat and receive responses to specific prompts, simulating a conversation with a real person.

Content reorganization

Copilot aids in reorganizing digital notebooks, adjusting formatting, and highlighting key points, enhancing the overall look and utility of the notes.

Availability

Available to users with a Microsoft 365 Copilot license, Copilot in OneNote is a game-changer in the realm of note-taking and organization.

Additional reading on Copilot in OneNote

- Copilot in OneNote: `https://packt.link/Copilot-in-OneNote`
- Summarize your OneNote notes with Copilot for Microsoft 365: `https://packt.link/Copilot-OneNote-summaries`
- Create a to-do list and tasks in OneNote with Copilot: `https://packt.link/Copilot-OneNote-to-do-lists`
- Allow Copilot to create project plans in OneNote for you: `https://packt.link/Copilot-OneNote-project-plans`
- Chat with Copilot about your notes and research questions: `https://packt.link/Copilot-OneNote-chat`

Copilot in Microsoft Stream

Microsoft Stream, an integral part of the Microsoft 365 suite and a video powerhouse, has been significantly enhanced with the introduction of Copilot. This AI-powered tool redefines how organizations interact with video content, facilitating quick and meaningful information extraction.

Video summarization and insights

Copilot in Stream stands out for its ability to summarize videos, pinpointing key points necessary for viewers. This feature is especially beneficial for quickly absorbing information from long or detailed videos. Furthermore, Copilot can answer specific questions about video content, offering valuable insights and facilitating a deeper understanding of the material.

Intelligent content location and calls to action

Another innovative aspect of Copilot in Stream is its capability to locate where certain people, teams, or topics are mentioned in a video, allowing users to jump directly to relevant sections. Additionally, it can identify calls to action within the video, guiding users on where their involvement or input might be required.

Accessibility and getting started

Copilot in Stream is accessible across Microsoft 365, including from within SharePoint, Teams, Viva Engage, and the Stream web app. To get started, users first need to access a video on the Stream start page. If a transcript is not available for the video, it needs to be generated beforehand. Copilot then offers suggested prompts, such as `Summarize the video`, and provides linked timestamps to navigate directly to the pertinent sections of the video.

Built on security and privacy

Ensuring security and privacy, Copilot in Stream leverages LLMs in Azure OpenAI to comprehend video content with transcripts. Importantly, user data, questions, and Copilot responses remain within Microsoft's secure environment. The technology adheres to Microsoft's AI principles and Responsible AI Standard, ensuring a secure and privacy-compliant solution.

Additional reading on Copilot in Microsoft Stream

- Introducing Copilot in Microsoft Stream: `https://packt.link/Copilot-in-Stream`

Copilot in Microsoft SharePoint

Copilot in SharePoint Online will be new as of March 2024. At the time of writing, information about this feature is limited. Once again, we must iterate this message: those who are willing to research and adapt will be the ones who make the most of AI!

Microsoft SharePoint, a cornerstone of the Microsoft 365 suite, has been transformed by the integration of Copilot. This new addition propels SharePoint into a new realm of user experience, enhancing collaboration, search capabilities, and data security, and offering deeper insights and analytics.

Enhanced site and page creation

Copilot in SharePoint takes the creation and editing of sites and pages to a new level. By simply providing a brief prompt, Copilot can create a starter site, incorporate information from across the organization, and align with the brand's aesthetic. This feature significantly streamlines the site setup process and ensures alignment with organizational standards.

Content editing and web design

As a web design partner, Copilot in SharePoint converts existing documents or presentations into engaging SharePoint pages, complete with modern web design visuals. It also offers the ability to rewrite key passages of text, ensuring the tone is appropriate and engaging for the intended audience.

Simplicity in authoring

A key theme in the latest SharePoint innovations is simpler authoring. Copilot in SharePoint enables users to author SharePoint pages faster and more easily using natural language and AI. It works alongside users to conversationally configure sites, iterating on navigation and look and feel settings.

Compelling content and deeper engagement

SharePoint is also undergoing a major aesthetic update to create visually appealing sites and pages. The integration of Copilot supports deeper engagement through new integrations into email, Teams, and Microsoft Viva, making content more accessible and impactful.

Availability

Copilot in SharePoint is built on the Copilot system, leveraging LLMs and data in Microsoft Graph. It is accessible to users with a Microsoft 365 Copilot license.

Additional reading on Copilot in Microsoft SharePoint

- Welcome to the new era of SharePoint and OneDrive in Microsoft 365: `https://packt.link/SharePoint-OneDrive-new-era`
- SharePoint in the AI Era: Introducing Copilot in SharePoint & 10 more innovations for creators: `https://packt.link/SharePoint-AI-era`

Copilot in Microsoft OneDrive

Microsoft OneDrive, a fundamental component of the Microsoft 365 suite for individual productivity, is revolutionized with the integration of Copilot. This enhancement transforms OneDrive into a more intelligent and efficient platform for interacting with files stored in the cloud.

File summarization and insights

Copilot in OneDrive introduces the capability to quickly summarize changes in shared documents. This feature keeps users informed about the latest modifications in shared files, enhancing collaboration and file management. Additionally, Copilot provides insights into file sharing and usage, offering a deeper understanding of how files are utilized within an organization.

Effortless file management

The next generation of OneDrive simplifies file management, providing easy access to both personal and shared files. Innovations like a redesigned home experience, AI-powered file recommendations, meetings view, people view, shared view, colorful folders, favorites, shortcuts, and simplified sharing collectively streamline file access and enhance collaboration.

File finder

Locating files in OneDrive, especially amid a vast collection, is now more efficient with Copilot's assistance. This feature simplifies the process of finding the needed files quickly and accurately.

Content integration

Copilot's content integration in OneDrive is particularly noteworthy. It can seamlessly pull in relevant images, insert information from confirmation emails and calendar appointments from Outlook, and generate PowerPoint decks from Word documents. This capability significantly eases the creation of comprehensive and informative presentations.

Additional reading on Copilot in Microsoft OneDrive

- Unveiling the Next Generation of OneDrive: `https://packt.link/next-generation-OneDrive`
- Welcome to the new era of SharePoint and OneDrive in Microsoft 365: `https://packt.link/SharePoint-OneDrive-new-era`

Copilot in Microsoft Viva

Microsoft Viva, enhanced by Copilot, brings a new dimension to employee engagement and productivity within the Microsoft 365 suite. This integration offers a novel approach to managing workforce engagement and performance.

Unified experience across Viva apps

Copilot in Viva, built on the Microsoft 365 Copilot system, utilizes LLMs with data from Microsoft Graph and Viva apps, offering a comprehensive and intelligent experience across the platform.

Goal setting with Viva Goals

In Viva Goals, Copilot simplifies the creation and management of **objectives and key results (OKRs)**, providing recommendations based on existing documents, summarizing OKR statuses, identifying challenges, and suggesting next steps.

Engaging communications in Viva Engage

Copilot in Viva Engage assists leaders in crafting compelling posts, personalizing messages, and analyzing engagement metrics to enhance community interaction and storytelling.

Tailored learning in Viva Learning

In Viva Learning, Copilot suggests learning collections and knowledge summaries, customized to specific roles or development needs, streamlining the skill and training process for the workforce.

Topic exploration in Viva Topics

Copilot in Viva Topics facilitates a conversational interface for employees to explore important topics, enhancing knowledge management and collaboration.

Enhanced feedback analysis with Viva Glint

Viva Glint, integrated with Copilot, offers advanced tools to analyze employee comments and engagement data, providing leaders with deeper insights and understanding.

Additional reading on Copilot in Microsoft Viva

- Introducing Copilot in Microsoft Viva—A new way to boost employee engagement and performance: `https://packt.link/Copilot-in-Viva`
- Introducing the Microsoft 365 Copilot Early Access Program and new capabilities in Copilot: `https://packt.link/Copilot-early-access-program`
- Announcing Copilot in Viva Engage: `https://packt.link/Copilot-in-Viva-Engage`

Copilot in Power Platform

In the rapidly evolving digital landscape, the ability to automate and optimize business processes is paramount. Microsoft's Power Platform, a suite of high-productivity development tools, has been at the forefront of this transformation. One of the key innovations within Power Platform is Copilot, an AI-powered assistant designed to simplify and accelerate the process of building and automating workflows, apps, bots, and dashboards.

This topic delves into the capabilities of Copilot across various components of Power Platform:

- **Copilot in Power Apps** aids in rapid app development, enabling users to create and modify Microsoft Dataverse tables using natural language prompts.
- **Copilot in Power Automate** can streamline the creation of automated workflows, from setting up connections to applying necessary parameters.
- **Copilot in Power Virtual Agents** aids in the rapid development of Power Virtual Agents by building out decision trees based on natural language inputs.
- **Copilot in Power BI** can assist in data analysis and visualization, making it easier to derive insights from complex datasets.
- **Copilot in Power Pages** can help in creating interactive webpages that communicate data and insights effectively.

Next, we will look at Copilot's capabilities in Power Platform in more detail.

Copilot in Power Apps

Copilot in Power Apps is an AI companion that guides you through the app creation process. With Copilot, you can build an app, including the data behind it, just by describing what you need through multiple steps of conversation. Your apps will have Copilot-powered experiences built in from the first screen—so your users can discover insights through conversation instead of mouse clicks. Copilot offers the following features:

- **Build apps through conversation**: Copilot allows you to describe what you want your app to do, and it generates the code for you. This feature significantly reduces the time and effort required to build an app.
- **Auto-setup connections**: Copilot can automatically set up connections on your behalf to get you to working automation as soon as possible.
- **Apply necessary parameters**: Copilot can apply the necessary parameters in the flow based on your prompt.
- **Respond to requests**: Copilot can respond to your requests to make changes to your flow, such as update actions and replace actions.
- **Answer questions**: Copilot can answer questions about your flow and product.

Chapters 9 and *10* of this book, *Creating Power Apps* and *Applying Power Apps* respectively, delve into the practical aspects of app development.

Copilot in Power Automate

The Copilot in cloud flows experience in Power Automate is a new way to build automation (currently, cloud flows specifically) with the help of an AI assistant—Copilot. Copilot in Power Automate accompanies you on your flow-building journey and builds, sets up, and runs an automation on your behalf through a chat experience. Copilot offers the following features in Power Automate:

- **Build automation through conversation:** Copilot allows you to describe what you want your flow to do, and it generates the flow for you. This feature significantly reduces the time and effort required to build a flow.
- **Auto-set up connections:** Copilot can auto-set up connections on your behalf to get you to working automation as soon as possible.
- **Apply necessary parameters:** Copilot can apply the necessary parameters in the flow based on your prompt.
- **Respond to requests:** Copilot can respond to your requests to make changes to your flow, such as update actions and replace actions.
- **Answer questions:** Copilot can answer questions about your flows and products. For example, you can ask Copilot questions about your flow like, "What does my flow do?" You can also ask Copilot product questions like, "How do I access child flows?" and "How do I access licenses?".

In *Chapter 8, Power Automate (Microsoft Flow)*, the focus shifts to the practical facets of automating workflows.

Copilot in Power Virtual Agents (Copilot Studio)

Microsoft Copilot Studio is a dynamic platform designed for customizing and constructing instances of Copilot. Through Copilot Studio, you can harness a connected environment to develop, deploy, analyze, and manage your Copilot instances, all within the same web experience.

Copilot Studio is an evolution of Power Virtual Agents, providing a solution that aligns with the capabilities of Power Virtual Agents for chatbot creation.

Overall, Copilot Studio offers the following features:

- **Create topics through conversation:** Copilot allows you to describe what you want your bot to do, and it generates the topic for you. This feature significantly reduces the time and effort required to build a bot.
- **Update existing nodes:** Copilot can respond to your requests to make changes to your bot, such as updating existing nodes.
- **Summarize information:** Copilot can summarize information collected from a user in an interactive, graphical adaptive card, with all the JSON for the card generated automatically.

Within *Chapter 18, Copilot Studio (Power Virtual Agents)*, you can find coverage of the practical aspects of creating bots.

Copilot in Power BI

Copilot in Power BI combines advanced generative AI with your data to help everyone uncover and share insights faster. Simply describe the insights you need or ask a question about your data, and Copilot will analyze and pull the right data into a stunning report—turning data into actionable insights instantly. Copilot in Power BI offers the following features:

- **Create visuals and insights:** With Copilot in Power BI, you can simply describe the visuals and insights you're looking for, and Copilot will do the rest. Users can create and tailor reports in seconds.

- **Generate and edit DAX:** Copilot in Power BI can generate and edit DAX (Data Analysis Expressions) suggestions just by saying what you want in natural language.

- **Create narrative summaries:** Copilot can create narrative summaries of your data.

- **Conversational language:** Copilot can seamlessly turn your conversational language into easy-to-understand text summaries.

To enable Copilot in Power BI Desktop, you need to enable quick measure suggestions and Q&A for live connected Analysis Services databases in Power BI Desktop or the Power BI service's admin page. To enable both, the user must be a system admin and follow the steps below:

1. Log in to your Power BI account first.
2. Once you log in to Power BI Desktop, click on **File** | **Options and Settings** | **Options** | **Global** | **Preview Features.** Then, you can check out the **Quick Measure** suggestions and Q&A for live connected Analysis Services databases.

Copilot in Power Pages

Copilot is a feature in Power Pages that allows users to generate natural language descriptions and create data-centric forms by using simple prompts. Namely, these prompts can be used to generate the following Power Pages content:

- **Generate webpages:** You can create a new webpage for your site by describing the type of webpage. Copilot generates the HTML for the page with relevant text copy and images from the description. The page is added to the main navigation of the site and can be refined and edited using Copilot and the WYSIWYG editor.

- **Create forms:** Copilot simplifies your form-building process using Copilot in Power Pages too. Just specify the form type, and Copilot will auto-generate tables in Microsoft Dataverse, creating the corresponding forms. You also have the flexibility to adjust, add, or fine-tune fields using natural language input. It's a more streamlined approach to form creation.

- **Generate text:** Use Copilot to generate text and add it to a webpage.

To use Copilot for text in a Power Pages workspace, you need to:

1. Go to the Power Pages workspace.
2. Add a text component.
3. Select the Copilot icon.

4. Describe the text that you want to generate using AI.

5. Generate text by pressing the **Enter** key on the keyboard, or using the **generate text** icon on the bottom-right side of the text box.

6. Select **Add to page** to add the AI-generated text.

Data privacy and security

Microsoft Copilot for Microsoft 365 is a service that provides AI-powered productivity capabilities by connecting LLMs to your organizational data and Microsoft 365 apps. This section briefly discusses how Microsoft Copilot for Microsoft 365 uses, protects, and stores your data, and how it meets regulatory compliance requirements:

- **Data usage:** Microsoft Copilot for Microsoft 365 accesses content and context through Microsoft Graph, such as emails, chats, and documents that *you have permission to access*. It can generate responses anchored in your organizational data, as well as public web content and third-party plugins, if enabled by admins and users. Prompts, responses, and data accessed through Microsoft Graph aren't used to train foundation LLMs, including those used by Microsoft Copilot for Microsoft 365.

- **Data protection:** Microsoft Copilot for Microsoft 365 is compliant with Microsoft's existing privacy, security, and compliance commitments to Microsoft 365 commercial customers, including GDPR and EU Data Boundary. Microsoft Copilot for Microsoft 365 only surfaces organizational data to which individual users have at least view permissions. It also honors the usage rights granted by Microsoft Purview Information Protection and Microsoft 365 sensitivity labels. Microsoft Copilot for Microsoft 365 uses Azure OpenAI services for processing, not OpenAI's publicly available services. Abuse monitoring for Microsoft Copilot for Microsoft 365 occurs in real time, without providing Microsoft with any standing access to customer data, for either human or automated review.

- **Data storage:** When a user interacts with Microsoft Copilot for Microsoft 365 apps, data about these interactions is stored in Microsoft 365. The stored data includes the user's prompt, how Copilot responded, and information used to ground Copilot's response. This data is processed and stored in alignment with contractual commitments with your organization's other content in Microsoft 365. The data is encrypted while it's stored and isn't used to train foundation LLMs, including those used by Microsoft Copilot for Microsoft 365. Admins can view and manage this stored data using Content search or Microsoft Purview. They can also submit an online support ticket to delete a user's history of interactions with Microsoft Copilot for Microsoft 365.

- **Data residency:** Microsoft Copilot for Microsoft 365 calls to the LLM are routed to the closest data centers in the region, but can also call into other regions where capacity is available during high utilization periods. For EU users, traffic stays within the EU Data Boundary, while worldwide traffic can be sent to the EU and other countries or regions for LLM processing. Microsoft Copilot for Microsoft 365 upholds data residency commitments as outlined in the *Microsoft Product Terms and Data Protection Addendum*. The Microsoft Advanced Data Residency and Multi-Geo Capabilities offerings will include data residency commitments for Microsoft Copilot for Microsoft 365 customers later in 2024.

- **Regulatory compliance:** Microsoft Copilot for Microsoft 365 is integrated into Microsoft 365 and adheres to all existing privacy, security, and compliance commitments to Microsoft 365 commercial customers. As regulation in the AI space evolves, Microsoft will continue to adapt and respond to fulfill future regulatory requirements. Microsoft has been on a Responsible AI journey since 2017, when it defined its principles and approach to ensuring this technology is used in a way that is driven by ethical principles that put people first. A multidisciplinary team of researchers, engineers, and policy experts reviews Microsoft's AI systems for potential harms and mitigations. Microsoft also shares resources and templates with developers and customers to help them build effective, safe, and transparent AI solutions.

The future of Copilot

As we look toward the future, the potential for further developments in Copilot is vast. The field of artificial intelligence is rapidly evolving, and with it, so too are the capabilities of AI tools like Copilot.

One area of potential development is the expansion of Copilot's capabilities to more Microsoft 365 applications. While it's already integrated with several key applications, there's scope for it to be incorporated into additional tools across the Microsoft 365 suite. If the tools you use don't have Copilot capabilities as of yet, you should look out for this development, possibly in the near future.

In addition, as part of its commitment to making Copilot a truly global productivity tool, Microsoft has outlined an ambitious roadmap for expanding language support. Currently, Copilot supports the following languages: English (US, GB, AU, CA, IN), Spanish (ES, MX), Japanese, French (FR, CA), German, Portuguese (BR), Italian, and Chinese Simplified, but it's expected to support many more languages in the future. If your business operates in multiple countries, this is a massive development in terms of adopting Copilot in your business processes.

Summary

To conclude this chapter, it's time to reflect on the transformative impact of Copilot on productivity and its role in reinventing the way we work.

One of the key ways Copilot enhances productivity is by leveraging AI to automate routine tasks. This includes everything from drafting emails and creating documents to scheduling meetings and managing tasks. By taking over these time-consuming tasks, Copilot allows users to focus on more strategic and creative aspects of their work.

In addition to task automation, Copilot also provides intelligent assistance to users. This includes providing contextually relevant suggestions, helping users to navigate complex software, and even generating code in Power Apps. These features not only make it easier for users to complete their work but also help them learn new skills and improve their efficiency.

Finally, Copilot enables more efficient workflows by integrating with various Microsoft 365 apps. This means users can leverage the power of Copilot without having to switch between different apps. Whether you're working in Outlook, Teams, or Power BI, Copilot is there to assist you.

The role of Copilot in reinventing productivity is a testament to the transformative power of AI in the modern workplace. By leveraging AI to understand, assist, and automate, Copilot is transforming the way we work. And with its ability to learn and adapt, as well as integrate multiple apps and services, Copilot is truly reinventing productivity for the modern workplace.

FAQs

Here are a few FAQs along with their answers relating to Copilot in M365 and Power Platform:

1. What's new in Microsoft 365 Copilot?

    •   Copilot, in general, is a very new technology; it will rapidly change over the coming months. Some of the latest developments include the new Copilot icon when using Copilot in Windows, the new Copilot user experience, and Bing Chat.

2. What is Copilot Lab?

    •   With Copilot Lab, you can learn how to improve your prompt writing. As we described earlier in this chapter, prompt writing is the most significant skill you can learn to get the most out of any natural language processing LLM. Improving your prompt writing will greatly improve the quality of what you generate; remember, what you get is only as good as what you give.

3. How do users interact with Copilot?

    •   Users can interact with Copilot by selecting prewritten prompts or writing their own questions. Responses include clickable citations that direct users to the relevant source content that was used.

4. What's the difference between ChatGPT and Copilot?

    •   ChatGPT is a general-purpose LLM trained by OpenAI on a massive dataset of text, designed to engage in human-like conversations and answer a wide range of questions on several topics. Copilot also uses an LLM and is also developed with OpenAI. The key difference is that Copilot was developed in collaboration with Azure, meaning that it can work with your business data while meeting your security and privacy requirements.

5. How does Copilot work in Dynamics 365 and Power Platform?

    •   With Copilot, Dynamics 365 and Power Platform apply foundation models to your business data with Search (using Bing and Azure Cognitive Search), which brings domain-specific context to a Copilot prompt, enabling a response to integrate information from content like manuals, documents, or other data within the organization's tenant.

6. How does Copilot use your proprietary business data?

    • Copilot uses both an LLM (like GPT) and your organization's business data to produce more accurate, relevant, and personalized results. Your business data is used to improve context only for your scenario, and the LLM itself doesn't learn from your usage. Microsoft recommends a "Zero Trust" approach to Copilot in your business, which you can read more about in the following resource: `https://packt.link/Copilot-zero-trust-policy`

7. Are Copilot's responses always factual?

    • Copilot's responses are generated based on the training data and the specific prompt given by the user. While the model strives to provide accurate and factual information, it's always important to verify the information from multiple sources.

8. What are the technical requirements for using Microsoft 365 Copilot?

    • The technical requirements for using Microsoft 365 Copilot can be found in the Microsoft 365 admin center. Here's a documentation resource to point you in the right direction: `https://packt.link/Copilot-technical-requirements`

Unlock this book's exclusive benefits now

This book comes with additional benefits designed to elevate your learning experience.

Note: Have your purchase invoice ready before you begin.   `https://www.packtpub.com/unlock/9781803243177`

13

Unlock Your Book's Exclusive Benefits

Your copy of *Microsoft 365 and SharePoint Online Cookbook* comes with the following exclusive benefits:

- ☁ Next-gen Packt Reader
- ✦ AI assistant (beta)
- 📄 DRM-free PDF/ePub downloads

Use the following guide to unlock them if you haven't already. The process takes just a few minutes and needs to be done only once.

How to unlock these benefits in three easy steps

Step 1

Have your purchase invoice for this book ready, as you'll need it in *Step 3*. If you received a physical invoice, scan it on your phone and have it ready as either a PDF, JPG, or PNG.

For more help on finding your invoice, visit `https://www.packtpub.com/unlock-benefits/help`.

 Note: Bought this book directly from Packt? You don't need an invoice. After completing *Step 2*, you can jump straight to your exclusive content.

Step 2

Scan the following QR code or visit `https://www.packtpub.com/unlock/9781803243177`:

Step 3

Sign in to your Packt account or create a new one for free. Once you're logged in, upload your invoice. It can be in PDF, PNG, or JPG format and must be no larger than 10 MB. Follow the rest of the instructions on the screen to complete the process.

Need help?

If you get stuck and need help, visit `https://www.packtpub.com/unlock-benefits/help` for a detailed FAQ on how to find your invoices and more. The following QR code will take you to the help page directly:

 Note: If you are still facing issues, reach out to `customercare@packt.com`.

packt.com

Subscribe to our online digital library for full access to over 7,000 books and videos, as well as in-dustry leading tools to help you plan your personal development and advance your career. For more information, please visit our website.

Why subscribe?

- Spend less time learning and more time coding with practical eBooks and Videos from over 4,000 industry professionals
- Improve your learning with Skill Plans built especially for you
- Get a free eBook or video every month
- Fully searchable for easy access to vital information
- Copy and paste, print, and bookmark content

At www.packt.com, you can also read a collection of free technical articles, sign up for a range of free newsletters, and receive exclusive discounts and offers on Packt books and eBooks.

Other Books You May Enjoy

If you enjoyed this book, you may be interested in these other books by Packt:

Learn Microsoft Power Apps – Second Edition

Matthew Weston

ISBN: 978-1-80107-064-5

- Understand the Power Apps ecosystem and licensing
- Take your first steps building canvas apps
- Develop apps using intermediate techniques such as the barcode scanner and GPS controls
- Explore new connectors to integrate tools across the Power Platform
- Store data in Dataverse using model-driven apps
- Discover the best practices for building apps cleanly and effectively
- Use AI for app development with AI Builder and Copilot

Microsoft Power Apps Cookbook – Second Edition

Eickhel Mendoza

ISBN: 978-1-80323-802-9

- Learn to integrate and test canvas apps
- Design model-driven solutions using various features of Microsoft Dataverse
- Automate business processes such as triggered events, status change notifications, and approval systems with Power Automate
- Implement RPA technologies with Power Automate
- Extend your platform using maps and mixed reality
- Implement AI Builder s intelligent capabilities in your solutions
- Extend your business applications capabilities using Power Apps Component Framework
- Create website experiences for users beyond the organization with Microsoft Power Pages

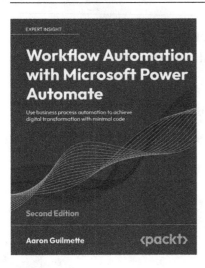

Workflow Automation with Microsoft Power Automate – Second Edition

Aaron Guilmette

ISBN: 978-1-80323-767-1

- Learn the basic building blocks of Power Automate capabilities
- Explore connectors in Power Automate to automate email workflows
- Discover how to make a flow for copying files between cloud services
- Configure Power Automate Desktop flows for your business needs
- Build on examples to create complex database and approval flows
- Connect common business applications like Outlook, Forms, and Teams
- Learn the introductory concepts for robotic process automation
- Discover how to use AI sentiment analysis

Packt is searching for authors like you

If you're interested in becoming an author for Packt, please visit authors.packtpub.com and apply today. We have worked with thousands of developers and tech professionals, just like you, to help them share their insight with the global tech community. You can make a general application, apply for a specific hot topic that we are recruiting an author for, or submit your own idea.

Share your thoughts

Now you've finished *Microsoft 365 and SharePoint Online Cookbook - Second Edition*, we'd love to hear your thoughts! Scan the QR code below to go straight to the Amazon review page for this book and share your feedback or leave a review on the site that you purchased it from.

https://packt.link/r/1-803-24317-1

Your review is important to us and the tech community and will help us make sure we're delivering excellent quality content.

Index

A

add-ins 113

AI chatbots
comparison 568

alerts
adding 198-200
notification emails 201, 202
properties and settings 198

app
adding, from SharePoint Store 108-113
removing , from site 114, 115
types 113, 114

Application Lifecycle Management (ALM) 394

application programming interface (API) 152

approvals, in Teams
using 337-345

artificial intelligence (AI) 447-552
prompt engineering 553, 554
terminologies 552

Asset Checkout 468

AutoSave
in client app 226, 227

Azure Active Directory (Azure AD or AAD) 536

B

Bing Chat 559

blank template
canvas app, creating from 437-444

breakout rooms
using, in Teams meetings 356-363

browser editing
advantages 219

business process automation 2

business process flow
creating 401-407

C

calculated columns 524

canvas apps
creating, from blank template 437-444
versus model-driven apps 420
versus Power Pages 420

cardinality
many to many 523
one to many 523
one to one 523

cascading menus 119

channel calendar tab
creating 345-349

channels and tabs
creating 304-307

ChatGPT 558, 559

classic list
versus modern lists 190

classic user interface
versus modern experience 39

ClearCollect function 426

Clear function 426

client app 249

co-authoring 221, 246

collaboration 1

Collect function 426